LLOYD GEORGE:

TWELVE ESSAYS

LLOYD GEORGE:

TWELVE ESSAYS

EDITED BY

A. J. P. TAYLOR

ATHENEUM
NEW YORK
1971

Preface

LLOYD GEORGE was the most dynamic figure in British politics during the first part of the twentieth century. He was the pioneer of the welfare state, the first man of the people to become prime minister, and the man who won the First World War. He carried the British Empire to a pinnacle of greatness. He solved the Irish question or at any rate came nearer than any other man to doing so. Even out of office, he continued to wield great influence —admired by some, feared by many. He was almost the man of destiny of 1931 and still dreamt of becoming the man of destiny during the Second World War. His career stirs the curiosity of historians, and fortunately this curiosity can be satisfied.

Lloyd George was the first prime minister to possess an efficient secretariat of his own, and he did not fear the cabinet office, which he himself had created. He took with him all his records when he left office. With their aid he wrote his *War Memoirs* and his account of the Paris peace conference. He died in 1945, leaving these papers to Countess Lloyd-George. In 1951 Lord Beaverbrook bought the papers. He in his turn inspired the biography of Lloyd George which Frank Owen wrote and drew on the Lloyd George papers for his own books, *Men and Power* and *The Decline and Fall of Lloyd George*. Beaverbrook originally intended to place the Lloyd George papers in the library of the University of New Brunswick at Fredericton. Later he decided to establish a centre for historical research at Cherkley, his country home near Leatherhead. The Lloyd George papers were housed in what had been the private cinema. They remained there until Beaverbrook's death.

Cherkley proved unsuitable as a research centre. It was difficult of access and had no adequate precautions against fire. The directors of Beaverbrook Newspapers, to whom the Lloyd George papers belong, and the trustees of the First Beaverbrook Foundation therefore resolved to set up the Beaverbrook

Library in St. Bride Street, London, at the heart of the news-paper world which bulked so large in Beaverbrook's life. All the papers which Beaverbrook had possessed were transported there, and the Library was opened on 25 May 1967.

The Library possesses the Lloyd George papers, magnificently calendared by Mrs. (Sheila) Elton; the Bonar Law papers, which Law bequeathed to Beaverbrook, also calendared by Mrs. Elton; the papers of Sir Edward Goulding, later Lord Wargrave; the papers of Sir Patrick Hannon; the papers of R. D. Blumen-feld, lately given to the Library by Sir John Elliot, Blumenfeld's son; and Beaverbrook's own papers. In addition owners of other collections have placed their papers here on permanent deposit. These include the papers of St. Loe Strachey, deposited by the *Spectator*; of Lord Lee of Fareham, deposited by his executors; and of Lord Davidson, deposited by his family. All except the Beaverbrook papers are open to *bona fide* researchers or will be when they have been catalogued.

The Library has been in constant use from the day it opened. Scholars have come from all over the world, particularly from the Dominions and the United States. The results of their work are already being shown in innumerable books and university theses. As Honorary Director of the Library I was too impatient to wait for these publications. I therefore arranged seminars during the university vacations at which users of the Library discussed their work, and the papers read there cried out for publication. The present volume is the result.

The selection is in a sense undesigned, determined by the chance whether a paper was available. In particular, there is comparatively little about Lloyd George's activities in foreign affairs both during the First World War and after it, though the majority of researchers have, I think, been working on these topics. These may well provide the central theme for a further volume. I add a personal comment. Two of the essays suggest that in my own writings I exaggerated Lloyd George's con-nection with the Radical critics of Grey's foreign policy, as Lloyd George himself exaggerated it later. Lloyd George took offence at German actions more readily than I supposed, and this may help to explain his rapid conversion to support of the war in 1914. Such revisions of outlook are the driving force behind historical studies.

Lord Beaverbrook asked at the end of *Men and Power*:

> What new assessments will tomorrow bring forth, and what judge-
> ment will posterity accord to David Lloyd George, born in a cottage,
> brought up in a shoemaker's shop, strayed from the fields of Llanys-
> tumdwy to that narrow street so many desire to tread, yet so few
> deserve to enter, the path that leads to No. 10?

This volume attempts to provide some answers. It is devoted to
a famous statesman. It is also a memorial to that great historian,
Max Aitken, Lord Beaverbrook.

A. J. P. Taylor

Beaverbrook Library,
London

Contents

ix

Abbreviations

ADM   Admiralty
B.D.   *British Documents on the Origins of the War*
D.B.F.P. *Documents on British Foreign Policy, 1919–1939*
CAB   Cabinet Minutes
CID   Committee of Imperial Defence
CP   Cabinet Papers
F.O.   Foreign Office
F.R.U.S. *Foreign Relations of the United States*
G.P.   *Grosse Politik*
H.C. deb. *House of Commons Debates* (Hansard)
H.L. deb. *House of Lords Debates* (Hansard)
IC   Imperial War Cabinet Conclusions
n.d.   No date
W.C.   War Cabinet Conclusions

Acknowledgments

The Editor and Contributors wish to thank the following:
For permission to quote from, and/or access to, Papers:
The Hon. Mark Bonham-Carter—Asquith Papers; The Earl of Halifax—Hickleton Papers; Viscount Harcourt—Harcourt Papers; the late Sir Basil Liddell Hart—Liddell Hart Papers; Lord Kennet (Wayland Young)—Papers of the first Lord Kennet; Mrs. Lloyd—Neville Chamberlain Papers; Lady Mottistone—Murray of Elibank Papers; Sir Steven Runciman—Runciman Papers; Mr. Laurence Scott—Scott Papers; Viscount Simon—Simon Papers; Viscount Younger of Leckie, O.B.E., —Younger Papers.
The custodians of the following Museums and Libraries for access to collections in their keeping:
Balliol College—Harold Nicolson Diary, 1938; Beaverbrook Library—Bonar Law and Lloyd George Papers; Birmingham University Library—Austen Chamberlain Papers and the Records of the Midland Liberal Federation; Bodleian Library, Oxford—Asquith Papers, H. A. L. Fisher Papers, Milner Papers; British Museum—Balfour, Campbell-Bannerman, J. Burns, Herbert Gladstone, Scott and Spender Papers, and the Newspaper Library, Colindale; Cambridge University Library—Hardinge and Templewood Papers; Churchill College, Cambridge—McKenna Papers; Conservative Research Department Library—Sir Robert Sanders Papers, lent by The Hon. Mrs. Butler, O.B.E., J.P.; Eastern Counties Liberal Federation; Leeds Public Library—S.C.A.L.A. Annual Report and Account Books; London School of Economics, British Library of Political and Economic Science—Dalton and Passfield Papers; House of Lords Library—Samuel Papers; National Liberal Club Library —Annual Reports of the Women's National Liberal Federation, 1918–1925; National Library of Scotland—Haldane and

Murray of Elibank Papers; Yale University Library—House Papers; Yorkshire Liberal Federation.

The Controller of H.M. Stationery Office for access to collections of Government records in the Public Record Office and elsewhere.

For permission to publish extracts from books published by them: William Collins, Sons, Ltd.—*Harold Nicolson, Diaries and Letters*; Victor Gollancz, Ltd.—Lord Riddell; *Intimate Diary of the Peace Conference and After*.

I

DAVID LLOYD GEORGE AND FOREIGN POLICY BEFORE 1914

M. L. DOCKRILL

MICHAEL LAWRENCE DOCKRILL

Age 34

London School of Economics 1957–61 B.Sc.
University of Illinois 1962–63 M.A.
London School of Economics 1964–66 Ph.D.
Currently Lecturer in War Studies
King's College, London

DAVID LLOYD GEORGE AND
FOREIGN POLICY BEFORE 1914

It is most unfair on Grey that he should be hampered and his
Department invaded by a couple of ignorant and irresponsible
men like L. George and Mr. Churchill, who are not loyal to their
Colleagues, who spend most of their time in unprincipled
intrigues and who act as they do for their own party purposes.[1]

LLOYD GEORGE took only a spasmodic interest in foreign
affairs down to 1914. He was chiefly concerned in this period
with domestic and Irish problems, and inevitably historians
have concentrated on these issues. Nevertheless his influence on
British foreign policy, at least after 1908, was much greater than
his biographers, or for that matter Lloyd George himself,
subsequently conceded, although of course considerable
attention has been paid to his Mansion House speech of 1911,
and to his reactions to the European crisis of July and August
1914.

His infrequent references to international questions both
before and during the Boer war provide some indication of the
attitude he was to adopt in the future to foreign affairs. Thus
after 1896 he chided the Salisbury administration for its weak
resistance to the encroachments of the other great powers on the
vital interests of Great Britain abroad, and for its failure to
uphold British prestige and honour all over the world. Nor,
during his campaign against the Boer war, did he neglect the
larger issues. The 'greedy despotisms of Europe', he declared,
were taking advantage of Great Britain's preoccupation with
the South African war, to make inroads into British commercial
and other interests in China and elsewhere. He feared that as a
result of her involvement in the war, Great Britain would have
to spend ever increasing sums on building up her army and
navy in order to defend the empire from the hostility of Russia,
France, and Germany. After the Boer war his references to
foreign affairs became increasingly rare, although he reacted

[1] Knollys to Hardinge, 24 Aug. 1908, Hardinge Papers.

3

indignantly to the Dogger Bank incident in 1904, castigating Russia's action as 'most insolent and unjustifiable'.[1] For the first two years after he became president of the board of trade in Campbell-Bannerman's Liberal ministry in December 1905 he took no interest in foreign policy; the responsibilities of his office consumed most of his energy. The other ministers were also, by and large, preoccupied with internal questions and reforms and, as a result, the foreign secretary, Sir Edward Grey, was not bothered by much cabinet interference with his foreign policy. Nor did he go out of his way to encourage such interference. Grey and Lloyd George had little in common. Reserved, cautious, and rather secretive, Grey was not a personality likely to appeal much to the mercurial Welshman.[2] Their methods were entirely at variance. In contrast to Lloyd George, Grey's approach to public affairs was based on a set of firmly held attitudes and assumptions, and as a result his foreign policy was rather inflexible and unambitious. His mind was dominated by a deepseated suspicion of Germany, and the threat which he believed that country posed to Great Britain's security.

His views were shared by his permanent under secretary, Sir Charles Hardinge, and, with few exceptions, by the rest of the foreign office staff. They firmly believed that Germany was seeking the hegemony of Europe, and that only by maintaining her naval supremacy and the *entente* with France could Great Britain frustrate the realization by Germany of her ambitions. Hence Grey concentrated, after 1905, on tightening the bonds between Great Britain and France in order to preserve the *entente* as a defensive combination against Germany. Inevitably Anglo-German relations deteriorated sharply after 1906, an outcome which gave Grey little concern. He feared, above all, that British efforts to remove the causes of Anglo-German ill-feeling might lead France to suspect British disloyalty to the *entente*, which in turn might drive France into the arms of Germany.

The brief period of calm in international affairs after the

---

[1] Quoted in the *North Wales Observer*, 28 Oct. 1904, Lloyd George Papers, A/12/2/38.

[2] Kenneth O. Morgan, *David Lloyd George* (1963), 40; Lucy Masterman *C. F. G. Masterman* (1939), 161.

Algeçiras Conference in 1906 further discouraged Liberal ministers from taking much interest in foreign policy. Despite its undertones of hostility towards Germany, Grey's policy was pacific and nonprovocative. The *entente* with France, the Russian Convention of 1907, and the reforms of Admiral Fisher at the admiralty and of Haldane at the war office, resulted in economies in defence expenditure, and many Liberals hoped that the second Hague peace conference in 1907 might result in a multilateral agreement on the limitation of armaments.[1]

Grey's relative immunity from interference and criticism by his colleagues came to an end, however, during and after 1908. The Hague conference failed to produce anything more than pious resolutions. To make matters worse the Germans decided to make substantial increases in the size of their navy towards the end of 1907. Accordingly the British admiralty demanded counter increases in the naval estimates, a demand which provoked the first of a series of acrimonious disputes in the cabinet between the 'economists' and 'big navalists' which threatened at times to lead to the break-up of the government.[2] Then, in April 1908, Asquith replaced the ailing Campbell-Bannerman as prime minister and, in the ensuing reshuffle, Lloyd George became chancellor of the exchequer and Winston Churchill replaced him at the board of trade. These two men now became staunch allies for a time in a campaign to secure reduced estimates, and to apply the savings to social reforms.[3] They both declared that they were not opposed to naval increases if these were essential in the interests of British security; what they did object to were what they believed to be the inflated demands of the admiralty.[4]

The cabinet economists failed to prevent naval increases in 1908. The new chancellor of the exchequer circulated a memorandum soon after his advent to the treasury, warning the cabinet that, unless there were cuts in the service estimates,

[1] G. W. Monger, *The End of Isolation, 1900–1907*, (1963), 257–331.

[2] Arthur J. Marder, *From the Dreadnought to Scapa Flow*, (1961), i, 138–140.

[3] Ronald Hyam, *Elgin and Churchill at the Colonial Office*, 1905–1908, (1968), 48–51.

[4] Herbert du Parcq, *Life of David Lloyd George*, (1914), ii, 391; David Lloyd George, *War Memoirs*, (1938), i, 5.

the government would either have to sacrifice educational reforms and old age pensions, or impose fresh taxation on the country.

> I need hardly remind my colleagues that we have repeatedly pledged ourselves both before we took office and since, to a substantial reduction of the national expenditure, and particularly that which depends upon the two armed services ... unless some definite assurances can be given ... I do not see how we are to repel the attacks which will certainly be made upon us, not only by our opponents, but by sections of our own supporters.[1]

For a time Lloyd George and Churchill tried, unsuccessfully, to secure cuts in the army estimates, but they soon returned to the question of excessive naval expenditure, which was in any case likely to yield more sizeable savings. Since both the admiralty and the foreign office justified increased naval estimates by reference to Germany's competition, the two men suggested that the problem could be solved if the government reversed what appeared to be a policy of hostility towards Germany, and sought instead an agreement with that country, which would enable both to reduce their naval expenditures. They both regarded Germany as their mentor in the successful application of social reforms[2] and they concluded, naturally enough, that she would be equally enthusiastic to reduce her naval budget.

Accordingly the two ministers proceeded to deliver speeches up and down the country advocating an Anglo-German naval agreement. Lloyd George declared that British suspicions of Germany were as ill-founded as her suspicions of France had been in the previous century, and since he could perceive no genuine cause for Anglo-German hostility, he could not understand why Anglo-German relations should not be as friendly as Anglo-French and Anglo-Russian relations had now become.[3] His activities did not endear him to Grey's officials who had, in any case, long regarded him as an ardent

[1] Memorandum by David Lloyd George, 'The Financial Situation—This Year and Next,' 18 May 1908, CAB 37/93/62.

[2] Churchill to Asquith, 29 Dec. 1908, Asquith Papers, vol 11.

[3] Speeches by Lloyd George at the peace congress meeting, London, 28 July 1908, and at the inaugural meeting of the Women's Anglo-German friendship union, 11 Downing Street, 22 July 1908, Daily News, 29 July 1908, and 23 July 1909, Lloyd George Papers, C/33/1/7 and C/33/2/10.

Germanophil who, they believed, would not be sorry to sacrifice either the *ententes* or British naval supremacy if he thought it necessary in the interests of an accommodation with Germany. They feared that his clamour for an Anglo-German *rapprochement* might upset France and Russia by casting doubts on Great Britain's loyalty to the *ententes*.

While Grey did not believe that Anglo-German relations could genuinely improve while Germany was forcing increased naval expenditure on Great Britain,[1] and while he shared to some extent the fears of his officials, political exigencies were forcing him to adopt a less rigid attitude towards relations with Germany. The Lloyd George–Churchill campaign was beginning to strike a responsive cord in the Liberal party. At the same time he realised that a satisfactory naval agreement with Germany would end the annual rumpus in the cabinet over the naval estimates, so dangerous to the unity of the government, assuage Liberal opinion in the country, and contribute to a relaxation in international tension. He always insisted however that any agreement with Germany must leave British naval supremacy intact and must not affect the *ententes*.

Although, unlike Lloyd George, he was somewhat sceptical about Germany's willingness to discuss an agreement, a scepticism which was amply justified by the events of the summer, he did attempt to satisfy Lloyd George that he was not standing in the way of an improvement in Anglo-German relations. Twice during July Lloyd George and Grey saw Count Metternich, the German ambassador, in an effort to convince him that there could be no real improvement in the relations between the two countries until Germany agreed to mutual reductions in naval expenditure. Their appeals, however, fell on deaf ears.[2] Grey next attempted to promote friendly discussions with Germany on the subject when the king visited the German emperor at Cronberg in August 1908. The king mentioned the question vaguely to the emperor but abandoned it when the latter displayed no interest. When Hardinge, who had accompanied the king, raised it subsequently, the emperor 'assumed

[1] Minute by Grey, on memorandum by Walford Selby, 1 Aug. 1908, F.O.371/461/Germany.
[2] Memorandum by Grey, 23 July 1908, Grey Papers, F.O.800/92; Lloyd George, *War Memoirs*, i, 7–17.

a most uncompromising attitude', and refused to discuss it.[1] Despite this set-back, which was not 'unexpected', Grey still thought that Germany might eventually agree to some slackening of her naval competition, but he decided to desist for the time being from further approaches to her since these appeared to embarrass the German government and exacerbate relations between the two countries.[2]

Lloyd George was unaware of this decision, and the motives which prompted it. In August he too visited Germany to study her old age pensions and poor law problems.[3] He soon began to lobby for an agreement on naval armaments, and in an interview, which was published in the Vienna *Neue Freie Presse* on 12 August 1908, he proposed an Anglo-German understanding on naval reductions which would enable both countries to spend more on social reforms. His initiative provoked a sharp reaction from the foreign office. Eyre Crowe, the senior clerk in the western department, protested to Grey that,

> It is somewhat alarming to see Cabinet Ministers with obvious imperfect understanding of foreign affairs plunge into public discussion abroad of an 'entente' with Germany . . . Presumably Sir E. Grey will lay down for Mr. Lloyd George's guidance what he should say . . . and what he should not say. How much better would it be if he said nothing at all.[4]

Accordingly Grey asked the prime minister to inform Lloyd George that in view of the German emperor's attitude, public discussion by British ministers of the naval question would be resented and would only harden opinion in Germany against an agreement. Lloyd George replied from Berlin promising not to meddle in international questions, but to confine himself 'exclusively to invalid and other pensions'.[5]

Consequently Grey was greatly irritated when Harold

[1] Hardinge to Grey, 15 Aug. 1908, and memorandum by Hardinge, 16 Aug. 1908. B.D.vi, nos. 116 and 117.

[2] Grey to Asquith, 17 Aug. 1908, Grey Papers, F.O.800/100. Notes drafted by Grey, 22 Aug. 1908, Grey Papers F.O.800/92; Minute by Crowe, on Lascelles to Grey, desp 349, 14 Aug. 1908, B.D.vi, no 115.

[3] Harold Spender, *The Prime Minister: The Life and Times of David Lloyd George*, (1920), 155.

[4] Minute by Crowe, 18 Aug. 1908, F.O.371/461/Germany.

[5] Asquith to Lloyd George, Berlin, tel, 20 Aug. 1908 (drafted by Grey); Lloyd George to Asquith, 21 Aug. 1908, Grey Papers, F.O.800/101.

Spender, who accompanied the chancellor to Germany, told the *Berliner Tageblatt* that Lloyd George 'would willingly and only too gladly, enter into . . . discussions with official circles if the latter would give him an opportunity'. Grey protested to the prime minister on 22 August 1908 that

> it is very risky for Cabinet Ministers to go abroad and make utterances about international affairs, when they are out of touch with the F.O. I shall make no fuss as long as no harm is done, but if any harm is done I should have to insist on the Minister in question being disavowed which would be very humiliating for him, or on my resignation being accepted, which would cause inconvenience.

He concluded that further initiatives of this kind might shake France's confidence in Great Britain's loyalty to the *entente*.[1] Asquith was equally irritated and he wrote to the chancellor making his views on the latter's activities 'pretty plain'.[2] In the event Lloyd George had little luck in Berlin. The emperor, who was annoyed because the naval question had been raised once more, refused to see him. He dined with Theobald Bethmann Hollweg, the future chancellor, but when Lloyd George mentioned a possible naval agreement, Bethmann lost his temper and complained of British efforts to encircle Germany with a ring of hostile powers. Lloyd George left Berlin 'gravely disturbed' by Germany's 'distrust and suspicion'.[3]

Lloyd George and Churchill failed to secure an agreement with Germany, an inevitable consequence of Germany's refusal to listen to British proposals. As Grey told Lord Sanderson, a former permanent undersecretary at the foreign office, it was difficult to convince his colleagues that 'there are such things as high walls; the most certain way of doing this is to let them run their heads against them'.[4] Anglo-German relations worsened during the winter of 1908 and 1909 as a result of the Bosnian crisis and a number of other incidents. British suspicions of Germany increased even further when, towards the end of 1908, the admiralty announced that Germany was secretly accelerating her naval building programme. The first lord, Reginald McKenna, accordingly

[1] Grey to Asquith, 22 Aug. 1908; Grey Papers, F.O.800/100.
[2] Asquith to Grey, 24 Aug. 1908, Grey Papers, F.O.800/100.
[3] Lloyd George, *War Memoirs*, 19.
[4] Grey to Sanderson, 12 Sept. 1908, Grey Papers, F.O.800/111.

demanded the addition of six dreadnoughts to the British
estimates as the minimum necessary to combat the German
manoeuvre. A new cabinet split loomed as the economists—
Lloyd George, Churchill, Lewis Harcourt, John Burns, John
Morley and Lord Loreburn, the lord chancellor—insisted that
the admiralty's suspicions were unfounded, and that in their
view only four extra battleships were necessary. Grey threw his
support behind McKenna and threatened resignation if the
cabinet rejected the six dreadnoughts. Eventually Asquith
persuaded both sides to accept the famous 4:4 compromise
whereby McKenna eventually secured two more dreadnoughts
than he had originally demanded.[1]

The economists suspected that they had been tricked,[2] with
the obvious danger, as far as the foreign office was concerned,
that they would turn once more to the sensitive question of
Anglo-German relations. Hence Grey's officials were greatly
perturbed when the German press and foreign office began,
in the spring of 1909, to campaign for the opening of negotiations between the two countries to settle their outstanding
differences. The foreign office believed that these approaches
were designed to encourage British Liberals to press for reduced
naval estimates on the grounds that Germany was not hostile to
Great Britain.[3] Nevertheless Asquith, Grey, and Hardinge
decided that, for political reasons, some official notice must be
taken of Germany's willingness to discuss an agreement. Thus
Grey gave a cautious welcome when, on 21 August 1909, the
new German chancellor, Bethmann Hollweg, suggested that the
two countries commence negotiations for a political and naval
agreement.[4]

Grey's confidence in Germany's desire for a genuine settlement of the difference between the two countries was soon
undermined when the German chancellor offered only a
reduction in the annual rate of German naval construction,
leaving the whole programme intact. In return for this paltry
concession Bethmann demanded an Anglo-German neutrality

[1] Grey to Asquith, 5 Feb. 1909, Asquith Papers, vol. 1; Marder, i, 159–
171.
[2] Lloyd George to Haldane, 27 Feb. 1909, Lloyd George Papers, C/4/17/1.
[3] Hardinge to the king, 4 May 1909, Hardinge Papers.
[4] Goschen to Grey, tels 93 & 94, 21 Aug. 1909, B.D.vi, 186 & 187.

and non-aggression pact.[1] Later, in 1910, he withdrew even his meagre naval offer on the grounds that a successful political agreement between the two countries would so improve their relations that a naval understanding would be unnecessary. Grey now began to pay more attention to the warnings of his officials, who charged Germany with initiating the conversations in order to destroy both Britain's naval supremacy and the triple entente. He was compelled, however, to persevere with the fruitless negotiations because of the interest that Lloyd George and the other cabinet economists were taking in them.

The progress of the talks during 1910 was impeded by the constitutional crisis in Great Britain, and by the difficulties Germany continued to make about naval reductions. The cabinet economists began to grow impatient. Lord Loreburn raised the matter in the cabinet on 20 July 1910,[2] while Lloyd George began to grumble, in the autumn, about the frequent delays in bringing the discussions to a conclusion.[3] Grey was also embarrassed when, towards the end of 1910, the radical Liberals launched a full-scale assault in press and parliament against the allegedly anti-German direction of British foreign policy. He was further irritated when, in December, interviews with Lloyd George on Anglo-French relations were published in French newspapers. When the French government expressed its displeasure, Grey commented testily that the interviews 'have caused far more annoyance at home than they even possibly caused' the French.[4] Haldane wrote to Grey to sympathize; 'Ll.G. is irritating in the extreme. Just when you are talking with Bethman Hollweg to have these interviews going on'.[5]

There was a fresh upheaval in the cabinet in 1911 over the 1911–1912 naval estimates. Again Lloyd George failed to prevent increases, although he extracted a pledge from McKenna that there would be substantial economies in 1912.[6] Faced with further increases the chancellor of the exchequer

---

[1] Goschen to Grey, desp 371, 4 Nov. 1909, B.D.vi, 204.

[2] Asquith to the king, 20 July 1910, CAB/41/32/67.

[3] Asquith to Lloyd George, 24 Sept. 1910, Lloyd George Papers, C/6/11/7.

[4] Bertie to Grey, 25 Dec. 1910; Grey to Bertie, 9 Jan. 1911, Bertie Papers, F.O.800/174.

[5] Haldane to Grey, 26 Dec. 1910, Grey Papers, F.O.800/102.

[6] Marder, i, 218.

turned his attention to the negotiations with Germany. The economists suspected that Grey was approaching the discussions in a half-hearted spirit,[1] and fortified by the rising tide of Liberal opinion in favour of improved relations with Germany, they embarked on a major effort to force the reluctant foreign secretary to accept an agreement with Germany. They persuaded the cabinet, on 20 January 1911, to set up a committee on foreign affairs, consisting of Asquith, Grey, Lord Crewe, Lloyd George, John Morley, and Walter Runciman. This was an unprecedented step during Grey's long tenure of the foreign office. According to Arthur Murray, his parliamentary private secretary,

> I have had lately to convey to Sir Edward Grey an alleged grievance of Lloyd George's. The latter said that although he was specially interested in Foreign affairs, in that he was called upon to provide the money for huge naval estimates, he was kept in the dark in regard to essential features of our Foreign policy. He knew nothing, he said, of what was going on and he demanded that papers should be sent to him. This was of course impossible, in the sense that he desired, but the matter has been satisfactorily settled by the setting up of a sub-Committee of the Cabinet, of which Lloyd George will be a member, periodically to discuss Foreign policy.[2]

The committee was not, however, packed with pro-Germans. While Runciman's position is unclear at this time—he had sided with McKenna in the 1909 struggle over the estimates—only Lloyd George can be regarded as a staunch critic of Grey's policy. Asquith normally saw eye to eye with Grey, Crewe usually took a moderate line, while Morley could never be relied upon to follow a consistent course, had supported Grey's policy, with reservations, hitherto, and deputized for him during the latter's absences from the foreign office early in 1911.

Nevertheless, as the lamentations of Sir Arthur Nicolson, who had replaced Hardinge as permanent under secretary in the previous autumn, indicated, the foreign office regarded the committee as a serious threat to the stability of British foreign policy. Nicolson complained that it would put the foreign office into commission, restrict Grey's liberty of action, and

---

[1] On 29 July 1910 the cabinet accepted revised proposals by Grey for an Anglo-German agreement as better than nothing. Asquith to the king, 30 July 1910, CAB 41/32/68.

[2] Diary of Arthur Murray, 27 Jan 1911, Murray Papers, 8814.

deprive 'us permanent officials of a certain amount of influence upon affairs'. He noted that its proceedings were not entirely 'harmonious', and thought that, while Grey was 'perfectly sound', the other members wanted an understanding with Germany, and were prepared to fall in with the German view that a political agreement was of more importance than a naval understanding.[1]

The committee concentrated on drawing up new British proposals for an Anglo-German agreement. Although Lloyd George wrote to McKenna in March that Grey felt 'very sanguine that we may be able to secure an understanding as to slowing down', Grey was minuting at this time that there appeared to be no hope of ending the naval race, 'except on terms that will leave them our rivals in sea power, and to such terms we cannot agree'.[2] Lloyd George proposed many amendments to Grey's initial draft,[3] which was much altered by the committee.[4] To his horror Grey discovered, on 17 February, that the committee had omitted a clause from his original draft which stated that the political and naval agreements must be concluded simultaneously, an omission which provided evidence for Nicolson's suspicions about the committee. Grey persuaded his colleagues to re-insert the clause.[5]

The draft memorandum was carefully considered by the cabinet on 8 March. It resolved that, while the British government was prepared to make an exchange of 'pacific declarations' with Germany, these must be so worded that they could not possibly be misinterpreted in France and Russia.[6] This was a clear victory for Grey's policy of maintaining the *ententes*, and a defeat for those ministers who, Nicolson believed, were prepared to make terms with Germany at any cost.[7]

---

[1] Nicolson to Hardinge, 2 Mar. 1911, B.D.vi, no. 440, and Nicolson Papers, F.O.800/347.
[2] Lloyd George to McKenna, 3 March 1911, Lloyd George Papers, C/5/12/7; Minute by Grey on Cartwright to Grey, desp 33, 24 Feb. 1911, F.O.371/1123/Germany.
[3] Tyrrell to Grey, 17 Feb. 1911, Grey Papers, F.O.800/101.
[4] Grey to Goschen, desp 60, 8 March 1911, B.D.vi. no. 444.
[5] Grey to cabinet committee, c. 17. Feb. 1911, F.O.371/1123/Germany.
[6] Asquith to the king, 8 March 1911, CAB 41/33/5.
[7] Nicolson to Goschen, 28 Feb. 1911, Nicolson Papers, F.O.800/347.

The negotiations were in any case brought to an end by the Agadir crisis in July 1911. Grey's officials suspected that Germany's action in sending the gunboat, the Panther, to Agadir, was designed to smash the *entente* by demonstrating to France that she could not rely on British support, and they feared that, as a result, France would be forced into an agreement with Germany for the partition of Morocco, which would affect Great Britain's strategic and commercial interests in that country. The cabinet, however, did not adopt such a dismal view of the situation. Meeting on 4 July, it resolved that Great Britain would not oppose the acquisition by Germany of an unfortified Moroccan Atlantic port in return for German recognition of a French protectorate over Morocco. At the same time it insisted that the British government must be consulted about any settlement which altered the *status quo* in Morocco, a reservation which Grey relayed to Paul Cambon, the French ambassador, and to Metternich on the same day.[1]

While Grey accepted the cabinet's decision, his officials were disgusted at what they considered to be the cabinet's feeble response to Germany's hostile policy. On 10 July Grey agreed to the opening of separate Franco-German negotiations at Berlin on the basis that Germany would receive compensation on the French Congo in return for giving France a free hand in Morocco.[2] The French promised to keep him informed as to the progress of the talks and to secure British agreement to the subsequent settlement. On 15 July, however, the Franco-German negotiations nearly collapsed when Germany demanded practically the whole of the French Congo.[3]

The foreign office believed that this inflated German demand was put forward in the expectation that it would be rejected by France, and that this would be followed by a German ultimatum insisting on a share in the partition of Morocco. Nicolson and the others were convinced that the *entente* could only be saved if Great Britain stood firmly by the side of France in resisting Germany's demands. Grey, too, was becoming anxious about these recent developments. Accor-

[1] Asquith to the king, 4 July 1911, CAB 41/33/20; Grey to Bertie, 4 July 1911, B.D.vii, no. 355.

[2] Goschen to Grey, tel 47, 10 July 1911, B.D.vii, no. 367.

[3] Bertie to Grey, tel 103, 18 July 1911, B.D.vii, no. 392.

dingly, when the cabinet met on 19 July to consider the crisis, he proposed that he should call a conference on Morocco. This was resisted by Loreburn, who feared that if Germany refused a conference, war might become inevitable. Deadlock ensued, and the cabinet decided to defer a communication to Germany until its next meeting on the 21st. France was to be told that Great Britain could not regard 'as a *casus belli*' a French decision to resist German territorial acquisitions in Morocco.[1]

The cabinet met on the morning of 21 July 1911 amid increasing international tension, mounting industrial unrest, and the crisis over the parliament bill. Details of Germany's Congo demands had been published in the *Times* on the previous day, and had led to anxious press speculation. The cabinet authorised the now thoroughly alarmed Grey to inform Germany that since she had not replied to his statement of 4 July, the British government must make it clear that should the current Franco-German talks break down, Great Britain would insist on being included in any discussions likely to lead to Germany's receiving compensation in Morocco.[2] Grey's declaration to Metternich after this meeting, and Lloyd George's Mansion House speech in the evening were both based on this cabinet resolution,[3] although Lloyd George's spech was not discussed by the cabinet. It was an independent initiative of the chancellor's, who felt that he might well utilise the opportunity provided by this speech to say something about the crisis.[4] It echoed speeches he had made in the 1890's, when he had complained that Salisbury had neglected British prestige and honour overseas:

> If a situation were to be forced on us in which peace could only be preserved by the surrender of the great and beneficent position that Britain has won by centuries of heroism and achievement by allowing Britain to be treated, where her interests are vitally affected, as if she were of no account in the Cabinet of nations, then I say emphatically that peace at that price would be a humiliation intolerable for a great country like ours to endure.[5]

[1] Asquith to the king, 19 July 1911, CAB 41/33/22. Grey to Asquith, 19 July 1911, B.D.vii, no. 399.
[2] Asquith to the king, 21 July 1911, Asquith Papers, vol. 6.
[3] Grey to Goschen, desp 164, 21 July 1911, B.D.vii, 411.
[4] For a further elucidation of this point see Note A.
[5] Quoted in *Lloyd George*, ed. Martin Gilbert, (1968), 46.

Mr. A. J. P. Taylor in his book *The Struggle for Mastery in Europe*, suggests that the speech was addressed to Caillaux and the French rather than to the Germans.[1] Lloyd George, in his speech, was diplomatically reticent on this point, and in any case, if it was true, it failed in its intention. In fact all the available evidence points at its being directed at Germany. France had been reminded several times of the British position; the cabinet met on the 21st solely to decide on what Germany should be told. Lloyd George stated in his *Memoirs* that 'the German government, naturally, was furious, for its gunboat diplomacy had received a severe and well-merited rebuff.'[2] Lord Riddell wrote that the chancellor 'looked pleased', when, after the speech, Riddell told him that it would show the Germans that radicalism was not inconsistent with nationalism.[3] Few at the time regarded the speech as in any way addressed to France (except in so far as it put fresh heart into her to resist German pressure),[4] least of all Germany, as her angry reaction demonstrated. From Grey's point of view the conversion of the supposedly pro-German Lloyd George had two beneficial effects—the chancellor's speech had more influence on the Germans than any comparable effort by Grey would have done,[5] and it left the other pro-Germans in the cabinet rather isolated.[6] According to Churchill, who was now equally suspicious of Germany, the chancellor only made up his mind at the last moment, but once he had done so 'we were able immediately to pursue a firm and coherent policy'.[7] Little is known of Lloyd George's attitude to the crisis before 21 July, although Sir Edward Goschen, the British ambassador to Berlin, who visited London earlier in the month, wrote on

[1] A. J. P. Taylor, *The Struggle for Mastery in Europe, 1848–1918* (1954), 471.

[2] Lloyd George, *War Memoirs*, i, 43–45.

[3] Lord Riddell, *More Pages from My Diary, 1908–1914* (1934), 20–22. Lloyd George added that 'the policy of the jack-boot won't do for us. I am all for peace, but I am not going to be jack-booted by anyone.'

[4] Nicolson to Hardinge, Nicolson Papers, F.O.800/349.

[5] Grey, *Twenty-Five Years*, (1925), i, 225–226.

[6] Not that Lloyd George claimed to be any less pro-German than before. He told C. F. G. Masterman in July that 'I like the Germans but I hate the Junker caste.' Masterman, 199.

[7] Winston S. Churchill, *The World Crisis, 1911–1918*, (1931), 37.

15 July that 'luckily the backs of the left-wing of the cabinet were put up by the idea of England being left out of the Morocco conversations'.[1] The chancellor's reaction to the crisis on 21 July was quite consistent with views he had expressed before about Great Britain's role in world affairs. Before 1905 he had often asserted Great Britain's right to make herself heard in international questions. During July 1911 he found that Germany seemed bent on humiliating France, and at the same time, on ignoring Great Britain's vital interests in Morocco. For three years he had strenuously advocated an Anglo-German understanding. Not only had the Germans failed to offer Great Britain anything substantial in the shape of reduced naval estimates, but during July they appeared to be taking advantage of Great Britain's internal difficulties, and of what they conceived to be a split in the British cabinet over policy towards Germany, to secure a diplomatic success in Europe. The tone of his speech was one of intense indignation about Germany's behaviour.

Protests about the speech were not long in forthcoming. Lord Morley saw Lloyd George, Grey, and Churchill on 27 July, and wrote afterwards to Asquith to complain that the speech was unnecessarily provocative towards Germany.[2] On the same day Loreburn asked Grey to say something in parliament 'to undo the effect of Lloyd George's speech' otherwise he feared that 'something irreparable might happen before long'.[3] Grey had a stormy interview with Metternich on 24 July. The ambassador complained that Lloyd George's speech had 'a tone of provocation'; that instead of using the normal diplomatic channels the British government had made a public declaration which had encouraged the chauvinism of the French and British presses, and had been widely interpreted as a threat to Germany. As a result the poisoning of the atmosphere would interrupt the Franco-German negotiations, and might even lead to an 'explosion'. Grey retorted that German complaints about the speech were in fact its justification—the speech was intended to assert Great Britain's right to be treated as a great power and the speech would not have occasioned such

[1] Goschen to Hardinge, 15 July 1911, Hardinge Papers.
[2] Morley to Asquith, 27 July 1911, Asquith Papers, vol. 13.
[3] Loreburn to Grey, 27 July 1911, Grey Papers, F.O.800/99.

surprise in Germany unless there had been a tendency there to think that Great Britain might be disregarded.[1]

The Liberal radicals also protested. C. P. Scott, the editor of the *Manchester Guardian*, had breakfast with Lloyd George, Churchill, and the chief whip on 22 July. Scott was critical both of the speech and of the policy which lay behind it. Lloyd George told Scott that neither he, Grey, nor Asquith would remain in office unless they could assert the country's right to be treated with diplomatic courtesy. Germany had ignored Grey's request that she recognize Great Britain's treaty right to be a party to a Moroccan settlement. France, he claimed, was weak and terrified of Germany, while the latter sought European predominance, and, if she humiliated France, would be well on the way towards achieving it. Scott commented sadly that 'the impression I got was that he is not immune from the microbe of Germanophobia'.[2]

The foreign office was, of course, overjoyed by the turn of events that had brought the chancellor to accept their views on the nature of German policy. Nicolson wrote to Hardinge in July that,

> Lloyd George especially has grasped the situation thoroughly, and is confident that if we adopt a firm attitude there is every possibility that peace will be assured, but if we show any weakening the chance of war is immeasurably increased. I must confess that I am pleasantly surprised at the attitude which both Lloyd George and Winston have adopted, as I regarded them as not likely to be advocates of a firm and determined policy.[3]

In August he added that

> Lloyd George and Winston, the two members of the Cabinet whom we always regarded as dubious and uncertain factors, were those who took up the strongest line, and who were the readiest to go to the utmost extremities.[4]

Certainly during the summer Lloyd George and Churchill became absorbed in foreign and defence policies to an extent which amazed the foreign office. The British remained anxious until the end of September that the Franco-German negotia-

---

[1] Grey to Goschen, desp 168, 25 July 1911, B.D.vii, no 419.
[2] Hammond J. L. *C. P. Scott of the Manchester Guardian*, (1934), 154–158.
[3] Nicolson to Hardinge, 27 July 1911, Nicolson Papers, F.O.800/349.
[4] Nicolson to Hardinge, 17 Aug. 1911, Hardinge Papers, (1911).

tions might break down, and war ensue. While the cabinet was in recess its functions were usurped by an unofficial directorate consisting of Asquith, Grey, Lloyd George, Churchill, and Haldane, who held frequent meetings at Haldane's London home to discuss the crisis.[1] Churchill and Sir Henry Wilson, the energetic director of military operations at the war office, persuaded the prime minister to call a meeting of the committee of imperial defence on 23 August to discuss British military and naval strategy in the event of war. Lloyd George attended—the first time he had done so. There he learnt of the detailed plans of the general staff to despatch 166,000 troops to France in the event of war, plans that were eventually adopted by the committee.[2]

After this meeting Lloyd George, Churchill, and Haldane threw themselves into the tasks of ensuring that Britain was ready for war with an enthusiasm which caused Grey some anxiety. Many observers commented on Lloyd George's bellicosity during the autumn.[3] Nicolson described both the chancellor and Churchill as

> a little disappointed that war with Germany did not occur ... I was struck with the determination of both of them not to permit Germany to assume the role of bully and at their belief that the present moment was an exceedingly favourable one to open hostilities.[4]

Grey was bombarded with letters from them about various aspects of the situation. Lloyd George believed that the crisis had demonstrated the need for 'great expenditure' on national defence, which had 'been stinted up to now'. He feared that

---

[1] Haldane to his mother, 15 & 21 Aug. 1911; 26 and 30 Oct. 1911. Haldane Papers, 5986.

[2] Committee of Imperial Defence, Minutes of 114th meeting, 23 Aug. 1911, C.I.D., 38/19/49. The admiralty's poor performance at this meeting led the prime minister to appoint Churchill as first lord in the autumn. McKenna replaced him at the home office.

[3] C. F. G. Masterman wrote of Lloyd George pondering military maps of Europe at Criccieth, planning wars, and considering alliances. And after meeting him at Balmoral, Lord Stamfordham, the king's secretary, exclaimed that he was 'far the most bellicose minister we have had here yet.' Masterman, 213–15, Stamfordham to Nicolson, 19 Sept. 1911, Nicolson Papers, F.O.800/350; also Austen Chamberlain, *Politics from The Inside, 1906–1914*, (1936), 363.

[4] Nicolson to Hardinge, 17 Aug. 1911, Hardinge Papers.

German public opinion might force its government to go to war with France, and he clamoured for information as to whether Russia was ready and willing to come to the assistance of her ally. He also supported Churchill's pressure for an Anglo–Russian–French alliance to guarantee the independence of the low countries.[1] These activities caused Grey no little alarm, since if they became public knowledge, Germany might regard them as a further provocation. While he was determined that, if Germany forced war on France, Great Britain would come to the assistance of her *entente* partner, he now hoped that Germany, made cautious by Lloyd George's warning against going too far, would conclude her negotiations with France in a more amenable spirit.

He therefore took steps to restrain the ardour of Lloyd George and Churchill. He dined with Churchill on 4 September and told him that he intended to call a conference if the Franco-German negotiations broke down, and he wrote to Lloyd George that he did not think Germany wanted war, and that he had been encouraging France to offer Germany reasonable concessions in the Congo. He also instructed Nicolson to keep Lloyd George informed of the progress of the Franco-German negotiations.[2]

The Moroccan crisis was settled early in November by a Franco-German arrangement whereby Germany received compensation in the French Congo, and France her coveted protectorate over Morocco. The Germans were acutely dissatisfied by their meagre gains in Africa, and they became convinced that had it not been for British interference they could have extracted more from France. During the autumn German press and politicians bitterly attacked British policy during the crisis. British radicals soon took up the cry and Grey was faced with a widespread campaign in the British Liberal press and in parliament against what was described as the pro-French orientation of his foreign policy. Both Lloyd George and Grey became extremely depressed about the poor state of

[1] Lloyd George to Churchill, 25 Aug. 1911, Churchill to Grey, 30 Aug. 1911; Churchill to Lloyd George, 31 Aug. 1911, Lloyd George Papers, C/3/15/6 and 7; Lloyd George to Grey, 1 Sept. 1911, B.D.vii, no. 462.

[2] Grey to Lloyd George, 5 Sept. 1911, Lloyd George Papers, C/4/14/5; Grey to Nicolson, 15 Sept. 1911, Nicolson Papers, F.O.800/350.

Anglo-German relations as the autumn progressed. As early as 5 September, Grey wrote to Lloyd George that the 'whole question of future developments in Foreign policy will have to be considered very carefully and coolly in the light of recent events.' The two men met at Aberdeen on 13 September, in Grey's words, 'to talk things over'. According to Grey they both concluded that 'a patched up peace between France and Germany, violent animosity worked up against us in Germany ... and a large increase in naval expenditure is not a pleasant prospect but that is the way things are tending'.[1]

Plainly some effort to remove the ill-feeling in Germany would be all to the good, not only in reducing international tension, but in conciliating British Liberal opinion, and restoring Lloyd George's somewhat tarnished image amongst his radical supporters.[2] Even the cabinet was now becoming restive about the implications of British defence and foreign policies.[3] Lloyd George, Grey and the others were provided with a practical opportunity to do something to improve the atmosphere when, early in January 1912, the Germans invited Churchill to visit Berlin to discuss Anglo-German relations. The invitation was discussed by Grey, Haldane, Churchill, and Lloyd George towards the end of January. They decided that Haldane should go to Berlin instead of Churchill, and they drew up a programme for the latter's guidance during the talks.[4] Their conclusions were subsequently endorsed by the cabinet. Grey was concerned that his colleagues were too over-optimistic about the prospects, for he cautioned them against going too far and too fast. An agreement, he insisted, would be valueless unless Germany recognized Great Britain's naval supremacy and agreed to reductions in naval expenditure.[5] He became even more doubtful that the negotiations would succeed when he discovered that the Germans were planning large naval increases, and he wrote again to Lloyd George and Churchill to

[1] Grey to Lloyd George, 5 Sept. 1911, Lloyd George Papers, C/4/14/5; Grey to Asquith, 13 Sept. 1911, Asquith Papers, vol. 13.
[2] Churchill, i, 73.
[3] Chiefly the secret Anglo-French military conversations; Asquith to the king, 2 Nov. 1911, CAB 41/33/28.
[4] Haldane to Mrs. Haldane, 23 Jan. 1912, Haldane Papers, 5987.
[5] Grey to Churchill, 29 Jan. 1912, Lloyd George Papers, C/3/15/14.

remind them of the need to secure a cessation of Germany's naval competition.[1]

The details of the Haldane mission may be found elsewhere.[2] The Germans would only promise to consider a reduction of the rate of their ship-building, and they again proposed that a neutrality and non-aggression agreement would provide the only secure basis for a genuine *rapprochement*. When he discovered that the Germans intended to proceed with their naval increases, Churchill decided that further negotiations with them would be useless,[3] but Lloyd George continued to hope that some naval reductions might still be arranged.[4]

The British ambassador to France, Sir Francis Bertie, became increasingly anxious that the cabinet would accept a political agreement, which, he was convinced, would spell the end of the *entente* with France. He hurried to London in the middle of February to warn the ministers of the dreadful consequences that would result for Great Britain's continental security if they accepted an agreement on the lines drawn up by the Germans. To his horror he found that even Grey was willing to consider the conclusion of a political agreement, while, of the other ministers, only Churchill was totally opposed to it. He discussed the question with Lloyd George on 19 February at the house of commons. Lloyd George spoke in favour of obtaining 'something binding from Germany for the limitation of her naval expenditure in return for territorial concessions from us', and he reminded Bertie that there was a growing feeling in Great Britain in favour of an Anglo-German *rapprochement*. He then proceeded to attack the French for throwing away, in 1911, 'the best opportunity they had ever had or were ever likely to have again, to try conclusions with Germany'. Great Britain and Russia would have supported her and 'it would have brought home to the Germans that they could not ride roughshod over Europe as they appeared to think'.[5]

[1] Grey to Churchill, 31 Jan. 1912, Lloyd George Papers, C/3/15/15.

[2] B.D.vi, no. 506; S. E. Koss, *Lord Haldane, Scapegoat for Liberalism*, (1969), 68–86.

[3] Memorandum by Churchill, 17 Feb. 1912, Lloyd George Papers, C/13/15/15.

[4] Riddell, *More Pages*, 36–7.

[5] Memoranda by Bertie, 16 & 19 Feb. 1912, Bertie Papers, F.O.800/171.

Lloyd George did not take a leading part in the ensuing discussions with Germany, which ground to a halt in the late spring owing to Germany's refusal to accept naval reductions unless Great Britain incorporated a neutrality clause in the political agreement, a demand which Grey rejected.[1] Nevertheless the Haldane mission did lead to a considerable improvement in the relations between the two countries, which by 1913 became more cordial than they had been for years. Lloyd George and Grey were now on reasonably good terms. They cooperated in trying to settle the coal strike in the early months of 1912, and both were now in agreement about foreign policy. A friendly correspondence sprang up between them on internal and foreign problems.[2] Lloyd George's complaint in his *Memoirs* that he was kept in the dark about 'the realities of the foreign situation', was certainly unjustified as far as he was concerned after 1911, when he began to play a leading part in the formulation of foreign policy.[3]

He took a keen interest in the wars between Turkey and the Balkan allies which broke out in October 1912. He was delighted when the Turks were decisively defeated, and the cause of the Balkan nationalities at long last triumphed.[4] However he became increasingly alarmed when the war in the Balkans nearly involved Austria and Russia and the other great powers on opposite sides.[5] There were anxious meetings between Lloyd George, Grey, Churchill, and Asquith to discuss British policy in the near east,[6] and Grey kept the chancellor informed of the efforts he was making to preserve peace.[7]

The crisis dragged on until the late summer, when the Balkan wars ended without serious complications arising between the great powers. The cabinet ascribed the peaceful outcome to

---

[1] According to Harcourt, Lloyd George proposed in the cabinet on 20 February that Germany should be told that further negotiations for a political agreement could not be continued unless she abandoned her naval increases, but his suggestion was rejected by the cabinet. 'Rough notes of a cabinet meeting,' 20 Feb. 1912, Harcourt Papers, Box 14.

[2] G. M. Trevelyan, *Grey of Fallodon*, (1937), 176–7.

[3] Lloyd George, *War Memoirs*, i, 29.   [4] Masterman, 244–7.

[5] Riddell, *More Pages*, 98–9.

[6] Asquith to Grey, 4 Nov. 1912, Grey Papers, F.O.800/100.

[7] Grey to Lloyd George, 21 Dec. 1912, Lloyd George Papers, C/4/14/8.

Grey's successful mediation between Austria and Russia, and as a result his reputation as foreign secretary was enhanced. In subsequent speeches Lloyd George made fulsome references to Grey's efforts to preserve peace during the Balkan crisis.

Lloyd George's interest in foreign affairs waned as he became immersed in his land campaign and with the crisis in Ulster. In any case Europe was, in general, deceptively peaceful after August 1913. The chancellor was now quarrelling with Churchill about the latter's escalating naval estimates. The friction between the two men became serious when, at the end of 1913, the first lord demanded the addition of four dreadnoughts to the British navy. Lloyd George thought that only two were necessary, and he mustered a formidable array of cabinet supporters in support of his opposition to Churchill. The chancellor pointed to the more friendly relations with Germany as an argument against large naval increases, and protested that

> It would be construed as a direct challenge to Germany, and such a policy, at a time when our relations with that country are better than they have been for years, is, to say the least, highly inopportune.[1]

Grey had made no fresh approaches to Germany about a naval agreement after 1912. He did not wish to become involved in renewed arguments about political formulae and, in any case, the Germans made it clear that they would not welcome further British proposals on the subject. Nor did Lloyd George revive the question of an Anglo-German naval agreement in his speeches, although he continued to demand reductions in naval expenditure. Grey attempted to find a compromise of the dispute over the naval estimates which would satisfy both Lloyd George and Churchill. The foreign secretary feared that the adoption of an over-large naval programme by Great Britain might encourage a renewed agitation in Germany for additional naval expenditure, which might lead, in turn, to fresh Anglo-German recriminations on the subject, and thus destroy his efforts to improve relations between the two countries. However, when Lloyd George tried to rally public support for his stand in an interview published in the *Daily Chronicle* on 1 January 1914, Grey became somewhat

[1] Memorandum by Lloyd George, 24 Dec. 1913, CAB 37/117/97.

irritated. The chancellor appealed for reductions in naval
expenditure on the grounds that Anglo-German relations were
better than they had been for years, and because the continental
nations were spending more money on building up their armies,
and would in consequence have less to spend on their navies.[1]
There were reports that Grey was 'furious' with Lloyd George,[2]
but this probably resulted from Lloyd George's failure to consult either the foreign office or the cabinet before he allowed the
interview to be published, rather than with its contents.[3] There
was a friendly enough exchange of letters between the two men
later in the month about distorted accounts of the interview
which appeared in the German press.[4] When Cambon protested
about the effects of all this on French public opinion, Grey
merely referred him to a passage in the interview which made
friendly reference to the *ententes*.[5]

The dispute between Lloyd George and Churchill raged
throughout January and early February, accompanied by the
usual threats of resignation on both sides. However the
chancellor was unwilling to provoke a final breach with
Churchill, for he eventually gave way, and accepted Churchill's
programme in return for the latter's promise to make substantial
reductions in the following year. Lloyd George's cabinet
supporters, deprived of their leader, reluctantly acquiesced.[6]

Lloyd George took no interest in foreign affairs during the
spring and early summer of 1914. He made two speeches in
July in which he took a fairly optimistic view of the state of
international relations, reaffirmed his belief in the possibility
of future reductions in armaments, and again extolled the good
relations which existed between Great Britain and Germany.[7]
These remarks merely reflected a general feeling of satisfaction
in the foreign office about the relative calm that had descended

---

[1] Lloyd George Papers, C/36/2/1.

[2] Riddell, *More Pages*, 195.

[3] Bertie to Grey, 8 Jan. 1914, Bertie Papers, F.O.800/166.

[4] Grey to Lloyd George, 23 Jan. 1914, Lloyd George to Grey, 26 Jan.
1914, Lloyd George Papers, C/4/14/12 and 13.

[5] Grey to Bertie, 6 Jan. 1914, F.O.371/1973/Germany.

[6] Randolph S. Churchill, *Winston S. Churchill*, ii, (1967), 655–683.

[7] Mansion House, 18 July 1914, in the *Daily Telegraph*, 18 July 1914,
Lloyd George Papers, C/36/2/27; Speech in the *House of Commons*, 23 July
1914.

on Europe during the spring and early summer of 1914 by comparison with previous years. Indeed Grey was formulating, during the summer, a role for Great Britain of mediator between the two alliance groupings.[1]

Neither he nor Nicolson believed that the assassination of Francis Ferdinand at Sarajevo on 28 June 1914 would lead to a serious international confrontation until they read the terms of Austria's peremptory ultimatum to Serbia on 24 July 1914.[2] Even then Grey remained hopeful that, with German cooperation, a peaceful settlement of the Serbian problem could be arranged that would be satisfactory to both Austria and Russia.[3] The cabinet, which had been preoccupied by the Ulster crisis, was abruptly informed by Grey of the serious implications of the note on 24 July;[4] days of confusion and uncertainty followed. Not until 27 July, when Austria rejected Serbia's conciliatory reply to her ultimatum, and Germany displayed her unwillingness to fall in with Grey's suggestion for mediation by the four less interested powers,[5] did it become clear that the crisis was unlikely to be settled by the methods employed during the Balkan wars.

Thus on 27 July the cabinet was made fully aware of the prospect of a European war in which Germany and Austria would be pitted against France and Russia. The ministers were also informed of the strong possibility of a German attack on France through Belgium, and that as a result Great Britain might be drawn into the struggle.[6] Thus British obligations towards Belgium became an important subject of subsequent deliberation, and while the cabinet ruled on the 29th that 'the matter if it arises will be rather one of policy than of legal obligation', the problem of what policy to adopt should Belgium be invaded remained a deeply contentious one.[7] The issue was further complicated by doubts, which persisted

[1] Memoranda by Bertie, 25 June, 4 and 16 July, 1914, Bertie Papres, F.O.800/161 & 171.

[2] Crackenthorpe, Belgrade, to Grey, tel. 48, 24 July 1914, B.D.xi, no. 94.

[3] Grey to Sir H. Rumbold, tel. 196, 24 July 1914, B.D.xi, no. 99.

[4] Asquith to the king, 25 July 1914, CAB 41/35/20.

[5] Goschen to Grey, tel. 96, and Grey to Bunsen, desp. 124, 27 July 1914, B.D.xi, nos. 185 and 188.

[6] Asquith to the king, 28 July 1914, CAB 41/35/21.

[7] Asquith to the king, 30 July 1914, CAB 41/35/22.

until 1 August, as to whether Belgium would defend herself against invasion,[1] and whether she would appeal to the other treaty powers to come to her rescue. In his *Memoirs* Lloyd George chided Grey for his failure to make it clear to Germany from the start that Great Britain would come to the assistance of Belgium, but this was out of the question in view of the cabinet's evident inability to reach a decision as to British policy, and the uncertainty about Belgium's attitude in the event of a German invasion,[2] An early British declaration on these lines might, in any case, have destroyed Grey's continued efforts to find a peaceful settlement to the Serbian dispute, a task which at least united a cabinet that was deeply divided on almost everything else. However as the crisis developed and reports of mobilizations and counter-mobilizations descended from all sides, his hopes rapidly diminished, although even on 1 August there was still a faint possibility that a settlement might be achieved by direct Austro-Russian negotiations.[3]

While Grey was privately convinced that British security depended on her joining France and Russia in the event of war, he could not force a decision on this question in the cabinet without provoking the resignation of at least half its members. Even Grey recognized the difficulty of justifying to British public opinion British intervention in a war over Balkan questions.[4] Under the circumstances he had to remain content for the time being with the cabinet's decision to preserve Great Britain's freedom of action in the crisis, however unhappy this might make the French.[5]

Lloyd George, as Asquith recognized, was the key to the situation. Once he became converted to British intervention, most of the other ministers would probably follow suit.[6] The strategy adopted by the prime minister and the foreign secretary was one which Masterman advocated to Lloyd George on either 1 or 2 August,

> I am with Runciman and McKenna in fighting for *time* sooner than

[1] Villiers, Brussels, to Grey, tel. 8, 1 Aug. 1914, B.D.xi, no. 415.
[2] Lloyd George, *War Memoirs*, 1, 43; see also Trevelyan, 254–8.
[3] Grey to Goschen, tel. 250, 1 Aug. 1914, B.D.xi, no. 411.
[4] Grey to Bertie, tel. 299, 1 Aug. 1914, B.D.xi, no. 426.
[5] Asquith to the king, 30 July 1914, CAB 41/35/22.
[6] Roy Jenkins, *Asquith*, (1964), 326.

break up the Cabinet. Twelve hours might find us united. Our collapse will be unthinkable—what is to happen to the Empire if we break to pieces!!
Do *fight* for unity.[1]

The chancellor appeared to have set himself against British involvement from the outset. He told C. P. Scott on 27 July that he was convinced that war would break out on the continent, and that Germany would then strike hard at France. He assured Scott that 'there could be no question of our taking part in the first instance'.[2] Nevertheless the problem of Belgium agitated him just as much as it did his colleagues. He wrote in his *Memoirs* that, 'I never doubted that, if the Germans interfered with the integrity and independence of Belgium, we were in honour bound to discharge our duty to that country'.[3] But descriptions of his reactions to events during the crisis suggest that he remained undecided on this question until 3 August. Of course there was no certainty that Germany would, in the last resort, attack Belgium at all—he may have assumed that Germany's strategic plans were as flexible as his would have been under similar circumstances. The Belgians themselves persisted in their belief that Germany would not violate their neutrality even as late as 2 August.[4]

At the cabinet meeting of 1 August Asquith found the chancellor, 'all for peace—is more sensible and statesmanlike for keeping the situation still open',[5] while at the cabinet meeting on the following morning (Sunday the 2nd), one of the non-interventionists, Harcourt, was evidently still doubtful as to the strength of Lloyd George's commitment to British neutrality. In a scribbled note he appealed to the chancellor, 'you must now speak for us. Grey wants us to go to war *without any violation of Belgium*.'[6] This at least provided an issue on which the non-interventionists and the waverers in the cabinet could come together. During the morning the cabinet had agreed,

[1] Note by Masterman, 1 or 2 August 1914, Lloyd George Papers, Cabinet notes, C/Box 12.
[2] Memorandum by C. P. Scott, 27 July 1914, Scott Papers, 50901.
[3] Lloyd George, i, 31.
[4] Villiers, Brussels, to Grey, tel 10, 2 Aug. 1914, B.D.xi, no 476.
[5] Quoted in Jenkins, *Asquith*, 327.
[6] Rough note by Harcourt, 2 Aug. 1914, Lloyd George Papers, C/Box 12.

not without protests, that Grey could promise the French that the British navy would protect the northern shores of France,[1] a comparatively cheap method of satisfying the consciences of those ministers who felt that Great Britain had incurred at least a moral obligation to give some assistance to France. After the meeting Lloyd George, Beauchamp, Samuel, Harcourt, and some of the others met for lunch and settled a scheme whereby they hoped Great Britain would be able to escape further involvement in the continental struggle. A declaration of Great Britain's determination to defend both the northern coasts of France and Belgian neutrality might, it was thought, deter Germany from invading Belgium. Both Lloyd George and Samuel believed that this would be of real service to France by enabling her to concentrate her forces on the defence of her narrow frontier with Germany, while Lloyd George suggested that later on Great Britain might utilize the resulting stalemate to force the belligerents to make peace.[2]

Neither Burns nor Morley would agree even to this degree of British interference, while Simon and Beauchamp expressed doubts about it. Nor was the success of the manoeuvre by any means certain. Germany's reply on 1 August to Grey's request that she respect Belgian neutrality was, to say the least, evasive.[3] In the evening the cabinet duly resolved that any substantial violation of Belgian neutrality would entail British intervention.[4] The effort to preserve Belgian neutrality collapsed on the rock-like refusal of the German army leaders to vary their strategic plans. In any case they contemplated British intervention with equanimity, and were not to be put off their course by British protests.[5] On 3 August the cabinet, learning of Germany's ultimatum to Belgium and of Belgium's determination to resist the invader, decided on the path that was to lead to Britain's involvement in the continental war on the following night. Only Morley and Burns refused to follow Lloyd George into the interventionist camp, and, as Asquith had

[1] Jenkins, *Asquith*, 328.
[2] Rough notes by Harcourt and Lloyd George, 2 Aug. 1914, Lloyd George Papers, C/Box 12; Samuel to Mrs. Samuel, 2 Aug. 1914, Samuel Papers, A/157; Lloyd George, i, 43.
[3] Grey to Goschen, 256, 1 Aug. 1914, B.D.xi, 448.
[4] Lord Crewe to the king, 2 Aug. 1914, CAB 41/35/23.
[5] Taylor, *Struggle for Mastery*, 525.

anticipated, all the other ministers eventually fell into line behind the chancellor.[1]

The invasion of Belgium was the deciding factor that impelled Lloyd George into supporting British intervention. He told Riddell on the 2nd that he would favour intervention in certain circumstances, although he would resign if Great Britain went to war in the face of a German promise to respect Belgian neutrality.[2]

But strategic and other considerations also played a part in his decision.[3] There were certain parallels with the 1911 crisis. Germany was trying to force her will on Belgium in the same way that she had attempted to bully France three years before. Then, as now, she had shown a contemptuous disregard for British interests. He told Scott after the fateful cabinet meeting of 3 August of 'the provocative attitude of German diplomacy', and of how the violation of Belgian territory had completely altered the situation.[4]

Walter Runciman later reported the chancellor as saying that, if Great Britain intervened and he resigned, he would not lead an anti-war party in the country, but would retire to Criccieth for the duration of the war—'there appeared to be nothing for a Liberal to do but to look on while the hurricane raged.'[5] This act of self-abnegation was in the end unnecessary. Despite Morley's subsequent assertions[6] Lloyd George was sincere in his advocacy of non-involvement before the 2nd. Masterman spoke 'strongly' to Scott 'of the way in which George had fought in the cabinet all through the week for peace'.[7] As Lloyd George told Bertie on 19 February 1912, 'to bring the British people to fighting point it would be requisite that Germany should have passed into Belgium for the purpose of attacking France or should have crossed the French

---

[1] Asquith to the king, 3 Aug. 1914, CAB 41/35/23.

[2] Lord Riddell, *War Diary*, 4.

[3] Kenneth O. Morgan, *Wales in British Politics 1868–1922*, (1944), 275.

[4] Memorandum by Scott, 3 Aug. 1914, Scott Papers, 50901.

[5] Runciman to Spender, 1929, Spender Papers, 43386.

[6] Morley, John, Viscount, *Memorandum on Resignation* (1928), 16–18. Even Morley admitted on the 2nd that Germany's high-handed actions were hindering the work of the peace-makers. Sir Almeric Fitzroy, *Memoirs*, (1925), ii, 560.

[7] Memorandum by Scott, 3 Aug. 1914, Scott Papers, 50901.

frontier'.[1] By 3 August Germany had announced her intention of invading Belgium, and this, as far as he was concerned, was decisive.

NOTES

Note A. *The Mansion House speech.* According to the chief whip's brother, writing in 1944, Lloyd George approached Grey after the cabinet with a draft of what he intended to say. Asquith was called in and the three men drew up a suitable form of words. Lord Tyrrell of Avon confirmed this account of events, which was based presumably on what Lloyd George told Murray on 17 January 1912, i.e. that he drafted the speech 'of his own accord'. Churchill wrote later that the speech was also shown to him. Nicolson informed Hardinge on 27 July 1911 that the speech was 'not a sudden improvisation, as it was written down and submitted to Grey previously, and it was read out and not spoken on the occasion on which it was delivered'. Grey told the commons on 27 November 1911 that he, Asquith, and Lloyd George had felt that for a 'first rate' cabinet minister to make a speech after Grey's interview with Metternich, without saying anything about foreign affairs, 'would be misleading to public opinion here and everywhere'. Arthur Murray to Lord Tyrrell of Avon, 24 Feb. 1944, min, by Tyrrell, F.O.371/1160/Morocco/1911; Diary of Arthur Murray, 17 Jan. 1912, Murray Papers, no 8814; Nicolson to Hardinge, 27 July 1911, Nicolson Papers, F.O. 800/349; Grey, i, 224; Lloyd George, *War Memoirs*, i, 26–27; Parliamentary Debates (Commons), vol. xxxii, cc. 43–65.

Portsmouth Polytechnic   M. L. DOCKRILL

[1] Memorandum by Bertie, 19 Feb. 1912, Bertie Papers, F.O.800/171.

II

THE LAND CAMPAIGN: LLOYD GEORGE AS A SOCIAL REFORMER, 1909–14

H. V. EMY

H. V. EMY

Age 25

London School of Economics B.Sc. 1963–66
Ph.D. 1966–69
Currently Lecturer in politics at Monash
University, Melbourne

THE LAND CAMPAIGN:
LLOYD GEORGE AS A SOCIAL
REFORMER, 1909-14

AFTER three years in office, Liberalism by 1909 had reached an impasse. Thus far the government had given legislative blessing to those demands whose priority had been established by 1906—Trade Disputes, Pensions and the Miners' Eight Hours Act. Yet the government might justifiably be accused, firstly of failing to recognize the gravity of the social problem, and secondly of being too open to pressure from interested groups. A cry was raised amongst the Radical ranks for a more constructive approach to reform, for a definite commitment to a social ideal in which positive social values would themselves be taken as the abiding criteria of legislation, overthrowing the limitations of time and money which so seemed to mesmerize the 'practical' politicians.

Nor was this spirit of criticism the prerogative of Labour alone. A Liberal-Radical group, varying in size from 20 to over 50 in any one division, urged the government strongly to reduce 'unproductive' (military) expenditure, and to divert the money saved to poor-law and educational reform, to financing works of public utility for the unemployed, including therein a programme of land-based industries, afforestation, reclamation schemes and scientific farms. This new growth of Liberal-Radicalism after 1906 brought into parliament a spirit of inquiry which questioned whether retrenchment and economy, as strictures upon government expenditure, were in themselves ends at all, but merely the means to a greater end, namely, the need to secure the most productive use of a society's resources.

In this context, the Radicals insisted that a wider approach to social reform was inseparable from a reappraisal of prevailing economic determinisms, choosing to doubt the benefits of the undisputed sway of Capital as the fount of the entire productive process, and preferring instead to view Land and Labour as the first agents in production, with Capital as the secondary outcome of their twin energies. Broadly, the Radicals believed that social reform was a matter of removing the restrictions and inequalities which characterized the present state of both Land and Labour, that by removing the abuses of monopoly ownership and exploitation from these two factors, true freedom of production and equality of opportunity might be obtained. The existing pre-eminence of Capital they saw as an encouragement to claims to wealth, to social and economic power, which were both unjust in that they ignored the questions of how that wealth had been acquired and the uses to which it might be put, and uneconomic in that it was within the power of wealth in an imperfect market to extort a progressively greater reward for itself, a reward which bore little relationship to the economic value of the service performed.

If Labour was associated with the unearned increment of production, so Radicalism had by now developed the analogous device of 'social value', whereby what was sought was to distinguish between the private and the social origins of wealth, between a reward that was due to ability (i.e. a payment necessary to induce the services of a particular factor of production), and that reward which was either unearned or unnecessary, the outcome of an unduly favourable market position; for example, the exploitation of rising urban land values, or the use of unorganized, sweated labour. The origins of this Radicalism lay both in the traditional Liberal preoccupation with the land, with the feature of economic rent, and in the teachings of Hobsonian economics. By 1909 Radicalism was demanding a changed role for government expenditure in order to increase the joint productive capacities of Land and Labour, calling upon the Government to establish the undisputed right of society to determine the conditions upon which private use of these two original, natural, resources should take place.

Such Radicalism, however, was removed from the tenor of official Liberalism, which by 1909 was more concerned with the uneasiness upon the right of the party than upon the left. The business fraternity, including Liberals like Sir Christopher Furness, Sir James Kitson, Sir Walter Runciman, Lords Pirrie, Cory, Lupton and Walton, were increasingly disturbed by the favours shown to trade unions, and by restrictions on hours and wages imposed by a free-trading government. Furness and

Walton thought the Liberals were giving way to socialistic pressure,[1] while isolated Liberals of a whiggish persuasion, Harold Cox, Major Renton and Carlyon Bellairs voted consistently against Liberal reforms.

In the country, the Conservatives sought to identify the 'New Liberalism' with socialism, questioning the sincerity of previous Liberal pledges of retrenchment and seeking to identify themselves as upholders of financial orthodoxy. The Conservatives accused the Liberals of having made insufficient allowance for the future liabilities of old-age pensions, of maintaining the income-tax at a war level, of refusing to broaden the basis of taxation, of destroying the elasticity of the taxable reserves and thereby throwing too heavy a burden upon the class most responsible for the maintenance of production and employment.[2] The Conservatives lent unofficial support to the plethora of indignant groups aroused to protest by Liberal reforms—the Municipal Reformers in London, the Middle-Classes Defence Society and the Income-Tax Reduction League. 1908 witnessed a string of Liberal by-election defeats.

Rising unemployment in October 1908, and the mixed prospects of further reform precipitated a crisis of confidence amongst the Liberal sections. In response, cabinet speeches began to appear more positive, Asquith promising on 21 October and again on 15 December that the government would deal 'with the permanent causes and conditions of unemployment'. The scale of the government's commitments began to broaden, chiefly owing to the growing knowledge of German insurance schemes common to both Churchill and Lloyd George. While Lloyd George, on 1 October, spoke of a comprehensive programme to combat the social evils of the aged, the infirm, the weak and unemployed, Churchill at Dundee asserted the government's responsibility to provide for the central organization of industry, and on 11 December, presented his scheme for unemployment insurance and labour exchanges to the cabinet as part of a 'tremendous policy of social organization'.

[1] E.g. Ripon to Campbell-Bannerman, 9 Sept. 1906. Campbell-Bannerman Papers, Add. MSS. 41225. Walton to Campbell-Bannerman, 9 Oct. 1907. Campbell-Bannerman Papers, Add. MSS. 41240.

[2] E.g. *H.C. deb.*, 4s. cxciii, c.665 25 July 1908 (A. Chamberlain).

In the winter of 1908–9, Lloyd George was reported to be moving in search of a more democratic policy.[1] His position was more than a little ambiguous, for the real character of the impasse was primarily financial. Lloyd George had already posed as the champion of economy in the face of demands from both McKenna and Haldane, and one of his first acts as chancellor had been to remind the cabinet that they were collectively pledged to the reduction of expenditure, and 'sections of our own supporters will attack unless we do so act'.[2] While he had for the while surrendered the major responsibility for insurance to Churchill, following his own visit to Germany in August his interest in health insurance had been aroused, and indeed, he later claimed that the only reason why he had not personally superintended the whole insurance scheme from the beginning was due to Churchill appropriating his ideas in 1908.[3]

There is no reason to doubt that Lloyd George fully supported the expansion of the Liberal commitment to social reform and, being well aware that no money could be saved from existing expenditure, opted for a Radical rather than an orthodox financial policy. The necessity for imposing fresh taxation (the necessity being underlined by the further demands of the navy in 1909), at a time of electoral unpopularity, could only be justified by the prospect of additional social reform. There were, however, two factors which influenced Lloyd George in his choice. Firstly, there was the Liberal belief in the superiority of direct to indirect taxation, their willingness to impose direct taxation upon property, and their tacit admission of the principle of graduation in their constant tinkering with the scales of abatement, and Asquith's introduction of the differentiation between earned and unearned income in 1907. (A strong demand for a fully graduated income tax was a feature of the Radical case, especially in the hands of Chiozza Money.)

Evidence exists to suggest that the Liberals after 1906 were consciously developing a progressive system of taxation as a

[1] L. Masterman, *C. F. G. Masterman* (1939), 112.

[2] CAB 37/93 no 62, 19 May, 1908, 'The Financial Situation'.

[3] Lloyd George to the Master of Elibank, 17 April, 1911. Elibank Papers, MSS. 8802.

necessary infrastructure to any programme of social reform. A treasury minute of 1907 stated:

> The present Government have recognised the pressing need for social reforms which must entail heavy additional expenditure. No one now expects that reductions of existing expenditure will provide the necessary means.[1]

It went on to say that the only real way of expanding revenue sufficiently lay in a super-tax on large incomes. Asquith in 1907 also gave warning of a break with orthodoxy when he said:

> The country has reached a stage in which, whether we look merely at its fiscal or at its social exigencies, we cannot afford to drift along the stream and treat each year's finance as if it were self-contained. The Chancellor ought to budget, not for one year, but for several years.[2]

while Haldane submitted to Asquith, in 1908, a memorandum which identified financial and poor-law reform as the two chief problems facing the Government. He too advocated a policy of taking 'such toll' from the evident increases in wealth through direct taxation as would provide for both social reform and national defence:

> The more boldly such a proposition is put the more attractive . . . will it prove. It will commend itself to many timid people as a bulwark against the nationalisation of wealth.[3]

Clearly, precedent existed for the course Lloyd George took in 1909, and support from these sources may well have proved invaluable in helping him overcome opposition within the cabinet. Yet for the land clauses themselves one must look to the second factor at work upon Lloyd George, the long-standing relationship between Liberals and the land.

Policy towards the land had always marked a point of difference between Liberals and Conservatives. The Liberal antipathy to privileged landlordism, to a semi-feudal system of land tenure, and their emphasis upon the obligations of property rather than its rights, was in strong contrast to the Conservative respect for land as the basis of all property rights. By 1906, Liberal views had moved considerably from their campaigns

[1] CAB 37/87 no 22, 26 Feb. 1907.
[2] *H.C. deb.*, 4s., clxxii, c1186 18 April 1907.
[3] 8 Aug. 1908. Asquith Papers, volume II.

for free trade in land. Agricultural decline and rural depopulation were swelling the pools of casual labour in the cities, adding
to the housing shortages and aggravating the problems of local
authorities who were expected to finance both their own very
necessary improvements and a large share of the cost of national
services like education and the poor rate. In the face of rising
urban land values, the authorities found it difficult to secure
land for redevelopment and housing at reasonable prices, hence
there was a strong demand for rating reform, for compulsory
acquisition powers to allow local authorities to buy land on the
fringes of expanding towns in advance of their immediate needs.[1]

To reformers, it seemed that many inter-related problems
had their roots in the land, the provision of land for unemployment schemes, the recovery of farming, and urban development.
Land reform featured prominently in all Liberal policy statements after 1900. In 1902, land reformers of all opinions
combined to form the United Committee For The Taxation Of
Land Values, which campaigned for the comprehensive
valuation of all land, in which site value would be set apart from
the separate value of property and improvements. This policy
rested on the belief that if, instead of taxing the letting value of
property, the local rate was to be laid upon the selling value of
the land, where that was defined as the price a willing seller
might obtain in the market, and if vacant land were also rated,
more land would be diverted on to the market for sale as the
speculator's motives for holding it were discouraged, (i.e. he
would no longer profit by the gap between the nominal letting
value of the property, and the real value of the land in a seller's
market). Moreover, by transferring the primary incidence of
local taxation from property to land, all tenants might be
stimulated to improvement and development, for except in so
far as they were increasing the value of the land at sale, they
would no longer be rated directly upon the value of their own
improvements.

Their emphasis upon the land is often taken as proof that the
Liberals never truly understood the nature of the industrial
problem. This criticism was certainly true for many Liberals
whose obsession with the landowning class caused them to lay

[1] Cf. W. Ashworth, *The Genesis of Modern British Town Planning* (1954)
Ch. 7.

the blame for all modern problems at the door of the 'land monopoly'. One Liberal, writing on unemployment in 1908, refused to accept that agricultural depression was in any degree due to international price movements and the influx of cheap wheat, or the fall in the capital value of the land and the absence of capital for agricultural development; 'the only cause of rural depopulation is the power of the landowner to refuse to let his land in as many cases as he likes, and to exact too high a rent in all other cases'. If it were true, he claimed, that economic causes were alone to blame, then rents should have fallen by as much as prices. As it was, they had not, and the tenant farmer was being squeezed between falling prices and a higher level of rent. The burden of the ground rent was an inflated and unnecessary cost in agriculture, in building, mining and quarrying.[1] In reply, the Conservatives stressed that rent reductions had undoubtedly taken place in many cases, and pointed out that the return to a landowner was often barely sufficient to provide him with the capital to improve the land and to build new cottages. Conservatives were also curious to know how the taxation of an element of cost (i.e. site value) would in fact reduce total cost.

Contemporaries themselves distinguished between three categories of land value taxation advocates. Firstly, there were those like the Land Law Reform Association who simply wanted to make all land accessible and to divert part of its value into public hands, but had no intention of attacking private property. Secondly, there were the single-taxers, the followers of Henry George, who believed that wealth was primarily the outcome of the application of labour to land, and that the real obstacle to increasing production and employment was the existence of a tribute in the form of economic rent which the landlord was able to extort from an individual producer by virtue of his ownership of a scarce commodity. Taxation of economic rent, being a tax upon a non-necessary cost of production, could not be passed on by the landowner, and if steadily increased, must, they believed, destroy the selling value of land, so leading to a virtual state of common property in land, although this would not involve the complete denial of private ownership.

[1] J. Orr, *Unemployment* (1908).

The third group, the land nationalisers, wanted to abolish all private property in land and favoured site value taxation as the means by which to arrive at a fair basis upon which the actual transfer of land to public ownership might be effected. They viewed the resultant tenure of land from the state as analogous to a conditional freehold, with all revenues from the use of land going to the state. The nationalizers thought it impossible to tax landowners out of existence, pointing out that such taxation, if first intended to break-up the large estates, must also increase the number of landowners and hence the opposition. The nationalizers took the most positive view of the state development of land resources. A. Williams, for example, Liberal M.P. for Merioneth until 1910, suggested that if all land were under public supervision, it would become an easy matter to instigate forestry and reclamation schemes, and to develop housing and roads while allowing for the full requirements of town and country planning.[1]

It was some indication of the new Radical influence within the parliamentary party after 1906 that the Land Nationalisation Society could claim nearly 130 M.P.s to be their supporters.[2] In the parliament of 1906, it was evidently the single taxers who were in a minority, Wedgwood, their spokesman, later wrote of 'only' seven adherents.[3] A valuation bill being essential to all three groups, unity reigned amongst them, although after their eventual success in 1909 the groups separated to complicate Lloyd George's Land Campaign. The land reformers, 280 strong under J. H. Whitley, maintained unremitting pressure upon both Campbell-Bannerman and Asquith in the form of memorials and petitions, but although they gained promises of a valuation bill, and although three fairly radical land measures were brought forward by the Government in 1907 (two of which were lost in the Lords) they gained nothing tangible. By 1909 their frustration was acute.

The effect of this pressure, combined with a strong demand now being made by the Central Chamber of Agriculture for rating reform, provided Lloyd George with an invaluable context in which to set his land clauses. Not only did they

---

[1] A. Williams, *Unemployment and Land Nationalisation* (1909).
[2] Land Nationalisation Society Annual for 1906.
[3] J. C. Wedgwood, *Memoirs of a Fighting Life* (1940) 67.

provide Radicalism with an opportune enemy, an enemy with which Lloyd George was himself well acquainted, but they promised to provide an expanding source of revenue in the years ahead. The Conservatives were especially resentful that free trade finance had found a further lease of life at the very moment when its prospects seemed most limited. The sight of an expanding social programme with its attendant attacks upon wealth and property might well have convinced the Conservatives that they had everything to gain by fighting the budget and little to lose.[1]

In the first place, the land clauses were politically inspired, and so Lloyd George told Spender:

> I do not agree with you that we ought never to have introduced the land clauses in the fourth session. The Party had lost heart. On all hands I was told that enthusiasm had almost disappeared at meetings, and we wanted something to rouse the fighting spirit of our own forces. This the land proposals have undoubtedly succeeded in doing.[2]

Yet the clauses can also be seen as an integral part of Lloyd George's own developing ideas on social policy. From his speeches in 1909, he was already looking to a constructive land policy to provide the solution to the problem of surplus urban labour, draining the most inefficient casuals off to 'regenerative' land and labour colonies, while providing alternative sources of employment for the more capable, which was, in fact, very much on the lines of the Minority Report's suggestions. A land policy he saw as the corollary of unemployment insurance; the latter, initially at least, could succour those trades where there was a real prospect of regular, if discontinuous, work. But it could only do so if the numbers were limited and clearly organized. The budget speech provided a clue to his intentions, for Lloyd George listed a series of aims for which the budget was to provide the revenue: Labour exchanges, Insurance, the Development Commission, and the reform of local government finance. Over the next five years his policies unfolded in precisely that order.

The establishment of the Development Commission revealed Lloyd George as willing to devote state funds to agricultural

---

[1] Cf. J. S. Sandars to A. J. Balfour, 21 Sept. 1909. Balfour Papers. Add. MSS. 49766.

[2] 16 July 1909. J. A. Spender Papers. Add. MSS. 46388.

education and research, and to miscellaneous matters relating to internal improvements, (two million pounds were set aside here in 1909). This Commission further suggests that Lloyd George was, politically, closer to the land nationalisers amongst the Radicals, in that he was giving effect to a policy of national development which such reformers had urged as being the most effective answer to tariff reform. Such a policy also found favour with certain Liberal businessmen, notably those who had subscribed to the 'Brunner memorandum' in 1904, a memorial which asked for national funds to be devoted to promote industrial purposes 'which will bring an adequate return in an increase of trade and prosperity'.[1]

Neither the existence of these sources of support, however, nor the admittedly congenial nature of the choice he made, must be allowed to obscure the significance of Lloyd George's decision to found his forthcoming policies, and career, upon a Radical base. For it was among the Radicals alone that he could now expect to find consistent support for further rises in direct taxation, for his repeated raids upon the sinking fund—a very distinct break with orthodoxy—and for the imminent expansion of the idea of a minimum wage, which Lloyd George supported in 1909, became a leading exponent of in 1912, and adopted for his campaign in 1913. The feeling aroused by the 1909 budget, among Liberals as well as among the Conservatives, suggested that in terms of support, the political consequences for the parties were likely to be considerable.

By March, 1909, Lloyd George had decided upon a separate valuation of site values and buildings, and in order that this might be accepted as a part of the finance bill, (constitutionally), he intended to attach two clauses for the taxation of mining royalties and ground rents, and the taxation of vacant land valued below £50 per acre.[2] Out of the latter proposal sprang the increment and development duties, a 20 per cent tax on the incremental value of land accruing from the date of valuation, (April 30, 1909), to the date of sale, and a tax of a half-penny in the pound on the capital value of undeveloped land; agricultural land was to be exempt. The land taxes were to

[1] Copy, Campbell-Bannerman Papers, Add. MSS. 41242 ff.1–7.
[2] CAB 37/98, no 44, 13 March 1909. There was also a 10% Reversion Duty, but this was negligible.

bring in an estimated £500,000 in a full year, and to meet the full deficit of £16 million Lloyd George increased the death duties, imposed a super-tax, raised the taxes on unearned incomes, on spirits and tobacco, stamp duties and licenses.

In the cabinet, Murray opposed the reversion duty, the concession to the 'brats', and forecast trouble over the evasion of the super-tax.[1] He and Runciman thought Lloyd George had purposely underestimated the yield of the new taxation and that there was no need to raid the sinking fund. Runciman wanted to drop one of the direct taxes at least. Lewis Harcourt forecast the budget would mean the 'triumph of tariff reform'.[2] Burns thought it 'the most kaleidoscopic budget ever planned' and recorded that Lloyd George had 'nearly all against him for good and sound reasons'.[3] Within the party, it was rumoured that nearly 100 Liberals were 'irreconcilably opposed' to the development duty, although only seven apparently voted against it in the lobbies and only eight voted against the increment value duty.[4] Yet this was not the whole story. Sir Walter Runciman, Chairman of the Northern Liberal Federation, wished to resign as soon as he heard of the 'destructive' character of the budget; he too believed in unemployment resulting from 'a lack of funds that have been exhausted by taxes'. Prominent Liberals, such as Furness and Alfred Pease, were much disturbed by the budget's implications, while Fitzmaurice wrote to Bryce, in some disgust, that 'the house of commons was never so full of financial cranks as it is now'. Undoubtedly, the budget appealed most clearly to the Radicals, and it was significant that amongst the high proportion of Liberal M.P.s, (about 70), retiring in 1910, nearly half were disgruntled with the radicalism of reform.[5]

The Conservatives bitterly opposed the land clauses as a discrimination against one class of property, 'the fundamental right of ownership was at stake' they declared. They opposed

[1] Memo. by Elibank, 7 April 1909, Asquith Papers vol. 22.
[2] Cabinet notes from Elibank and Harcourt to Runciman, Runciman Papers, General Correspondence.
[3] J. Burns Papers, Add. MSS. 46326, 1 and 28 April, 1909, (diary).
[4] Runciman Papers, General Correspondence, note to Asquith from Elibank, n.d. H.C.Div. Lists nos. 400 and 413, 1909.
[5] Also, N. Blewett, *The General Elections of 1910*, unpublished Oxford D.Phil. Thesis, 1967.

the dated valuation as a fictitious concept, producing costly
and arbitrary decisions. They denied that it was possible to
distinguish social value from the values due to individual effort,
especially in the case of agriculture, and instanced the case of
builders who would legitimately expect their work to increase
the value of land. The Central Board of Agriculture opposed
the increment values because, they said, to tax any recovery in the
value of agricultural land, after the value had been declining
for forty years, would be unjust. In so far as this was a direct
tax upon the landowner, it was yet another increase in his
costs which might possibly be met by a further decline in the
money he was willing to invest in the land. Hence there might
be an uncertain market for land which would accentuate the
already low prices and discourage future development.

The government admitted the validity of some of these
criticisms. It was agreed that agricultural land should be
exempt from increment duty in respect of increases in value
due to expenditure upon the land, while owners of agricultural
land were further allowed to claim a 25 per cent deduction
against income tax in respect of the cost of improvements, including cottages upon their land. The latter was estimated to cost
£550,000, 'and its effect is calculated to leave the owners of
agricultural land better off as regards the total taxation
exacted from them than they were before the present budget'.[1]

Meanwhile the land reformers had achieved their objective
of a national valuation, and it was this, rather than the actual
land clauses, which gained their immediate support. Indeed,
both then and later, Wedgwood, for the single taxers, made it
quite clear that they opposed the increment value duty as this
could still be included in the final selling price of land.
Wedgwood later blamed McKenna for the loss of a single tax in
1909, Lloyd George being too concerned with the revenue
aspects alone.[2] Within the parliamentary party after 1910, the
balance apparently inclined more to the single taxers, for
although the Land Nationalisation Society still claimed
98 supporters in the Commons, in the light of later events this
seems to have been an exaggeration, and moreover the

[1] Asquith to King Edward VII, (copy), 18 Sept. 1909. Asquith Papers,
vol 5.
[2] Wedgwood, *Memoirs*, 68–69.

Parliamentary Land Values Group now included such leading single tax speakers as C. E. Price (the chairman) P. W. Raffan, Dundas White, Neilson and Spicer. Further evidence of a tilt in the balance was provided when the Group submitted a new memorial on August 3, 1910. They now asked not only for power to be given to the local authorities for them to adopt site value as the uniform standard of rating, but also for a national tax on full site value. Part of the proceeds of the national tax would go in relief of the rates, but it was primarily designed to finance the abolition of the food taxes and to provide a national fund out of which newly-allocated, fully national services could be financed, education, poor relief, roads, police and asylums.

Previously, valuation had been considered within the confines of local finance. A national tax was something new and was now evidently to be promulgated as the joint answer to national financial needs and to rating reform. The Land Values Group now took the view that valuation, not expected to be completed before 1915, was taking too long. In a memorandum submitted on 18 May, 1911, and signed by 174 M.P.s, they called for its expediting. By 1912, they were suggesting that valuation should omit a separate assessment of buildings and improvements, and be simply a record of the whole land value, which might then be capitalized for purposes of taxation. On 24 April, 1912, Francis Neilson introduced a land values rating bill which adopted such a system as its basis, and on 12 July, the Group agreed to adopt the text of their previous memorial as a statement of policy. This new emphasis upon the taxation of the land itself seemed to be a move away from policies of positive state development, and although Wedgwood described it as more than a financial reform, i.e., as a social and economic reform, reducing the rating burden upon productive industry, increasing the availability of the land for settlement, and encouraging the promotion of land-based industries, yet it was surely doubtful whether land taxation would achieve such ends by itself. In this lay the seed of the emerging quarrel between the single taxers and the nationalizers.

In 1912, the more significant conflict lay between the land reformers and the moderates within the party. In the country, by May 1912, both the General Council of the Scottish Liberal Association and the General Council of the N.L.F. had declared

in favour of the Land Values Group. On 31 May, 1912,
E. G. Hemmerde succeeded Sir George White in North West
Norfolk, and on 13 July, R. L. Outhwaite won Hanley from
Labour. Both were advocates of the single tax, and both
campaigns were won on the land issue. The style of their
campaigning, however, aroused opposition, A. C. Murray,
brother of the Master of Elibank, writing in his diary:

> This group is running for all it is worth an extreme land policy, which
> in effect, although they deny it, amounts to a single tax on land values.
> The members of the group are becoming more arrogant every day,
> one of them having the audacity to say that there was no place in the
> Liberal party for anyone who did not accept their policy!

He recorded the moderates' dislike of a 'raging, tearing
campaign' and forecast the loss of many of the party's 'best
supporters if such a campaign is allowed to mature'. He also
remarked on the isolation of Lloyd George in the Cabinet—
'he is making a mistake if he thinks he can run a land campaign
single-handed'.[1]

Lloyd George was, in fact beginning to encounter increasing
hostility. Bonar Law was informed that Lloyd George had lost
popularity with the business Liberal and that 'the better-class
Liberal is—sick and tired of Lloyd Georgian finance, and the
"People's Budget" is beginning to be felt'.[2] Lloyd George had
also lost ground in these quarters over his willingness to
incorporate the '5 and 2' in the Miners' Minimum Wage Act.
The Conservatives publicized the anomalies arising out of the
progress of the valuation and stepped up their attacks upon
the quality of Lloyd George's financial abilities:

> Consols below 78. Other gilt edged securities similarly depressed.
> The sinking fund reduced. Taxation at war level. The elasticity of our
> tax revenue almost destroyed. Enormous increase in the exportation
> of capital . . . Every interest threatened and harassed.[3]

Such was his proximity to the Radical reformers that on
8 October, 1912, he took the opportunity of affirming, through
the medium of George Lambert, a respected Liberal farmer,
that he was no single taxer, but land should contribute to

[1] A. C. Murray's Diary, 19 July and 8 August 1912. Elibank Papers,
MSS 8814.
[2] Memo. dated 8 March 1912, Bonar Law Papers, 26/1/76.
[3] *Morning Post*, 9 Feb. 1912.

taxation in proportion to its value-at-sale. In private, he told A. C. Murray that he would 'Twist the necks' of Hemmerde's group in October, although if Wedgwood's estimate was accurate, that group, by now, was 70 strong. This was, no doubt a reference to the newly-established Land Enquiry Committee.

During 1911, with the passage of the Parliament Bill and the preparation of Insurance, there was little time for Lloyd George to contemplate a large land programme. A departmental committee on local taxation was set up to review financial developments since the Royal Commission of 1901, a move which derived in part from the growing pressure for rating reform; the Conservative Hayes Fisher moved an amendment to the Address on this issue every year after 1910, and in 1912 he received support from Wedgwood and W. P. Byles who tabled a similar amendment of their own which was talked out.

Against the backcloth of industrial unrest, and with the Irish problem looming once again, Lloyd George could not afford to delay the opening of the land campaign unduly. The origins of the unofficial Enquiry Committee dated from a breakfast given by Lloyd George to a group of leading Radicals, including Seebohm Rowntree, C. P. Scott, C. R. Buxton and C. F. G. Masterman, in June 1912. It was agreed that the Enquiry would investigate rural and urban conditions separately; each enquiry would have a chief organiser in London and a team of investigators. The full committee would consist of five M.P.s, Ellis Davies, Baron de Forest, E. G. Hemmerde, Ian Macpherson and R. Winfrey, under the chairman, A. H. D. Acland, with Seebohm Rowntree and his lawyer also in attendance. The Enquiry relied upon financial contributions from wealthy Liberal sympathizers such as W. H. Lever, Joseph Rowntree and de Forest himself. Operations began in August with the rural areas, a sub-committee of three (Hemmerde, de Forest and E. R. Cross, Rowntree's lawyer), being delegated to begin the urban enquiry. Progress was delayed in October by the ill-health of the secretary, Heath, and in November, by the Balkan situation. The initial findings tended to substantiate Conservative allegations that there existed widespread depression and uncertainty in the property market, due not only to the 1909 budget but to the whole trend of Liberal social legislation. From Leeds, Newcastle and the

North, came reports of a 'revision of mortgage loans and—
increasing investment in foreign and colonial securities of
money hitherto lent upon the security of English properties'.
The evidence also confirmed the findings of the 1907 agricultural census of long hours and low wages, a sixty- to seventy-hour
week for a cash sum ranging from 12s.–14s. per week in many
southern counties, to 17s.–20s. per week in the north. Acland
instanced the case of one landowner who had bought up all
neighbouring property 'because I do not want any undesirable
person in the village'. Cases of farmers being driven off their
farms by uncontrolled game, of landlords' failure to repair their
cottages, and of a farmer forced to quit when his rent was
raised on his own improvements, underlined the need for
reform.[1]

When the Enquiry was established, there do not seem to have
been any specific terms of reference beyond the general question
of the 'condition of the land'. The general air of indecision can
fairly be attributed to the very confused state of the party in the
latter half of 1912, which was exhibiting severe signs of strain
after the efforts of previous years and remained in part uncon-
vinced of the merits of an all-out land campaign;—'the Liberal
party cannot be in power for ever, and this is a fact that should
be recognized by some of the wild men on our side'.[2] It seemed
to the moderates that political considerations, amongst which
Lloyd George's own aspirations were numbered, were becoming
too dominant and that in the struggle for popular power, an
ever-expanding social commitment might well become a
dangerous liability. While, by this time, there were few in the
party who were not full supporters of the social programme,
there was a sizeable group who could fairly be described as
'orthodox' in their views of matters financial, economic, and
constitutional. When A. C. Murray, for example, organized a
petition to Asquith pointing out the risk to the party of continual
reform, he obtained about forty signatures.

It is evident that it may have been Asquith's support for
Lloyd George that was the determining factor here. In 1911,
Asquith had moved Runciman to the Board of Agriculture in
order, as he said, to rejuvenate the administration. 'The

[1] Lloyd George Papers, C/2/1.
[2] Elibank Papers, MSS 8814, 8 Aug. 1912.

Government', he wrote, 'has lost much ground in the English rural counties, largely because we have not been able to present to them an intelligible and attractive land policy'.[1] The land campaign may well have appeared to him, as it appeared to Lloyd George, as the means whereby to confirm the Liberal party as the constructive party of reform. Lloyd George had in fact heard from Llewellyn Davies, a Radical supporter, that Ramsay MacDonald, Keir Hardie, and Snowden, had 'admitted that land reform was the economic bedrock of [social] reform, but could not identify themselves with it for fear of losing their independent position and bringing grist to the Liberal mill'.[2] At Ladybank, on 6 October, 1912, Asquith pledged that the coming campaign would not be of a confiscatory nature, and finally, on 10 February, 1913, Lloyd George was able to tell Runciman that 'the P.M. has now unleashed me'.

As the evidence accumulated, two major questions emerged, housing and wages. Runciman was primarily concerned with the former where the joint failure of Burns and the local authorities to use what powers they possessed, plus the Liberal refusal to consider making loans to private landowners for housing, pointed the finger increasingly towards the assumption of a direct responsibility by the state to provide cottages. In the rural areas. the landowner was traditionally the chief provider of cottages, but at a time when the rent from such building was so low, the landowner was reluctant to build unless he retained full control of the cottage. The rural district council could obtain loans from the Public Works Commissioners, repayable at $3\frac{1}{2}$ per cent over 80 years, but the rent was often not enough to cover full repayment with the result that the deficit fell upon the rates, which again the local landowners resented. The sum of such loans had fallen from £350,000 in 1900 to £49,000 in 1909, Burns refusing to put any pressure upon the local authorities, (although in opposing a state housing scheme, Burns claimed that loans had risen to £130,000 in the first nine months of 1913). Finally, various land societies, operating on a commercial basis, charged rents of three shillings a week, which labourers

[1] Asquith to Runciman, 14 Oct. 1911, Runciman Papers, General Correspondence.

[2] Lloyd George Papers, C/9/3/10. 4 Aug. 1912.

could rarely afford. In August 1913, Runciman suggested a state housing programme of 10,000 cottages, costing up to £2 million, perhaps being let at a commercial rent. In November, he appointed an advisory committee on rural cottages, principally to examine methods of construction and in April, 1914, he asked for a grant of £100,000 to build 'a few hundred cottages as an experiment'. A state housing bill was one of the measures lost on the outbreak of war.

It was clear however that state-sponsored housing would certainly be dearer than renting from a private landlord, which raised the issue of wages—in particular, the feasibility of securing a minimum wage for the agricultural labourer. A difference of opinion emerged here between Runciman and Lloyd George, the latter being quite willing to fix a national figure for such a wage, which would serve as the guide-line for local wages-boards. He apparently envisaged a central wages tribunal to which there would be 'a statutory direction' to 'award a wage which should secure the physical efficiency of the labourer and his family, and also enable him to pay a commercial rent for his cottage'. Lloyd George and the Land Enquiry thought it necessary to endorse the principle of a living wage, for otherwise wage awards might fail to do more than cover the increased cost of rent.[1] Runciman believed a national minimum in any form to be impossible, and considered the only practical commitment could be to a fair wage. Lloyd George, he told Asquith, only wanted a living wage 'because Rowntree has invented a protein standard!'. Runciman did not admit that the Minimum Wage Acts of 1909 and 1912 were parallels for the case of agriculture.[2]

To the structure of wages boards was next opposed the idea of a Land Commission, which Haldane suggested in July 1913. This was to consist of men with a practical knowledge of agricultural conditions, who would be able to decide wage awards and all matters relating to landlord-tenant relations. By mid-August, Lloyd George had come to support the idea of a Commission, or 'Arbitration Panel', and when on 21 August

---

[1] Lloyd George to C. R. Buxton, 17 July 1913, Lloyd George Papers, C/2/2/30.

[2] Runciman to Asquith (copy), 18 Aug. 1913, Runciman Papers, General Correspondence.

the cabinet attempted to sum up the land policies so far adopted, it was agreed that 'the cardinal point of the present proposals is that a Commission should have discretionary power to intervene in any case where it was alleged that an unfairness of contract existed. . . .'

> The Commission would decide these questions, not as matters of law, but as matters of general equity, and would be able to interfere with contracts in accordance with powers given to them by the Bill . . . in the interests of the State.

The major practical point to be decided was how best to apply the principle of the minimum. Would the Commission, for instance, receive a discretionary power by law to fix a minimum wage for each district, or would such a power be obligatory?

Within the English agricultural trinity—landlord, tenant farmer and labourer—wage and housing concessions to the labourer accordingly put pressure upon the tenant farmer. Hence the next stage was to win the support of the farmers through securing for them security of tenure, compensation for improvements, and assurances of the right of appeal against both high rents and prohibitive wage increases. The Land Commission was quite capable of arbitrating in all such cases, and the Cabinet memorandum dwelt upon this, pointing out that there was no desire to call into being inflexible rules on behalf of the State:

> It is not proposed that there should be any general system of fixing fair rents between landlord and tenant, any more than there should be any general system of fixing fair wages between farmers and labourers. It is only proposed that the Commission should have power to adjust rents in certain circumstances.

At this time, it was thought that the Commission's very flexibility would enable it to sit as an informal, administrative body: 'it would decide questions in a friendly way, without the paraphernalia of a legal inquiry'. Only later was it seen that this was to risk confusion between its judicial and administrative functions, and it was decided that the Commission would be a judicial body.[1]

---

[1] Lloyd George Papers, C/9/4/81, and Bonar Law Papers, 32/3/13, and no. 56. 'The General Form of the Land Proposals'.

While debate continued in the cabinet, in the country the land succeeded the Insurance Act as the prime social issue. The summer of 1913 saw a resurgence of agricultural trade unionism. The Agricultural and Rural Workers' Union increased in number by nearly 8,000, and claimed 232 branches in 26 counties. There were strikes in Lancashire and in Somerset for a minimum wage, overtime payments, and a Saturday half-holiday. Both Labour and Conservative parties set up policy committees on agriculture. The Labour report in June caught up proposals which had been in the air for some time— state credit banks, agricultural research, the application of co-operative methods on the Danish model, and county wages boards. For the Conservatives, Lord Lansdowne advocated state loans at low interest rates to landowners and private associations who were prepared to make their land available for housing purposes. This was denounced by the Liberals as yet another dole to landlords. A further group of Conservatives were disturbed at their leaders' own lack of appreciation of the gravity of the land problem, and themselves advocated local agricultural wages boards under an impartial chairman to sanction wage awards on the grounds of efficiency, and recommended a necessary reform of local taxation. They faulted the Liberals for making 'little, if any, attempt to stimulate production, while actively discouraging the employment of more capital on the land by making the position of the present holder, or of the prospective investor, precarious and unremunerative'. The Conservative leadership was split on the issue of wages boards, and tended to favour an independent inquiry as the best solution. Especially, they feared that to devote too much attention to the land would be to play into Liberal hands by removing the focus of attention from Home Rule. In July 1913, Conservative Central Office gave official blessing to a national campaign against 'Home Rule, Socialism, and Radical Land Robbery'.[1]

In the late summer of 1913, concern was undoubtedly growing that the Liberal emphasis was forsaking 'production and development' for the uncertain ends of a single tax campaign. At a land conference in July, attended by delegates

[1] Lloyd George Papers, C/9/4/81, and Bonar Law Papers, 32/3/13, and 40/5/4.

from the Central Chamber of Agriculture, the Farmers' Club, and by surveyors, land and estate agents, doubt was expressed as to why agricultural land was being valued despite its immunity from existing taxes. This, they feared, was the harbinger of a national land tax. Agriculturalists were perturbed at how the full site value of their land was being calculated; they wished to exempt all improvements that were made to the land in the course of its working—hedging, drainage, manuring —from the full value. They pointed out that full site value did not allow for various forms of capital expenditure involved in clearing a site, in the redemption of a fixed charge upon the land, or in the cost of land appropriated for public use, and although an owner was allowed to claim for the consideration of such matters, there was no uniform standard here, and the rule that the owner should be assessed upon the 'man-made value of the top nine inches of the soil' was inherently unfavourable to agriculturalists.[1]

Much expert opinion was prepared to acquiesce in a policy of development. Lord Haldane, chairman of the Development Commission, saw reform as intended to make land 'a more fluid form of capital'. Lord Ashley and Lord Milner saw reform as encouraging the most productive use of agricultural land. Liberals like A. C. Murray and Lord Eversley (Shaw-Lefevre), declared that a tax placed upon the capital value of the land would penalise those societies and individuals whose savings were invested in some form of land. The National Farmers' Union favoured above all a state-aided land purchase bill to protect the tenant-farmer against insecurity of tenure consequent upon the breaking-up of large estates—a feature evident since 1909. They were encouraged to look to the Conservatives for this measure, while the Central Chamber of Agriculture also supported the Conservatives in their call for an independent investigation into the land.

The single-taxers and the nationalizers were by now clearly split over the purposes of land reform. For the single-taxers, Wedgwood and Outhwaite held to a highly residual theory of distribution with the traditional tri-partite distinction between the capitalist, (interest), the labourers, (wage-fund), and the

[1] 'The Land Conference', Private Memo. dated 23 July 1913. Copy, Bonar Law Papers, 40/1/52.

landowner, (rent); if the nationalizers bought out the landowners, 'what today goes as rent to the landowner will then go
as rent to the owners of the bonds of the debt created. The
labourer . . . will never be able in that way to add the rent-fund
to his wages-fund'. The true course was to take the rent-fund
by the process of taxation, assuming that such taxation would
free resources and allow more money to be devoted towards
national services. For the nationalizers, Chiozza Money
disputed the residualists' emphasis upon the landlord as the
favoured 'last receiver', upholding instead an Hobsonian view
of distribution as primarily a struggle between unequal interests
wherein the important thing was to translate the wealth that
was created into demands upon consumption, especially the
demand for necessities. The taxation of economic rent was a
necessary but not a sufficient policy, and he wanted 'wage-
parliaments' in every industry to have regard to the efficiency,
the interests, and the division of wealth in that industry.[1]
The single-taxers were, by virtue of their residual beliefs, very
close in their economic views to those of the orthodox school;
Wedgwood, for example, opposed the idea of a legally enforce-
able minimum wage as likely to reduce employment, and
opposed 'doles to buy land for building or for small-holdings'
as 'a combination of sloppy socialism and landlord bribery
ten times worse than the insurance bill'.[2]

Throughout 1913, Lloyd George was under increasing
pressure to raise money both nationally and locally. Forster
informed the Commons in March, 1913, that 'already in the
counties they are insisting upon returning members who are
pledged to economise rather than carry out in their fullest
development the various measures of social amelioration which
the house of commons insists upon thrusting upon them'. By
November, it was evident that with Churchill's demand for
further naval construction and a new commitment to educational reform, the estimated deficit for 1914–1915 would be a
large one. On 18 November, Lloyd George reported to the
cabinet that increases in expenditure were estimated at £10
million, and a part of this expenditure, on education and roads,

[1] *H.C. deb.*, 5s. l, 13 March 1913.
[2] Wedgwood to Runciman, 22 Feb. 1912. Runciman Papers, General
Correspondence.

would require complementary local taxation. Clearly, the reform of local finance could be postponed no longer, a fact which made Lloyd George vulnerable to single tax pressure, this group having intimated in August that their support for a land campaign was conditional upon the adoption of full site value for both national and local taxation. In September, an attempt by Lloyd George to insert clauses into a revenue bill to define more closely the procedure for valuation, widening its scope with regard to agricultural improvements, was defeated by the single taxers, led by Price and Dundas White. Until this time, the cabinet appears to have barely discussed the issue of land taxation; the August memorandum touched only on the rating of improvements, and recommended merely that the Commission be empowered to grant exemptions or relief where necessary. It concluded:

> Some scheme of this sort is probably better than the more ambitious scheme of levying rates to a considerable extent on site value, though the effect of such a scheme would no doubt be incidentally to reduce the amount on which improvements would be rated.

With such disagreements in the background, the first report of the Land Enquiry Committee was released in early October in a blaze of publicity. Dealing with rural conditions alone, the report found that over 60 per cent of the ordinary agricultural labourers received less than 18s. a week from all sources; 20 to 30,000 received less than 16s. a week, and the rise in the cost of living since 1907 had brought a general halt to the rise of living standards. The report commented upon the long hours worked, the low standard of physical efficiency achieved, the impossibility of dealing with the housing problem before raising wages, and the great unsatisfied demand for land. It found housing standards to be deplorably low, the incidence of disease seriously high, the tied cottage a drawback to the labourer's independence, and the powers and activities of the local authorities inadequate. At least 120,000 new cottages were needed. It recommended the building of cottages on crown lands, loans to public utility societies of up to 80 per cent of the cost of a cottage, and future grants-in-aid to local authorities to be conditional upon a measure of performance. As the root of the trouble lay with wages, the report recommended a physical living wage to be enforced by 'some sort' of wages tribunal. In addition, there might be a land court to which farmers should have a judicial right of appeal against wage awards, and for purposes of security of tenure. The fact of security alone would probably reduce the demand for state-aided land purchase schemes. The land court could, it was suggested, be modelled upon the Scottish court set up in 1911 to provide rights of appeal on tenure and rents to farmers whose rent was under £50 or whose holding was under 50 acres. With regard to rating, the Enquiry announced its intention of dealing with it fully in a subsequent, urban, volume.

On 11 October, 1913, Lloyd George officially opened the land campaign at Bedford although he was unable to announce specific policies as the cabinet had not yet finalised their ideas. On 22 October, at Swindon, he was able to proclaim the Government's intentions: a new Ministry of Lands and Forests, which would supersede the Ministry of Agriculture, assume all responsibility for land valuation, small-holdings, land-purchase, and the development of land-based industries. Through Land Commissioners it would implement and deal with all matters of wages, rents and tenure. The Commissioners would be empowered to authorize loans for housing and development schemes, and when the new Domesday Book of land values was complete in 1915, it would form the basis for the Commissioners in their powers of land-acquisition. Lloyd George was careful that they would in all these matters act judicially, although their functions would rest as much in conciliation as in the exercise of their legal authority. The Government had adopted the figure of 120,000 as the number of cottages required.

The proposals gained an enthusiastic reception; some farmers, it was reported, found the offer of a secure tenure 'too good to be true'. The policies were swiftly borne over the country by Lloyd George, Runciman, and Herbert Samuel, Lloyd George retailing to the Chief Whip, Illingworth, the electoral possibilities in store. Already in November, an inner Cabinet group had discussed the possibility of a July 1914 dissolution; Asquith and Grey were favourable, but Lloyd George, backed by Haldane and Crewe, wanted longer, and apparently it was the prospect of the land campaign that swayed the issue.[1] By December, Rowntree was training 80 men as lecturers at a private cost of £800, and these were joined by a voluntary force of 150. On 9 December, at the National Liberal Club, Asquith endorsed the campaign, including the Liberal commitments to the living wage and the compulsory acquisition of land by public authorities in anticipation of development. His audience consisted of delegates from the local Liberal associations of England and Wales, and here they elected an executive, the Central Land and Housing Council, who were to have overall charge of the campaign.

Meanwhile the single-taxers maintained their pressure. In November, both Trevelyan and Outhwaite pressed Lloyd George to grant a national land tax. The latter had already learnt from the Board of Inland Revenue that the valuation was behind schedule in the towns, but some 60 per cent of the total work having been completed, the Board submitted a scheme for a local penny rate on site values which, it was estimated, would produce a further £9½ million in local revenue. By 13 December, Lloyd George had accepted that land reform should include a measure of rating reform, and he admitted the case for national aid for national services. In reply to P. W. Raffan's request for the two land taxes, Lloyd George, on 1 January, 1914, wrote him an open letter in which he assured him that the government were even then considering the most appropriate methods:

> You may depend upon it that the Government definitely intend to utilise the valuation which they are putting through at great expense for the purpose of compelling the owners of the sites which are not now bearing their share of local taxation, to contribute on the basis of the real value of their property.[2]

The land nationalizers, however, felt that the government were in danger of making too many concessions, even though Lloyd George had apparently ruled out a national land tax. Rowntree was anxious that the Campaign should not become a mere vendetta against the landowners, and he pressed for consideration for the unemployed. Chiozza Money wanted the principles of town-planning recognized as compulsory, and the establishment of a body of housing commissioners with powers

---

[1] Memo. dated 12 Nov. 1913. Lloyd George Papers, C/14/1/10.
[2] Lloyd George Papers, C/2/4/1.

of enforcement. On 4 December, Heath, the secretary to the Enquiry, wrote to Lloyd George:

> I feel that a large section of the Liberal party who are in favour of nationalisation are really disappointed with the land proposals. It is true that we have done everything possible to make it easy for municipalities to acquire land, but the difficulty is that no-one ... really expects that municipalities will exercise these powers.[1]

Finally, the farmers, although favouring proposals for security of tenure and rent appeals, remained cautious. Trustram Eve, the secretary of the Farmers' Club, disliked the intended 'scrapping of supply and demand as the basis for wages', and considered the Land Enquiry's idea of 'some sort' of wages tribunal dangerously vague. Any attempt to set aside economic laws 'invariably' created muddle; he was, he said, 'a natural causes man'.[2]

The progress of the campaign next waited on the urban report. The Town Tenants' League had presented their especial grievances to Lloyd George on 4 October, 1913, who agreed to adopt their own bill directly—full compensation for improvements made by the tenant, a greater measure of freedom for the tenant to adapt his property without being unduly hindered by restrictive covenants, and the right of appeal against excessive rent increases. In a preview of the urban report in November, Lloyd George proposed to Asquith a national survey of slum housing with grants-in-aid to local authorities being conditional upon their acting upon the problems exposed. He suggested that town-planning principles be compulsory within all urban development, and that the Trade Boards Act of 1909 be extended to urban areas in general to enable the many poor to afford a commercial rent; also that further (unspecified) measures be provided to afford a greater regularity of employment to casual labour. The Land Commissioners would deal with the compulsory acquisition of land by municipalities; vacant and undeveloped land would be rated, and parliamentary grants would be provided for the general purposes of re-development.[3]

From the beginning of 1914, Lloyd George began to draw the threads of his campaign together in preparation for the budget.

[1] Lloyd George Papers, C/2/3/57.   [2] *The Times*, 4 Nov. 1913.
[3] Lloyd George Papers, C/2/3/37.

To the Commons on 12 February, he promised that the Government would submit rating reform proposals. In March the departmental committee on local taxation reported. The majority group of seven agreed that state relief for semi-national services was overdue, especially for education and the poor-law, and agreed too that ministerial supervision of local expenditure was desirable. The majority rejected the rating of site values, but the minority group of six favoured this idea, and thought that half of all future increases in local expenditure should be met by a rate on site values, while relief might also be given on all improvements by reducing the charge levied on the present basis of rateable value, and making good the deficiency by a second, extra-ordinary, rate on site values.[1]

In April, with budget day delayed until 4 May, the urban report was published. Its emphasis fell upon housing. One-tenth of the total population was declared to be living in over-crowded and unsanitary conditions; the 1909 Housing and Town Planning Act had failed materially to increase the supply of houses. While in this case the state should not embark upon a direct building programme, it should increase the borrowing facilities available to public utility societies, and all block-grants to local authorities should be made conditional upon their observing obligatory principles of town planning—a reduction in the number of houses per acre, the promotion of building estates and transit schemes. It should be, the report went on to say, a statutory duty upon local authorities to provide proper sanitary housing accommodation for their working-class population, and to this end each authority should embark upon an immediate survey of its housing needs for the Local Government Board. Although the terms of reference had excluded the direct investigation of wages, the report called on the Government to 'take means to secure that within a short and defined period a minimum wage shall be fixed for all low-paid wage earners', and 'take steps to regulate the labour market with a view to decreasing the amount of casual employment'.

The report devoted much space to the compulsory acquisition and leasing of land, very much on the lines of the Town Tenants' League's suggestions. It accepted the case for rating reform,

[1] Report of the Departmental Committee on Local Taxation Cd.7316, xl, 1914.

and suggested that all future increases in local expenditure, chargeable to the rates, could be met by a site value rate. Furthermore, part of the existing expenditure could be met by a penny rate on capital site value, and the authorities should have the option of increasing the proportion of their expenditure that might be financed locally in this way, with the one proviso that no new burdens should be placed on agricultural land. Further relief in the form of grants-in-aid up to a value of £5 million should be provided by the Imperial exchequer.

The similarities between this report and the departmental minority report were promptly hailed by the Land Values Group, collectively, as the admission of their case, although in their statement they still insisted that their minimum condition of support remained the national land tax. The influence of the land nationalisers however also seems to have been present, for the statement regretted that the case for rating site values had been couched in terms of financial necessity:

> What the reports lack is a frank avowal that the new system, in applying public values to public purposes, is in itself right and necessary as a matter of social justice. Nor is there any clear statement to be found as to the liberating effect of the change in opening up opportunities for Labour and thereby enabling it to secure its fair reward.[1]

In the event, the 1914 budget did not admit a national land tax, and Lloyd George was content to announce that 'the taxation of site values must henceforth constitute an integral part of the system of local taxation'. He explained to the Commons that of all the objects listed in 1909, only local taxation reform was left. The valuation was almost complete, the main task remaining was to ascertain the value of agricultural improvements and certain urban centres, and then he proposed to adapt this national valuation for local use in order that site value rating might be introduced. This would first necessitate a new rating bill to establish a uniform, national criterion by which full site value could be assessed by the valuation authorities; it would establish what improvements were to be included in full site value, and on what improvements, and at what rate, rating relief would be granted. He

[1] Recommendations for the Taxation of Land Values Explained and Criticised, By The Land Values Group, (1914).

agreed with the suggestions that all such relief should be financed by means of an extra rate on site values. He announced large increases in national grants-in-aid to the local authorities, and in future such grants were intended to form the only financial link, for all assigned revenues, the local taxation account, and the Agricultural Rates Relief Act of 1896, were to be abolished. The future grants would be assessed upon a percentage basis and would be liable to two conditions: they would be related to the efficiency of the service provided by the local authority, and the authority's view of its own responsibility in the matter; secondly, they would be distributed proportionally in order to take into account those areas most in need of assistance, and where the services to be provided constituted a heavy burden in relation to the rateable value. The grants to the police forces and for the upkeep of the main roads were to be raised to at least half the total cost; the educational grant was to be raised by up to £4 million, including therein further provision for school meals, grants for open-air schools for tuberculosis victims, for schools for the deformed, and for the training of specialist teachers; provision was made for new financial aid for the sanitoriums, maternity centres, and ancillary health services established by the 1911 Insurance Act. The total cost in a full financial year was estimated at £11 million, (including the cost of the local valuation scheme).

Not the least of the budget's interest lay in the proposals for further increases in direct taxation. 1914 saw the first introduction of a graduated income tax on earned incomes, rising to 1/4d. in the pound on incomes (earned) over £2,500. The upper rate on unearned incomes also became 1/4d. The overall limit of the super tax was lowered from £5,000 to £3,000, and all incomes over £3,000 would now pay on their excess over £2,500. The rate would be 5d. on the first £500, 7d. on the next £1,000, increasing at 2d. per £1,000 until all incomes over £9,000 paid at 1/4d. in the pound, at which point the maximum tax on income over £9,000 would be 2/8d. in the pound. For the death duties, 1 per cent was added to all estates worth over £60,000; over £250,000 the scale steepened to impose a maximum of 20 per cent, as against 15 per cent, on estates worth over £1 million. Finally, the income tax relief in respect of children was doubled from £10 to £20 for each child under sixteen.

Radicalism welcomed the budget enthusiastically, but moderate opinion was disturbed lest, in the words of an eminent backbencher, Sir Richard Holt, 'national expenditure [had] increased more rapidly than national wealth and income'. Again, there was the suggestion of Lloyd George in opposition to the moderate or orthodox opinion of the cabinet. He wrote to Samuel over the rumour of a budget leak, disturbed that such a leak 'gravely imperils our chances of getting this plan through the Cabinet'. He continued:

> I have worked for years to carry through this policy and I am . . . very upset at anything which puts it in jeopardy in the hour of fruition.

The budget's prospects were at once threatened by the formation of a Liberal 'cave' of about 40 members led by Sir John Jardine who were disturbed that Lloyd George should attempt so much legislation under the nominal cover of a Finance Bill. In particular, they wanted the local government reforms properly discussed in a separate bill, and on 22 June, in answer to a Conservative query, the Speaker ruled that that part of the Finance Bill relating to the reform of local government was, indeed, out of order. On 23 June, the cabinet decided that the Bill should be divided into two parts. Firstly, they would proceed with necessary taxation, meanwhile abandoning the grants-in-aid for the present session except for those for Insurance and Education; and secondly, in a later session, they would deal with the grants and with a Revenue Bill. On 26 June, however, on the second reading of the Finance Bill, the Government majority fell from a nominal 94 to 38; 35 out of 37 Labour M.P.s abstained, and one Liberal, Sir Luke White, voted against the Government at their decision to delay the local reforms.[1]

The Liberals were in fact faced with a saturated legislative timetable. E. S. Montagu had already warned Lloyd George on 29 April that legislative prospects were bleak, especially with both Home Rule and Welsh Disestablishment in the pipe-line. On 14 July, the cabinet decided that the present session would be terminated as soon as the Finance Bill and Home Rule had been dealt with. At the end of November

---

[1] *The Times*, 18 and 26 June, 1914. Asquith to King George V, 23 June, 1914. Asquith Papers, Vol. 7.

a new session was planned to dispose of outstanding legislation.

It was evident that the Ministry of Lands could not be established that year, although the Board of Agriculture had been working on the transfer of powers and the creation of the Judicial Commissioners since January. Several practical details of the campaign were still outstanding: the hours of work for agricultural labourers, including half-holidays; whether or not the new ministry should build cottages for townsmen who wished to settle in the country, and how wages were to be arrived at in country districts. It was intended to establish a cabinet committee to deal with these and with the vexed issue of which criterion of site value to adopt for taxation, either present-use value, or some estimate of capital-value. If the latter was adopted, it would have to include the value of some improvements and have regard to the optimum-use value as measured by market price; for agricultural land, this promised an increase in its rateable value. Yet if capital-value were ignored, there would be no criterion of measurement from which to gauge future, incremental, increases in value, for present-use value was a purely relative standard of measurement, the value of agricultural land: for example, varying according to the state of the market and the demand for a particular crop.

Lloyd George's parliamentary preoccupations were, as he told Rowntree, diverting his attention from the campaign in the country. On 12 May, Rowntree sent him a list of seven points needing elucidation; these included the machinery necessary to establish a minimum wage, the extent of such a wage in the towns, the agricultural half-holiday, and the date of the housing programme. On 25 May, Rowntree asked 'whether you want us to slow down or hurry up. At present we are counting on a 1915 election and organising accordingly'. On 28 May, Lloyd George received a highly favourable account of progress from the secretary of the Central Land and Housing Council who spoke of 'unprecedented enthusiasm' in the rural areas, even among farmers, for the Liberal proposals: 'the complete success of the rural campaign is assured'.

In the urban areas of the north east, the eastern counties, Lancashire, Devon and Cornwall, the campaign was going 'fairly well', 'but for the rest of the country the campaign in the boroughs has been disappointing. Public attention has been so occupied with gun-running, army revolts . . . that it has been difficult to arouse interest in land and housing'. If, the secretary suggested, Lloyd George were to give a public undertaking that 'the principle of the Trade Boards Act will be extended to include all low-paid workers, it would place our urban campaign on an entirely different level'. So far, he reported, there had been little opposition from any quarter.[1]

This was confirmed by reports from regional Liberal associations, difficulty being experienced in winning support from the more diverse urban audiences where again the commitment to the minimum wage appeared to be the crucial factor. On 12 June, Lloyd George told Runciman that Asquith was 'highly gratified' at the progress of the campaign, but a decision upon a living wage for the towns had not been taken by the end of June when the campaign was overshadowed by more momentous issues.

The promise of the intended land reforms was so much greater than their eventual outcome that evaluation becomes necessarily something of an academic exercise. It can be claimed, however, that the scale of the reforms confirmed the arrival of the 'New Liberalism' which had been forecast ever since 1906. The proposals for the Ministry of Lands, for minimum wage regulations, for a state housing programme, certainly ushered in a socialistic form of Liberalism which was apparently willing to increase government expenditure beneath the criterion of the social or collective good. Within the financial field, the steepening scale of direct taxation and the introduction of a graduated income tax in 1914 finally established the supremacy of direct over indirect methods of taxation, and it has to be stressed that this was no automatic development, but a policy carried through in the teeth of fierce Conservative opposition. Lloyd George was, perhaps, the first chancellor to expand the traditional functions of the budget from a purely accounting significance to a prime weapon of policy, and especially social policy. His two main budgets, 1909 and 1914, were both on a scale whose modernity far overshadowed their orthodox (Gladstonian) background. His

[1] Ref. Lloyd George Papers, C/2/4.

willingness to end the old system whereby the realized surplus of a past financial year was by law automatically devoted to the redemption of debt, and his readiness to link the justification of taxation to concepts of social justice rather than to purely economic criteria, laid him open to bitter attacks, for example, by G. E. Raine, that he had no economic knowledge whatsoever. Lloyd George was willing enough to allow money to 'fructify in the pockets of the people', but he evidently did not believe in the hitherto unquestioned supremacy of private to public expenditure. He had, for instance, to be converted to sound actuarial methods in 1910–11, and he was unwilling to see the Insurance Reserve Fund lying idle when it might be financing cottage-building by the state.

To the accusation that Lloyd George was a pure opportunist, it is possible to answer that few people had as yet a clear idea of the society they wished to create, and Lloyd George's main significance was anyway as a politician engaged in seeking solutions to urgent legislative problems. In this context, consideration of the work and planning involved in both the insurance and the land campaigns, in addition to the statement of intent in his 1909 budget speech, would suggest that Lloyd George himself had a clearer insight than many into the type of reform necessary. Haldane later wrote that 'Lloyd George had boundless energy and quick intelligence, but he was really an illiterate with an untrained mind'.[1] This seems to be typical of many statements about Lloyd George between 1909 and 1914, statements which seem to reflect more upon Lloyd George's ability to extract the maximum from a given political situation than upon his own intrinsic qualities as a creative legislator. Certainly he was dependent upon his Radical base in the Commons for both ideas and support, and when that base was itself divided, Lloyd George's path often appeared a little tortuous. Undoubtedly his methods of playing to the most promising political gallery offended the moderates within the party, some of his rhetoric in support of his policies (for example, about the deer forests) appeared absurd under scrutiny, but it has to be said in his defence that his actual policies scarcely reflected the bias with which his opponents credited him. It is wiser to quibble at the actual worth of the

[1] Haldane Papers, MSS. 5923 f.7.

policies themselves, the largely mythical 'land-based' industries, the hope that an extensive 'land campaign', as the answer to modern economic problems, would deal with urban casual labour—this reflects upon an essential weakness in his own position and in that of many Radicals who supported him. The crucial question is how much weight Lloyd George put upon the policies for 'development', how far he was prepared to go in following the nationalizers and the under-consumptionists not merely in extending the sphere of state social and legal regulation but in intervening in the field of private economic management, in hours and wages, in following up Radical proposals for railway and mines nationalization, and this, in common with the final effects of the land campaign, must remain a matter for speculation.

Monash University   H. V. EMY

III

LLOYD GEORGE AND THE STRUGGLE FOR THE NAVY ESTIMATES OF 1914

F. W. Wiemann

FRIEDRICH WILHELM WIEMANN

Age 28

Universities of Bonn, Cologne, Hamburg
History and English Literature 1962
Currently 'Referendar' at University Library
of the Free University of Berlin (West)

LLOYD GEORGE AND THE
STRUGGLE FOR THE
NAVY ESTIMATES OF 1914

To generations of historians, Lloyd George was during the years preceding the outbreak of World War I, a leading pro-German and pacifist—the prototype of a Radical. It is mainly Lloyd George's attitude during the Agadir crisis which makes it doubtful whether this judgment is applicable to the three years that follow—if indeed it had not already lost its validity before the Panther's spring brought him to the height of militancy.

In 1908 Lloyd George had tried to enter into private talks with the German Chancellor on a naval agreement.[1] Six months later he brought the Cabinet to the brink of a split as he fought the navy estimates which McKenna, then first lord of the admiralty, had proposed and which both Lloyd George and Churchill thought extravagant.[2] In 1910, however, his Unionist friend F. E. Smith wrote that Lloyd George 'does not like being wagged by his Radical tail'.[3] This was not a surprising judgment as Lloyd George in the same year put forward a plan for coalition with the Unionists which came close to including universal conscription.[4]

Then came the Agadir crisis of the summer of 1911, and with it the famous Mansion House speech by Lloyd George. It has been stated that Lloyd George was warning the French that Great Britain wanted her share of Morocco if France, Germany and Spain agreed on partition.[5] It has also been argued that he may have been speaking to his own countrymen to keep them from unpatriotic strikes.[6]

Both opinions may contain some truth. However, this speech

[1] G.P. XXIV 8232 ff. [2] Roy Jenkins, *Asquith* 215 f.

[3] Austen Chamberlain Papers 12/28 letter by F. E. Smith to A. Chamberlain 20 Oct. 1910.

[4] Petrie, *The Life and Letters of the Right Hon. Sir Austen Chamberlain*, 381–8.

[5] A. J. P. Taylor, *The Struggle for Mastery in Europe 1848–1918*, 471.

[6] A. J. P. Taylor, *The Panther's Spring*, in *Politics in Wartime and other Essays*, 59.

was primarily meant and taken as a threat of war against Germany. The threat had become necessary in the eyes of Lloyd George and some of his colleagues because Germany a few days before had made demands on France that were unacceptable. The whole British cabinet agreed[1] and it was feared that either war would ensue or that France would surrender without war if Great Britain kept her silence. The following weeks were filled with rumours of war and with military preparations. And by September, when a peaceful solution seemed imminent, Lloyd George, far from being either pro-German or pacifist, said at court that it was a pity that war had been avoided this time.[2]

Lloyd George was not alone in the Cabinet in his preparedness for German aggression. He was one of five or six cabinet ministers who formed a group within the cabinet discussing British foreign and military policy. Members of this group, which one might describe as an inner cabinet, were besides Lloyd George: Asquith, the prime minister; Grey, the foreign secretary; Haldane, the secretary of state for war; Churchill, the home secretary; and rather isolated as he did not really believe in the danger of war, McKenna, the first lord of the admiralty. Churchill seems even to have surpassed Lloyd George's militancy during this crisis. Thus, he seemed the right man to take over the admiralty from McKenna and introduce reforms that better assured Great Britain's security against aggression by her strongest rival at sea.

By the end of 1911 Lloyd George seems to have changed his position somewhat. According to a German source he replied to reproaches on account of the Mansion House speech that he was completely innocent. Grey, he said, was the author of this speech and had ordered him to memorize it. Lloyd George, who was not interested in foreign affairs and knew nothing about them, had obeyed without giving much thought to what he was repeating to his audience.[3]

---

[1] Asquith to George V, 19 July 1911, CAB 41/33/22.
[2] Randolph S. Churchill, *Winston S. Churchill*, ii, 529—Companion Volume II, Part 2 (1969) 1128. The help which I have obtained from this biography and its Companion Volumes is acknowledged by the frequent quotations drawn from it.
[3] GP 29 10621 Note.

Although this was pure fiction and did not bear the slightest relation to the events preceding the Mansion House speech, it may faithfully represent Lloyd George's intention to impress on others that it was not he but Grey who deserved any blame for the poor state of Anglo-German relations consequent to the Mansion House speech.

Lloyd George was not content with this situation and actively intervened to end the antagonism. On 7 January 1912, the day on which Churchill declined to follow an invitation for talks on naval and political questions in Berlin,[1] Lloyd George advocated in private conversation with Grey's private secretary, Murray, a change in British foreign policy. Murray noted in his diary that Lloyd George wanted to allow Germany 'almost unrestricted freedom in Asia Minor right down to the Persian Gulf' so that Great Britain might profit in her trade and so it would be possible 'to play off Russia against Germany and vice versa'. The prerequisite of this policy was that 'Germany had to learn firstly that we intended to maintain the supremacy of our Navy at whatever cost, and secondly that we did not propose to allow her to "bully" whomsoever she pleased on the continent of Europe'.[2]

During the weeks following this conversation talks were held by four members of the inner cabinet, Lloyd George, Grey, Churchill and Haldane—Asquith was on holiday—and ways and means to implement this policy were sought. The outcome of these discussions and an exchange of views through undiplomatic channels with Germany received the approval of the Cabinet on 2 February. Haldane was to be sent on a diplomatic mission to Berlin to discuss the possibilities of an understanding on naval and colonial questions. The diplomatic service bitterly resented both the mission and the undiplomatic channels by which it had been prepared, as expressions of distrust in both Foreign Office and diplomatists abroad. Perhaps Grey shared this resentment and gave in only as attacks on him in the radical press and in parliament made it dangerous for him to resist the pressure from his colleagues—especially Lloyd George. We do not know details about the

[1] B.D.vi, 492.
[2] Murray Diary, 7 Jan. 1912. National Library of Scotland, Elibank Papers, 8814.

talks preceding the Haldane mission, but it is possible that there were quarrels and that Lloyd George intended to weaken Grey's position. These quarrels may explain the fact that Asquith thought it necessary to deny that he intended to resign or that there were struggles for the succession between Lloyd George and Grey.[1]

If it had been Lloyd George's intention to weaken Grey's position and to bring about a change in Anglo-German relations, nothing came of it. The Germans were not willing to recognize British superiority at sea by concessions in their naval plans, and demanded one counterconcession which Great Britain could not give: Great Britain was to declare her neutrality in a future conflict between France and Germany. Lloyd George seems to have lost all interest in the discussions shortly after Haldane's return from Berlin. Perhaps his interest was absorbed by a great strike movement, or he was soon convinced that Germany was upholding her intransigent attitude on the fleet question which he had experienced since 1908.

Not long after the end of the discussions of the Haldane mission the British Cabinet decided how far its contingent in the Mediterranean could be reduced without endangering British interests or increasing British dependence on France. These discussions, which led to an Anglo-French exchange of letters, would have offered a genuine opportunity for Lloyd George to prove himself a pacifist and pro-German. Yet Lloyd George did not seem much interested and left the brunt of the fight to McKenna and his supporters on one side. and to Churchill and his supporters, among whom was Grey, on the other.

Perhaps the *Observer* was right when it stated on 16 June 1912 that Lloyd George was discontented with his position in the Government and was thinking of resignation to form a coalition between his radical followers in the Liberal Party and a remodelled Labour Party. If Lloyd George was discontented then, he became even more so when he was harassed for his part in the Marconi scandal. Only in the second half of 1913 does he seem to regain his old activity. He then became interested in proposals for land reforms, the Irish question, and the increase in the navy estimates of 1914/15.

[1] Runciman Papers, Runciman to his wife, 14 Feb. 1912.

On 1 January 1913, Churchill had written that the demands for 1913/14 would certainly be 'substantially exceeded, perhaps to the extent of £2,000,000 by the estimates of the year 1914/15'.[1] However, this statement did not arouse much opposition within the Cabinet as the estimates of 1913/14 were still being discussed, and not much thought was spent on the possibility of conflict over later estimates.

Churchill was not very eager to put forward this increase in his estimates, so he proposed that Germany and Great Britain should both take a naval holiday and slow down or interrupt their programmes of construction. Although Germany gave no public answer to this proposal, privately she left no doubt of her resistance to any naval agreement. Therefore, Churchill was told by Asquith and Grey that he should not repeat his offer.[2]

In spite of this Churchill referred to his proposal in a public speech at Manchester on 18 October 1913—not long before the cabinet began the discussion of the coming navy estimates. The gist of Churchill's speech was that there would have to be an increase in the navy estimates for the next year unless both Great Britain and Germany would agree to put back for one year the construction of the four and two dreadnoughts, respectively, they planned to build in 1914. To most contemporaries this was a mere propaganda trick, as a German refusal of the offer would have eased Churchill's task of defending his increase against the protests of the radical and socialist supporters of the Government.[3]

Churchill probably had obtained approval for his speech from Grey and Asquith, and he may have been helped therein by the above mentioned propaganda effect. He himself, however, seems to have been genuinely convinced that the acceptance of his offer was in the interest of both countries, and therefore he may have been moved by a last ray of hope that it would be accepted.

On 24 October Churchill wrote to Grey that both Great Britain and Germany suffered enormously from this competition. In spite of all her efforts Germany had not improved

---

[1] CAB 37/114 Nr 11.　　　[2] B.D.x, 2480, 481.
[3] GP 39 15578; Hardinge Papers, Cambridge University, 71/86. Nicolson to Hardinge, 29 Oct. 1913.

her position in relation to the *Entente*—to the contrary, in fact. Nevertheless, England could not be complacent as the increased Russian fleet, which formed part of the *Entente* superiority, might suddenly support the Triple Alliance.[1] If there really had been hopes that a German refusal of the naval holiday proposal might ease Churchill's task, they were not realized. Germany did not give any official answer that might be used against her and neither the British radicals nor their German counterpart seem to have taken much notice.

In a Guildhall speech on 10 November Churchill was to make a big mistake by neither repeating his naval holiday proposal nor using any other arguments that might have helped him put over his increased estimates. Instead he boasted that British naval power had increased both actually and relatively in recent years. There was less danger to European peace than before, but in answer to foreign armaments there would be 'expenditure and exertions greater than we have ever made in times of peace' and 'it will be my duty, if I should be responsible for this important Department of State, to present to Parliament Estimates substantially greater than the enormous sums originally voted in the present year'.[2]

The effect of such a speech on radicals and socialists was obvious. One can hardly understand why Churchill, who in 1909 had himself been leading the fight for 'economy', could not have foreseen it. Churchill was attacked for this speech in the press and in public meetings. Even the prime minister's wife was upset. She wrote to Lloyd George on 17 November: 'Don't let Winston have too much money it will put our party in local war,—Labour and even Liberals. If one can't be a little economical when all foreign countries are peaceful then I don't know *when* we can.'[3]

Lloyd George had other reasons to be discontented with Churchill's demands. On the day he received Mrs. Asquith's letter, the chancellor of the exchequer had to inform his colleagues in the cabinet that their present demands involved a deficiency of 10 millions for the coming estimates. Of these 10 millions at least 4 millions (and probably 6) were accounted for by the increases in the navy estimates. There were other

[1] B.D.x, 2487.   [2] *The Times*, 11 Nov. 1913.
[3] Randolph S. Churchill, *Winston S. Churchill*, ii, 655 f.

increases, too, which Lloyd George 'recited with the object of warning the spending departments of the calamities their extravagance brings on us'.[1] These increases were: £800,000 for the Army; £2,000,000 for education; £1,250,000 for the Civil Service.[2]

The next fortnight brought some serious thinking about this deficiency in the budget and how it could be met. There were two alternatives; either cut spending or increase taxes. If the latter unpopular solution were to be avoided, then it was tempting to begin by chopping the biggest increase. This was all the more tempting as the reaction to Churchill's Guildhall speech showed how popular economies in the navy estimates would be. Closer scrutiny of Churchill's proposals could not begin until after he submitted a detailed memorandum on 5 December asking for 50·7 million pounds in the ordinary estimates and about 2 million in a supplementary estimate.

While his colleagues were no doubt studying this memorandum and looking for possible cuts, Churchill once again 'put his foot in it' by attending a private dinner with members of the shadow cabinet. They met to discuss the Irish question and Churchill's presence, along with Morley, Austen Chamberlain and F. E. Smith, must have appeared treasonable to his colleagues.

Churchill and Morley had long been concerned over tensions caused by the government's intention to accord Home Rule to the whole of Ireland. Churchill, in fact, was more compromised than Morley. He had once been a Unionist and the tariff question, over which he had changed political allegiance, had ceased to form an important part of Unionist policy. He had never severed all links with his old party and now suspicion was aroused that he might intend to return to it if he failed to persuade the Liberals to compromise over the Irish question. As the Liberals were on the brink of making it the main plank in their platform, Churchill's defection at this point must have been particularly annoying.

Lloyd George, with whom Churchill should have been particularly friendly, was personally affronted because Austen Chamberlain had pointedly refused to include him in the talks.[3]

---

[1] Runciman Papers, Cabinet note, 17 Nov. 1913.   [2] Ibid.
[3] Austen Chamberlain, *Englische Politik*, 500.

News about the dinner—which took place on 8 December, the same day the discussion of the navy estimates began in the cabinet—soon leaked to the press. Though it did not create a sensation there, it seems to have done within the cabinet. Not only was McKenna 'very bitter about it',[1] but Lloyd George, Simon (attorney-general with a seat in the cabinet) and Trevelyan (undersecretary of state for education) were to argue in January that a resignation of Churchill over the navy estimates would be far less dangerous than a resignation over the Home Rule question.[2]

By 13 December according to Riddell, a journalist friend of Lloyd George's, Churchill's enemies within the cabinet formed a group working for a reduction of the estimates and possibly the resignation of the first lord. Members of this group were Samuel, the postmaster general, Runciman, president of the board of agriculture and Pease, president of the board of education. These three were perhaps united in their opposition to Churchill because his demands endangered the funds which they needed for reforms initiated in their own departments. Others in opposition included Hobhouse, chancellor of the duchy of Lancaster, and above all McKenna, who probably had never forgiven Churchill for replacing him after the Agadir crisis. Lloyd George told his friend that although he would not join the colleagues who wanted to drive him from the Cabinet, he would be more strict with his demands than in previous years. He hoped that Churchill would amend his figures and meet the views of the party.[3]

Lloyd George's hopes seemed justified at a cabinet meeting on 15 December. Churchill offered reductions totalling 700,000 pounds on his original estimates. Lloyd George and then the cabinet agreed to the new figure of 49·7 million pounds.[4]

With this agreement the fight might have ended before it really started. That it did not end was due partly to the

[1] Randolph S. Churchill, *Winston S. Churchill*, ii, 659.

[2] Lloyd George: C. P. Scott Papers, Add. 50.901, 21 Jan. 1914; Simon and Trevelyan: Runciman Papers, letter to Runciman 5 Jan. 1914.

[3] Lord Riddell's Diary, 13 Dec. 1913, cited in Randolph S. Churchill, op. cit., 659.

[4] Runciman Papers, Cabinet note of 15 Dec. 1913.

animosities Churchill had raised by his Guildhall speech and the private dinner affair, and partly by the deficit that still had to be met after Churchill's concession.

Haldane proposed that new taxes be introduced to deal with this deficit. Lloyd George, on whom the unpopularity of such a measure would have centered, vigorously opposed this. Only one solution remained. Samuel proposed that there be further cuts in the navy estimates. A great deal of money might be saved without endangering the British superiority of 60 per cent over the German navy, if instead of four, only two dreadnoughts were constructed in 1914.[1] The meeting ended with this proposal.

On the following day the discussion was resumed. Samuel repeated his attacks and was joined by Pease. More significantly, Lloyd George withdrew his agreement of the previous day. McKenna demanded savings by reducing the oil reserves and by putting several ships on reserve. Even Grey, who in former struggles had always been on the side of the defenders of a large navy, supported further reductions. He proposed withdrawing some ships from the Mediterranean even if this meant leaving protection of British interests there entirely to the French.[2] Churchill reproached Lloyd George for not keeping his word, but Lloyd George replied that he wanted reductions to the new programme in view of the approaching 1915 elections. Churchill's refusal to agree to a delay in construction of only six months was just due to stubbornness.[3]

If Asquith had forced a decision at the end of this meeting, it is highly probable that Churchill would have resigned. But there was no decision taken as Grey intervened,[4] and probably the ministers were sent home for the Christmas holidays advised to reconsider their positions and try for agreement.

On 18 December Lloyd George once again met his journalist friend. Riddell noted afterwards that Samuel, Simon, Runciman and Co. did their best to force Churchill to resign. Lloyd

---

[1] Ibid.; CAB 41/34/39 Asquith to George V, 20 Dec. 1913; Asquith Papers, Box 109, 244 note of 15 Dec. 1913.

[2] CAB 41/34/39 Asquith to George V, 20 Dec. 1913; Asquith Papers, Box 109, 249.

[3] Randolph S. Churchill, *Winston S. Churchill*, ii, 661—Companion Volume II, Part 3 (1969) 1833.

[4] Randolph S. Churchill, *Winston S. Churchill*, ii, 633.

George, however, was far less explicit and seemed still to be considering his position and the strength of the resistance against Churchill.[1]

The Christmas holidays offered ample time for the Chancellor to come to a decision. He had many things to consider. In addition to the speech at the Guildhall, the private dinner blunder and the deficit, there were other problems. On 9 December there had been a meeting of Liberal MPs at the Westminster Palace Hotel. A deputation was formed to protest to the Prime Minister about the increase in the navy estimates. On 17 December this deputation was received by the prime minister—40 MPs took part and 60 more expressed their solidarity.[2] Much might be achieved if Lloyd George made himself leader of both these hundred MPs and of the Churchill-must-go movement within the cabinet.

As a result of Lloyd George's reflections during the Christmas holidays an interview appeared in the *Daily Chronicle* on 1 January 1914. In it Lloyd George openly challenged his colleague. If Churchill publicly stated that there must be an increase in the navy estimates for him to remain in office, then Lloyd George declared the time had come to overhaul British expenditure in armaments and take a bold and independent step towards disarmament. He referred to his predecessor, Lord Randolph Churchill, who had resigned from his post of chancellor of the exchequer rather than assent to estimates which he regarded as bloated and profligate. There were three reasons for this new policy: Anglo-German relations had improved recently; Germany and her neighbours concentrated on military rather than naval armaments; resistance against the organized insanity of competitive armaments grew everywhere.

This interview was militant enough to form a rallying cry for all enemies of Churchill and his demands for the navy. On the other hand it left open the policy Lloyd George might choose. If he considered six months delay in the construction of the planned four dreadnoughts as a bold, independent step, he might do so without breaking his word. He could also demand more or less just as his strength might indicate. This strength, his support in parliament and within the cabinet, had to come

[1] Randolph S. Churchill, *Winston S. Churchill*, ii, 659.
[2] *The Westminster Gazette*, 11 Dec. and 17 Dec. 1913.

into the open before it was safe to proceed any further. Therefore, it is not surprising that Lloyd George left for a Mediterranean holiday shortly after giving the interview.

Churchill had not been passive during the Christmas holiday.
He first assured himself of the support of his subordinates on the
question of the four dreadnoughts, and after he knew they
would follow him, he wrote to the prime minister saying he
would resign if only two dreadnoughts were provided for.[1]
Churchill also wrote many memoranda to argue his case. He
reminded his colleagues of the German aggressiveness in 1911,
and probably applied pressure in a variety of ways in order to
win the support of some of his colleagues.

When the *Daily Chronicle* interview appeared, Churchill did
not argue about it but left it to Grey, Illingworth (the chief
whip) and Seely (secretary of state for war) to complain to
Asquith.[2] Surprisingly Samuel also belonged to the group of
politicians protesting against the interview—he had heretofore
been a supporter of the Churchill-must-go movement. Perhaps
his appointment to the local government board which doubled
his salary was remuneration for this defection.

Grey's disagreement with the interview seems to mark no
change of attitude. His suggestion to lower the estimates by
reducing the British contingent in the Mediterranean had
probably been made only in an effort to find a peaceful
compromise. What annoyed Grey most about the interview
were the inroads Lloyd George had made on his position as
foreign secretary. Although it was true that relations with
Germany had recently improved and that Germany's military
armament made a further extension of her fleet improbable,
it was very undiplomatic for a British statesman to say so.
Both the *Entente* partners would take the speech amiss, and
Germany would hardly be delighted.

As far as Asquith and Illingworth were concerned, the foreign
policy implications were secondary to the influence the interview might have on the fate of the Asquith government and the
Liberal party in general. If a majority in parliament as well as
in the cabinet now rallied behind Lloyd George Churchill's
position was no longer the only one in question. The man who

---

[1] Randolph S. Churchill, *Winston S. Churchill*, Companion Volume II,
Part 3 (1969), 1834 f., 1838.   [2] Ibid., 1844.

had forced the government to dismiss one of its ministers and who had introduced a new policy of disarmament would not be far from pushing the prime minister from his seat. Merely by continuing to introduce bold independent measures he could make Asquith a mere puppet. Even if Lloyd George could not force Churchill's resignation he might be strong enough to resign himself and begin a campaign against the 'imperialist' and 'militarist' Liberal and Conservative parties, thus forcing his return to power as leader of a radical-labour coalition. Lloyd George might not succeed with this plan, but in the process he would split the Liberal party and doom the political future of Asquith and his friends. Although we do not know what opinions were exchanged between Asquith and Illingworth, these ideas surely were discussed.

In the fortnight following the Lloyd George interview no further action seems to have been taken by either party. The Liberal newspapers were trying to explain away any difference of opinion between cabinet ministers whereas most Tory papers gloated over the dissension within the Liberal party. On 16 January Churchill and Lloyd George met for two hours. Lloyd George's friend C. P. Scott noted in his diary that there had been no result, but Haldane got the impression from Churchill that there were no principal differences and both sides were willing to make an agreement.[1] If Lloyd George was in a mood to agree, he did not say so to his friends—quite the contrary. Two days later he informed C. P. Scott that he concurred with McKenna and Samuel [perhaps Samuel had once again changed his mind?] that Churchill should be made to resign.[2]

Asquith and Grey were not very optimistic. Therefore, on 20 January they came to the conclusion that 'sooner than have a smash-up and resignation . . . [they should] dissolve parliament and run the risk of the election'.[3] This plan formed a strong weapon in the hand of the prime minister, for a rebellion and break up of the Liberal party was not probable if the rift came into the open only on the eve of an election. Even if Lloyd

[1] C. P. Scott Papers, Add. 50.901; Haldane to Elizabeth Haldane, 17 Jan. 1914, National Library of Scotland, Haldane Papers, 6012.

[2] C. P. Scott Papers, Add. 50.901, 18.1.

[3] Spender and Asquith, *Life of Lord Oxford and Asquith*, 76.

George's policy had more than a hundred sympathizers in parliament and six or seven in the cabinet, it was highly unlikely that many of them would dare follow him into open rebellion in the face of an election. Such a rebellion would have been against not only Asquith, Grey, Haldane and the other ministers who supported Churchill, but also against the party machinery and strong if not overwhelming opposition in the constituencies. At best the rebels could hope to form the basis for a new government in the future. But the immediate result would surely be defeat for the fragmented Liberals and a large Unionist majority.

On 21 January the prime minster met both Churchill and Lloyd George in a private conversation. It was then that the climax of the crisis was reached. Although Lloyd George probably did not show it, he had decided by the end of their talk that it was not worth while to carry the fight to extremes. From the account of the conversation that Lloyd George gave to C. P. Scott it seems that he attacked Churchill rather strongly on both the navy estimates and the Irish question. Asquith, however, did not flinch in his support of Churchill, and when Lloyd George threatened resignation, he replied that the immediate consequence of such a step would be a general election. Although Lloyd George probably did not mention this to anybody, that was the beginning of the end. On the day after this conversation he was ready to agree to the four dreadnoughts Churchill had requested and even to go further; if it were announced in parliament that the estimates of 1915/16 would contain a great and assured reduction on those of 1914/15, Lloyd George would agree to all present obligations.[1]

Although there might be further debates on what was to be understood by the term 'present obligations', it was clear from this moment that Lloyd George did not feel strong enough to carry on his resistance. Whether or not the 100 or more Liberal MPs who were concerned about the increase in the estimates and the members of the cabinet who wanted to get rid of Churchill might choose to continue their fight, he would not lead them into open rebellion.

On 23 January the quarrel between Lloyd George and Churchill seemed to have been buried for good. In a private

[1] C. P. Scott Papers, Add. 50.901, 21 Jan. 1914.

conversation between them Churchill promised reductions for the following year, and although he still thought the demands for 1914/15 rather high, the chancellor of the exchequer accepted Churchill's figures. When Lloyd George informed C. P. Scott about this development, he explained apologetically that there was nothing for him but to accept this situation, as the alternative would have been to destroy both the government and the Liberal party. He reckoned it would take at least ten years to get another Liberal majority.[1] Not mentioned in Scott's diary nor probably by Lloyd George, was the assumption that his premiership would come more certainly and probably sooner if the rebellion were squelched. He could afford to await Asquith's resignation—either on the prime minister's own initiative or as a result of another crisis when Lloyd George would be strong enough directly to attack his leadership.

Asquith was informed of the agreement between Churchill and Lloyd George and the crisis seemed to be over, as he noted on 23 and 25 January.[2] Yet once again there was a break. On 26 January Churchill wrote to his colleague that he could not be bound by his promise 'in any extraordinary or improper sense. While I am responsible what is necessary will have to be provided ... No forecasts beyond the year have ever been made by my predecessors. I have no power even if I were willing to bind the Board of Admiralty of 15/16 to any exact decision . . .'[3]

Lloyd George felt betrayed. If Churchill were not willing to stick to his promise even though offered total victory for this year, there was nothing but defeat for Lloyd George. Once more the chancellor of the exchequer rallied his rebel colleagues round him and planned new moves against Churchill. One of the invitations to this new war council can be found in the McKenna Papers. '. . . important letter from Winston which puts to an end all my efforts for peace. Hobhouse and Simon and Beauchamp are coming here. Do make an effort . . .'[4]

To Churchill he wrote that Churchill's letter proved the failure of all efforts for conciliation undertaken by him in the hope of rescuing Liberalism from the 'greatest tragedy which had yet befallen it'.

[1] Ibid.   [2] Spender and Asquith, *Life of Lord Oxford and Asquith*, 258 f.
[3] Owen, *Tempestuous Journey*, 257.
[4] McKenna Papers 4/4, 27 Jan. 1914. Churchill College, Cambridge.

The following day brought a cabinet meeting in which Lloyd George once more reverted to his conciliatory mood. Asquith later wrote that the cabinet thought that Churchill was justified in making his reservations about his promise to reduce the estimates of 1915/16. Nothing could have demonstrated better the weakness of Lloyd George's position than this cabinet decision. One would think that Churchill's conclusive victory would end the quarrel. But on the following day Asquith found it necessary to make a personal appeal to both sides not to split the party on such a question at such a time.[1] Simon was not persuaded and wrote to Asquith that Churchill's resignation would not split the party but strengthen it.[2]

By then Lloyd George seems to have seen that further resistance was useless. Perhaps he was also willing to renew his friendship with Churchill or at least accept his good will. This attitude was expressed in a cabinet meeting on 29 January, when Lloyd George agreed to tax increases which were to be linked with the promise to parliament that the surplus expected from the reduced estimates of 1915/16 would be spent on education and land reform. Churchill told his colleagues that he would need 52·8 millions for 1914/15 and expected to spend 3·3 millions less in 1915/16. In view of the long term liabilities for which he had to provide, this was no mean offer. Even so he was asked to try for further cuts.[3]

After the cabinet meeting there was another meeting of the Churchill-must-go movement. A letter of protest was drawn up and sent to Asquith. But even this letter shows that—provided there were no further complications—the crisis was over: Lloyd George had not signed it.[4] The signatories, Beauchamp, Hobhouse, McKenna, Runciman, and Simon, did not bear enough political weight either within the cabinet or within parliament to try a rebellion on their own.

On 6 February Churchill produced another memorandum with cuts amounting to £920,000. McKenna still hoped for

[1] Spender and Asquith, op. cit., 77.

[2] Randolph S. Churchill, op. cit. 677—Companion Volume II, Part 3, 1859.

[3] Randolph S. Churchill, op. cit., 675—Companion Vol. II, Part 3, 1858 f.

[4] Randolph S. Churchill, op. cit., 676—Companion Vol. II, Part 3, 1857 f.

Churchill's destruction but to no avail.[1] At last, on 11 February, Asquith wrote to the king that the cabinet had approved Churchill's proposal of the 6th, and Churchill remained in his seat until the defeat at the Dardanelles proved his undoing.[2]

In the end Lloyd George escaped from the struggle for the navy estimates without severe loss of face. When the estimates came up for discussion in parliament and he might have been taunted for his failure to achieve the drastic cuts expected after his *Daily Chronicle* interview, other events took the headlines and drew the attention of both MPs and cabinet ministers. Civil war seemed imminent in Ireland—the Curragh mutiny led to the resignation of several military leaders and the secretary of state for war.

On 23 July, the day the Austrian ultimatum was delivered to Serbia, thus setting the time bomb that exploded a week later into World War, Lloyd George referred to the subject of the *Daily Chronicle* interview in parliament. Once again he spoke of the improved relations with Germany and the growing resistance to the cost of armaments. This time, however, Lloyd George was far more cautious. He did not mention the need for a bold independent step towards disarmament. On the contrary he stated, 'It is very difficult for one nation to arrest this very terrible development. You cannot do it. You cannot when other nations are spending huge sums of money . . .'[3] The immense caution that speaks from these sentences makes it difficult to believe that Lloyd George was once more challenging his colleague at the admiralty. He may have intended to do so later, when the navy estimates came up for discussion at the end of 1914, but this intention cannot be proved by this speech which is merely a faint echo of his statement on disarmament in the *Daily Chronicle* interview.

Other historians have seen this speech in quite a different light because they have been struck by the reference to the improved relations with Germany at a time when war with Germany was only a fortnight away. E. Halévy, who quotes from this speech only in a note, writes that Lloyd George 'down to the very eve of the crisis provoked by the Austrian ultimatum . . . had been

[1] Runciman Papers, McKenna to Runciman, 6 Feb. 1914.
[2] Randolph S. Churchill, *Winston S. Churchill*, ii, 681.
[3] *H.C. deb.*, LXV, c. 727.

the champion of a *rapprochement* with Germany and disarma-ment.'[1] A. J. P. Taylor also quotes this speech and argues that 'it is difficult to resist the surmise that Lloyd George was planning to fight [the next] . . . election as leader of a radical-labour coalition. Reconciliation with Germany, and resistance to Russia in Persia, must have been part of the coalition's programme.'[2]

To judge from these statements, the preceding interpretation of Lloyd George's struggle for a reduction of the navy estimates has missed an important motive which guided him in this fight —his desire to improve Anglo-German relations. Both the speech in July and the *Daily Chronicle* interview mention the improve-ment of Anglo-German relations. But in this essay it has scarcely been mentioned that Lloyd George was pro-German— on the contrary, this view has repeatedly been challenged. It would, however, be incomplete if we left things at the position reached so far, namely that Lloyd George was not a pro-German and that he was not particularly interested in foreign affairs when he fought against the estimates of 1914/15. Instead we shall try to depict on the following pages Lloyd George's outlook on foreign policy in December 1913 and the months that follow. Unfortunately, there is no record giving Lloyd George's views at this time—except that he was convinced of the improvement in Anglo-German relations. On the other hand, from both what Lloyd George said—and did not say— one can surmise that he was content with Grey's policy and shared Grey's interpretation of Great Britain's position in international affairs.

In 1912 Lloyd George had proposed that Great Britain should try to play off Germany against Russia and vice versa. This idea failed because the concession which would make Germany a rival for Russia's position in the Near East depended on an improvement in both Anglo-German relations, resulting from a naval arrangement stating Great Britain's supremacy, and on Germany's ceasing to bully, i.e. threaten, France.

By the end of 1913 it was no longer necessary to give Germany unrestricted freedom in Asia Minor right down to the Persian Gulf, for even without it she had become embroiled with Russia. The cause of this broil lay in the exaggerated fears of

[1] E. Halévy, *The Rule of Democracy 1905-1914*, ii, (1952) 671 f.
[2] A. J. P. Taylor, *Struggle for Mastery in Europe*, 513.

Russia over the mission of a German general to Turkey to reform the Turkish army. France and Great Britain were agreed that the fuss the Russians made about this mission bore no relation to its political importance, and therefore they were very slow to support Russia. But this lack of support was not without danger, for the Russians, once they saw that their *entente* partners would not back them up, threatened a complete change of policy—especially towards Great Britain. Churchill had feared such a change in Russian policy even before Russia threatened it in December and January of 1913/14.[1] Probably Lloyd George, too, now saw that it was not easy to play off Russia and Germany as both were potential enemies and might unite unless Great Britain took sides.

There were two possible solutions to avoid this Russian policy change. Either Great Britain could increase her support for Russia or she could try to persuade France and Germany to combine against Russia. Grey it seems, and the cabinet with him, found a third solution. This was to support Russia as far as possible, but at the same time tell Germany that there were limits to this support and Great Britain was not interested in harming the good relations with Germany. In fact, Great Britain was willing to improve these relations by concluding the impending agreements with Germany.

At the end of the Russo-German struggle in Turkey, it was obvious that Anglo-Russian relations had suffered a great deal by the lack of British support, and there seemed the danger that Russia might once more turn against Persia. In this situation Grey found a means to bind Russia closer to the *Entente*. During a Paris visit he agreed to the proposal of a naval convention between Great Britain and Russia on the model of the Anglo-French convention of 1912. When he informed the cabinet of this plan, he met with no opposition. One of those present noted in his diary that it was 'one of the most interesting, amusing, kindly and enjoyable gatherings I have ever attended.'[2] This was a very shrewd step, as it made the Russians conciliatory in Persia and enabled Grey to begin talks on a revision of the Anglo-Russian agreement of 1907. These talks began so successfully that even Nicolson, one of the least optimistic members of

[1] B.D.x, 2487 Churchill to Grey 24 Oct. 1913.
[2] Burns Papers, Add. 46336, 13 May 1914.

the foreign office, wrote in July '. . . We certainly meet with a very conciliatory and friendly disposition on the part of the Emperor and Sazonoff . . . there is no real reason for the fears . . . that the Anglo-Russian understanding is likely to be endangered . . .'[1]

Both the lack of resistance against the naval convention and the hopeful beginning of talks for a revision of the agreement of 1907 make it extremely improbable that anybody in the cabinet, including Lloyd George, was thinking of a change in foreign policy. There was no better way of defending British interests in both Persia and India than by making agreements with Russia, as Russian enmity—which would have been accentuated by an Anglo-German *entente*—would have put Great Britain in an extremely awkward position. Great Britain had no land force to speak of to set against the Russian forces that might invade Persia. Although Germany could have provided this force, it was probable that the Germans would demand such a price for their support that it would be almost as costly as Russian aggression itself. However, if the policy to conciliate Russia failed Great Britain would have been forced to look for German support. If Germany and Great Britain were in a state of tension, as they had been in 1911, Great Britain would have to submit to Russian threats. If on the other hand there were an improvement in Anglo-German relations this would provide a counterbalance to Russian threats against Persia. This explains a certain ambiguity in British foreign policy in 1914. On the one hand a naval convention with Russia was prepared and a revision of the treaty of 1907, and on the other, agreements with Germany on the Bagdad Railway and on the future partition of the Portuguese colonies in Africa.

Churchill seems to have been a particularly active supporter of both sides of British foreign policy. He was responsible for the preparation of the naval convention providing for the cooperation of the British and Russian navies in case of war with Germany, and at the same time he tried to discuss the possibilities of a naval agreement with his German counterpart, Tirpitz. It was only after considerable persuasion by Grey and Asquith that Churchill gave up this renewal of the effort of February 1912.[2]

[1] B.D.xi, 33 incomplete PRO 800/375. [2] B.D.xii, 511 ff.

Before either the agreements with Russia or those with Germany had been ratified, the Austro-German aggression on Serbia brought an end to the improvement in Anglo-German relations. Great Britain would have preferred to remain neutral if the war had been limited to Austria, Serbia, Russia and Germany, but it could not remain so in a war that involved a full scale German attack on France via Belgium, as was anticipated in 1905/6 and 1911.

Lloyd George realized that such a war was imminent even before the Austrian attack on Serbia had begun. On 27 July he told C. P. Scott, 'there could be no question of our taking part in the first instance'—but at the same time he foresaw 'that a difficult question would arise if the German fleet were attacking French towns on the other side of the Channel—if there was to be war it would come quickly so that Germany could mobilize in a week and gain the initial advantage over France which took a fortnight and over Russia which took a month. Germany would probably seek to strike hard at France and cripple her in the first instance, then swing back and strike at Russia. By sea she might use her superiority in order (1) to land a force behind the French force advancing to meet the German invasion across Belgium . . .'[1]

Lloyd George could hardly have been sincere either to himself or to his friend if he advocated neutrality in spite of these facts, all pointing to the necessity of British support against Germany. For what reason had he demanded the unflinching British support against Germany in 1911 if not to avoid such a crippling blow against France? Why had he demanded universal conscription in 1910—only to please the Unionists or because he thought the German danger rested not so much on her fleet as on land? Since the summer of 1911 his friend Churchill had been preparing against the possibility of a 'bolt from the blue', a German surprise attack on the British fleet. Even if Lloyd George had disagreed about the necessary size of British armaments, was he so certain of Germany's intentions towards Great Britain that he was willing to accept a German attack on the ports on the other side of the Channel? This seems incredible for the man who in 1911 had declared that it was a pity war with Germany had been avoided at that time.

[1] C. P. Scott Papers, Add. 50.901, 27 July 1914.

If we contrast Lloyd George's views on foreign policy with those of his colleagues, we come to the conclusion that there were no important differences. Lloyd George may have differed from some of them in that he did not think that the German fleet was as dangerous as they thought, and thus was more prone than they to take up the fight for disarmament. He may also have been more inclined to believe in German reasonableness when he tried for naval agreement in 1908, 1911 and 1912. But during the Agadir Crisis and during the time of his fight for the navy estimates in 1914/15, and on the eve of the war there are no signs of any great divergence in their views.

F. W. WIEMANN

University Library of the
Free University of Berlin.

IV

THE RISE TO THE
PREMIERSHIP, 1914-16

PETER LOWE

PETER LOWE

Age 29

University of Wales B.A. 1963, Ph.D. 1967
Lecturer in History, Manchester University

THE RISE TO THE PREMIERSHIP
1914-16

BEFORE August 1914 Lloyd George was widely regarded as the champion of social reform and as the opponent of imperialism and jingoism. Admittedly his trenchant words in the Mansion House speech of 1911 could be set on the other side, as could the proposal for limited national service put forward in his suggestion of a coalition government in 1910, although the latter was not generally known and would have shocked many of his radical supporters had they heard of it. Thus Lloyd George possessed an interest in foreign affairs and defence before the outbreak of war but this was overshadowed by the domestic controversies surrounding social, constitutional and Irish issues. Between 1912 and 1914 Lloyd George's interest in social reform was exemplified in the land campaign, designed to assist the tenant farmer and agricultural labourer while simultaneously improving land utilization; it was a project dear to his heart, for one of the consistent themes in his long career was his hostility to the system of landownership and his dislike of landowners. Land was to be the issue which would win the Liberal party the next general election, expected in 1915. All was completely transformed by the events of late July and early August 1914. Lloyd George, the scourge of the landowners and Tory peers, soon became the scourge of Prussian militarism and of ineptitude in the British war effort. The period from August 1914 to December 1916 witnessed the gradual rise of Lloyd George's reputation and popularity with the public at large but there was nothing inevitable in his attainment, in December 1916, of the premiership. It was the product of diverse elements and paradoxically Lloyd George achieved the office of prime minister, long the ultimate object of his ambition, at a time when he did not want or expect to secure it. This essay will pursue the stages by which Lloyd George came to occupy the 'driver's seat'.

When the European crisis broke, Lloyd George, like most other Liberal cabinet ministers except Grey, was wrestling with the complexities of the Irish question. Suddenly in late July the

increasing possibility of Great Britain becoming involved in a
European conflict dawned on ministers and the general public
alike. According to C. P. Scott, the editor of the *Manchester
Guardian,* who saw Lloyd George on several occasions, Lloyd
George did not at first consider British intervention to be likely.
'As to the *European situation* there could be no question of our
taking part in any war in the first instance ... He [Lloyd George]
thought if there was to be war it wd. come quickly so that
Germany which cd. mobilise in a week cd. gain the initial
advantage over France which took a fortnight and Russia
which took a month ...'[1] In the cabinet discussions Lloyd
George adopted a middle path between those who favoured
British intervention regardless of Belgium and those who were
hostile to any intervention. He did not wish to intervene, since
he was doubtful of various aspects of Grey's policy and was not
convinced of the menace of German aggression but, as the days
went by, Lloyd George reluctantly recognized that British
involvement was bound to come. He told C. P. Scott on
3 August that, 'He had done his utmost for peace but events
had been too strong for him'.[2] Scott commented: 'He was
looking terribly worn & tired. He began at once by saying that
he had been entirely deceived about *Germany* & that I ought to
know that the evidence was overwhelming that the party which
had got control of the direction of affairs throughout the crisis
had deliberately played for & provoked the war.'[3] It does not
appear that there was anything Machiavellian in Lloyd
George's reaction: he had looked at the issue frankly and his
attitude had changed from one of deep suspicion to one of
resigned acceptance of war. In this he mirrored the response of
much British opinion and in particular of the majority opinion
in the Liberal party.[4] Later speculation that Lloyd George had
discerned the character of the war and grasped the opportunity
it afforded him possesses little justification. At the start of the
war Lloyd George was as overwhelmed as other ministers and

[1] Interview notes, 27 July 1914, C. P. Scott Papers, Add. MS. 50.901.
[2] Interview notes, 3 Aug. 1914, Scott Papers, Add. MS. 50.901.
[3] Interview notes, 3 Aug. 1914, Scott Papers, Add. MS. 50.901.
[4] See T. Wilson, *The Downfall of the Liberal Party 1914–1935* (1966),
49–50. The classic Liberal attitude is well illustrated in the changing tone of
the leaders in the *Manchester Guardian* for August 1914.

had little idea how long it would last or of the nature of the conflict.

As chancellor of the exchequer, Lloyd George had to face the economic issues which the war raised. The immediate aim was to calm the fears of the bankers and general public and to preserve the stability of the monetary system. This was achieved in the first week and contributed to the excessive praise lavished on Lloyd George in the early stages of the war. In the next month he did not figure very prominently in the headlines: Asquith, Kitchener and Churchill dominated the scene. Lloyd George's first significant statement came in his speech at the Queen's Hall, London, on 19 September when he addressed an audience of three thousand London Welshmen. It was an important occasion, for he committed himself wholeheartedly to support of the war and expressed his detestation of German militarism. The speech is worth citing for it illustrates the humour, skill and wit that were the essential ingredients in any address by Lloyd George. He began by explaining his personal position: 'There is no man in this room who has always regarded the prospect of our being engaged in a great war with greater reluctance, with greater repugnance than I have done throughout the whole of my political life. There is no man more convinced that we could not have avoided this war without national dishonour.'[1] He then emphasized the importance of observing treaty obligations, cleverly linking a Welshman's sympathy with smaller nations like Belgium and Serbia with his castigation of Germany. 'The Prussian Junker is the road-hog of Europe. Small nationalities in his way are flung to the roadside bleeding and broken; women and children crushed under the wheel of his cruel car; Britain ordered out of his way. All I can say is this. If the old British spirit is alive in British hearts, the bully will be torn from his seat.... They think we cannot beat them. It will not be easy. It will be a long job. It will be a terrible war. But in the end we shall march through terror to triumph.' Lloyd George had stressed the consistency in his thinking in his remarks on the international application of Liberal principles, on the suffering of war and on the change in attitudes that would result—in short, his belief that the war would eventually produce a greater willingness to remedy the failings

[1] *Manchester Guardian*, 21 Sept. 1914.

of British society. His great speech was a call, as he said, for 'a new patriotism'. This became the theme of Lloyd George's career for the remainder of the war—the need for internal unity and efficiency, coupled with a new spirit which would not only help to win the war but produce new solutions to internal problems.

The same thinking was reflected in the speech with which he introduced his first war budget on 17 November. Lloyd George began by discussing the gigantic financial demands of the war: already it was the most expensive conflict in which the country had been involved and he estimated that the first full year of the war would cost at least £450 million. He implied that the war would be a long one: 'We are fighting an enemy that cannot submit to any terms we can accept—to any terms we can prudently accept—without a smashing defeat. Let us bear that in mind when we are making our calculations. Therefore if there is any doubt about the length of the War, I am bound, as Chancellor of the Exchequer, to assume a longer rather than a shorter period in making my plans . . .'[1] When he came to discuss his proposed tax increases, including the doubling of income tax and sharp increases in taxation of unearned and earned income, he returned to the theme of civilian sacrifice at home and the sacrifices of servicemen:

> War is the time for sacrifice in nations. They are in the spirit of sacrifice and that makes a difference. It is a time when men know that they are expected to give up comforts, possessions, health, limb, life— all that the State requires in order to carry it through the hour of its trial. It is a time of danger, when men part willingly with anything in order to avert evils impending on the country they love, and I am perfectly certain that when there are millions of our countrymen volunteering to risk their lives, men who cannot volunteer are not going to grudge a fair share of their possessions. It is not merely a time for sacrifice, it is a time for the temper of self-denial, it is a time to ask the nation to make sacrifices. People who cannot go and give their lives are anxious to do something else to assist, and I am perfectly certain that I should be committing an unpardonable blunder against the highest interests of this country if as Chancellor of the Exchequer, however disagreeable the task may be, I did not take this, the earliest possible opportunity, for submitting proposals that would enable people to contribute something towards carrying on the War in which the honour and life of their country are so deeply involved.[2]

[1] *H.C. deb.*, lxviii, c. 353.
[2] *H.C. deb.*, lxviii, cc. 355–6.

At the end of 1914 Lloyd George's restless, inventive mind was looking beyond the tasks of the treasury, formidable as these were, and towards the strategy of the war and the mobilisation of resources necessary to wage it effectively. He reacted more quickly than his colleagues to the problems of the war and was less overawed by the generals. Basically Lloyd George favoured a more flexible approach, an alternative to the policy of attrition combined with heroically useless attempts to break through the German lines on the western front. This is not to say that he was a convinced 'easterner' but rather that he was critical of any policy that did not produce swift success. Therefore he looked more enthusiastically at the possibility of eliminating Austria-Hungary or Turkey while not surrendering hope of an eventual break-through in the west. These thoughts were clearly revealed in two important memoranda written for the war council of the cabinet, the body of more prominent cabinet ministers which met periodically but not, in the early months of the war, frequently, to consider policy. In the first paper Lloyd George called for reconsideration of existing policy now that the new 'Kitchener army' was being trained:

> In intelligence, education, and character it is vastly superior to any army ever raised in this country, and as it has been drawn not from the ranks of those who have generally cut themselves off from home ties and about whose fate there is therefore not the same anxiety at home, the people of this country will take an intimate personal interest in its fate of a kind which they have never displayed before in our military expeditions. So that if this superb army is thrown away upon futile enterprises, such as those we have witnessed during the last few weeks, the country will be uncontrollably indignant at the lack of prevision and intelligence shown in our plans. I may add that operations such as those we have witnessed during the past few months will inevitably destroy the *morale* of the best of troops. Good soldiers will face any dangers and endure any hardships which promise ultimate progress, but this intermittent flinging ourselves against impregnable positions breaks the stoutest hearts in the end.[1]

He went on to suggest two operations, the first comprising an attack on Austria-Hungary 'in conjunction with the Serbians, the Roumanians and the Greeks'; the new British army could be used in an offensive on the Dalmatian coast. The second

---

[1] 'Suggestions as to the military position', 1 Jan. 1915, CAB 42/1/8; also reprinted in D. Lloyd George, *War Memoirs* (6 vols. 1933), i, 369–80.

operation would be directed against Turkey, the essential point being a landing of British troops in Syria to cut off the Turkish forces gathering for an invasion of Egypt. He ended by attacking the tendency to allow matters to drift, which was to be the hallmark of his pronouncements during the war and the essence of his growing dissatisfaction with Asquith's lethargic leadership.

In the second paper, dated 22 February 1915, Lloyd George renewed the attack with greater bluntness, beginning with a dramatic warning: 'I am anxious to put before my colleagues a few considerations on the general situation. It must be acknowledged to be one of the utmost gravity, and one which, if it is not taken in hand at once firmly and boldly, may end in irretrievable disaster for the cause of the Allies and for the future of the British Empire'.[1] He reviewed the position castigating the misleading optimism engendered by official statements, which in turn were magnified by the press. No German territory was occupied by the allies and most of Belgium was under German control. The Russian position was disturbing, since the Russian reserves had been consumed in repelling the German counter-attack and the Russians were very short of rifles. After examining the relative strengths of the armies involved, Lloyd George urged more cooperation among the allies: 'Who can present a reliable estimate of the military resources of the Allies? We ought to have a conference between the military authorities of the three countries, at which a candid exposure of the position of each country is made and some military convention agreed to as to our future action'.[2] In particular more information was required on Russian resources. Great Britain must increase the size of her armies:

> Every effort must be made to increase the number of men whom we can put into the field and to shorten the period in which they could be put into the fighting lines. How is this to be done? If France could put 3,000,000 of men under arms and Germany 5,000,000, then the whole of the Allied countries ought to be able, on the basis of population, sooner or later to arm 20,000,000. That may be an impossibility, but it is an indication of the enormous reserves of men fit to bear arms that the Allies have to draw upon.[3]

[1] 'Some further considerations on the conduct of the war', 22 Feb. 1915, CAB 42/1/39; also reprinted in Lloyd George, *War Memoirs*, i, 168–70, 422–30.   [2] Ibid.   [3] Ibid.

The problem concerned the training and equipping of the men as speedily as possible and the maintenance of the *status quo* until the allies were prepared to move decisively. The provision of war munitions was imperative and so far Great Britain was lagging:

> I do not believe Great Britain has even yet done anything like what she could do in the matter of increasing her war equipment. Great things have been accomplished in the last few months, but I sincerely believe that we could double our effective energies if we organized our factories thoroughly. All the engineering works of the country ought to be turned on to the production of war material. The population ought to be prepared to suffer all sorts of deprivations and even hardships whilst this process is going on. As to America, I feel confident from what I have heard that we have tapped only a small percentage of this great available reserve of supply.[1]

At this stage Lloyd George did not consider compulsory service to be necessary: he was confident that sufficient numbers of men would enlist once the gravity of the situation was grasped by the country. Towards the end of his memorandum, Lloyd George returned to the strategy of the war. During 1915 the allies would have to concentrate, in the west, on defending the existing position, since they were not powerful enough to begin a new offensive. In the east the situation was changing with the allied attempt to force the Dardanelles. Lloyd George supported the operation, for it was consistent with his advocacy of a more flexible strategy, but it is interesting to note that he regarded the new campaign objectively and envisaged the possibility of failure as well as success:

> If this great movement succeeds—then, if we are prepared to take immediate advantage of it—its influence may be decisive as far as the Balkan States are concerned. This means that if we have a large force ready, not merely to occupy Gallipoli, but to take any other military action which may be necessary in order to establish our supremacy in that quarter, Roumania, Greece and, I think, very probably, Bulgaria will declare for us. If, on the other hand, we have no force on the spot adequate to cope with the Turkish army, it may be that most of the effect of such a brilliant *coup* might be lost ...
> Now let us take the other contingency—the failure of the Dardanelles effort. Unless it is at once countered, such a failure will be disastrous in the Balkans, and might very well be disastrous throughout the East. The Bulgarian general pointed out that not merely Bulgaria, but

Roumania and Italy have a good deal to gain in the way of territory
by throwing in their lot with Germany.[1]

Lloyd George ended with the opinion that the only realistic
policy was to send a large British force to the Dardanelles
reinforced by a powerful diplomatic mission, which would
attempt to bring Greece and Roumania into the war; the
ordinary diplomats were regarded contemptuously, 'their
qualities are not of the first order.'

Lloyd George's ideas were bold, imaginative, conceived on
the grand scale. In the main he was undoubtedly accurate in
his analysis and forecast; the war was going to be a long one,
old ideas and incompetent methods could not be tolerated,
throughout new, more vigorous methods must be adopted.
The principal defect, subsequently to be reflected in his policy
as minister of munitions, was that he underestimated the human
problems involved in adjusting to total warfare, especially in
the case of Great Britain with the peculiarly tenacious attachment to the principle of the liberty of the individual and
suspicion of the state. In addition Lloyd George was not
conversant with the complexity of the Balkans and the task of
winning the Balkan countries to the side of the *entente* was more
difficult than he believed.

Thus in February 1915 Lloyd George was already fast
emerging as the man of dynamism and efficiency. The unsatisfactory nature of munitions production and other war work
deeply worried him. He had belonged to one cabinet committee
set up in October 1914 to promote efficient production and he
was shortly to belong to a second committee charged with the
same function. The obduracy of Kitchener and the secrecy of
the war office had seriously hampered matters however. Lloyd
George considered that restrictive practices of trade unions and
excessive drinking by workers were two of the most significant
reasons for failure to expand production more rapidly. In
March 1915 he helped to negotiate the 'Treasury agreement'
whereby the trade union leaders agreed to suspend restrictive
practices for the duration of the war and to cooperate with the
government, provided that employers made a similar contribution to the national effort through taxation of excessive

[1] Ibid.

profits. Lloyd George's zeal then advanced to the issue of drink. He received much information from employers describing drink as the chief factor delaying production: workers arrived late for work, did not return after 'refreshment' or failed to appear at all for days at a time. This was allegedly responsible for hindering production of munitions and of military and naval equipment. There was much truth in the allegation but drink was not the all-embracing explanation of inefficiency which employers stated and which Lloyd George himself so readily accepted. He threw himself into a campaign to reduce the amount of alcohol in beer, and limit hours when drink could be obtained. Already in his speech at Bangor on 28 February he had assailed 'neglect' and 'sloth' in the war effort. The number of workers failing to work honestly was not large but nevertheless significant: 'What is the reason? Sometimes it is one thing, sometimes it is another. But let us be perfectly candid; it is mostly the lure of the drink . . . Drink is doing us more damage in the war than all the German submarines put together.'[1] He voiced the same sentiments a month later when meeting a deputation of shipbuilding employers, '. . . I must say that I have a growing conviction, based on accumulating evidence, that nothing but root-and-branch methods will be of the slightest avail in dealing with this evil . . . We are fighting Germany, Austria, and drink, and as far as I can see the greatest of these three deadly foes is drink'.[2] Lloyd George's enthusiasm was so vocal that Churchill wrote to him in alarm, 'I fear that if your energies are dissipated in a great prohibition campaign, the comparatively small practical measures which wd. deal with the local evils & the misbehaviour of minorities in particular places will be overlooked. . . . After all the French are drinking their wines & Germans their beer & we have never been a drunken and inefficient nation as the Russians were'.[3] When he realized the depth of feeling in the country and the hostility of vested interests, Lloyd George gave up his idea of the state assuming control of the liquor industry and instead reverted to the problem of munitions. Strict measures were

[1] *Manchester Guardian*, 1 March, 1915.
[2] *Manchester Guardian*, 30 March, 1915.
[3] Churchill to Lloyd George, 7 April 1915, Lloyd George Papers, C/3/6/25.

taken, however, to limit the amount of alcohol in beer and spirits and wines were heavily taxed; public houses could also be closed or controlled in certain areas.

At this point, in May 1915, lack of success in the war, accentuated by the development of a press campaign against shell shortages, and the sudden resignation of Lord Fisher as first sea lord, produced the downfall of the Liberal government and the formation of the Asquith coalition.[1] Lloyd George played an important part both in persuading Asquith to agree to the coalition and in the lengthy discussion which ensued with the Unionist leaders on the allocation of offices. Why did Asquith and Lloyd George agree so readily to the coalition? On Asquith's side, the indications are that he appreciated that he must agree if he was to retain the premiership, for Bonar Law and his colleagues were now adamant on the need to improve the effectiveness of war policy. Lloyd George's enthusiasm stemmed fundamentally from his belief in maximum unity for waging successful war. He had never been a narrow party politician and he regarded the almost fanatical attachment to liberty of the individual, so prevalent among many Liberals, as positively dangerous when fighting a war on an unprecedented scale. Perhaps equally important was a growing pessimism about the trend of developments which made it all the more necessary to have the Unionists in the government; if the Unionists were not in the government, Lloyd George might sink with the ship should the situation further deteriorate. This analysis is underlined by the discussion at the war council on 14 May. Kitchener gloomily observed that Sir John French had failed in his attack on the German lines:

> It appears to me [Kitchener] that we are therefore forced still to maintain the defensive role hitherto imposed on us, and prepare for a concentration and attack by Germany on our and the French lines such as the Russians had recently shown they could not withstand. It would then be a good moment for Germany to hamper our sending support to our line of defence in France by an attack on these shores.[2]

Lloyd George followed expressing his grave doubts on the

[1] The most recent examination of the crisis is S. E. Koss, 'The destruction of Britain's last Liberal Government', *Journal of Modern History*, xi, (1968) 257–77.

[2] Minutes of war council, 14 May 1915, CAB 42/2/19.

Dardanelles operation, 'Personally he felt very doubtful whether the army could force the position. . . . It was very dangerous to go on from day to day merely drifting'.[1] Lloyd George pressed strongly for a coalition and, according to Churchill, was largely responsible for Asquith's swift decision to agree to a coalition.[2] In the discussions between the Liberal and Unionist leaders, he was prominent; the aim of the Liberals was to exclude the Unionists from the major offices in the cabinet, with the exception of the admiralty. The Unionists would incur the responsibility of power but their share in wielding it would be kept to the minimum. Lloyd George was passionately interested in the production of munitions which had been so ineptly handled by the war office: it was an urgent question and, as he no doubt appreciated, one which would be very rewarding to a successful minister. However, it was a definite risk to leave the treasury for a new post, which would be lower in the official hierarchy. Lloyd George determined to take the risk, confident that in his hands the danger would be minimal; the personal motive blended with the desire of other Liberal leaders to prevent the Unionists from controlling the new ministry of munitions or the exchequer, Lord Crewe writing to Lloyd George: 'Like you, I regard it as imperative for different reasons that both the Exchequer and Munitions should not fall into opposition hands. Then let you take Munitions and let McKenna come to the exchequer. . . .'[3] Suspicion was profound on both sides at the start of the coalition but the simple political distinctions were soon to dissolve and be replaced by new tensions, particularly those stimulated by the growing disagreements between Lloyd George and Asquith. The first coalition was not a happy government.

There was much support in the press for the idea of Lloyd George assuming direction of munitions production. As the *Manchester Guardian* observed on 26 May: 'Mr. Lloyd George has sacrificed a great position for one officially small and hitherto even non-existent. But the post is not the measure of the man, but contrariwise, the man of the post, and in Mr.

[1] Ibid.

[2] See interview notes, 1 Oct. 1915, Scott Papers, Add. MS. 50.902, and W. S. Churchill, *The World Crisis*, (6 vols. 1923–31) ii, 365.

[3] Crewe to Lloyd George, 24 May 1915, Lloyd George Papers, C/4/1/22.

George's hands the Ministry of Munitions should become the most important administrative office in the State. Its possibilities are great, almost unlimited. . . .'[1] The ministry of munitions was crucial to the rise of Lloyd George to supreme power. In a government grappling with stalemate on the western front, failure at Gallipoli and muddle at Salonica, the organization of munitions production on vastly improved lines was a dramatic success. Lloyd George radiated energy and vigour, conveying an air of confidence and zeal to the public and indeed many politicians; his private papers include many letters of congratulation and praise from men as diverse as L. S. Amery, Charles Bathurst, Lord Devonport, J. L. Garvin, H. A. Gwynne, Alfred Mond, R. E. Prothero and F. E. Smith, apart from a number of serving officers. Lloyd George's performance contrasted markedly with the fumbling of Asquith, the weariness of Grey, the enigmatic stubbornness of Kitchener, although the latter remained a popular hero, and the eclipse of Churchill. Lloyd George toured the major industrial areas of the country, making fiery speeches on the need for improved production, sacrifice and change. He was not always successful in securing his aims but he personified the desire of the nation to proceed more rapidly and energetically with the war. The difficulties he faced in forming the ministry of munitions were considerable, comprising the previous ineptitude, the existing resentment and continued hostility of the war office, the suspicions of trade unions and still more of their members, the need to coordinate all branches of munitions work, the problem of obtaining skilled labour and the introduction of much expanded use of female labour. The control of munitions had previously been exercised by Kitchener and the appropriate members of the army council, the quartermaster-general, master-general of ordnance and the finance member.[2] Kitchener tried to centralize everything and keep control in his own hands: it was hardly surprising that he was known in the war office as 'K of Chaos'. Kitchener had fought a rearguard action against

[1] *Manchester Guardian*, 26 May 1915.

[2] 'History of the Ministry of Munitions' (12 vols. unpublished, 1922), i, 46, Mun. 5 321A, P.R.O. ['History of Munitions']. Although unpublished, copies of the work may sometimes be found on library shelves, I have considered it wiser, in addition, to give the P.R.O. reference.

increasing intervention of civilian ministers but the manifest failures of ammunition production, especially of shells, undermined his position. Lloyd George set to work at the end of May 1915 and organized the new ministry. As he observed in his *War Memoirs*, he conceived his role as analogous to that of the head of a large business organization: it was his task to superintend policy, find the right man for the right job, carefully examine every facet of the ministry and apply pressure wherever it was needed.[1] He began by summoning the assistance of leading businessmen from a number of different industries: these were to provide the 'push and go' in improving efficiency.[2] Plans were made for beginning national factories; firms new to the industry were encouraged rather than discouraged, as had been the case under the war office. Vast orders were laid down regardless of cost. He built on firm foundations and established the basis for the great success of the ministry. As the official history states:

> This wide view of his position and responsibilities is reflected throughout his career as Minister of Munitions and his vision of the character and probable length of the conflict that lay ahead not only had a profound effect on the munitions programmes actually adopted in his period, but enabled the Ministry to meet much larger programmes later on. He laid the foundations of the Ministry's productive capacity on a scale so vast that it was almost sufficient—as far as guns, gun ammunition, rifles, machine guns, and trench warfare supplies were concerned—to carry the country to the end of the war.[3]

The flavour of Lloyd George's leadership of the ministry is admirably conveyed by the surviving minutes in his papers. These were usually succinct, crisp and urgent in character. On the delay in production at the new Leeds national factory he wrote:

> This was started eight weeks ago, but I am amazed to hear now that not a single lathe will be working for the turning out of the first shell

[1] Lloyd George, *War Memoirs*, ii, 654.

[2] For an example of Lloyd George's letters to businessmen, see his letter to his old colleague, D. A. Thomas of Cambrian Collieries Ltd., requesting the help of Thomas and of his able managing director, Leonard Llewellyn, Lloyd George to Thomas, 8 June 1915, D/12/1/1, and 14 June 1915, D/12/1/3 and Thomas to Lloyd George, 12 June 1915, D/12/1/2, Lloyd George Papers.

[3] 'History of Munitions', ii, part i, 11–12, Mun. 5 321A.

until about the second or third week in July, and only then on forgings being supplied from elsewhere. Not much 'push and go' in all this! I am disappointed to learn further that even when in full swing this factory is only expected to turn out 5,000 shells a week—a contemptible output for one of the largest and best equipped engineering centres in England . . .

I trust that the slowness with which the resources of Leeds are being mobilised will not be copied in the other districts. It is no use making good starts: our success depends not on these successful impulses but on continuous steady pressure being applied; otherwise you and I will be open to the charge that we just fussed about and achieved nothing in the end.[1]

Other minutes reflect the same tone. Lloyd George could be bitingly sardonic but his comments were very effective in producing results. The bulk of his intense work was carried through in his first four months at the ministry, when the lines were laid down which were pursued thereafter. He was so occupied in this period that he often missed cabinet meetings or meetings of the new Dardanelles committee, which had replaced the war council at the formation of the coalition. The work was successful and figures of munitions output steadily grew. The statistics of shell production may be cited as an example. Walter Layton, in a minute sent to Lloyd George shortly after he left the ministry in July 1916, noted that one year's output in 1914–15 could be obtained as follows: 18-pdr ammunition in three weeks, field howitzers in two weeks, medium guns and howitzers in eleven days and heavy howitzers in four days. The weekly output in the first three classes was practically equivalent to the whole stock in existence before the war.[2] A more detailed statement of the achievements in production during and after Lloyd George's period of office is given as an appendix below.

Labour was one of the gravest problems when Lloyd George took office. This partly resulted from the loss of men to the armed services in the early months of the war and partly from a shortage of skilled labour. The trade unions were suspicious of the government and afraid that advances made in the years before 1914 might be swept aside and workers treated like soldiers and forced to obey employers through the coercion of

[1] Minute by Lloyd George, 22 June 1915, Lloyd George Papers, D/3/3/35.
[2] Minute by Layton, 6 July 1916, Lloyd George Papers, D/5/2/11.

the state. In addition the introduction of dilution, that is the replacement of skilled labour by semi-skilled or unskilled labour, would threaten the status of the craft unions. When he became minister, Lloyd George met the union leaders and reluctantly agreed to an extension of voluntary methods including the fuller utilization of the 'King's Squad'.[1] Little improvement was secured, however, and in September 1915 Lloyd George declared that existing methods had failed and dilution must follow. The introduction of unskilled labour, including large numbers of women, resulted and was in general very successful. Not surprisingly some resistance was encountered in particular regions, notably on Clydeside where a militant movement flourished among some of the workers.[2] At Christmas 1915 Lloyd George visited Clydeside and endeavoured to use his oratorical powers to overwhelm the malcontents. It was a stormy meeting: both Lloyd George and Arthur Henderson, who chaired it, were vociferously heckled and eventually Henderson had to close the proceedings, which occurred amidst further uproar. Angered at this experience, Lloyd George helped to ban the militants' paper, *Forward*, for publishing an essentially accurate account of the meeting. He could derive some comfort from the *Manchester Guardian* which praised his courage:

> It is impossible not to admire at once the intrepidity and the ardour of the man who thus chooses to spend himself on the day of all other days when he might most easily have been excused for taking a brief rest and seeking peace and refreshment after exhausting labours. It is just this dynamic quality in Mr. Lloyd George, the demonic impulse which compels him to do at once and with all his might the thing which at the moment most needs doing, that constitutes his greatness and marks him out as a fit leader in times of danger and of difficulty.[3]

He was then rightly urged to display more patience in dealing with workers and employers. Clydeside was a storm which passed, even if it was always liable to erupt again. Some skilled labour was regained from the services, some from other sources

---

[1] 'The King's Squad' was a body of munitions workers which volunteered to travel wherever required for a period of three months provided wages remained the same and expenses were paid.

[2] See W. Kendall, *The Revolutionary Movement in Britain 1900–21* (1969), 120–3.   [3] *Manchester Guardian*, 27 Dec. 1915.

but the largest single segment from females.[1] During Lloyd George's term of office, more than half a million persons entered munitions industries, of whom approximately one half comprised women or girls: the increase was particularly swift in 1916.[2]

Lloyd George was accused of extravagance in ordering munitions by McKenna and to some extent by Kitchener; of riding roughshod over the workers by parliamentary critics like W. M. R. Pringle. There was some substance in these charges, especially concerning his attitude to labour: Lloyd George tended to be too critical of unions and workers and not critical enough of employers. Viewed in the context of the war and of the huge problems which he faced, the criticisms pale into insignificance. He had presided over a remarkable achievement; at the end of his year at the ministry the army was receiving ever increasing supplies of ammunition and guns and the urgent problems of May 1915 had mostly been solved. Lloyd George's prestige in the country was higher than that of any of his colleagues, and even they were compelled to pay grudging tribute to his success when munitions production was discussed at the war committee in June 1916.[3]

Now to revert to Lloyd George's attitude to the wider issues of the war, from the autumn of 1915 to the spring of 1916. He was pessimistic about the progress on both fronts and was still deeply dissatisfied at the British failure to mobilize all resources. C. P. Scott, owner and editor of the *Manchester Guardian*, saw him frequently in 1915–16. Scott was dazzled by Lloyd George's mercurial qualities but simultaneously critical of certain trends in his thinking, notably the emphasis on compulsion and force which was becoming the dominant theme in Lloyd George's pronouncements. Scott noted on 3 September, 1915:

> Ll. G. wired me to come to breakfast. He was alone. Stayed an hour. He at once broached subject of prospects of the war & probable need of compulsory service. Russia done for. Germans wd. probably take

[1] Jellicoe blamed delays in naval shipbuilding, in January 1916, on Lloyd George's having commandeered labour for munitions work, see A. Temple Patterson, *Jellicoe* (1969), 94.

[2] This paragraph is largely based on 'History of Munitions' iv, parts i, ii, iv, Mun. 5 321A.

[3] See minutes of war committee, 21 June 1916, CAB 42/15/10.

over Petrograd & Moscow ... The Russians were desperately short
not only of munitions but of rifles ... He was confident that we wd.
have to come to compulsion; the danger was that we shd. adopt
it too late.[1]

In the cabinet Lloyd George and Churchill were two of the
foremost advocates of compulsion but the cabinet was seriously
divided. Asquith was personally opposed to compulsion while
being prepared, as Lloyd George remarked to Scott, to accept
it as a last resort to preserve his position.[2] Leading Liberals
like McKenna, Runciman and Simon were strongly opposed
both on the grounds that the economy could not withstand the
strain and because of an attachment to the rights of the
individual. Labour circles were extremely suspicious of
compulsion, indeed Henderson was later to submit his resign-
nation on the issue. Kitchener was slowly coming round to the
view that compulsion might be necessary but in the autumn of
1915 was still upholding the voluntary principle, in which he
was further bolstered by Asquith who appreciated that his own
position would be seriously weakened if Kitchener changed his
mind. Lloyd George was firmly convinced that compulsion was
essential to winning the war: he was correct but did not give
sufficient allowance for minds that worked more slowly than
his own. On 5 September Scott lunched with him at Walton
Heath and received a clearer explanation of his views. Scott
wrote, 'That though he had not unlimited faith in compulsion
he regarded it as practically our only chance of winning the
war. ... He had quite made up his mind that if defeated on
compulsion he wd. decline to be further responsible for the war'.[3]
Scott continued that Lloyd George realized that his resignation
would involve the fall of the government and the disintegration
of the Liberal party:

> It was obvious that in all this he was thinking quite sincerely & simply
> of the military situation & the winning of the war. But when I put it
> to him he said at once that of course conscription wd. simplify very
> much his difficulties with labour by enabling him to reach the
> 100,000 enlisted munitn. men and as a means of disciplining the small
> minority who make all the trouble in the munitions work.[4]

[1] Interview notes, 3 Sept. 1915, Scott Papers, Add. MS. 50.901.
[2] Interview notes, 5 Sept. 1915, Scott Papers, Add. MS. 50.901.
[3] Ibid. [4] Ibid.

The struggle raged in the cabinet. Lloyd George made his position patently clear. He told a cabinet committee investigating manpower: 'You will not get through without some measure of military compulsion or compulsion for military service. The longer you delay the nearer you will be to disaster.'[1] Great Britain, he added, needed to raise larger armies if victory was to be secured and the weakness of Russia was always liable to throw extra pressure on the western front. 'Not only that, it is murder, because to send a number of men who are obviously inadequate is just murdering our own countrymen without attaining any purpose at all.'[2] He ended by urging that compulsory service should, if possible, be extended throughout the British empire. In mid-October Scott saw him again and learned that the grave crisis in the cabinet was approaching a climax. Lloyd George stated that eight members of the cabinet were determined to stand firm. Scott thought that his real aim was to reduce Asquith's power and himself replace Kitchener at the war office:

> It was evident that there was more involved in the controversy than the immediate matter in dispute & that it had been made a battle ground of parties one object of which was either to get rid of Asquith (of whom LG spoke with great bitterness) or to break his influence, and another object was to get rid of Kitchener whom G. proposed to send to France as C.-in-C. in place of French.[3]

Lloyd George said that whoever succeeded to the war office should have full powers, as Scott had suggested restoring the office of C.-in-C. to supervise strategy; he declined to comment when Scott asked who should replace Kitchener. Scott wrote, 'I think he desires the Office for himself.'[4] Lloyd George shrank from resignation, however; he held much respect for Asquith's political skill and was reluctant to challenge him openly. The only resignation was that of the attorney-general, Sir Edward Carson, who was thoroughly dissatisfied with the conduct of the war and in particular with the failure to send adequate help to Serbia, then being crushed by the enemy forces.[5]

---

[1] Report of war policy committee (chairman, Lord Crewe), 12 Oct. 1915, CAB. 42/4/8.   [2] Ibid.

[3] Interview notes, 14–15 Oct. 1915, Scott Papers, Add. MS. 50.902.

[4] Ibid.

[5] See Carson to Asquith, 12 Oct. 1915, Asquith Papers 15 fol. 17.

Thus Lloyd George remained in the government, profoundly unhappy with Asquith's leadership and with the failure to adopt compulsion. In the war committee, on 6 December, he attacked the 'piecemeal policy' of conducting war exemplified by Gallipoli, Salonica and Egypt and pressed for careful consideration of future strategy. In the house of commons, while discussing the progress of munitions production, he made his famous reference to 'the mocking spectre of "Too Late"', which he said had become the recurrent theme of the allied war effort.[1] On 28 December he supported Balfour in expressing doubt as to the possible success of a new allied offensive, which had been approved at the Chantilly conference. '*Mr. Lloyd George* said he agreed with the First Lord. General Joffre had always favoured this idea of a great offensive in the West: he had always been confident and he had always been wrong'.[2] Lloyd George once more pressed for meticulous appraisal of all aspects before new offensives were agreed upon. He kept contemplating resignation unless the direction of affairs improved but drew back from the final step. When Scott met him in February 1916 he thought he seemed 'worn and old'.[3] Lloyd George was attracted by the thought of joining Carson and Churchill in launching a formidable attack on Asquith, a course later advocated by the *Manchester Guardian*.[4] In the war committee he continued to demand more efficiency and repeatedly implied his doubts about decisions made by Kitchener and Robertson. On 7 April a long discussion took place in the committee on the coming summer offensive. Lloyd George was opposed to the committee giving *carte blanche* to the military in France, which was a bad principle: in addition he did not consider that the allies were strong enough. '*Mr. Lloyd George* referring to the question of a "Great Offensive" said we must have a superiority in men and material. He did not see how we could enter on a very great offensive *now* ... *Mr. Lloyd George* personally held to the plan of holding the Germans up, and smashing the Turks. That would be very unpleasant for Germany'.[5]

[1] *H.C. deb.*, lxxvii, c. 121, 20 Dec. 1915.
[2] War committee minutes 28 Dec. 1915, CAB 42/6/14.
[3] Interview notes, 17–19 Feb. 1916, Scott Papers, Add. MS. 50.902.
[4] *Manchester Guardian*, 21 April 1916.
[5] War committee minutes, 7 April 1916, CAB 42/12/5.

Meanwhile the battle for general conscription had been renewed in the cabinet. When C. P. Scott encountered Lloyd George at the ministry of munitions:

> He told me of his strong & increasing dissatisfaction with the conduct of the War & his intention to bring matters to a head by resigning if a measure of general compulsory service were not adopted on the lines of the motion of which Carson had given notice . . . He repeated & developed this statement at breakfast next morning, adding that he was going to meet Sir W. Robertson Nicoll, editor & proprietor of the 'British Weekly' at Sir George Riddell's house that afternoon to discuss his position & he pressed me to come, as he said he would like me to meet Nicoll.[1]

Nicoll and Scott both urged resignation on Lloyd George; Scott was so disillusioned with Asquith that he believed the existing coalition must fall if the war was to be won. Again, however, Lloyd George paused at the brink and retreated. He told Scott that there were several reasons why he did not resign: he did not wish to alienate further his radical supporters, many of whom were distressed by his advocacy of compulsion, the time was not appropriate and personally he felt that he had not yet extracted the maximum political advantage from his strenuous work at the ministry of munitions. Probably, as before, the most important reason was Lloyd George's respect for Asquith's position. Also, as Scott noted: 'he may be partly influenced by the fact that he has no independent means. He several times spoke of this more or less laughingly, but as he also said that he had received from an American agency an offer of £5,000 for 10 political articles the pressure of circumstances was not too severe . . .'[2] Asquith in turn had recognized that compulsion was now inevitable and supported what he had previously resisted. The issue which had threatened the break-up of the government ended on a note of anti-climax. Lloyd George defended his opinions in a scintillating speech at Conway on 6 May, repudiating the allegation that he was indulging in intrigue for ulterior purposes:

> There is no indignity in compulsion. Compulsion simply means that a nation is organising itself in an orderly, consistent resolute fashion for war . . .

[1] Interview notes, 13–20 April 1916, Scott Papers, Add. MS. 50.902.
[2] Ibid.

There are people who say—'What is he up to now? I am going to tell you what I am up to. I am up to winning this war . . .

I came into politics to fight for the underdog, and it has been all the same to me whether he was an under-paid agricultural labourer, a sick workman, an infirm and broken old man or woman who had given their lives to the country, a poor slum-dweller, or a small nation harried by voracious empires. In fighting this war I have simply, in my judgment, been carrying out the principles which I have advocated on this platform for thirty years of my life . . .

Time is not an ally. It is a doubtful neutral at the present moment, and has not yet settled on our side. But time can be won over by effort, by preparation, by determination, by organisation. We must reckon fearlessly the forces of the enemy.[1]

Ireland then intervened to divert the attention of the country and of Lloyd George. Redmond's magnanimity in pledging full support for the war effort had been insufficiently appreciated and the growth of the Sinn Fein movement gradually undermined the authority of the Irish parliamentary party. The Easter rebellion was the catalyst: British leaders suddenly realized the Irish question had entered a new and dangerous phase and that it was imperative that a settlement should, if possible, be reached. Lloyd George showed an early awareness of the need to curb the brutality of the military authorities, who were engaged in suppressing the insurrection. At the war committee on 28 April he 'expressed his fear lest the whole of Ireland be set ablaze by the unconsidered action of some subordinate officer.'[2] After visiting Ireland to assess the situation, Asquith decided to invite Lloyd George to undertake the task of attempting on behalf of the cabinet to negotiate a settlement: it was 'a *unique* opportunity, and there is no one else who could do so much to bring about a permanent solution'.[3] Margot Asquith and Walter Long quickly followed with letters appealing to him to take up Ireland, Margot's letter being written in typical vein: 'You will settle it & the whole Empire will be grateful for ever. There is no more to be done in Y. Department *make no mistake* there is a lot to be done for Ireland. If you want to please Henry and me & do a *big thing* settle Ireland. Any one with wit & a sense of humour must

[1] *Manchester Guardian*, 8 May 1916.
[2] War committee minutes, 28 April 1916, CAB 42/12/12.
[3] Asquith to Lloyd George, 22 May 1916, Lloyd George Papers, D/14/1/5.

enjoy Ireland, trying as the Irish are'.[1] It was obvious why
Asquith was so anxious that Lloyd George should accept his
request; it would occupy his time for some weeks to come and
prevent a renewed attack by him on Asquith's leadership. If
Lloyd George accepted and succeeded it would boost the
popularity of the government and if he failed it would diminish
his reputation. Lloyd George it appears was willing to accept,
although he may have pretended otherwise. He was becoming
weary of the ministry of munitions since his constructive work
was over, and Ireland offered an opportunity to raise his
prestige even higher. If successful he would rehabilitate himself
in the eyes of many Liberals who were critical of his antagonism
to Asquith and of his increasing identification with the Unionists
in the cabinet. He accepted but his position was ambiguous
from the start.[2] The cabinet had not delegated authority to
Lloyd George to arrange any settlement he thought best: rather
it had empowered him to conduct negotiations and make
recommendations to the cabinet. It was an important point
and one on which his efforts foundered. Lloyd George entered
the discussions with characteristic vigour, organizing meetings
with most shades of Irish opinion—orthodox and unorthodox
nationalists, Ulstermen, southern Unionists. The aim was to
discover a solution acceptable to the majority of Irish and
Ulster opinion, to reconcile the profound differences which
had come so near provoking civil war in July 1914. Lloyd
George's solution was simple yet simultaneously and deliberately
vague; the Government of Ireland Act was to be brought into
operation immediately but the six counties were to be excluded.
The solution was accepted by the leaders of the parliamentary
party, Redmond, Dillon and Devlin, and by the Ulster leader,
Carson. Their supporters generally showed less enthusiasm but
were won round by an arduous campaign waged by Redmond
and Devlin for the nationalists and by Carson for the Ulster
Unionists. During the negotiations Lloyd George had perhaps
unavoidably conveyed the impression that whatever solution

[1] Margot Asquith to Lloyd George, 23 May 1916, Lloyd George Papers,
D/14/1/7; Long to Lloyd George, 23 May 1916, Lloyd George Papers,
D/14/1/9.
[2] For a recent illuminating account of the 1916 negotiations, see F. S. L.
Lyons, *John Dillon: a Biography* (1968), chapter 13.

was reached would be accepted by his cabinet colleagues; in this way he was impressing all concerned with the urgency of matters while gambling on his ability to sell the scheme successfully to his colleagues. The Unionist leaders were mostly unhappy with the settlement, however, and a few incensed. Lansdowne and Selborne opposed any settlement which would give tangible recognition to the nationalists while Long repented his earlier encouragement of Lloyd George.[1] Letters of protest descended on Lloyd George and Asquith from their Unionist colleagues. As Lloyd George wrote to Dillon, 'the whole of the Unionist members are in a state of mutiny, and say they will not assent to any proposals to bring the Home Rule Act into operation during the war'.[2] It was not quite as bad as this, for Bonar Law, Balfour and F. E. Smith stoutly defended the settlement at an acrimonious cabinet meeting but the terms Lloyd George had made were amended to make it clear that the exclusion of the six counties was permanent and the Irish members would not sit at Westminster once the act came into operation. This destroyed the inherent ambiguity of Lloyd George's proposals, for nationalists had only accepted exclusion on the assumption that it was temporary while the Ulstermen had taken it to be permanent. Although Lloyd George again considered resignation when his terms were not accepted, he and Asquith subsequently retreated. To both the war and the need to preserve national unity took precedence over Ireland. Lloyd George had once more revealed his astonishing dexterity in negotiation and he derived some benefit in the English context, as it underlined his courage in facing controversial and intractable problems, but in the Irish context his reputation declined, Redmond and Dillon feeling that they could never trust him again.[3]

[1] See Long to Lloyd George, 11 June 1916, Lloyd George Papers, D/14/2/28; Asquith to Lloyd George, 17 June 1916 enclosing Selborne to Asquith, 16 June 1916, Lloyd George Papers, D/14/3/9; and Austen Chamberlain to Asquith (copy), Lloyd George Papers, D/14/3/34.

[2] Lloyd George to Dillon, 17 June 1916, Lloyd George Papers, D/14/3/11. Lloyd George personally believed exclusion should be permanent. According to C. P. Scott, he said 'that exclusion was largely a matter of words, since all agreed Ulster could not be forced', Interview notes, 27 July 1916, Scott Papers, Add. MS. 50.903.

[3] Lyons, *Dillon*, 302.

Long before the Irish negotiations were completed, Lloyd George's attention was diverted to another issue of far greater personal significance: the issue of whether or not he should accept the war office and, if so, on what terms. On 5 June Lord Kitchener was drowned when the *Hampshire* struck a mine shortly after leaving for Russia. His last months at the war office had been singularly unhappy, since he had been reduced to a figurehead, effective power lying with Sir William Robertson, the chief of the imperial general staff. Asquith had to offer the war office to Lloyd George, once it was clear that Bonar Law would not accept it, if he was to keep Lloyd George in the government and this was essential if the government was to survive. Lloyd George was caught in a similar dilemma. He was vitally interested in the military issues and genuinely concerned to improve efficiency and reduce the futile slaughter on the western front but how could this be achieved while Robertson held the reins of power? C. P. Scott accurately summarized Lloyd George's predicament:

> He was afraid of the soldiers & Robertson was indispensable. On the other hand he wd. not dream of taking the post without the power. The soldiers wd. crawl before the man who they knew had the ultimate power over them & treat any one who hd. not with contempt.[1]

The obvious course to pursue was to secure the reduction of Robertson's power. Accordingly Lloyd George prepared a long memorandum for Asquith on 17 June. It was an astute blend of Lloyd George's continuing dissatisfaction with the war record of the government combined with a statement of the reasons why the secretary of state for war should possess genuine power and not be 'a mere cipher'.[2]

Determination of strategy would still be decided by the generals but they needed to be 'checked by the common sense of the civilian'.[3] He continued: 'Great strategical enterprises ought to be submitted not merely to the Secretary of State but to the War Committee. The soldiers in this war have not been a conspicuous success. Up to the present there has not been a plan

---

[1] Interview notes, 10 June 1916, Scott Papers, Add. MS. 50.903.

[2] Lloyd George to Asquith, 17 June 1916, Lloyd George, *War Memoirs*, ii, 762–8.

[3] Lloyd George to Asquith, 17 June 1916, Lloyd George, *War Memoirs*, ii, 762–8.

conceived and carried out by them which has not ended in bloody failure.'[1] He ended with a reiteration of his opposition to 'the progress and conduct of the war'. As his work at the ministry of munitions was now at an end, it might be best if he resigned:

> I propose now to take a course which I had determined upon long ago. I had been profoundly dissatisfied for a long time with the progress and conduct of the war. I had expressed my dissatisfaction in writing and orally to you, the War Committee and the Cabinet. Had it not been for the fact that I had undertaken a task the carrying out of which was vital to the success of our army I should long ago have joined Carson, with whom I have been in the main in complete sympathy in his criticism of the conduct of the war . . .
>
> I therefore feel that my position in the Ministry is an anomalous one, as I am completely out of sympathy with the spirit and method of the war direction. I feel we cannot win on these lines. We are undoubtedly losing the war, and nothing can save us but the nation itself. The people do not realise how grave the situation is. I feel they ought to be told . . .
>
> It is with deep regret that from an overwhelming sense of public duty I feel that I must sever my association with you and with some of my other colleagues who have shown me great kindness and good-will, but I am profoundly convinced that I can render better service to my country in a very dark hour by standing outside and telling them what I know . . .[2]

Asquith would not reverse the existing arrangement at the war office and called Lloyd George's bluff. After further thought, Lloyd George decided to accept the *status quo* and seek to undermine Robertson's authority from within. He had little choice and as previously, his threat of resignation was not intended seriously. Lloyd George therefore became secretary of state for war. It was to be an unsatisfactory period of office for him. 'Wully' Robertson proved a much tougher proposition than he had hoped, the Somme offensive largely failed at tremendous cost, and Roumania was swiftly defeated. The culmination was the struggle with Asquith to change the methods of war government which surprisingly ended with Lloyd George replacing Asquith as prime minister.

Before assuming the war office, Lloyd George had been a frequently bitter critic of the complete reliance of the military,

[1] Ibid.
[2] Lloyd George to Asquith, 17 June 1916, Lloyd George, *War Memoirs*, ii, 762–8.

with Asquith's acquiescence, on the concept of victory on the western front. In the spring and summer of 1916 France was urging the value of an offensive from Salonica, where 350,000 allied troops were idle. At a meeting of the war committee on 17 May, a discussion had been held on the French approach. Robertson opposed it on military grounds as a convinced westerner while McKenna and Runciman were hostile because the allies did not possess enough ships to transport men and equipment. '*Mr. Lloyd George* said that they should make their real challenge on military grounds. He could not suppose that they would let a matter of forty ships stand in their way. They ought to challenge the proposal on military grounds.'[1] Lloyd George was not committing himself to automatic support of operations in the Balkans or on the western front but rather emphasizing that likelihood of military success should be the sole criterion: it was ludicrous to say that men's lives should be squandered in a hopeless offensive simply because shipping was in short supply. On the other hand it was equally necessary to examine the French proposal critically. Meanwhile his ire with the arrogance of the generals was made abundantly clear at the next meeting of the war committee. It arose from relatively trivial origins—an enquiry from Curzon, chairman of the shipping committee, concerning a request from the army for shipping to take horses to France. The army council replied indignantly that the matter was one for them alone and Robertson unwisely read out a private letter from Haig to the same effect. Lloyd George launched a savage attack on the military mentality:

> *Mr. Lloyd George* agreed [with Curzon] that it was most surprising to receive such a letter which amounted to the Army Council setting itself up against the Government. After referring to somewhat similar transactions in connection with the Admiralty, he said that he considered it a perfectly insolent letter from Sir D. Haig. The latter talked about his responsibility—to whom was he responsible? He was responsible to them, to the Government and through Parliament to the people. The effect of this letter was to tell the War Committee 'to mind their own business' and not interfere with his. He thought that the documents of the Army Council and of Sir D. Haig were most improper.[2]

[1] War committee minutes, 17 May 1916, CAB 42/13/1.
[2] War committee minutes, 18 May 1916, CAB 42/14/2.

Lloyd George then censured the military authorities for being too secretive:

> There was another matter to which he wished to direct their attention. That was the way the War Committee was treated in the matter of information, which was withheld from them. They had a perfect right to investigate any matter connected with the war that they pleased. If they said that they wished to investigate anything no one had the right to say that he objected, and to tell them to mind their own business.[1]

Lloyd George was therefore highly critical of the way in which the generals acted and of their reluctance to allow civilian intervention in military matters.[2] As secretary of state, he had to cooperate with them although the cooperation was soon to wear thin. The Somme offensive was beginning and Haig was, as usual, optimistic. It is difficult to assess Lloyd George's attitude but it is likely that he was sceptical of success. The Balkans claimed more attention in the war committee, where the desirability of opening a new offensive was being debated. In June Lloyd George opposed the contemplated eastern offensive which he termed 'a mad proposition'.[3] By July his opinion had changed, following the imminent entry of Roumania into the war. On 18 July he thought it would be worth considering a move designed to 'cut out Bulgaria and clear a road to Roumania'.[4] It would also isolate Turkey. Robertson was hostile, however, and stubbornly adhered to his belief that large-scale operations should only take place on the western front. Lloyd George showed increasing enthusiasm for an advance in the Balkans to assist Roumania, for action against the recalcitrant Greek court, and for the Arab revolt against the Turks. He made little headway. Within the cabinet great weariness was growing and there were some indications that a compromise peace was possible. On 30 August, when Lloyd George was absent, Asquith told the war committee that it was necessary to give consideration to the possibility of peace, 'Everything indicated that M. Briand considered that we

[1] Ibid.
[2] Haig disliked Lloyd George, while recognizing his great ability, see R. Blake (ed.) *The Private Papers of Douglas Haig 1914–1919* (1952), 166, 172.
[3] War committee minutes, 7 June 1916, CAB 42/15/6.
[4] War committee minutes, 30 Aug. 1916, CAB 42/18/8.

should be face to face with this question before the end of the autumn'.[1] He requested each member of the committee to prepare papers on their respective attitudes. There was no suggestion of approaching the Germans directly but of preparing for possible contingencies. Lloyd George had always deplored talk of compromise peace. It is true that he had often been pessimistic about the trend of the war but this was a reflection of his alienation from the incompetence of the political and military leadership within Great Britain, reinforced by the failure to secure closer cooperation among the allies; Lloyd George travelled abroad frequently for conferences and was impressed with the desirability of establishing closer relations with France and Russia at all levels. In September he loudly, even harshly, voiced his belief in the need for overwhelming victory in the famous 'knock-out blow' interview given to Roy Howard, of the United Press of America. Great Britain, said Lloyd George, desired no neutral mediation, she would fight to the end:

> But the British determination to carry the fight to a decisive finish is something more than the natural demand for vengeance. The inhumanity and the pitilessness of the fighting that must come before a lasting peace is possible is not comparable with the cruelty that would be involved in stopping the war while there remains the possibility of civilisation again being menaced from the same quarter.
> Peace now or any time before the final and complete elimination of this menace is unthinkable.[2]

There was nothing new in these sentiments, for such trenchant expressions had occurred in most of his speeches, including an address at Criccieth a month earlier.[3] It was, however, very different when such outspoken words were directed at the United States, whose president, Woodrow Wilson, was eager to promote peace in Europe. Several motives coalesced in the interview: Lloyd George's sincere belief in the more vigorous prosecution of the war with his determination to eschew the

---

[1] War committee minutes, 30 Aug. 1916, CAB 42/18/8.

[2] *Manchester Guardian*, 29 Sept. 1916.

[3] 'We must have such a victory as will be a warning to any ruler that now sits or will ever sit on a throne, to any kings or councillors of kings, that they will be called sternly to account by the conscience of civilisations for every outrage they perpetrated against international right and fair dealing', *Manchester Guardian*, 21 Aug. 1916.

possibility of making an unsatisfactory peace, and possibly a desire to cultivate better relations with the British generals in France whom he had antagonized by criticism voiced to General Foch.[1] Grey had apparently approved the idea of the interview but afterwards he wrote to Lloyd George deprecating the terms used:

> It has always been my view that until the Allies were sure of victory the door should be kept open for Wilson's mediation. It is now closed for ever as far as we are concerned.
>
> I may be quite wrong in my view but a public warning to the President of the United States is an important step & I wish I had had an opportunity of putting these considerations before you & discussing them with you.[2]

Lloyd George replied in breezy terms defending his opinions:

> If the hands of Wilson had been forced—and there is every indication that the Germans and Irish in cooperation could do so—then we should be in a very tight place. Any cessation of hostilities now would be a disaster; and although we could always refuse or put up impossible terms, it is much better that we should not be placed in the predicament. *You* could not have warned off the United States without doing it formally. I could commit a serviceable indiscretion: you could not. It would ruin you; I am inoculated . . .[3]

Lloyd George had further consolidated his reputation with the British public and with those politicians who were weary of Asquith's flaccid leadership.

In the war office his relations with Robertson were deteriorating. He had hoped to persuade Robertson to return some at least of the authority which he exercised. His hopes were doomed to disappointment, for Robertson firmly resisted Lloyd George's interference. Lloyd George tried to send him to Russia on a mission intended to assess the Russian war effort and to put more vigour into the Russian contribution, since she was leaning too heavily on Britain for financial assistance. The real aim from Lloyd George's viewpoint was to steer Robertson

[1] Interview notes, 2–3 Oct. 1916, Scott Papers, Add. MS. 50.903. Scott considered that either Lloyd George wished to regain popularity with the generals or that there was a serious division of opinion on the peace issue within the cabinet.

[2] Grey of Fallodon to Lloyd George, 29 Sept. 1916, Lloyd George, *War Memoirs*, ii, 856–7.

[3] Lloyd George to Grey of Fallodon, 2 Oct. 1916, *War Memoirs*, ii, 857–8.

away from the war office for a considerable period during which he could establish control. Robertson discerned the manoeuvre and refused to go, consistently opposing all attempts to persuade him.[1] On 12 October Lloyd George sent him a masterly letter, drawing Robertson's attention to the appearance in the press of highly confidential information, stating that this was intolerable and, while recognizing Robertson's authority to speak on strategy, maintained his own right to comment at the war committee. 'Believe me, there is no man who has more sincere admiration for you than I have and there is no one more anxious to cooperate with you so as to make the most of these gifts for the benefit of the country: but you must not ask me to play the part of a mere dummy. I am not in the least suited for the part'.[2] Robertson was immovable, however, and received strong support from Lord Northcliffe and H. A. Gwynne of the *Morning Post*; Lloyd George's exasperation increased. He was extremely unhappy at the development of military operations and pressed for a conference of allied leaders. The conference was held at Paris in mid-November: Lloyd George called for changes in policy but the conference approved the decisions of the military for a new offensive on the western front in 1917.[3] It was the final straw: angered and disturbed by the atmosphere of apathy and resignation around him, possessing no effective power with the implacable Robertson resisting, he at last decided to stand firm for a fundamental reform of the British constitutional machinery for waging war. The existing policy of drift could not be continued: either Asquith would agree to the changes he envisaged or this time he would resign.

Great controversy has surrounded the events of late November and early December 1916, particularly as to the respective aims of the two men principally involved, Lloyd George and Asquith.[4] Before examining the developments in detail, brief discussion of Asquith's leadership is necessary. Asquith has, on the whole,

---

[1] Robertson to Lloyd George, 27 Sept. 1916, Lloyd George Papers, E/1/5/2; see also war committee minutes, 21 Nov. 1916, CAB 42/25/2.

[2] Lloyd George to Robertson, 12 Oct. 1916, Lloyd George Papers, E/1/5/3.

[3] See *War Memoirs*, ii, 913–62 for Lloyd George's views of the Paris conference.

[4] For a recent revisionist interpretation, see C. Hazlehurst, 'The conspiracy myth' in M. Gilbert (ed.) *Lloyd George* (1968), 148–57. Independently I have come to largely the same conclusions as Dr. Hazlehurst.

been treated kindly by the historians. Cultivated, intelligent, urbane, he appears as a man gradually overwhelmed by the magnitude of the war and finally displaced in an atmosphere of cut-throat intrigue by the unprecedently devious Lloyd George. Asquith was in many respects admirable and likeable but as war-time prime minister, he was disastrous. His most valuable contribution had come at the beginning of the war in ensuring the amazing unity with which Great Britain entered the conflict and it is doubtless true that no other Liberal politician could have elicited the affection and loyalty which Asquith received. His defects were numerous, however, and handicapped the determination of policy. Asquith retained the large cabinet as the ultimate source of decision while using the smaller war committee, in its various manifestations, as the body which dealt more closely with war policy. The large cabinet was hopelessly unsatisfactory for effective discussion. The smaller war committee was no marked improvement. Usually at least ten were present, sometimes more: discussion was discursive with rambling, often irrelevant statements and little coordination. The war office and admiralty were reluctant to provide sufficient material for discussion. Asquith presided benignly, sometimes writing letters while meetings proceeded but conspicuously failing to show real decision and grasp. It was hardly surprising that a man with Lloyd George's drive and initiative felt so frustrated. He was not alone; Bonar Law was profoundly dissatisfied, other Unionists like Austen Chamberlain increasingly worried and even loyal Asquithians such as Lord Crewe, believed that the system had to be changed.

The detailed story has been told by Lord Beaverbrook in his *Politicians and the War*, although he is at times misleading.[1] Bonar Law had for long chafed at the conduct of the coalition from the comparative backwater of the colonial office. His vague uneasiness was accentuated during 1916 by the emergence of Sir Edward Carson as a formidable critic of the government and as a growing power within the Unionist party. Bonar Law was also suspicious of Austen Chamberlain and thought he might be working to obtain the leadership. Encouraged by Aitken,[2]

[1] Lord Beaverbrook, *Politicians and the War* (1960), one-volume edition of the original two volumes first published in 1928 and 1932 respectively.

[2] Later Lord Beaverbrook.

Bonar Law made up his mind to support Lloyd George in making representations to Asquith. Lloyd George's proposal was that the war committee should be reduced to three members, two of whom must be the first lord of the admiralty and the secretary of state for war, with a third minister without portfolio, one of the three acting as chairman; the committee would have full powers, although the prime minister and the cabinet would have the right to intervene; the committee would possess the authority to invite any minister and his advisers to attend its meetings.[1] Asquith's immediate response was moderately favourable. His reply to Lloyd George included a damaging admission of the failure of the existing war committee:

> The two main defects of the War Committee, which has done excellent work, are (1) that its numbers are too large (2) that there is delay, evasion, and often obstruction on the part of the departments in giving effect to its decisions. I might with good reason add (3) that it is often kept in ignorance by the departments of information, essential and even vital, of a technical kind, upon the problems that come before it, and (4) that it is overcharged with duties, many of which might well be delegated to subordinate bodies.[2]

Asquith stipulated that the prime minister must be chairman of the new committee and believed that it should be enlarged to five members, including the minister of munitions and another minister either without portfolio or with light departmental duties. In addition a 'Committee of National Organisation' should be set up to transact purely domestic business. The cabinet was to be the final court of appeal. Lloyd George was prepared to accept Asquith's proposal, subject to agreement on personnel. It seemed that the government would continue on a reorganized basis. Lord Crewe wrote to Asquith welcoming the virtual abolition of the full cabinet: 'I do not see how anybody can regret it, for no meeting for some time past has been of any service to the country or the Govt. If it is possible to substitute two small Boards of three each, with you as President of both, business ought to be promptly done. . . .'[3] On 3 December Scott

---

[1] Lloyd George to Asquith, 1 Dec. 1916, Lloyd George, *War Memoirs*, ii, 982–3.

[2] Asquith to Lloyd George, 1 Dec. 1916. Beaverbrook, *Politicians and the War*, 388.

[3] Crewe to Asquith, 4 Dec. 1916, Asquith Papers, 17 fol. 179.

lunched with Lloyd George at Walton Heath. Lloyd George admitted that he had consistently been a thorn in Asquith's side but maintained that this was defensible because of his concern with efficiency:

> When I remarked to Ll. G. that he might be accused of always making trouble & attacking the P.M. he admitted that he was the disruptive element in the Cabinet but was of opinion that he hd. really done the P.M. a service, as if he had not goaded him to action he wd. have come to disaster long ago.[1]

The Unionist leaders, meeting on 3 December, decided in view of increasing discussion in the press of Lloyd George's proposal, that reform of the government from within was now impossible and that Asquith should be advised to tender the resignation of the government; if Asquith refused to do so, Bonar Law was empowered to submit the resignations of the Unionist ministers. Much speculation has surrounded the precise objectives of the Unionist ministers: was their statement intended to strengthen Asquith, to support Lloyd George, either or neither according to the attitude of each individual or was it intended as a statement of neutrality? Bonar Law was the most favourable to Lloyd George but not uncritically so. Austen Chamberlain was neutral: as he wrote in a long letter to the viceroy of India, personally he liked Asquith but Lloyd George was the man of drive and the continuation of the Asquith government had become impossible—either Asquith or Lloyd George had to form the new government and if Lloyd George could succeed, the Unionists would support him.[2] Curzon was personally inclined towards Asquith also but would support whoever triumphed. Lord Robert Cecil was prepared to serve under Lloyd George if necessary but as Lord Milner wrote in a private letter, was 'deflected by an almost insane dislike of Carson, and in a lesser degree of B.L.'[3] Balfour was ill but, like Curzon, was ready to support the victor, although one of Lloyd George's aims had originally been to remove Balfour from the admiralty. Lansdowne was the only senior

[1] Interview notes, 2–5 Dec. 1916, Scott Papers, Add. MS. 50, 903.

[2] A. Chamberlain to Chelmsford, 8 Dec. 1916, Austen Chamberlain Papers, AC/15/3/8; the letter is reprinted, in sections, in A. Chamberlain, *Down The Years* (1936), 115–28.

[3] Extract from Milner to Lady E. Cecil, 5 Dec. 1916, Milner Papers 143.

Unionist who warmly favoured Asquith while Carson was the only extreme opponent of Asquith but he was an outsider among prominent Unionist politicians. Fundamentally the Unionist formula was a declaration of neutrality: the Unionists probably could not provide a prime minister and it had to be seen which of the two leading Liberals could form a viable administration.

Thus the Unionists understood Lloyd George's memorandum to be an attempt to overthrow Asquith. The belief was most probably erroneous. Lloyd George was not trying to supplant Asquith but ironically the action of the Unionists helped to secure that he did. Asquith was angered by the tone of press comment, especially by *The Times* of 4 December, for he wrongly suspected Lloyd George of having inspired the article. He protested to Lloyd George and reiterated the conditions which he had previously drawn up under which the new war committee would function. Lloyd George replied in conciliatory vein denying responsibility for Northcliffe's activities.[1] Asquith was already regretting his decision to compromise and was encouraged by his Liberal colleagues to assert his authority. It has been suggested that Lloyd George's advocacy of Carson's inclusion in the new war committee was intended to insult Asquith: that Lloyd George was not sincere in stating that he wished Asquith to remain prime minister.[2] Lloyd George had genuine respect for Carson; they had long held similar views on the conduct of the war and had closely cooperated in the abortive Irish negotiations earlier in the year. Carson's peculiar failure to shine in office was not as clear in December 1916 as it became subsequently. Further, the Asquithian Crewe envisaged the possible inclusion of Carson in a letter written to Asquith on 5 December: would he have put down Carson's name had he believed that it was so obnoxious to the prime minister?[3] Asquith had already decided to accept the resignations of his colleagues and form a new government. He now felt it to be essential that the prime minister should be the permanent chairman of the committee and he could not agree that Carson should be a member. Indeed the matter of personnel was one

---

[1] Lloyd George, *War Memoirs*, ii, 987–9.

[2] Wilson, *Downfall*, 94–5.

[3] Crewe to Asquith, 5 Dec. 1916, Asquith Papers 17, fol. 184.

'which I must reserve for myself to decide';[1] his objection to Carson stemmed from growing antagonism to Lloyd George's wish to help determine the personnel of the committee and was not in itself responsible for the new line he adopted. Lloyd George received the letter with surprise and indignation. He replied in a brilliantly argued letter, underlining the inconsistency of Asquith's reasoning and finishing with a blunt statement of dissatisfaction:

> We have thrown away opportunity after opportunity, and I am convinced, after deep and anxious reflection, that it is my duty to leave the Government in order to inform the people of the real condition of affairs and to give them an opportunity, before it is too late, to save their native land from a disaster which is inevitable if the present methods are longer persisted in. As all delay is fatal in war, I place my office without further parley at your disposal.[2]

Asquith, tired but perhaps still believing that no one else could form a government, resigned as prime minister. Asquith's attitude was at this stage similar to that of the Unionist leaders —let Lloyd George accept the responsibility of his actions and try to form a government. Bonar Law was invited to assume office but preferred that Lloyd George should do so: Bonar Law had little if any personal ambition left and had privately stated his willingness to serve under Lloyd George a year earlier.[3] Could Lloyd George form a government without Asquith's inclusion? Lloyd George had not set out with the intention of securing the premiership: he faced grave difficulties in doing so given the antagonism of many Liberals, the uncertain attitude of Labour and of some Unionists. As Montagu[4] wrote to Asquith on 5 December, 'I found him in almost as great a condition of misery and unhappiness as I am myself. Believe me or not as you will, he wanted to work with you . . . He does not want, I am confident, to be Prime Minister . . .'[5] C. P. Scott was also struck by Lloyd George's genuine indignation and

---

[1] Asquith to Lloyd George, 4 Dec. 1916, cited Lloyd George, *War Memoirs*, ii, 990–2.

[2] Lloyd George to Asquith, 5 Dec. 1916, cited Lloyd George, *War Memoirs*, ii, 994.

[3] R. Blake, *The Unknown Prime Minister* (1955), 275–6, 296.

[4] The Hon. E. S. Montagu, Asquith's Minister of Munitions.

[5] Cited Gilbert, *Lloyd George*, 104.

chagrin when he saw him on 5 December.[1] It was now too late. Lloyd George had frequently considered resignation in 1915–16 but this time he had resigned and could do no other than endeavour to form a government. He succeeded and reached the end of the road to the premiership, attaining his life-long ambition unexpectedly and in complex circumstances. It was, however, not the product of intrigue but rather the product of accident, as so often in history.

Between August 1914 and December 1916, David Lloyd George established a record of solid achievement unequalled by any of his colleagues: no one could rival the success of the minister of munitions. No other minister possessed the astonishing dynamism and resilience of Lloyd George. He personified action: as he had written to Asquith in his final letter of resignation, 'Vigour and vision are the supreme need at this hour'. Lloyd George knew he possessed these qualities and even more important that large numbers of people in the country believed he possessed them and therefore gave him their trust. Lloyd George's success was founded on his swift and accurate appreciation of the frightening character of the new warfare, of the demands it made and would make and on its demolition of the old Britain and the old Europe. As he had remarked—and perhaps appropriately in the circumstances—in his much interrupted speech to the Clydeside workers on Christmas Day 1915, 'It is the deluge ... It is an earthquake which is upheaving the very rocks of European life.'[2] He did not care for old traditions and habits or for old Liberal principles. Men were sacrificing their lives in vast numbers and the nation had to be organized so that she could support these men with maximum efficiency. Naturally Lloyd George considered his own prospects and the role he should play in the war but he was not spurred on by unscrupulous personal ambitions. He was devious, as all supremely successful politicians have to be devious, but he was not unique in this respect. He cared deeply and genuinely about the suffering and carnage of the struggle. He had no all-embracing solution in mind which would win victory more rapidly. What he did have was a flexible approach to problems coupled with the adoption of competent, forceful

[1] Interview notes, 2–5 Dec. 1916, Scott Papers, Add. MS. 50. 903.
[2] *Manchester Guardian*, 27 Dec. 1915.

methods of government. Should he have resigned earlier and could he have secured the premiership had he done so? He did not resign sooner because he did not consider his political strength sufficient to justify it, justification connoting more efficient government. He consistently exaggerated Asquith's power and was understandably reluctant to indulge in futile resignation. It is possible that he could have become prime minister sooner but he would not take the risk involved. Until the final crisis, Lloyd George believed Asquith must remain prime minister. What Lloyd George desired was better, more effective government. He did not force a crisis earlier because he was not aiming at the premiership. Lloyd George was regarded with distaste and distrust by many: the speed with which his mind worked, his readiness to criticize others—a quality in which he was never deficient—accentuated by his mysterious relations with the press, all caused suspicion and enmity. Thus these traits partly cancelled out the favourable impression given by his arduous work. Lloyd George became prime minister because the war was going badly and distrust of him was outweighed by disillusionment with Asquith. There were doubts among many but the feeling that however Lloyd George performed, he could scarcely be worse than Asquith was common by December 1916. The *Manchester Guardian* decided to hope for the best: 'Our future for perhaps many a long day rests largely in Mr. Lloyd George's hands. Let us hope that he will show himself worthy of so mighty a trust'.[1] The hope was to be justified.

[1] *Manchester Guardian*, 9 Dec. 1916.

APPENDIX

The following table illustrates the great increase in production of munitions following the creation of the new ministry.

MUNITIONS DELIVERIES IN 1915, 1916 AND 1917

	July–Sept. 1915	July–Sept. 1916	July–Sept. 1917
Guns and Howitzers (no. delivered to service)			
Light	997	501	1,187
Medium	193	449	285
Heavy	—	256	370
Very heavy	16	134	234
Total	1,206	1,340	2,076
Gun ammunition (no. of rounds filled and completed)			
Light	1,680,400	11,229,500	13,170,800
Medium	407,300	4,011,100	5,055,400
Heavy	63,000	922,200	3,902,800
Very heavy	21,700	693,000	995,600
Total	2,172,400	16,855,800	23,124,600
Trench mortars (no. accepted after proof)			
Light	93	1,094	799
Medium	59	124	786
Heavy	—	74	122
Total	152	1,292	1,707
Trench warfare ammunition (no. of rounds filled and completed)			
Grenades	2,355,076	8,969,694	7,668,206
Trench howitzer bombs			
Light	39,790	1,230,609	1,337,320
Medium	41,893	211,475	363,730
Heavy	—	60,906	64,913
Total	81,683	1,502,990	1,765,963

	July–Sept. 1915	July–Sept. 1916	July–Sept. 1917
Machine guns (no. accepted)	1,719	9,572	18,985
Rifles (no. accepted)	173,317	457,732	324,423
S.A.A. (no. of rounds)	395,881,000	807,639,000	318,609,000

(Reproduced from 'History of Ministry of Munitions', II, part I 44–5, Mun 5 321A, P.R.O.)

Manchester University   PETER LOWE

A number of the extracts from C. P. Scott's diaries cited in this essay may now be found in T. Wilson (ed.), *The Political Diaries of C. P. Scott, 1911–1928* (1970). This work appeared too late for me to incorporate references in the text.

The research for this article was generously facilitated by a grant from the Twenty-seven Foundation, London.

V

HOW TO SETTLE THE IRISH QUESTION: LLOYD GEORGE AND IRELAND 1916–21

D. G. BOYCE

GEORGE BOYCE

Age 27

Queen's University, Belfast
B.A. 1965, Ph.D. 1969
Currently Assistant in the Department of
Western MSS., Bodleian Library

HOW TO SETTLE THE IRISH
QUESTION: LLOYD GEORGE AND
IRELAND 1916-21

HOWEVER much historians differ in their assessment of Lloyd George's career, and their evaluation of his character, few would deny his achievement in disposing of one of the most distracting problems in British politics—the Irish question; and what makes it all the more remarkable is the fact that, whatever Lloyd George's mission in life may have been, it was not to pacify Ireland. He was, to be sure, a Liberal and a home ruler, and he acknowledged the justice of Ireland's claim to self-government; but the cause of Irish home rule was never one that aroused Lloyd George's enthusiasm or fighting spirit, and he was not deeply concerned about Ireland, nor was he particularly interested in Irish affairs. 'He was never', remarked Thomas Jones, 'as Gladstone was, a crusader for Home Rule':[1] yet Lloyd George found the key to the Irish puzzle where all before him had failed. It is the purpose of this essay to follow the twists and turns of Lloyd George's Irish policy between 1916 and 1921, to examine his motives and methods, and, finally, to explain how he earned himself the epithet: 'The solver of the insoluble.'

Lloyd George had served his political apprenticeship in the parliament which, in 1893, had rejected Gladstone's second home rule bill, and his ministerial experience was acquired in the last Liberal governments before the First World War. As a result, he had witnessed the pernicious influence which the Irish question could exercise on the course of British politics and the careers of British statesmen; and when, on 22 May 1916, Asquith entrusted him with the task of finding a solution, Lloyd George must have felt some misgivings. On the same day he wrote ruefully to his brother William: 'P.M. and Bonar Law want me to take Ireland with full powers to effect settlement. Rather interesting that when there is a special difficulty they always pick on me!'[2]

The 'special difficulty' that confronted the minister of

---

[1] Thomas Jones, *Lloyd George* (1951), 187.
[2] William George, *My Brother and I* (1958), 254.

munitions in May 1916 was essentially the legacy of the prewar
home rule struggle, when Asquith's Liberal administration,
in alliance with the Irish Parliamentary Party led by John
Redmond, attempted to introduce a measure of self-government
into Ireland. The powers of the proposed Irish legislature were
to be of a very limited kind, with important services reserved
to the imperial parliament, whose ultimate authority was
carefully preserved; but the Protestants of Ulster, fully supported by the British Conservative party, pledged themselves to
resist 'by all means that may be found necessary' the establishment of a home rule parliament in Ireland. The example which
they set encouraged the emergence of a more militant Irish
nationalism, which rejected the constitutional methods and
limited aspirations of the home rulers, and professed to admire
the warlike preparations of the Ulster Volunteers. The onset
of the Great War in August 1914 postponed the home rule
crisis; but in Ireland a group of separatists, including members
of the Irish Republican Brotherhood and of James Connolly's
Citizen Army, resolved to strike a blow for their country's right
to independence. Their act of defiance and self-sacrifice began
on Easter Monday, 24 April 1916; and although the British
suppressed the rebellion within a week, they could not ignore its
implications. The rising, after all, had taken place in the middle
of a war which was being fought ostensibly for the rights of
small nations and, apart from this embarrassing predicament,
it was imperative to attempt some kind of settlement so that the
British war-effort would not be hampered by a serious internal
crisis. It was at this point that Lloyd George entered the scene,
charged with the task of picking up the pieces and patching up
an Irish settlement.

Lloyd George was not a man likely to be for long overawed
by a political problem, however intractable, and his complaint
to his brother on hearing about his new job of peace-maker in
Ireland was tempered by a sense of anticipation. He must have
known that the successful accomplishment of his mission would
enhance his reputation and improve his political prospects.
There were other considerations besides those of personal
advantage. Lloyd George was passionately concerned to win the
war. 'In six months', he exclaimed to Sir Edward Carson, 'the
war will be lost . . . The Irish-American vote will go over to

the German side. They will break our blockade and force an ignominious peace on us, unless something is done, even provisionally, to satisfy America'.[1]

The phrase 'unless something is done, even provisionally' explains what Lloyd George tried to do in 1916, for he was primarily concerned, not to devise a settlement that would last for all time, but to make an arrangement that would paper over the cracks and leave England free to get on with the war. He therefore hoped to shelve the contentious question of partition which had jeopardized earlier attempts to find a compromise. Lloyd George offered immediate home rule for 26 counties of Ireland, with the corollary of exclusion of the remaining six;[2] and to secure acceptance of his proposals he did not shrink from making contradictory promises to Carson, who negotiated on behalf of the Ulster unionists, and to the nationalist leader John Redmond. In order to induce Redmond to modify his instinctive aversion to partition, Lloyd George allowed him to gather the impression that exclusion was only a temporary arrangement; but at the same time he assured Carson that 'We must make it clear that at the end of the provisional period Ulster does not, whether she wills it or not, merge in the rest of Ireland'.[3]

Redmond could not accept the permanent division of Ireland, Carson would in no circumstances tolerate less: Lloyd George must therefore appear to satisfy both. He was probably not much concerned about the number of parts into which it was possible to divide Ireland; partition was a means to an end, for, as he explained to Redmond, 'If I am allowed to make some arrangement about Ulster I can promise to get you Home Rule for all the rest of Ireland'.[4] Lloyd George had made a similar suggestion in February 1914, when he urged the cabinet to offer to each Ulster county an option to vote itself out of the operation of the home rule bill for a period of six years, and thus 'put the other side entirely in the wrong';[5] but the bargain that Lloyd George struck with Carson and Redmond in May

---

[1] Thomas Jones, *Lloyd George*, 81.
[2] The counties to be excluded were Antrim, Armagh, Down, Fermanagh, Londonderry, Tyrone.
[3] F. S. L. Lyons, *John Dillon: a biography* (1968), 388.   [4] Ibid., p. 385.
[5] Robert Blake, *The Unknown Prime Minister* (1955), 183.

1916 needed to be underwritten by the party whose opposition to home rule he had hoped to undermine in 1914. Partly at Lloyd George's instigation, Asquith, in May 1915, had broadened the base of his administration by admitting representatives of the Conservative party to power, and now Lloyd George's home rule proposals met with opposition from his recently recruited colleagues. The immediate prospect of a Dublin parliament was, perhaps, more than most unionists could bear; and British unionists were under pressure from southern Irish unionists who, in Lloyd George's own expression, were 'moving heaven and the other place to thwart settlement'.[1] On 11 June Walter Long warned him that the unionists in the south of Ireland were being driven to a settlement which they knew to be 'morally wrong and wrong politically', and that the nationalists were 'sullen and hostile'.[2] The Lloyd George plan had run into trouble.

Lloyd George had given the Irish nationalists 'the most emphatic assurance, saying he had "placed his life upon the table and would stand or fall by the agreement come to"';[3] and it appeared, for a moment, that he meant what he said. On 12 June Lloyd George drafted a letter of resignation to the prime minister, stating that 'without a united Government settlement is impossible'. On the same day he reaffirmed his promise to Redmond to resign if his terms were not accepted by the cabinet, and he informed Walter Long of his intention to quit the government.[4] Perhaps Lloyd George hoped that his threat would cause Long to back down, and would thus strengthen the hand of the home rulers in the cabinet; if so, he was mistaken, because Long promptly called his bluff: 'I cannot believe that you seriously intend to base your resignation upon this excuse'.[5] Long was right: the copy of the letter of resignation in the Lloyd George papers is endorsed with the words 'not sent'.[6]

[1] Lloyd George to John Dillon, 12 June 1916, Lloyd George Papers, D/14/2/31.
[2] Walter Long to Lloyd George, 11 June 1916, ibid. D 14/2/28.
[3] Denis Gwynn, The Life of John Redmond (1932), 506.
[4] F. S. L. Lyons, John Dillon, 394; Lloyd George to Walter Long, 12 June 1916, Lloyd George Papers, D/14/2/32.
[5] Walter Long to Lloyd George, 12 June 1916, ibid. D/14/2/33.
[6] Lloyd George to Asquith, 12 June 1916, ibid. D/14/2/29.

Unionist opposition was not overcome: indeed, it grew more determined. 'They are all in it', Lloyd George complained bitterly to John Dillon on 20 June, 'except Balfour, Bonar Law and F. E. [Smith]. Long has behaved in a specially treacherous manner'.[1] Once again Lloyd George seems to have hovered on the brink of resignation, and once again he drew back. Instead, he conducted a half-hearted rearguard action, and negotiations dragged on until the end of July, when the exposure of Lloyd George's contradictory promises to Carson and Redmond finally ended the episode. But it was the behaviour of unionist members of the cabinet that was the fundamental cause of failure, and Lloyd George must take his share of the blame for running away.[2] Lloyd George knew that he was not yet politically indispensable, and he was resolved not to suffer the fate of other British statesmen who had faced, and failed to solve, the Irish question. However we may judge his conduct, there can be no doubt that, from the point of view of his career, he was well-advised to sacrifice his Irish settlement and live to fight another day: for in six months he was to become prime minister.

The negotiations which Lloyd George initiated in May 1916 in the end achieved nothing; nevertheless, they were not without significance for the future. One of the main unionist grievances was that Lloyd George, in coming to terms with Carson and Redmond, had exceeded his mandate which, they argued, had been to discover a possible basis of agreement between the contending parties, not commit the cabinet to a definite settlement. Lloyd George repudiated this insinuation, replying that he had always kept his unionist colleagues informed about the nature of his settlement plan;[3] but the experience of 1916 taught him his lesson: never again did he over-reach himself, never again did he outpace his Conservative colleagues when working out an Irish policy. From now on he proceeded with caution—a method of procedure which was obligatory after

[1] Lloyd George to John Dillon, 20 June 1916, ibid. D/14/3/22.
[2] So too, of course, must Asquith.
[3] Asquith to Lloyd George, 17 June 1916, enclosing a letter from Lord Selborne to Asquith, 16 June 1916, Lloyd George Papers (D/14/3/9); Lloyd George to Asquith, 23 June 1916, enclosing a letter from Austen Chamberlain to Asquith, 22 June 1916, ibid. (D/14/3/34).

his assumption of the premiership in December 1916. The party
political rebellion against Asquith which brought Lloyd George
to power originated in the ranks of back-bench unionists led
by Carson, and owed its successful outcome largely to the
influence of Bonar Law. It would be misleading to suggest that
Lloyd George was dependent on the unionists to the extent
that he later became; nevertheless, unionists provided the most
substantial element of support, even if a Liberal-Labour alliance
was a remote possibility. Lloyd George had not only to lead the
second coalition, he had also to induce its members to follow
him; and, at any rate as far as Ireland was concerned, unionists
would not follow him whither he went. In March 1918 Lloyd
George complained to Riddell that:

> It is no use being Prime Minister unless you can do what you want to
> do. It is useless for me to say that I can, because I can't. I have to make
> compromises all the time in order to conciliate different sections . . .
> Take the Irish question. If I had a clear majority in the House of
> Commons I could soon settle it, but I have not.[1]

This accounts for the apparent lack of direction in Lloyd
George's Irish policy between December 1916 and the end of
the First World War. The exigencies of the political situation at
Westminster did not permit Lloyd George to decide upon a
particular course of action and see it through to a successful
conclusion, and on the first full day of his premiership he had
announced to a group of prominent unionists, including
Austen Chamberlain, Lord Robert Cecil, Lord Curzon and
Walter Long that 'he was free from commitments to the Irish
Members, and that the hands of the Government would in no
way be tied on this issue'.[2] In early 1917 Lloyd George was
reluctant to reopen the Irish question, and pessimistic about the
chances of success; but the decision of the United States to enter
the war on the Allied side made it necessary to make another
attempt at settlement, in order to unite American opinion
firmly behind the war effort. It was with this consideration
chiefly in mind that Lloyd George examined several possibilities
before deciding, almost as an afterthought, to adopt the
suggestion of a convention, in which representatives of all

---

[1] Lord Riddell, *War Diary* (1933), 317.
[2] Lloyd George, *War Memoirs* (2 vols. 1938), i, 633.

important shades of Irish opinion should meet, and—it was hoped—settle their own problem for themselves.

The Irish Convention deliberated from July 1917 until April 1918, and eventually produced a report;[1] but the refusal of Sinn Fein to send representatives vitiated its authority, and its report was peppered with minority protests against the recommendations on which the majority found agreement. The experiment, however, was not entirely unproductive, because a section of the southern Irish unionists led by Lord Midleton consented to an all-Ireland parliament firmly established within the United Kingdom. The southern unionists had been instrumental in sabotaging Lloyd George's attempted settlement in 1916; but now the prime minister perceived an opportunity to use his former enemies to defeat the present opponents of peace, the Ulster unionists, who stubbornly blocked any proposal that would place them under the authority of a Dublin parliament. The conciliatory attitude of Midleton's supporters reinforced Lloyd George's case for Irish home rule, and in a carefully phrased letter to Bonar Law on 12 January 1918 he tried to exploit the advantages of the situation:

> This is the opportunity for Ulster to show that it places the Empire above everything, and if the little Protestant Communities of the South, isolated in a turbulent sea of Sinn Feinism and Popery, can trust their lives and their property to Midleton's scheme, surely the powerful Communities of the North might take that risk for the sake of the Empire in danger.[2]

In his letter to Law, Lloyd George hinted at resignation 'if Ulster declines'; but when Ulster did decline to assist in settlement Lloyd George retreated once again. The tug-of-war between the prime minister and his unionist colleagues continued. Now it was Lloyd George's turn to find himself under pressure, for by the spring of 1918 the Conservatives had convinced themselves that the time had come for the government to compel Irishmen to face up to their responsibilities and submit to military conscription. Lloyd George had earlier

[1] *Report of the proceedings of the Irish Convention*, Cmd. 9019 of 1918; an account of the Convention is given by Stephen Gwynn, *John Redmond's Last Years* (1919), ch. viii.
[2] Lloyd George to Bonar Law, 12 Jan. 1918, Bonar Law Papers, 82/8/4.

expressed strong misgivings about the wisdom of such a course,[1] but after the German offensive in March 1918 he could scarcely resist it any longer, and in April 1918 a new act empowered the government to extend conscription to Ireland by order in council. Lloyd George conceded this point; but he also sought another opportunity to turn the tables on the Conservatives. At a cabinet meeting on April 23 he developed an argument congenial to unionist philosophy. The Irish nationalists, he maintained, in opposing conscription were challenging the right of the imperial parliament to impose upon them an act which they disliked: 'That was a challenge to the unity of the Kingdom'. But Lloyd George then proceeded to stand this argument on its head: the cabinet, he explained, should be in a position to say 'These domestic issues we hand over to you, but conscription we mean to enforce'.[2] In other words, Ireland must be given home rule and control over her domestic affairs, but if she then failed the test of loyalty by refusing to submit to conscription, the government would know that she should never have been entrusted with home rule in the first place.

By this stratagem, Lloyd George hoped to enlist fresh troops in Ireland, and also inveigle the unionists into conceding Irish home rule: 'Conscription', he told C. P. Scott, 'was a political necessity now if the Tories were to accept Home Rule'.[3] It was too clever by half, and it was also too late, for it is difficult to see how the Irish Parliamentary Party could have exercised the authority to govern Ireland in the unlikely event of the establishment of an Irish parliament; and unionist Ulster's relationship to such a parliament was, as yet, undefined. Lloyd George's attempt to combine conscription with the enactment of a home rule bill only convinced Irishmen of the poverty of the whole home rule movement, and served to confirm the political ascendancy of Sinn Fein. The government's decision, announced on June 20, not to proceed with the dual policy was an admission that it was no longer dealing with nationalists who were prepared to accept the supremacy of the imperial parliament, but was now confronted with a revolutionary movement that

[1] Lord Riddell, *War Diary*, 239–40.
[2] War cabinet minutes, 23 April 1918, CAB 23/6.
[3] C. P. Scott's diary, 21–23 April 1918, Add. MS. 50.905, fol. 36.

rejected co-operation with Great Britain and condemned the union itself as a crime against the Irish nation.[1] A general election in December 1918 resulted in the return of 73 Sinn Fein candidates, while the Irish Parliamentary Party could secure only six seats, and the successful members on 21 January 1919 assembled in their own parliament, Dail Eireann, where they adopted a provisional constitution and reaffirmed the declaration of independence of Easter 1916. Lloyd George was now faced with new and more resolute adversaries than the body of constitutional nationalists with whom he had negotiated since May 1916.

The general election that swept the home rule party out of political existence also swept Lloyd George back into power; and the circumstances in which Lloyd George returned to office were no less significant for Ireland than for Great Britain, for he was now the head of a coalition in which Conservatives were the dominant party, numbering 338 out of a total coalition complement of 484, and comprising in all about three-fifths of the entire House. The Conservatives were the victors, even if they had to endure the leadership of a Liberal, and, what was more important, they need only endure that leadership as long as it suited them, for if Lloyd George broke with the coalition they could set up a government of their own. It was within this framework of Conservative domination that Lloyd George had to discover a solution to the Irish question. His wartime experiences in this field hardly indicated that such a solution would be easily forthcoming.

The political topography at Westminster obliged Lloyd George to exercise circumspection in any moves he might contemplate towards an Irish settlement; but at least it did not altogether bar his path. The Conservative party with which Lloyd George had now chosen to work was not of the same calibre, nor was it in the same mood, as the party that had screwed its resistance to the sticking point in 1914 and 1916. It was, perhaps, more conservative and less unionist, because it was gradually drawing away from its Irish unionist allies. And the British political environment was changing. In May 1918 Austen Chamberlain wrote with a touch of awe that

---

[1] See Lord Curzon's speech on 20 June 1918, *H.L. deb.*, 5s., xxx. 323–41; War cabinet minutes, 19 June 1918, CAB 23/6.

'a new world has come into existence with new problems of profound gravity and with the settlement of old problems made more urgent by the rapid progress of events';[1] and one of the 'old problems' that the Conservative leadership acknowledged must be settled after the war was the problem of Ireland.

It was for this reason that Lloyd George, in a letter addressed to Bonar Law on 2 November 1918, was able to claim the right to bring an Irish settlement into effect, although he was also compelled to admit that 'in the present condition of Ireland such an attempt could not succeed, and that it must be postponed until the condition of Ireland makes it possible'.[2] The condition of Ireland only grew worse in 1919, as clashes between members of the self-styled Irish Republican Army and the crown forces became more frequent and serious; and the proviso inserted in the coalition declaration of intent, if insisted upon, would have postponed home rule indefinitely. But if circumstances in Ireland were not conducive to a new attempt at settlement, in England they were working, albeit slowly, to Lloyd George's advantage. In October 1919 Bonar Law explained to A. J. Balfour that something had to be done, because the 1914 home rule act would automatically come into force on the ratification of the last of the peace treaties.[3] Lloyd George, he went on, was in favour of introducing new legislation; Law had not yet made up his mind about the best course of action; but on 4 November a cabinet committee on Ireland, under the chairmanship of Walter Long, reported that

> it is essential, now that the war is over, and that the Peace Conference has dealt with so many analogous questions in Europe, that the Government should make a sincere attempt to deal with the Irish question once and for all.[4]

And it was this committee, which included the Conservatives Lord Birkenhead, Sir Laming Worthington-Evans, and Sir Robert Horne, which was responsible for framing the home rule

[1] Austen Chamberlain to Lord Salisbury, 22 May 1918, A. Chamberlain Papers, 31/1/12.
[2] Lloyd George to Bonar Law, 2 Nov. 1918; published in *The Times*, 18 Nov. 1918.
[3] Bonar Law to A. J. Balfour, 9 Oct. 1919, Bonar Law Papers, 101/3/159.
[4] Cabinet committee on Ireland, first report, 4 Nov. 1919, C.P.56, CAB 27/68.

plans that Lloyd George expounded to the House of Commons in December 1919.

When, on 22 December 1919, Lloyd George explained his government's new proposals, he admitted that no home rule scheme could now be produced that would in any way satisfy nationalist Ireland.[1] But it was always his method to leave for the present the intractable problem, and turn his attention to a situation where something might be achieved; and Lloyd George had always been aware that one of the essential conditions of peace in Ireland was to dispose of the Ulster question. Lloyd George was never guilty of the solecism of underestimating the Ulster protestants' abhorrence of a parliament in which Roman Catholics would be in an overwhelming majority. Perhaps, as he himself admitted, his nonconformist upbringing gave him 'a thorough appreciation of the Ulster anxieties about Home Rule',[2] for in March 1917 he declared that there was, in the north-eastern corner of Ireland, a population 'As alien in blood, in religious faith, in traditions, in outlook—as alien from the rest of Ireland in this respect as the inhabitants of Fife or Aberdeen'.[3]

Lloyd George's nonconformist upbringing, however, was less influential in determining his attitude to the Ulster Unionists than was his conviction that exclusion in some form was an essential preliminary to a general settlement; a conviction that was sharpened by the reaction in Ulster to his speech of 7 March 1917. 'The atmosphere for settlement', he told C. P. Scott,

> which had been very bad in Ulster had become better since he had made his speech in the H of C repudiating any idea of coercion against Ulster. After that he was able to go to them and say 'You have no longer anything to fear; now let us do business'.[4]

By 1919, when home rule for Ireland was regarded as a foregone conclusion, the Ulster unionists were fully prepared to 'do business' with the British government, and concentrate on making favourable terms for themselves. But the Ulster Unionist Council was resolved to drive a hard bargain with the

---

[1] *H.C. deb.*, 5s., 123, c.1169.
[2] Lloyd George to R. J. Lynn, 5 June 1916, Lloyd George Papers. D/14/2/13.   [3] *H.C. deb.*, 5s., xci, c.459 (7 March 1917).
[4] C. P. Scott's diary, 2–4 April 1917, Add. MS. 50.903, fols. 215–17.

prime minister in return for accepting the new government of
Ireland bill, with its provision for a home rule parliament for
northern as well as southern Ireland. Lloyd George listed four
ways to delimit the new 'Ulster': the province as a whole might
be excluded; counties in Ulster might be excluded on the basis
of county option; the six counties which Lloyd George had
planned to exclude in 1916 might be taken as a unit, or these
counties might be excluded with some adjustment of their
boundaries.[1] Lloyd George seems to have preferred placing the
whole province under the northern parliament,[2] although he
did not believe, in any case, that the 'Protestant North would
ever amalgamate completely with the Catholic South'.[3] The
Ulster Unionist Council, however, envisaged only one way to
settle the problem: the idea of governing the three Ulster
counties which had substantial nationalist majorities 'was not
relished', and it would not co-operate in working the government's bill unless it were given the six county bloc as an area
which would ensure a permanent unionist ascendancy.[4]

Lloyd George could hardly have otherwise resolved the
Ulster question in 1920. Many, perhaps most, Conservatives
had lost their pre-war enthusiasm for the cause of the Ulster
Protestants, but they felt themselves under some obligation to
make a special provision for their former allies; and Lloyd
George, for his part, had long since reconciled himself to the
fact that some special provision for Ulster must be made. But
he had taken an important step nearer a final settlement, for, as
the Government of Ireland bill passed through its various legislative stages, it was becoming increasingly clear that the Irish,
northern and southern, willingly or unwillingly, were to have
home rule. Now a new question arose: how much home rule
were they to have? The Ulster unionists might be prepared to
make the best of their side of the bargain, but in the rest of
Ireland the immediate outcome was to intensify the hostility of
the republicans. The British government had no alternative
but to counter this challenge to its authority: but Lloyd George

[1] *H.C. deb.*, 123, c.1175.
[2] C. P. Scott's diary, 12–14 Aug. 1919, Add. MS. 50.905, fol. 205.
[3] Ibid., 20–3 Dec. 1919, Add. MS. 50.905, fol. 218.
[4] Cabinet conclusions, 10 Dec. 1919, CAB 23/18; cf. Sir James Craig's
speech in the House, 29 March 1920 (*H.C. deb.*, 127, c.989–93).

realized that there could be no formal declaration of war on
the I.R.A. because, in his own trenchant phrase, 'You do not
declare war against rebels'.[1] The alternative was to treat the
operations of the insurgents as those of a 'murder gang', whose
criminal activities were so widespread that the military was
obliged to act in support of the civil power; and, in order to
reinforce the civil power, it was decided to enlist men in Great
Britain, provide them with a rudimentary training in police
duties, and merge them with the hard-pressed and under-
strength Royal Irish Constabulary. Since there were not enough
police uniforms available, the recruits were fitted out in a
mixture of military khaki and R.I.C. rifle-green. These motley
outfits earned them their nickname of 'Black and Tans';[2] they
also symbolized their para-military function, for it was upon the
mixed force of regular policemen and Black and Tan recruits
that the brunt of the fighting fell.

In July 1920 Lloyd George confessed that it was 'very difficult
to control an unfriendly population' unless 'very violent
measures' were resorted to;[3] but the methods favoured by the
Black and Tans were, perhaps, more violent than Lloyd George
had anticipated. I.R.A. raids and ambushes were answered by
reprisals on the part of the police, the Black and Tans, and,
occasionally, the military, who hit back indiscriminately at the
enemy and the civilian population, and hardly a day passed
without an ambush, an assassination, a raid or a reprisal, and
all this in a country which was, at any rate nominally, part of
the United Kingdom. Lloyd George privately urged restraint
on the crown forces,[4] but in public he defended them against
all criticism. At Caernarvon in October 1920 he declared that
'the police naturally feel that the time has come for them to
defend themselves, and that is what is called reprisals'; 'There
is no doubt that, at last, their patience has given way, and there
has been some severe hitting back.'[5]

[1] Minute-sheet on Ireland, 30 April 1920, CAB 23/21.
[2] After the Scarteen hunt, a pack of hounds in County Limerick.
[3] Lord Riddell, *Intimate Diary of the Peace Conference and After* (1933), 225.
[4] At a cabinet meeting on 29 Dec. 1920 Lloyd George 'hoped that
General Tudor [police adviser] would realize the importance of preventing
such incidents' (CAB 23/23); cf. Lloyd George to Sir Hamar Greenwood,
25 Feb. and 21 April 1921, Lloyd George Papers, F/19/3/4, 17 f.
[5] *The Times*, 11 Oct. 1920.

Why did Lloyd George, the professed champion of the rights of small nations, allow himself to be tied to repression in Ireland, and condone methods similar to those he had condemned in South Africa twenty years before? Partly, no doubt, because his opinions were coloured by those of his Conservative supporters who were bitterly hostile to the separatist ambitions of Sinn Fein; Lord Birkenhead, for example, declared that the only reason he felt able to support the government's home rule proposals in 1919 was because he felt certain that Sinn Fein would refuse them, 'Otherwise in the present state of Ireland I could not even be a party to making the offer, for I believe that the Sinn Feiners if they did accept their Parliament, would only use it for the purpose of forwarding separation'.[1] But it was also Lloyd George's instinct to fight a nationalist movement, whose declared aim was secession from the United Kingdom, for even in his Welsh nationalist phase he had never demanded for Wales anything more than equality within the existing political framework of the British Isles.[2] At Caernarvon, Lloyd George demonstrated that, by any test of nationality, the Welsh were as much a 'separate nation' as the Irish, indeed more so:

> I have been listening to Welsh music ... I have been listening to a Welsh address which every one of you understands. Go to a county council in Ireland and, I have no doubt, Mr. Arthur Griffith would be presented with an address written in Gaelic which neither he nor anyone else in the place would understand.

It was 'a sham and a fraud, the whole of this nationality'. Moreover, although Lloyd George was, on his own admission, 'a home ruler all my life', the Liberal home rule policies on which he had been brought up were designed to strengthen, not fragment, the United Kingdom and the empire. It is doubtful whether these Liberal policies would have involved the employment of the Black and Tans; but, as far as Lloyd George was concerned, the ends justified the means, for, he remarked to Bonar Law in May 1920, de Valera and his associates had 'practically' declared war against the British empire 'and we

[1] Joint note by the lord chancellor and the minister of pensions (Sir Laming Worthington-Evans), 11 Nov. 1919, C.P.103, CAB 27/68.

[2] Kenneth O. Morgan, *David Lloyd George* (1963), 33; W. Watkin Davies, *Lloyd George, 1863–1914* (1939), 120.

ought not to stint anything that is necessary in order to crush the rebellion'.[1]

C. P. Scott once observed that Lloyd George had a 'love of and exaggerated belief in the value of force';[2] an exaggerated belief, perhaps, but not an overwhelming one. Lloyd George publicly affirmed his resolve to persevere with coercion in Ireland until the last revolver had been plucked out of the hand of the assassin; but, he asked himself in November 1920, 'would settling the gunmen settle the Irish question? It has not done so in the past';[3] and he was already casting round for some means whereby the Irish claim to self-determination might be safely reconciled with the interests and security of the British empire. As early as February 1919 Lloyd George reminded C. P. Scott that he 'stood by the terms of the letters "which you helped me to compose in this room" which contained, along with the Convention, a far-reaching scheme of Dominion Home Rule minus Customs and Excise'.[4] It is doubtful whether this definition of dominion home rule would have tallied with that of the dominions themselves; anyway, if the idea of a dominion solution did pass through Lloyd George's mind at the time of the Irish Convention, it was not one that he entertained for very long. 'The demand for Dominion status', he told C. P. Scott in April 1918, 'was really a demand for the right of secession, since the Dominions were virtually independent States and could secede at any time if they chose'.[5]

In July 1920, however, Lloyd George reconsidered the problem in the light of information supplied by his Dublin Castle advisers, Sir John Anderson and James MacMahon, Joint Under-Secretaries, and W. E. Wylie, Law Adviser, who suggested that Sinn Fein would not find unacceptable an offer of dominion home rule. Lloyd George probed: what was the price that his government would have to pay for peace, and what would it get in return? What measure of dominion home rule 'would produce the desired results? No Sinn Feiner had

[1] Lloyd George to Bonar Law, 10 May 1920, Bonar Law Papers, 103/4/2.
[2] J. L. Hammond, *C. P. Scott* (1934), 241.
[3] Stanley Salvidge, *Salvidge of Liverpool* (1934), 187.
[4] C. P. Scott's diary, 21–2 Feb. 1919, Add. MS. 50.905, fol. 186.
[5] Ibid., 21–3 April 1918, Add. MS. 50.905, fol. 37.

ever said that he would accept Dominion Home Rule.'
MacMahon replied that Sinn Fein might be content with
customs and excise, with the army and navy remaining under
the control of the British, and he also recommended that the
six counties of Northern Ireland be retained under the juris-
diction of the imperial parliament. Lloyd George probed
further: if dominion home rule on these lines were conceded,
and Sinn Fein told that the six counties were excluded, having,
if they wished, a parliament of their own, would this be
acceptable? MacMahon replied that it would not, because if
the six counties remained under the rule of Westminster Sinn
Fein believed that there was still a possibility of reunion,
whereas if they had a separate parliament all hope of unity
would disappear.[1]

Lloyd George's conversation with the officers of the Irish
government was largely exploratory; but, in any case, some
Conservative cabinet ministers moved quickly to dispel any
notion he might entertain of a move in the direction of dominion
home rule for Ireland. In a memorandum dated 24 July 1920,
and entitled 'The future of the Home Rule Bill', A. J. Balfour
refuted the suggestion that the powers of the government's bill
should be augmented; it would, he felt sure,

> be folly to suggest that it is but a half-way house to some new Utopia.
> This would supply a most powerful motive to continued agitation,
> and would deprive the measure of such chance as it still possesses of
> settling the Irish question.[2]

This opinion was endorsed by Walter Long the following day,[3]
and a few months later Long elaborated his reasons for objecting
to dominion home rule: it was impossible to grant this, he
argued, 'unless we are prepared to go the whole length and
accept the inevitable conclusion, namely, practical, if not legal
independence'.[4]

This was a conclusion that very few Englishmen, whatever
their political complexion, were ready to accept; but as the
military struggle in Ireland intensified in the autumn of 1920

---

[1] Notes of a conference with the officers of the Irish government, 23 July
1920, C.P. 1693, CAB 24/109.

[2] C.P. 1683, CAB. 24/109.

[3] Memorandum by Walter Long, 25 July 1920, C.P. 1688, CAB 24/109.

[4] Memorandum by Long, 29 Sept. 1920, C.I. 87, CAB 27/70.

the idea of a dominion solution found an increasing number of adherents, and letters to the newspapers from Lord Grey of Fallodon on September 29 and Asquith on October 5 in support of this thesis brought the subject to the forefront of public discussion. Dominion status lacked precision, because the self-governing dominions had acquired their powers gradually and almost imperceptibly over a period of time, and the pace of this development had quickened during the First World War; but the idea was an attractive one to many Englishmen, because it had roots in the past, and because it had been applied successfully elsewhere. Its supporters drew a parallel between Ireland and other parts of the empire, such as Canada and, more particularly, South Africa. But could the remedy that had reconciled defeated and far-away South Africa to the empire be applied with equal success to England's defiant neighbour on the other side of the Irish Sea? Lloyd George, apparently, thought not; and at Carnarvon in October 1920 he took the advocates of dominion home rule to task. He quickly dismissed Asquith's argument that economic considerations would deter the Irish from abusing the powers entrusted to them under dominion status:

> You do not need to spend much on submarines. They are vicious little craft, they are dangerous and perilous, but they are not expensive. I am not sure they cost as much as a respectable yacht. And mines you can have, and they are cheap, and those under full and complete Dominion Home Rule the Irish Republic can have.

The Irish might give their word of honour that they would not use dominion powers to the detriment of the empire, and Lloyd George did not despise 'the word of a nation'; but there was no-one in Ireland who could give that promise, or who would 'stand up for the Empire as General Botha stood up for the Empire in South Africa'.

But Lloyd George never ceased to hope that someone in Ireland would come forward and 'stand up for the empire'; and he was reluctant to exclude the possibility that a place might be found for Ireland within the imperial framework. In November 1920 Sir Archibald Salvidge, former chairman of the National Unionist Association, reckoned that Lloyd George 'was clearly not hoping for very much from the latest attempt at a Government of Ireland Act, and was increasingly leaning in the direction of Dominion Home Rule'. Salvidge suspected that he was 'being sounded on the constructive side of the matter', but Lloyd George's overtures met with a non-committal response from Salvidge, who 'was guarded throughout this part of the discussion, merely replying that for me and my friends the safety of Ulster was still, as it had always been, the first consideration'.[1]

By the end of 1920, therefore, the idea of a settlement more generous than home rule, but with adequate safeguards for imperial security was again passing through Lloyd George's mind; and his reluctance to move forward was based, partly upon the fear of provoking his Conservative supporters, and partly upon tactical grounds. If Lloyd George were to offer something more than the limited measure of self-government embodied in his government of Ireland act, and Sinn Fein were to reject such an offer, then the prime minister would no longer possess anything with which to bargain; hence Lloyd George's rough handling of his Liberal ministers who recommended the concession of fiscal autonomy. According to H. A. L. Fisher, Lloyd George was 'secretly convinced' that this would have to be conceded in the end, but would only part with it for value received.[2] At a cabinet meeting on 13 October 1920 the prime minister declared that

> If Customs had to be conceded in order to obtain peace, it might be considered: but he would only consider it if it was impossible to get other terms. Sinn Fein would have to come forward and bargain.[3]

And in April Tom Jones's assessment was that Lloyd George appeared to be 'as firm against any fiscal concessions as he was last autumn—saying they might be the ground for fresh demands'.[4]

Lloyd George wanted to retain hold on as many cards as possible, and it was prudent for him to conceal his hand from British Conservatives and Irish Sinn Feiners alike; but by the spring of 1921 the moment when he must make some decisive move in Ireland could not be long delayed. Elections to the parliaments of northern and southern Ireland, held in May,

[1] Stanley Salvidge, *Salvidge of Liverpool*, 187.
[2] H. A. L. Fisher, *An Unfinished Autobiography* (1940), 126-7.
[3] Cabinet conclusions, 13 Oct. 1920, CAB 23/23.
[4] Keith Middlemas (ed.), *Thomas Jones: Whitehall Diary* (1969), i, 154.

resulted in an emphatic victory for Sinn Fein in the south, and since the government of Ireland act provided for crown colony government in the event of the southern parliament's failure to function, the issue of peace or war had to be decided once and for all. Winston Churchill wrote that the prime minister was ready to fight, 'relying on the age-long loyalties of the Conservative Party'.[1] In the past, certainly, that party had not been indisposed to the use of coercion in Ireland; but never before had it been compelled to witness the lawless and irresponsible behaviour of the Black and Tans. Some leading Conservatives, including Oswald Mosley, Lord Robert Cecil and Lord Henry Cavendish-Bentinck, publicly rebuked the government for the conduct of its Irish policy, and a group of Conservative Members under the leadership of Sir Samuel Hoare began to seek an independent plan of settlement.[2] Lloyd George was under pressure from other quarters to make a new departure in his Irish policy; but the decisive influence was exerted by one of the dominion prime ministers, General Smuts, who was in London to attend an imperial conference. On 13 June Smuts lunched with King George V and found him 'anxiously preoccupied' with his visit to Belfast to open the first session of the Northern Ireland parliament. Smuts suggested that the king take the opportunity to make a plea for reconciliation, and when George V declared himself willing, Smuts drafted a speech and forwarded it to Lloyd George with a recommendation that it should 'foreshadow the grant of Dominion status to Ireland': the promise of dominion status '*by the King* would create a new and definite situation which would crystallize opinion favourably both in Ireland and elsewhere'.[3]

Lloyd George agreed that the Belfast ceremony 'was an occasion for a big gesture'; but he feared that Sinn Fein would not listen to any appeal, and he reiterated the hazards of dominion self-government, which would 'enable Ireland to

[1] Winston Churchill, *The World Crisis: The Aftermath* (1929), 291.

[2] Lord Beaverbrook, *The Decline and Fall of Lloyd George* (1963), 82 and appendices 38 and 39.

[3] Harold Nicolson, *King George V* (1952), 348–54; W. K. Hancock, *Smuts*, vol. ii, *The Fields of Force, 1919–1950* (1968), 51–5; Smuts to Lloyd George, 14 June 1921, Lloyd George Papers, F/45/9/48.

raise its own Navy and Army, possibly for use against Great Britain, and to levy customs duties against Great Britain'.[1] Lloyd George was not convinced that the British people were prepared to run these risks; nevertheless, a new speech was prepared by Balfour and Edward Grigg, and when, on 22 June, the king made a moving appeal for peace, the enthusiastic response from all sections of opinion quickly resolved Lloyd George's doubts. Before making a bold move, however, the prime minister was careful to divine the mood of his cabinet; and on 24 June he reminded his ministers of the king's speech and of the public reaction to it. He stated that there was some evidence to suggest that de Valera would accept less than a republic and that he would agree to certain military and economic conditions, and he inquired whether an invitation should be sent to the spokesmen of northern and southern Ireland to discuss the situation and, if possible, to reach agreement.[2] Even Lloyd George's Conservative colleagues were easily persuaded of the wisdom of this course, and their leader, Austen Chamberlain, had already made up his mind that 'the King's speech ought to be followed up by a last attempt at peace before we go the full lengths of martial law'.[3] Between 14 and 21 July 1921 Lloyd George and de Valera met four times in conference, and on 20 July the British prime minister submitted in writing his proposals for an Irish settlement. When Lloyd George had first made a tentative examination of the possibilities of a dominion settlement, the difficulties had seemed to outweigh the advantages. But now that both sides had fought each other to a standstill, now that even Conservatives were prepared to acquiesce in this alternative, Lloyd George did not hesitate to offer to Ireland the status of the dominion of Canada, with safeguards for the Protestants of Ulster and for the security of the United Kingdom.

On 28 July Lloyd George confided to C. P. Scott that the cabinet had gone further in supporting him than he had ever thought possible;[4] but Sinn Fein's reaction to his offer seemed

---

[1] Irish Situation Committee, conclusions, 17 June 1921, CAB 27/107.

[2] Cabinet conclusions, 24 June 1921, CAB 23/26.

[3] Austen Chamberlain to Hilda, 26 June 1921, Austen Chamberlain Papers, 5/1/202; see also Frank Pakenham (Lord Longford), *Peace By Ordeal*, (1967), 69.   [4] C. P. Scott's diary, 28 July 1921, Add. MS. 50.906, fol. 61.

to indicate that Lloyd George had overplayed his hand. He had always emphasized the danger of a British initiative which, if rejected, would leave the government high and dry; and his worst fears were realized when de Valera informed him within 24 hours of his offer that 'Dail Eireann could not, and the Irish people would not, accept the proposals of your Government'.[1] But Lloyd George quickly began to manoeuvre for lost ground. On 21 July he had confidently predicted to the king that 'we shall have public opinion overwhelmingly upon our side throughout the Empire and even in the United States when our proposals are published'.[2] And here Lloyd George's sense of timing was of vital importance. On 10 August Irish counter-proposals were received by the British government, which confirmed de Velera's initial rejection of the British offer, dismissed dominion status as 'illusory', and insisted that 'true friendship with England . . . can be obtained most readily now through amicable but absolute separation'.[3] Lloyd George replied on behalf of his government on 13 August that he was unable to go beyond the proposals that he had put forward on 20 July, which intended 'no derogation from Ireland's status as a Dominion, no desire for British ascendancy over Ireland, and no impairment of Ireland's national ideals';[4] and on the same day the cabinet decided to publish the correspondence, which had so far been confidential, in time for Monday morning's newspapers.[5] These documents comprised the official correspondence that had passed between Lloyd George and de Valera since the British offer of dominion status on 20 July; but Lloyd George took the opportunity to reinforce his case by the publication of a letter which General Smuts had addressed to de Valera on 4 August, urging him to accept the government's terms, pointing to the example of South Africa 'where the republican ideal for which we had made unheard-of sacrifices had ultimately to give way to another form of Freedom', and pleading with him not to insist on a republican

[1] *Correspondence relating to the proposals of His Majesty's Government for an Irish settlement*, Cmd. 1502 of 1921, no. ii.

[2] Lloyd George to King George V, 21 July 1921, Lloyd George Papers, F/29/4/60.

[3] Cmd. 1502 of 1921, no. ii.   [4] Cmd. 1502 of 1921, no. iii.

[5] Cabinet conclusions, 13 Aug. 1921, CAB 23/26.

form of government 'which means your final and irrevocable severance from the British League. And to this, as you know, the Parliament and people of this country will not agree'.[1]

The government's decision to publish was a tactical move taken, as Lloyd George admitted, 'because of the importance of ranging on the side of our proposals all sane opinion, not merely in this country and in Ireland, but throughout the world';[2] and the set of letters which was released to the public on 15 August aimed a formidable broadside against Sinn Fein's case for independence. As far as Irish allegiance to the crown and membership of the empire were concerned, Lloyd George could count on public approval for his contention that there could be no fundamental departure from his offer of 20 July: justice had not only been done, it had been seen to be done. But, having established this point, Lloyd George was anxious to impose few formal conditions on a conference, because de Valera might be persuaded to make privately concessions that he dared not make publicly. After the failure of his first attempt on 7 September to inaugurate a conference 'to ascertain how the association of Ireland with the community of nations known as the British Empire can best be reconciled with Irish national aspirations', Lloyd George was not sanguine about the chances of repeating the offer: 'I could not, if I would, offer better terms, and I could not carry consent to another unconditional conference.'[3] Nevertheless, a fortnight later, Lloyd George tried again, because, he explained to Austen Chamberlain, 'the country expects a conference to take place, and will not be quite satisfied that everything has been done to prevent rupture unless a conference is held . . . It is to some extent a question of presentation of the issue . . .'[4] On 21 September the cabinet agreed to repeat the invitation of 7 September, with the suggestion that 'conference, not correspondence, is the most practical and hopeful way to an understanding'.[5]

[1] W. K. Hancock, *Smuts*, ii, 59–60; the official documents are reproduced in Cmd. 1470 of 1921 and 1502 of 1921. The letter of General Smuts is omitted from these Command Papers.

[2] *H.C. deb.*, 5s., 146, c. 1874 (19 Aug. 1921).

[3] Lloyd George to C. P. Scott, 12 Sept. 1921, Add. MS. 50.909, fols. 224–8.

[4] Lloyd George to Austen Chamberlain, 21 Sept. 1921, Lloyd George Papers, F/7/4/27.   [5] Cabinet conclusions, 21 Sept. 1921, CAB 23/27.

Lloyd George thus scored two points: he managed to carry his cabinet with him in making another conciliatory overture to Sinn Fein; and he placed the full burden for any breakdown in discussions squarely on the shoulders of de Valera, since de Valera could scarcely reject a second invitation couched in such terms without appearing doctrinaire and unreasonable. Nor did he reject it, for on 30 September he agreed to send representatives to a conference in London to begin on 11 October. And this conference was unconditional only in a formal sense, because Lloyd George had pledged his government to discuss no settlement that would involve Ireland's refusal to enter the commonwealth, whereas de Valera had not once demanded British recognition of a republic as an essential preliminary to a conference, nor had he insisted that a British refusal to grant this recognition would inevitably lead to a renewal of fighting. It was, therefore, natural for the British to assume that Sinn Fein would, in the long run, submit to inclusion in the empire; in Frank Pakenham's words: 'in the race to secure opinion favourable to the settlements that they respectively contemplated, de Valera was still waiting for the pistol while Lloyd George was half-way home'.[1]

Whether or not Lloyd George finished the course depended upon a number of things. It depended upon Lloyd George's skill in negotiation, which Pakenham has emphasized—and rightly emphasized—in his book *Peace by ordeal*.[2] But it also depended upon the degree of success with which Lloyd George manipulated the political situation at Westminster: for Lloyd George was no freelance; and, after all, he had outsmarted a different set of Irishmen in 1916, only to see his efforts set at nought by the junketing of the Conservative party. In 1921 Lloyd George made no attempt to repeat the solo performance of five years ago; on the contrary, he was careful to select colleagues from the Conservative ranks who were too dangerous to be left out, men such as Lord Birkenhead and Austen Chamberlain, and he also took the precaution of sounding out the opinions of Bonar Law.[3]

Trouble could also be anticipated from the Conservative rank and file—in August 1921 the cabinet was reluctant to

[1] Pakenham, *Peace By Ordeal*, 79.   [2] London, 1935, and later editions.
[3] Lord Beaverbrook, *The Decline and Fall of Lloyd George*, 93–4, 101–2, 105–6.

hold a debate on Ireland in the House, lest the government's followers take the opportunity to attack their own front bench[1] —and the first serious revolt came at the end of October, when a Conservative Member, Colonel John Gretton, moved to censure the government for 'entering into negotiations with delegates from Southern Ireland who have taken an oath of allegiance to an Irish republic and have repudiated the authority of the Crown'. Lloyd George responded by making the die-hard resolution a vote of confidence in his Administration. He and his colleagues wanted to know if the House wished them to make peace; if the House did not want them to do so, Lloyd George would at once resign and leave others to face the music. The Conservatives did not relish facing the music; and only 43 members of the party rallied in support of the die-hards.[2]

It was one thing for the prime minister to scatter leaderless die-hards in the house of commons; but it was quite a different matter when Conservatives closeted themselves in their annual conference, and a dangerous situation when discontented back-benchers were presented with an alternative leader in the person of Andrew Bonar Law. Lloyd George had anticipated trouble from Law, whom he designated as 'the hardest task'; and when, in November 1921, Lloyd George began to press the Ulster unionists to submit to the rule of an all-Ireland parliament in return for Sinn Fein allegiance to the crown and membership of the empire, Law sprang to the defence of Northern Ireland: 'If L.G. goes on with his present proposals I will oppose them. I shall try to get the Conservative party to follow me'.[3] And there was a likelihood that a section of the party would follow Law in 1921, because Conservative distrust of Lloyd George's intentions towards Ulster, and resentment of his concessions to Sinn Fein, were reinforced by an increasing dissatisfaction with the prime minister and the coalition that he led.[4] At the National Union of Conservative Associations' conference in Liverpool on 17 November an attempt was made

[1] Cabinet conclusions, 17 Aug. 1921, CAB 23/26.
[2] *H.C. deb.*, 5s. 147 cc. cxlvii, 1367–1480 (31 Oct. 1921).
[3] Bonar Law to J. P. Croal, 12 Nov. 1921, Bonar Law Papers, 107/1/83.
[4] Sir Charles Petrie, *Life and Letters of Austen Chamberlain* (2 vols., 1939–40), ii, 164–5; Stanley Salvidge, *Salvidge of Liverpool*, 197–8.

by a group of Conservatives to break with the coalition and bring down the government, and Lord Salisbury reported to Bonar Law on 18 November that 'a great majority disliked the Coalition. L.G.'s name was hardly mentioned; it certainly never got a cheer'.[1]

But however strong the temptation to knock the prime minister from his perch, the Conservatives dare not yield to it; for, if Lloyd George fell, the hopes of an Irish settlement fell with him, and ordinary people above all wanted peace. Even at Liverpool, Lord Salisbury discerned 'a very strong desire to avoid civil war and a general wish not to break up the Irish Conference until everything had been tried to secure peace with honour'; and the Conservative chieftains, Austen Chamberlain, Birkenhead, Lord Derby, Salvidge, threw their support firmly behind Lloyd George's peace-making efforts. Lloyd George had at last achieved the seemingly impossible: by lashing himself firmly to the wheel of the Irish conference, he had made himself indispensable to the Conservative party. But he must steer carefully, because Conservatives were resolved that Lloyd George should not break up their party as he had broken up the Liberal party,[2] and, in order to forestall the intervention of Bonar Law, Conservative spokesmen were compelled to warn Lloyd George that any attempt to force Ulster into subjection to an all-Ireland parliament would cause 'a tremendous rally to Ulster's side'.[3] Lloyd George had now to persuade the Irish delegates to accept dominion status without the solatium of Irish unity.

Nevertheless, he was not displeased with the outcome of the Liverpool conference. After all, the Conservatives had given him a mandate to proceed with his negotiations for an Irish settlement, a mandate which they had denied him in 1916. There was, certainly, the important reservation that agreement must only be reached 'consistently with . . . the pledges given to Ulster'; but even before the Conservatives at Liverpool had pronounced their verdict, Lloyd George was looking for a loophole, and to find that loophole he reverted to methods of

[1] Lord Beaverbrook, *Decline and Fall of Lloyd George*, 119–20.

[2] Ibid., 120–1.

[3] Lord Derby to Lloyd George, 18 Nov. 1921, Lloyd George Papers, F/14/5/33.

secret diplomacy similar to those that he had employed in his
earlier negotiations with Carson and Redmond. Lloyd George
knew that it was imperative to avoid any disclosure about
whether or not the country was to be permanently partitioned.
In 1916 he had attempted to gloss over the issue by postponing
a final decision until after the war; in 1921 the device he
adopted was a 'boundary commission' which Thomas Jones,
his confidential agent, suggested to Arthur Griffith on 8 and 9
November. Jones pointed out that if Sir James Craig refused a
delimitation of the area of Northern Ireland (as he was likely
to, since he would forfeit so much territory) then his impossi-
bilist attitude would be revealed to the world, and Lloyd
George's hand would be strengthened against him.[1] On
12 November Lloyd George elaborated these tactics before
Arthur Griffith, and succeeded in obtaining from Griffith an
undertaking that, if Lloyd George were to proceed with the
boundary commission plan, Griffith would not afterwards
'let him down', and repudiate this arrangement;[2] and, on
5 December, the last full day of the conference, Lloyd George
further weakened the Irish resolve to break off the negotiations
on the Ulster question by allowing Michael Collins to believe
that, in the event of a delimitation, political 'Ulster' would lose
so much territory that she must come within a united Ireland,
and that in accepting a boundary commission Collins was, in
effect, achieving Irish unity.[3]

In this way, Lloyd George gave the appearance of having
guaranteed Irish unity, and at the same time he avoided a
breach with the Ulster unionists and their champion Bonar
Law. When Arthur Griffith on 5 December made a final
attempt to break on Ulster he was confronted with the promise
that he had made on 12 November not to let the prime minister
down. And now Lloyd George judged the appropriate moment
for an ultimatum, the threat of 'war, and war within three days'
if he did not get the Irish signatures to a treaty there and then.
The ultimatum was well-timed, and was delivered with all the
resources of Lloyd George's personality; and the Irish repre-

[1] Pakenham, *Peace By Ordeal*, 167–71.
[2] Ibid., pp. 174–82; see also Pakenham, 'The treaty negotiations', in
T. Desmond Williams (ed.), *The Irish Struggle, 1916–26* (1966), 109–12.
[3] Pakenham, *Peace By Ordeal*, 220–9.

sentatives, worn down by months of alternate threats and promises, submitted to their fate, signed the articles of agreement, and thereby sacrificed the republican ideal.[1] But the concession and sacrifice were by no means one-sided: for the Anglo-Irish treaty obliged British unionists, no less than Irish nationalists, to abandon the principles that they had sworn to cherish and defend. Not only did Lloyd George browbeat the Irish: he also hoodwinked the English. The Conservatives had been assured that Lloyd George's methods would break Sinn Fein and maintain the unity of the kingdom; yet, in December 1921, they were persuaded for the sake of peace to modify their traditional hostility to Irish nationalist claims, concede a generous measure of dominion home rule to Ireland, and assist Lloyd George to implement an Irish settlement that Conservatives in the past would have bitterly opposed.

And herein lies the explanation of Lloyd George's success in settling the Irish question: for Lloyd George realized that the key to a solution did not lie exclusively, perhaps not even mainly, in Ireland, but that it was to be found in England, and particularly in the attitudes and policies of the Conservative party. He was not the only Liberal statesman to appreciate this, nor was he the first: Gladstone in 1885 was convinced that only a Tory government, with Liberal support to counterbalance the defection of extremists, could carry home rule as it had carried Catholic emancipation, repeal of the corn laws, and the second reform bill;[2] and in the 1890's Lloyd George himself had suggested 'home rule all round' as a means of disarming Conservative hostility to Irish self-government.[3] As early, perhaps, as 1912, and certainly since 1917, his Irish policy was guided by the conviction that he must first resolve the Ulster question, and then make the best terms that could be made with nationalist Ireland. The precise nature of these terms, of course, he could not foresee; but whatever the final shape of the settlement, it could only be applied if Lloyd George had the

---

[1] The most vivid description of the presentation of the ultimatum is that of Winston Churchill in *The Aftermath*, 305–6.

[2] P. N. S. Mansergh, *The Irish Question, 1840–1921* (1965), 129–32.

[3] Thomas Jones, *Lloyd George*, 24–5; W. Watkin Davies, *Lloyd George*, 138–40.

backing of British conservatism, and it was for this reason that he was careful to implicate the Conservatives in everything that he did in Ireland between 1917 and 1921. All Lloyd George's negotiating skill would have been to no avail (as the experience of the 1916 negotiations demonstrated) had he not been able to carry with him the coalition Conservatives, and thus insist, in December 1921, that Irishmen, unionist and nationalist alike, accept a solution that none of them desired.

Bodleian Library, Oxford   D. G. BOYCE

VI

LLOYD GEORGE AND THE CONSERVATIVE CENTRAL OFFICE, 1918–22

D. D. CUTHBERT

DR D. D. CUTHBERT

Age 39

University of Canterbury, New Zealand
Balliol College, Oxford
London University Institute of Historical
Research
Currently Senior Lecturer in History,
Monash University, Melbourne

LLOYD GEORGE AND THE CONSERVATIVE CENTRAL OFFICE, 1918–22

LLOYD GEORGE's association with the Conservative Central Office must be counted as a failure: a generally unfortunate affair. A genuine partnership offered dramatic possibilities, for a formidable man would be doubly so if assisted by a formidable machine. But it was not to be. There was little partnership in the early months of the Lloyd George coalition, and even less in the forlorn concluding stages, and things were not so very different in between. Apparently Lloyd George could never overcome the ingrained Conservative conviction that he would always be a radical and wrecker.

Lloyd George's strength in Conservative circles was always at the very top: a personal influence, sometimes almost shading into ascendancy, over the most prominent Conservatives, such as Austen Chamberlain and Balfour, Birkenhead and Bonar Law.

This influence was partly based on Lloyd George's quite remarkable charisma, but it depended principally on the Tory chiefs' conviction that Lloyd George's leadership, and of course his band of Liberal supporters in the house of commons and the country, were necessary for the achievement of the causes which the Tories had at heart: victory in the world war, a postwar settlement that should be deserving of the title, the quietening of labour, and the 'foiling' or 'containment' of the Labour party.

Unfortunately for Lloyd George's fortunes, the less eminent Conservatives were less accustomed to see the Lloyd George–Conservative alliance in this light. In essence Lloyd George remained politically unattractive to the great mass of his allies: to the Conservative backbenchers who were about two thirds of the men who sustained the Lloyd George coalition in the house of commons; to the party activists in the Conservative constituency associations; and—above all—to the party activists in the Conservative associations in the hopeless or the doubtful seats, who were about to be relegated to the undesired position of actually sustaining and supporting a Coalition Liberal member.

In this uneasy situation the key figures at the Conservative Central Office (and they were a remarkably symbolic trio: Sir George Younger, Scottish brewer, banker and railway director, Sir Robert Sanders, west-country colonel of yeomanry and master of staghounds, and the London newspaperman Sir Malcolm Fraser)[1] occupied a sort of middle ground.

As servants of the party leader they were bound to play the constituencies and the constituency associations in the interests of the Coalition. As servants of the party, counsellors to, and confidants of, the constituency organizations, they were increasingly encouraged to denounce the Coalition and strike out for independence.

Moreover, just as the leading men at Central Office were likely to stand somewhere between the party leaders and the activists in the matter of coalition sentiment, so too they stood somewhere between the leaders and the activists in the matter of exposure to the Lloyd George charm. Although they had, or came to have, frequent contact with the premier's lieutenants, they had much less contact with the premier himself. For, rather imprudently perhaps, considering the extent to which the line to Central Office became the line to Conservative votes and political survival, Lloyd George allowed his association with Central Office to be conducted very largely through the Coalition Liberal whips.

Thus even at the best of times the men of Central Office were not quite under the magician's spell, and after a comparatively short struggle they appear to have escaped it altogether.

Initially however, in the first phase of the Lloyd George Coalition—which ran from December 1916 to the early spring of 1918—Lloyd George had no great need to contact or conciliate his partner's Central Office, and this for three main reasons:

First, though neither partner, Coalition Liberal or Coalition

[1] Younger was Chairman of the Conservative Party, 1916–23; Sanders his deputy from 1919 to 1921 and before that, in 1918, had had special responsibility for settling candidates in seats; and Fraser was Honorary Principal Agent 1920–3.

Tory, could control the house of commons on its own, the Coalition had a majority, and this was unchallengeable, or at any rate unchallenged. In these circumstances there was little need for the 'horse trading' which might well be inescapable if the Government should be forced to appeal to the electorate.

Second, Parliament's life had been extended, partly in the interests of national unity in time of war, and partly to enable both Houses to discuss and enact a new reform bill, which was likely to involve an advance to manhood suffrage and a massive re-arrangement and re-districting of the parliamentary seats. As a consequence there was no constitutional need to appeal to the electorate.

Thirdly, the party truce took care of by-elections. The constituency associations of the party in possession—Liberal, Conservative, or Labour—nominated to vacancies as these occurred, and the other parties in effect endorsed such nominations by allowing the nominees an unopposed return.

In these circumstances the Lloyd George Liberals could enjoy their pivotal position in the house of commons, protected from the more terrible and wholesale electoral hazards, and even, in so far as they could hold their own constituency associations for the Coalition, safeguarded from any appreciable measure of erosion to their numbers.

But on 6 February 1918 the passage of the Representation of the People Bill opened a new era for the Coalition. The extended franchise and the new redistribution provided fairly compelling reasons for proceeding to what was by now a long delayed election; and the tooling up for the election provided a compelling reason for Lloyd George to negotiate an electoral compact with the Conservative Central Office.

Why should this be so?

First many Lloyd George Liberals were electorally hobbled and restricted by the doubtfuls, neutrals and crypto-Asquithians behind them in their own constituency associations. They needed immunity from the Conservative Central Office, for even with the new and appreciably less restricted franchise they were in no position to face a Conservative attack.

And secondly, many Lloyd George Liberals were particularly vulnerable if they should come up against a Labour challenge.

Even under the old restricted franchise many of the Lloyd George Liberals had been particularly vulnerable to a challenge from the left. Almost a quarter of the members on the Coalition Liberals' lists[1] were returned for mining districts. Another quarter sat for working class divisions in the east end of London or across the river in the inner south, or had been elected in double harness with a Labour member for one of the twenty or so double-member constituencies characteristic of the larger to medium-sized provincial towns.

Now with Labour's claims, and confidence strengthened by the war (or more exactly the wartime expansion of the unions, and the wartime extension of the franchise) these Lloyd George Liberals were more vulnerable than ever.

It was a reasonable assumption that they could only overcome the likely challenge from their erstwhile Labour allies if they could secure the assistance of the Coalition Conservatives on their right.

Accordingly Lloyd George and his Chief Whip, F. E. Guest, promptly confronted Central Office with a set of conditions for leading the Coalition in an appeal to the electorate:

In the first article it was suggested that the Conservatives should assist the 'secure placement' of the two Liberal ministers and the six dependable supporters who had been displaced by redistribution.

Secondly, the Conservatives should assist the re-election of the twenty-five Liberal members of the Government.

Thirdly (and, along with section two, this was the really vital part) the Conservatives should assist the re-election of seventy-three backbench Liberals whom Guest listed as 'reliable supporters'.

Fourthly, the Conservatives should render similar support to forty-four, more cautious, backbench Liberals whom Guest now listed as 'unknown', but who had indicated 'a strong disinclination to pledge themselves to the official ... [i.e. Asquithian] machine'; this on condition that these one-time fence sitters were prepared to march under the Coalition banner and publicly endorse its programme.

Fifthly, both Conservative and Liberal coalitionists should

[1] E.g. those enclosed in Guest to Lloyd George. 20 July 1918, Lloyd George Papers, F/21/2/28.

support 'all Labour ministers and members'—it was apparently not expected that there would be many—who were prepared to accept the Coalition programme.

Sixthly, all Conservative supporters of the Coalition Government (provided they accepted the Coalition programme) should receive the full support of 'Lloyd George Liberals', and furthermore—at least by implication—similar support should be forthcoming for Conservative supporters of the Coalition challenging Liberals whom Guest now black-listed as irrevocably committed to the Asquithian machine.

Seventh and finally, the election should be organized and managed by a new and temporary body—Guest suggested the labels 'National', 'National Reform', or 'Government Coalition' —in an endeavour to overcome the traditional difficulty of getting Liberals and Conservatives actually to help one another at the polls.[1]

Of course Lloyd George's preliminary demands on Central Office were made more acceptable by the leading Conservatives' practical and ideological commitment to the Coalition, and by the Conservative leaders' fears of Labour, which made Central Office very prepared to welcome Coalition Liberal votes.

With Bolshevik revolution in Russia, war weariness and labour militancy in Britain, and a new, presumably more radical, and for the first time overwhelmingly *unpropertied* electorate, it was very far from certain that Conservatism—or at least naked Conservatism—would be shortly riding high.

In fact (as Lloyd George was almost certainly aware) the Tory whips were already in the process of conceding a number of working class electorates—including a fair number of what would once have been regarded as perfectly winnable electorates —to the modishly demagogic, but safely 'patriotic' political adventurers of the British Workers League.[2] Lloyd George's projected alliance between his Liberals and the Tories was

---

[1] Guest to Younger, 16 March 1918. Bonar Law Papers, 83/1/9. The enclosed lists have disappeared, but the numbers of Liberals in different categories can be regarded as approximately correct, on the basis of the similar—and possibly identical—lists of 20 July.

[2] Sanders' Memorandum on a proposal for an agreement with the British Workers' League, 18 March 1918, enclosed in Sanders to Bonar Law, same date. Bonar Law Papers, 83/1/15.

merely a further, if sizeable, extension of this type of Conservative insurance scheme.

And so Lloyd George's preliminary demands were fairly placidly received—if only slowly and selectively adopted.

Four stages may be noted:

First, Bonar Law appears to have instructed Central Office to keep the way open for a coalition election by warding off Conservatives from the Coalition Liberal seats;

Second, Younger blasted the front bench Conservative Walter Long for expecting to capitalize on Lloyd George's leadership and simultaneously enjoy a free run to attack the Lloyd George seats:

> In one sentence he talks about a coalition election & in the next demands absolute freedom to [sic. for?] the constituencies in putting up candidates.

Younger complained to Law in mid September.

> That would be a pretty way to play the game, & if he thinks LG would lead on such terms he is very greatly mistaken.
> ... So far the Central Office has gone no further than to act on the principle approved by you, that where a Liberal Member has consistently supported the present Govt. we can't run a candidate officially against him in a Coalition Election. That is surely an obvious obligation & it is the price we pay for LG as leader in the Election.
> If Walter objects to paying it he had better clear out, & the sooner the better.[1]

Third, Younger incorporated Lloyd George's principal demands in the counter proposals which—after six months of relative uncertainty, and harassment from Walter Long and others—he issued on behalf of Central Office:

> There are five classes of cases upon which a definite understanding must be arrived at,

he wrote to Law in the last week of September.

> Complications of all sorts are arising, and the difficulties are in some cases becoming aggravated, so that a clean cut arrangement must be concluded without any delay.
> The five classes of cases are as follows:
> 1. Liberal M.P.s who have loyally supported the Coalition Government since its formation.

[1] Younger to Bonar Law, 16 Sept. 1918. Bonar Law Papers, 84/1/13.

2. Vacancies caused by the retirement of Liberal Members who are recognised as supporters of the Government.

3. Seats held at present by Asquithian Liberals.

4. Vacancies arising where an Asquithian Liberal Member is retiring.

5. New Seats.

1. We have already arranged that where a Liberal Member has consistently supported the Coalition Government, we shall instruct our candidates to stand down in his interest and shall officially support the Liberal Member. We can, of course, only request them to do so, and there are one or two cases where it will be impossible to secure local assent to this arrangement. One is the case of Denman of Carlisle, a Member of the U.D.C. [i.e., the semi-pacifist Union of Democratic Control] and who now poses as a Lloyd George supporter. On no account whatever will our people have anything to say to him, nor will a large section of the [local] Liberals, who have already requested him to retire. Another, and much more difficult and unfortunate case is that of Mond at Swansea, but these I am happy to say, are exceptions. A man like Kellaway, for instance, who wouldn't have [had] a ghost of a chance of re-election if there had been no War and a General Election had been held in the Winter of 1914, will now have the support of our people, and there are a good many cases of a similar kind.

2. Our proposed action under No. 1. demands, in my opinion, reciprocal treatment of our existing candidates in constituencies where vacancies arise through the retirement of a Coalition Liberal. It appears to me that we must insist upon this, and so far as I am concerned, I cannot assent to asking candidates who have been working hard from 1906 and 1910 onwards, who have been spending large sums of money and maintaining the organisation, and who are quite good candidates, to stand aside now in favour of a new Lloyd George Liberal. If we accept a loyal Coalition Member, a loyal Coalition candidate is entitled to similar treatment, and ought to be adopted as the Government candidate. Where there is no Unionist candidate in the field in such cases we might, I think, assent to the substitution of a Lloyd George Liberal for the sitting Member if they desire to put one forward, and to recommend this course to our friends.

3. Where a Liberal supporting Asquith now sits the Unionist candidate in possession ought to be accepted as the Coalition candidate. Where there is no Unionist candidate there might be a policy of give and take in the matter.

4. Where an Asquithian Liberal retires, I should suggest the same course as under No. 3.

5. As to the new seats, some clear understanding should be arrived at. These mostly arise from sub-division. Where the original constituency is held by a Unionist, the Unionist might have the first claim in the sub-Divisions; where the reverse is the case, and a Liberal represents the original Division, the Lloyd George Liberals might have

prior claim, or there might be an arrangement of policy of give and take in certain cases where that seems to be the most desirable course to follow.

You have only to consider the grave disappointments now being occasioned by the large number of cases in which we have officially to give our support to the sitting Liberal Members to realise how essential it is that we must stand up for our rights in all other cases. . . .

I cannot go on much longer without a definite instruction on this subject. The complications are becoming intolerable, and the outside grumblings are being loudly voiced and are finding independent expression in appeals to certain of your colleagues. These come on here with charges against the Central Office of 'selling the pass' and so on, and I hope you will manage to find time today to consider the whole situation, and let me know . . . when Sanders and I could conveniently have a discussion with you about it. In the end, after we have had a talk, you will require personally to deal with Lloyd George himself, so that the necessary instructions should be given to his own Whips as well as to us.[1]

The fourth stage came when Younger (probably at Bonar Law's insistence) made a concession to the Lloyd George Liberals in the matter of his second class of cases—i.e. 'vacancies caused by the retirement of Liberal Members who are recognized as supporters of the Government'.

Under this new and much more generous version:

Such vacancies would be dealt with under the rule applied to No. 1. viz. that the retiring Member would be succeeded by a Lloyd George Liberal candidate. Cases of retirals are not likely to be at all numerous, but in some, already announced, we have had candidates in the field since 1906 and 1910, who have been spending time and money in maintaining the organisation, who are quite good candidates, and who would have won if there had been an election in 1914 under Peace conditions. It would be an ungracious thing to press those men to retire and it would create an embittered feeling in the constituencies which would probably lead to a refusal to fall in with the arrangement. In such cases there ought to be an exception to the rule, and if asked for, we should endeavour to give compensation elsewhere.[2]

The stage was now set for Lloyd George's revised demands on Central Office. These were based on Guest's opinion that in any agreement with the Tories Lloyd George had a right to up to 150 seats. This particular figure was apparently connected

[1] Younger to Bonar Law: Memorandum on Coalition arrangements re Seats, 26 Sept. 1918. Bonar Law Papers, 95/2.

[2] Younger to Bonar Law: Memorandum on Coalition arrangements re Seats, 27 Sept. 1918. Bonar Law Papers, 95/2.

with Lloyd George's current position and following, which Guest estimated as follows: 1. a tried 'War' following of 92 Liberals; 2. 27 Lloyd George candidates adopted by local Liberal associations; 3. 8 Labour ministers and 7 private Labour members; and, 4. 26 British Workers' League and 'Patriotic Labour' candidates (of whom, however, Guest doubted whether half would be successful).[1]

Lloyd George, now acted with uncharacteristic directness, and avoiding any inclination to chaffer with his allies, simply cut through Younger's five-fold class of cases, and asked for Coalition endorsement for his Liberals in up to 150 seats—of which 30 should be Scottish seats—leaving the detailed arrangements to be adjusted by the whips.[2]

Actually the request was not regarded as particularly unselfish, witness Younger's comment that he believed the request for 150 seats ('made be it remembered not by Guest but by LG himself') was governed by the number of candidates that the Lloyd George Liberals had available. Younger remained in little doubt that if they had been able to put up extra men they would have asked for extra seats.[3]

Nevertheless, while the demand was not regarded as particularly unselfish, it was fairly speedily accepted, after Law had checked with Central Office, and it was accepted without haggling,[4] though partly perhaps in the belief that the full price would not have to be paid. At least this came to be the Coalition Liberal view; Guest's initial enthusiasm for the agreement and gratitude to Bonar Law and Younger had rather faded some weeks later, and on 15 November 1918—i.e. three weeks after the agreement had been finalized—he reported to the premier that the Conservative whips had not yet delivered up the 'real goods'—i.e. Conservative support for Lloyd George Liberals in up to 150 seats as Lloyd George had requested. Guest doubted whether the Conservative whips really expected the Lloyd George Liberals to 'realize' more than about 125 of these, and wanted the premier to ask Bonar Law to tell his whips that the goods must really be delivered, in spite of all the difficulties.

[1] Guest to Lloyd George, 21 Oct. 1918. Lloyd George Papers, F/21/2/43.
[2] Younger to J. C. C. Davidson, 2 Dec. 1918. Bonar Law Papers, 95/4.
[3] Ibid.   [4] Ibid.

As a morale boosting conclusion Guest added that it must always be remembered that the Conservative party was 'quite helpless' if it had to go on without Lloyd George'.[1]

Seven days later Bonar Law reminded his Liverpool supporters that the net result of the agreement with the Lloyd George Liberals was that the Conservatives had 400 candidates and Lloyd George 'less than 150', and that, if the Coalition won the election, the result would certainly be the return of a much larger number of Conservatives than they could reasonably have expected if they had been fighting on their own.[2]

In the event, however, Guest actually secured 159 endorsements—or in Asquithian terminology 'coupons'—for the Coalition Liberals (though this concession was appreciably devalued by the presence of Independent Tory challengers in some eighteen of these seats) and the 159 coupons played a major role—perhaps the major role—in the return of the 137 Coalition Liberal members.

Thus the first phase in the association of Lloyd George and Central Office was apparently successful.

But this was only on the surface; in reality it was a relationship that was already turning sour.

Very largely this was due to conflicts over the distribution of the official Coalition candidatures in the seventy-four Scottish seats. More particularly it was because Younger had become the victim of Liberal inspired newspaper accusations that as grab man for the Coalition Tories he had been particularly greedy in the case of Scottish seats.

Now this was an accusation that Younger regarded as particularly unfair. For one thing he had agreed that the Lloyd George Liberals should have Coalition endorsement in up to 30 Scottish seats, which of course was the specific figure that Lloyd George had suggested and, for another, he had repeatedly told the Coalition Liberals' Scottish whip that he might have additional endorsements if he chose to put up candidates in an extra set of Scottish seats: viz. the eastern division of Edinburgh, the eastern division of Fifeshire (Asquith's seat), Forfarshire, Paisley, and the southern division of Midlothian and Peebles.

---

[1] Guest to Lloyd George, 15 Nov. 1918. Lloyd George Papers, F/21/2/47.
[2] Bonar Law to Sir C. Petrie and Sir A. Salvidge, 22 Nov. 1918. Bonar Law Papers, 95/4.

'I thought all along that in most of those Constituencies . . . it would be far better to put up a Coalition Liberal than a Coalition Unionist' he recalled. The history of the seats had made it a much better choice in the one way than the other. But he had been repeatedly rebuffed, and on each occasion the Coalition Liberal whip had categorically refused to take them.[1]

A second reason for dissension between the allies had been the fact that Younger had had to wage a bruising struggle—and in the event an only partially successful struggle—to obtain Coalition endorsement for Conservative candidates contesting Linlithgow, Forfarshire, and the southern division of Aberdeen.

In the case of Linlithgow a 'hands off' contest between a Liberal supporter of the Coalition and a Conservative supporter of the Coalition had been virtually agreed to, but the Liberal supporter of the Coalition had somehow failed to stay the course, and the Conservative candidate Kidd had been left to battle Shinwell of the I.L.P. Nevertheless (as Younger wrote— or exploded, to his leader):

> Miss Reid writes that she can't get a letter for Kidd . . . out of No. 12 [i.e. the office of the Coalition Liberal whips]. They say 'It must be fought out as a dog fight.' Can you imagine anything more idiotic? A dog fight between two sound candidates is one thing & that was the position when it was as settled, but a fight between a Coalitionist and an extreme Bolshevist is another. In the first place it didn't matter which won, but in the latter a Bolshevist victory would be a disaster.[2]

In the case of southern Aberdeen Younger emphasized that he had distinctly promised the coupon to the Conservative candidate, F. C. Thomson, whom he had shifted from another seat to make way for a Coalition Liberal, and he insisted that the Conservative's right to be standard bearer for the Coalition had never been in question.[3]

In the case of Forfarshire, Younger emphasized that the local Conservatives had only put up their candidate when they knew that no Coalition Liberal meant to stand, and Younger insisted that the Conservative party was under a definite obligation to see that their man received the coupon, since he had given up Dumfries at Younger's request, in the interests of a stronger

[1] Younger to Bonar Law, 28 Nov. 1918. Bonar Law Papers, 95/4.
[2] Younger to Bonar Law, 30 Nov. 1918. Ibid. 95/4.
[3] Younger to Bonar Law, 28 Nov. 1918. Ibid. 95/4.

local candidate, and this after he had been nursing and working-up the seat for years.[1]

In the event, Younger obtained Coalition endorsement for the Conservative candidates at Linlithgow and southern Aberdeen, but in the case of Captain Shaw and Forfarshire the Coalition Liberals steadily refused to be forthcoming. This was partly, so Younger was persuaded, because Lloyd George didn't want the coupon sent against the sitting Asquithian Liberal Falconer, who had rendered useful service in the Marconi affair in the years before the war.[2]

All told Younger seems to have emerged from the election reinforced in his distaste for the premier ('the P.M. seems always to be barging in, & not I should fancy with much knowledge')[3] and having acquired an extremely poor opinion of the capabilities and motivation of the Coalition Liberal whips:

> They have not played the game at all.[4]

This brings us to the second phase in the association of Lloyd George and Conservative Central Office which was one in which an uncomfortable relationship was fairly steadily becoming worse.

There were various reasons why this should be so, but most of all the post-election operation of the 'coupon' and, more particularly, the difficulties in defending the Coalition Liberal seats.

In the process Younger and Sanders became alarmed at the decay of the *Conservative* organization in the Coalition Liberal seats, and contemptuous of the Coalition Liberal organization in the constituencies.

The specific points were more or less as follows:

Firstly, they became persuaded that the general run of Coalition Liberal candidates was unimpressive (particularly in contrast to the virtual plethora of Tory talent):

For example:

> Batty [unsuccessful Coalition Liberal contender for South Norfolk] was a rotten candidate as most of the CL candidates appear to be. . . .

[1] Ibid.
[2] Younger to Davidson, 5 Dec. 1918. Bonar Law Papers, 95/4.
[3] Younger to Bonar Law, 30 Nov. 1918. Ibid. 95/4.
[4] Younger to Davidson, 2 Dec. 1918, Ibid. 95/4.

Had we been allowed to fight the seat with John Coke we should certainly have won easily.[1]

Secondly, they became persuaded that the Coalition Liberal organizations were almost useless.[2] This was partly because they were botched together in a hurry, i.e. in normal pre-election conditions there were no specifically Coalition Liberal organizations, merely undifferentiated Liberal organizations. Coalition Liberal members could hold these on the strength of personality and attachments from before the wartime coalitions, but on the death or resignation of a Coalition Liberal member they tended to be recaptured by the Asquithian machine.

Thirdly, Central Office was readily persuaded that the interventions of the Coalition Liberal officers seldom improved a situation, and on occasion actually made a situation worse:

> The invasion [sic.] of the Downing Street staff does no good. They arrive, spend money lavishly, but cut little ice. Indeed in some cases they have done positive harm.[3]

Fourthly Central Office came to the uncomfortable conclusion that, lacking a candidate of their own, the Conservative organizations in the Coalition Liberal seats were running down:

> When they [Conservative Constituency organizations] have not a Candidate of their own in the field it is very difficult for them to get subscriptions and without money an efficient Organisation cannot be maintained.[4]

and again:

> There have been a good many difficulties recently with our organizn. in CL seats & in many cases they are falling to pieces. Local subscriptions have fallen off . . .[5]

Additionally, Central Office could not disguise the evidence that disliking the task of sustaining a Coalition Liberal member, Conservative associations tended to perform the work indiffer-

---

[1] Younger to Bonar Law, 12 Aug. 1920. Bonar Law Papers, 99/4/16.

[2] Younger to Bonar Law, 12 Dec. 1919. Bonar Law Papers, 98/5/11.

[3] Younger to Bonar Law, 12 Aug. 1920. Bonar Law Papers, 99/4/16.

[4] Sanders to Younger: Memorandum regarding Seats held by Coalition Liberals, 2 Dec. 1920, enclosed in Younger to Davidson, 4 Dec. 1920. Bonar Law Papers, 99/8/4.

[5] Younger to Davidson, 4 Dec. 1920. Bonar Law Papers, 99/8/4.

ently, to the extent they were prepared to undertake the task
at all:

For example:

> Though our men did all they could to help [the return of the Coalition
> Liberal at South Norfolk] the rank & file were apathetic.

whereas

> In Woodbridge with a bad agent & a good many years neglect & with
> a very large number of abstentions from the poll we still held our seat
> comfortably. This was by no means an easy job . . . but we managed
> it. . . .[1]

The consequence was that Younger and his colleagues became
advocates of a palliative whereby the Coalition Liberals would
recognize their failure to capture the official Asquithian machine,
and set up *specifically Lloyd Georgian* associations in the Coalition
Liberal seats, or the Lloyd George whips should openly or
secretly subsidize the Conservative organizations in the
Coalition Liberal seats.[2]

They also became advocates of a more extreme and more
attractive measure, namely the attainment of organizational
efficiency through the formal 'fusion' of the Lloyd George
Liberals and the Tory party.[3]

However, in the face of the Coalition Liberal unreadiness to
undertake either of these measures, they tended to become
advocates of—or at the very least no very strenuous opponents
of—a return to normalcy, and normal organizational efficiency,
through a disruption of the Coalition.

There was a further cause of discord, namely the Coalition's
handling of the honours system, and in particular the new year
honours lists of 1920/21.

In the process Younger became digusted at the premier and
the Coalition Liberal whips, singling out their greediness, in
capturing appreciably more than half the honours lists; their
lavishness (which made the Palace raise difficulties over what
Younger regarded as extremely moderate Tory lists); their

---

[1] Younger to Bonar Law, 12 Aug. 1920, Bonar Law Papers, 99/4/16.
[2] Sanders to Younger: Memorandum regarding Seats held by Coalition
Liberals, 2 Dec. 1920, ibid., 99/8/4.
[3] Foreshadowed in Younger's Circular Letter to Conservative Constituency Agents, 14 Oct. 1919. Bonar Law Papers, 96/1.

poaching of Conservatives and potential Conservative sub-
scribers; and—most seriously perhaps—their recommendation
of unsavoury Conservatives whom Central Office had already
righteously cold-shouldered and rejected.

The upshot of the business was that Younger was found
wishing he were finished with the Coalition Liberal people.[1]

But in fact in the course of 1921 this became a general
Conservative demand. Independent Conservatives at Dover
and St. George's, Westminster actually defeated Conservative
supporters of the Coalition. The general run of Tory candidates
showed a strong desire to stand as Independent Tories. And by
the end of the year there were Independent Conservatives
challenging Coalition Liberals in fifteen English seats.

In these conditions Central Office virtually threw in the
Coalition hand. Sometime in the summer or the early autumn
it practically promised Conservative supporters that *the
Coalition would not be extended for a further term.*[2]

Now there is a definite possibility that this particular decision
(which of course almost necessarily converted Central Office
into the Coalition's most formidable opponent) was motivated
quite as much by personal inclination—i.e. its lack of patience
and lack of rapport with its allies—as by the actual requirements
of political survival.

Malcolm Fraser was still prepared to make the significant
admission that a 'National party' under Lloyd George's leadership would be sufficiently acceptable to Conservatives at
large:

> There is a general feeling for a party which is nebulously described as
> Constitutional, or National, or a Party of Law and Order. The local
> leading men to whom I have spoken would all subscribe, [although]
> some possibly not with much enthusiasm, to a moderate Party of
> sorts under the leadership of the Prime Minister.[3]

Moreover—and even more remarkably—Younger himself
was to make the highly significant admission that the Tory party
might still be won for a further term of Coalition Government,
provided the operation were conducted in an adept, unhurried,

---

[1] Younger to Bonar Law, 2 Jan. 1921. Bonar Law Papers, 100/1/2.
[2] Fraser to Austen Chamberlain, 31 Dec. 1921. Austen Chamberlain
Papers, AC 32/4/1a.
[3] Ibid.

way: 'It would have taken the most delicate handling . . . and it would need time.'[1]

But in a sense all this was by the by. Central Office had decided that the Coalition had to go, and as the future was to demonstrate was not above personally ensuring that it went.

The first move came in August 1921, when Younger impressed upon his leader Austen Chamberlain that at the next (query 1923?) election, the Conservatives would have to stand as Tories 'pure and simple'.[2]

Four months later Chamberlain alerted Central Office to the fact that Lloyd George and the Lord Chancellor, Lord Birkenhead ('F.E.') had an almost entirely different scheme in mind:

> The position is . . . that the Prime Minister is greatly attracted by the idea of an election [i.e. a new coalition election] early in the new year [in order to capitalize on the triumph of the Irish treaty, and to give the coalition and his own premiership an extra lease of life.] The Lord Chancellor is equally strongly in favour of it. I myself am opposed to it. . . .

But Chamberlain was very far from confident that this personal opposition would actually prevail:

> The Prime Minister professes not to have made up his mind and certainly has not come to a final decision, but there is no doubt where his inclinations point, and though I feel entitled to make the strongest representations to him as to the views of myself and my friends, I have to recognise that it is the peculiar prerogative of the Prime Minister to advise the King in such a matter; that he is not bound to consult the Cabinet or his colleagues . . . and, if he does consult some of his colleagues, he still retains the right to make the decision himself.
>
> If the Lord Chancellor and I were agreed that such an election would be a mistake, I think he would defer to our opinion; but if he continues of the same mind, and the Lord Chancellor sides with him, I expect that he will over-ride my objections.[3]

Chamberlain's report called forth a verbal lashing for the (supposedly) treacherous 'F.E.', and an eloquent assertion—

[1] Younger to Austen Chamberlain, 28 Dec. 1921. Austen Chamberlain Papers, AC 32/2/15a.

[2] Sanders' Diary, 21 Aug. 1921. Conservative Research Department Library.

[3] Austen Chamberlain to Younger, 22 Dec. 1921. Austen Chamberlain Papers, AC 32/2/2.

full of fighting words like 'flout' and 'smash'—of the doctrine that the Tory party and its leader still retained the upper hand:

> As to 'F.E.' he is as usual looking after 'No. 1'. I see his game quite clearly. He would like to keep the Coalition alive & go to the country again as we are. That would give him a better chance in the future than he has at present of securing the leadership.

As for the premier:

> Doubtedless the PM can act on his own view if he pleases to flout us, but we can smash his hopes easily & he'll have to get that made clear to him. I'm quite ready to do that part of it if the need arises.[1]

Central Office now moved on to what it claimed were settled judgments that a snap election, so far from reinvigorating the ailing Coalition, would almost certainly engender a formidable, and possibly fatal, Conservative revolt.

Thus Malcolm Fraser (writing for Lloyd George's eyes) laid particular stress on Tory unrest in the one hundred and thirty Coalition Liberal seats:

> In the 130 seats in which the Coalition Liberals nominate the Parliamentary candidate, the Unionist Organisation, both local and Parliamentary, has suffered. However hopeless the seat may be from a Unionist point of view the lack of a Parliamentary candidate means that there is no point around which the local Organisation can rally; while the financial position of the Organisation is affected both by lack of interest, and because there is no candidate to assist the local subscription list.
> ... It must not be forgotten that local politics are means by which local people may advance in the social scale. The offices of Councillor, Alderman, Mayor, Justice of the Peace etc. appear to possess attractions to which human nature cannot blind itself. Here, then, we have a large number of seats awaiting a suitable opportunity to break away from the Coalition. . . .

But of course the unrest was not just confined to Coalition Liberal seats: it was an undoubted fact that very many Conservatives regarded the Coalition with very strong disfavour. As a consequence, in the case of an immediate election, many Conservative constituencies would force their candidates to stand as independents. The Coalition would probably obtain a majority, but it would be a greatly reduced majority, and it was

---

[1] Younger to Austen Chamberlain, 24 Dec. 1921. Austen Chamberlain Papers, AC 32/2/11.

not at all certain that the members so returned would prove very 'tractable' or very reliable supporters in the day to day proceedings of the House.[1]

And again, and rather more candidly, to Austen Chamberlain:

> If the Prime Minister went to the country as a Coalition in February, he would probably get back with a majority, but the result would, I fear, split our party from top to toe. . . . In the West of England, which for so many years has been used to a form of Coalition in connection with the Liberal-Unionists, there would not be much trouble, but in the rest of England & Wales the feeling would run high.

Moreover Fraser was more or less persuaded that a very large number of their candidates would demand to stand as Independent Tories. At the recent by-elections they had invariably wished to do so, and it was only by giving them a large measure of independence that Central Office had been able to persuade them to at least pose as Coalition Tories too.[2]

So much for Malcolm Fraser.

Meanwhile Younger had made his own and distinctive contribution, with the lightly veiled suggestion that Central Office would feel obliged to assist and encourage the probable Conservative revolt:

> Malcolm Fraser will already have supplied you with the Office opinions [he wrote to Chamberlain—and through Chamberlain, Lloyd George]. He will no doubt have informed you of the difficulties which have faced us during the last few months in keeping the Party together in support of the Coalition, and how difficult it would be to secure general support in any circumstances for the continuation of the present condition of affairs.
>
> I am more concerned, however, to deal with the policy of making an appeal now to the constituencies. I do not think it could be justified unless there was an over-riding political necessity forcing it upon the Government. There is no such necessity. . . .

Additionally, the Government was committed to proceeding with the reconstruction of the House of Lords (or as Younger chose to call it, 'the restoration of the balance of the Constitution') and proceeding towards the commencement of the

---

[1] Fraser's Memorandum on election prospects, 30 Dec. 1921. Lloyd George Papers, F/48/5/4.

[2] Fraser to Austen Chamberlain, 31 Dec. 1921. Austen Chamberlain Papers, AC 34/4/1a.

coming session. This was an undoubted pledge. Nothing could excuse its non-fulfilment but a serious political crisis, and any 'betrayal' upon the question would be most bitterly resented and would prove the 'death knell' of the Coalition.

Moreover any possible fillip to the Government from the Irish treaty ought not to be taken advantage of for the advance of any personal or party interest:

> I feel very strongly about this . . . I cannot too strongly impress upon you that we ought to run a perfectly straight course in this matter. . . . A false step would bring the whole edifice to the ground. Anything which had the appearance of not being quite straightforward . . . would be fatal [to the Coalition].[1]

Characteristically, Younger ensured that he was even more explicit in his covering letter to the premier himself:

> I only came here [i.e. to Central Office] yesterday for a couple of days, but I have seen many of our Members, and one and all are opposed to any Election in the near future . . . and all declare that if an Election be forced upon them, they will not stand as Coalitionists, but as Independent Unionists. They tell me that so far as they have been able to ascertain, this intention is generally held. . . .

As for himself:

> I should regard it as a disaster to the best interests of the country if an Election were held in the present circumstances I see no justification for it, and no sufficient reason could be advanced in support of it. . . . Holding those views so strongly as I do, and believing that an Election now would rightly be regarded as an unfair advantage taken by the Party [sic.] in power, it would be my duty to use what influence I have to oppose it.[2]

Moreover Younger was almost equally explicit when he broached the whole election question to the public—or, as he preferred to see it, embarked upon an entirely defensive newspaper campaign, designed to counter Coalition Liberal attempts to manipulate and use the press:

> I purposely kept you & your name entirely out of my [newspaper] 'stunt', [he wrote to Austen Chamberlain]. I wanted you to have no kind of responsibility either for the matter or the manner of my action, but you can't believe how thankful I am that you do approve. I'll

[1] Younger to Austen Chamberlain, 28 Dec. 1921. Lloyd George Papers, F/48/5/4.
[2] Younger to Lloyd George, 4 Jan. 1922. Lloyd George Papers, F/48/5/4.

teach Sutherland [i.e. Lloyd George's press secretary] & Co. that they cannot regard our Party or myself as a negligible quantity. To invite our views [on the subject of a snap election] & then to start the Press as they did before the PM had even received them was an insolent & unpardonable thing to do & they have got it in the neck. So will LG when I meet him. . . .[1]

In the event Lloyd George was to maintain that Younger had behaved 'disgracefully' (breaking confidence when consulted on a most confidential matter),[2] but the premier possessed the wit to realize that, at least for the time being, Central Office had obtained the upper hand.

The intended February election was indefinitely postponed.

Perhaps inevitably, Central Office was only moderately appeased, and by the end of January, Younger and his lieutenants were coming back on the old line:

On looking through the letters of the last fortnight, [he wrote to Chamberlain], I am impressed by the growing number of candidates & Constituency Chairmen who say that they won't support the Coalition beyond the life of the present Parliament. Even a man like Douglas Hogg takes this line, though when I got him adopted [for St. Marylebone] he loyally accepted the Coalition. The feeling grows and grows & I feel more convinced than I even was this morning that our people will insist on severing the connection when an Election comes.

But it was not entirely the old line: there was perhaps, a new note of authority ('my care is to see that the Unionist Party is not broken up'), and there was certainly a very special interest in Chamberlain's probable reactions if the premier and his allies should attempt to spring an election once again:

Would Chamberlain at once come out as a leader of revolt, and be ready with the policy which would unite all sections of the party, or would he prefer to take some other line?[3]

And Chamberlain, it now appeared, really did prefer to take a different line. At any rate he was soon publicly proclaiming that it was not merely desirable but vital that the Lloyd George

[1] Younger to Austen Chamberlain, 9 Jan. 1922. Austen Chamberlain Papers, AC 32/2/23.

[2] Lloyd George to Austen Chamberlain, 10 Jan. 1922. Beaverbrook, *The Decline and Fall of Lloyd George*, (1963), 290–1.

[3] Younger to Austen Chamberlain, 30 Jan. 1922. Austen Chamberlain Papers, AC 32/3/4.

Liberals and the Tories, so far from severing connections, should maintain a firm alliance. Admittedly there should be no new issue of the famous 'coupons' but, apparently, there should be mutual withdrawals in the constituencies, and mutual support in the constituencies, much in the fashion of Liberal Unionists and Tories in the Home Rule struggle of thirty years before.

This could be taken as virtually a call for a new type Coalition, and as such was quite distinctly different from what Younger had in mind.

The next day Younger publicly revised his leader's doctrine, calling for 'a bill of divorcement' to end 'the matrimonial alliance' between the Lloyd George Liberals and the Tories, and implying that informal 'co-operation' with (selected?) Lloyd George Liberals was all that circumstances, or Conservative anti-Labour policy, required.

This of course lashed the Lloyd George-ites into fury.

Birkenhead denounced Younger as a presumptuous 'cabin boy' who aspired to run the ship, and Lloyd George inspired or authorized some more or less discreet enquiries as to whether Central Office could be placed in friendly hands. Or at any rate in less unfriendly hands!

On 3 March 1922 Sanders noted in his diary:

> Yesterday Guest came up to me and asked me to put up the conditions on which Conservatives would continue to support LG. He confessed that LG would not have me as [Conservative] Chief Whip [on the large scale Government reconstruction in the spring of 1921] because he thought I was too Tory; but Guest now suggested I should be Chief Whip & take Younger's place as well. I told him any ousting of Younger would be resented intensely.[1]

Younger of course stayed on at Central Office, and in the event the Lloyd George Coalition, perhaps surprisingly, managed to scrape on till the end of autumn. But Lloyd George's association with his partner's Central Office had already reached rock bottom—and it never really recovered from this early springtime low.

Monash University   D. D. CUTHBERT

---

[1] Sanders' Diary, 3 March 1922. Conservative Research Department Library.

VII

LLOYD GEORGE AND THE SEARCH FOR A POSTWAR NAVAL POLICY, 1919

J. KENNETH McDONALD

J. KENNETH McDONALD

Age 38

Yale 1951–54 B.A.
Oxford 1958–61 B.Litt., 1967–70 D.Phil.
Currently Associate Professor of International
Affairs, The George Washington University,
Washington, D.C.

LLOYD GEORGE AND THE
SEARCH FOR A POSTWAR
NAVAL POLICY, 1919

As prime minister in the first World war Lloyd George was not
only willing but anxious to organize national military policy
and to direct the strategic conduct of the war. In the closing days
of the war, and in the first few months after it, he demonstrated
a pugnacious determination to maintain British naval supremacy
against the challenge of President Wilson's policies. During the
allied negotiations over the pre-armistice agreement at Paris
in late October and early November 1918 the British prime
minister effectively eliminated the pernicious American doctrine
of the 'freedom of the seas', the second of Wilson's fourteen
points, from forming any part of the eventual peace settlement.
It was in these negotiations that he declared that 'Great Britain
would spend her last guinea to keep a navy superior to that of
the United States or any other power, . . .'[1] Again, in late March
and early April 1919 at the Paris peace conference Lloyd George
boldly attempted to use British acceptance of the league of
nations—or at least of Wilson's proposed 'Monroe Doctrine
Amendment' to the covenant—as a lever to force the United
States to abandon or modify her renewed 1916 naval construction programme.[2] In this Lloyd George was unsuccessful,
and within a few months of this failure his belief in the
possibility, or necessity, of continued British world naval
preponderance had begun to recede. By the end of the summer
of 1919, in several far-reaching decisions, Lloyd George's
coalition government set British naval policy in the direction of
reduction and retrenchment it was generally to follow until
rearmament began in the late 1930's.

The most famous of the decisions adopted at the cabinet's
memorable 15 August 1919 meeting was the 'ten year rule',
which stipulated that the British empire would be engaged in no

---

[1] House Diary, 4 Nov. 1918, House Papers, Yale University Library;
printed in Charles Seymour, *The Intimate Papers of Colonel House*, (Boston,
1928), iv, 180–1.   [2] Seymour, op. cit., 415–24.

great war during the next ten years.[1] Other decisions which drastically reduced naval expenditure were intended to support a new British diplomatic initiative to persuade the United States reciprocally to reduce her naval programme. When this diplomatic effort, in Lord Grey's mission to Washington in the autumn of 1919, failed, the government sought to combine the new policies to reduce naval expenditure with a determination to maintain at least a 'one power standard' of naval equality with the United States. It was not, of course, the logical inconsistency but the practical incompatibility of these two policies which made it seem impossible to pursue both for long. How Lloyd George arrived, by December 1919, at the position where he sought to pursue both is worth investigating. It was in the latter half of 1919 that the problems of organizing a coherent postwar British naval policy first emerged clearly, and the new documentary evidence available only in the past few years makes it now possible to give a more accurate account of this crucial period.

If naval supremacy could be defined simply as having the world's largest and strongest fleet, then Great Britain certainly had overwhelming naval supremacy at the end of the first world war. With the defeat of Germany, the internment of most of her high seas fleet and the surrender of the German submarines, the royal navy was nearly equal, in tonnage and in numbers of fighting ships, to all the remaining major fleets of the world combined. It was recognized, of course, that neither the men nor the money would be available to keep this entire navy intact after the peace; indeed, in its wartime planning the admiralty assumed that the postwar navy would revert to something around its 1914 size.[2] Yet, inside the admiralty and out, there was a general presumption at the war's end that Great Britain would remain the greatest naval power in the new postwar world.

By the opening of the Paris peace conference in January 1919, however, it had become apparent that the United States, now the world's second naval power, proposed to build a navy at least equal, if not superior, to the British fleet. Immediately after the conclusion of the armistice the United States prepared to continue work on the nineteen capital ships, including the

[1] CAB 23/15, W.C. 616A, 15 Aug. 1919, Secret, ('A' Minutes).
[2] ADM 116/1748, Admiralty Reconstruction Committee, 1918, Secret.

ten battleships and six battle cruisers of the 1916 building programme, on which work had been slowed or suspended during the war. Furthermore, before sailing for Paris President Wilson, in his 2 December 1918 message to congress, had requested a new three year naval construction programme for yet another sixteen capital ships.[1] When the Democratic 65th Congress expired on 4 March 1919 without passing the president's 1918 navy bill Great Britain was relieved of worry about this part of the American naval expansion programme, since the new Republican congress was not expected to support the president's naval proposals.[1] Indeed, in May 1919 Wilson withdrew support for the proposed 1918 programme.[2] The continuing 1916 programme remained, however, and this prospect alone proved enough to sustain British alarm over American building competition. Indeed, it was this 1916 programme that Lloyd George sought unsuccessfully to force the United States to abandon or modify at the peace conference, in the negotiations which the American secretary of navy Josephus Daniels later called the 'Naval Battle of Paris.'[3]

The principal motive for Lloyd George's pressure on the United States to reduce her naval building was the increasingly urgent necessity for his government to reduce British naval expenditure. The admiralty had been made aware of this necessity from the time of the armistice.[4] On 25 March 1919, the day before the first lord, Walter Long, went to Paris to quarrel with the American naval representatives about their building programme, he complained to his admiralty board of the size of their proposed estimates, and reminded them that the nation was going through a period of 'great financial stringency'.[5] The next day Bonar Law warned Winston Churchill,

[1] Ray Stannard Baker and Wm. E. Dodd (eds.), *The Public Papers of Woodrow Wilson: War and Peace 1917–1924*, (New York & London: 1927), v. I, 318; *Congressional Record*, v. LVII, Part 1, 7 (2 Dec. 1918).

[2] Harold and Margaret Sprout, *Toward a New Order of Sea Power*, (Princeton: 1940), 107–8.

[3] Josephus Daniels, *The Wilson Era, 1917–1923*, (Chapel Hill, N.C.: 1946), chapter 35.

[4] ADM 116/1809, B. Law (chancellor of the exchequer) to E. Geddes (first lord of the admiralty), 23 Nov. 1918.

[5] ADM 167/58, W. Long Memo. to the Board, 'Future Naval Programme', 25 March 1919.

then both war secretary and air minister, that the country must be convinced that 'we are not in for a big army and navy', and he continued by threatening—'half jocularly'—to move in cabinet to reduce service expenditures to £20 million per annum.[1] Estimates for the three services for 1919–1920 eventually totalled nearly £600 millions.[2]

The conflict between the immediate pressure to reduce navy spending and the prospect of an impending naval race with the United States vastly complicated the admiralty's efforts to produce a new peacetime policy. The implications of this conflict did not escape Winston Churchill, who as first lord in the prewar Asquith government had had experience in justifying increased peacetime navy estimates to a sceptical chancellor of the exchequer, Lloyd George. Now, on 1 May 1919, in his dual capacity as secretary of state for war and air minister, Churchill wrote Lloyd George in a new vein about the problem of peacetime defence estimates. Referring to the limit of £110 million which the chancellor of the exchequer, Austen Chamberlain, had recently proposed for all three service estimates in the 'first normal year', Churchill asserted that 'a large reduction in naval expenditure is essential to any satisfactory solution of the combined problem'. While he hoped that the postwar army would not need to be much larger than the prewar model he explained that its responsibilities—and its cost—had been increased by the war. Finding additional money for the army depended, he wrote, 'entirely upon a saving from the navy', a saving he considered quite possible, 'at any rate until some entirely new competition develops'. Churchill therefore told his chief that it was 'absolutely vital to persuade President Wilson not to start building new big ships'. If the United States began building superior ships Britain could not fall behind in quality, and he warned that matching the American ships would soon revive naval building competition 'in the most painful and embarrassing form'. Churchill told Lloyd George that such competition would be criminal, and that a naval agreement with the United States, to eliminate the need for new construction, should be possible 'with the great

[1] Thomas Jones, *Whitehall Diary*, (1969), i, 82.
[2] CAB 24/5, 'Memorandum by the Treasury on the Financial Position and Future Prospects of This Country'. G.257, 18 July 1919.

hold you must now have over President Wilson'. Only such savings in the navy estimates, Churchill concluded, 'will enable us to reconcile Imperial defence and national economy'.[1]

Although at the end of May 1919 the admiralty board was still cautiously confident that 'according to present indications it should be possible in coming years to reduce the Fleet below its 1914 strength', the board complained that it was impossible

> in the present unsettled state of International affairs to arrive at any final conclusion as to the Naval strength which will be required in the future, more particularly owing to the uncertainty in regard to the American Programme and our future policy in the Far East. . . .[2]

On 19 June the board therefore asked the cabinet, in view of these international uncertainties, to approve large estimates of over £170 millions in order to maintain 'for the present year . . . a relatively strong fleet in a state of readiness for action'. In this memorandum for the cabinet Walter Long admitted that the fleet's capital ships were concentrated in European waters for convenience and economy rather than for strategic needs, but he said the naval staff recognized they were providing for a purely transitional period.[3]

When approval for the admiralty's proposed policy and estimates was not immediately forthcoming the first lord wrote again to the war cabinet, pressing for action. In this memorandum of 5 July Long told the war cabinet that he was aware that the question would be asked 'Against what possible enemy are you preparing?' After admitting that the enemies of Europe had disappeared, Long referred vaguely to 'constant risks of unexpected and unforeseen troubles' and then advanced a more specific argument for maintaining a strong fleet ready for action. 'Is it not at least prudent to bear in mind', he asked,

> that if trouble arises in Ireland—and this seems almost inevitable— it is at least within the bounds of possibility that the United States of America may be forced by political exigencies of their own to assume hostile action towards ourselves; I do not mean, to make war—but to attempt to dictate. . . .

[1] Lloyd George Papers, F/8/3/46, Churchill to Lloyd George, 1 May 1919, Personal and Secret.

[2] ADM 167/56, Board Minute No. 802, 29 May 1919, Secret.

[3] CAB 24/82, Admiralty Memo. to War Cabinet, G.T. 7517, 19 June 1919, Secret.

Great Britain could ignore this kind of action, Long declared, so long as she kept command of the seas, but once this supremacy was lost, '. . . we should undoubtedly find ourselves in a very unpleasant and unsatisfactory position'. To this argument for naval supremacy over the United States Long added a testimonial to the royal navy as the 'cheapest and most efficient police force that the Empire can possess'. Thus the first lord justified the proposed 1919–1920 estimates to the war cabinet solely on general grounds of prestige: the diplomatic or deterrent value of having the world's largest fleet in any quarrel with the United States, and the imperial benefits of showing the flag. It was clear that at this time the admiralty had no expectation of any warlike use of the fleet in the foreseeable future.[1]

Strategic grounds, however, provided the basis for a vigorous treasury attack on the admiralty's planning. On 8 July 1919 the chancellor of the exchequer, Austen Chamberlain, in a sharply worded memorandum for the war cabinet, expressed 'profound shock' that the proposed postwar reduction in the navy's costs and manning levels was so slight compared with prewar figures. 'The British Navy is intended for Defence not aggression', he wrote, and offered his own strategic analysis of the powers or combinations of powers which might endanger Great Britain. Having dismissed each of the major European powers, Chamberlain then noted that two powers remained, the United States and Japan. 'Both these Powers emerge from the war with enhanced strength;' he wrote, 'and both are rather enigmatic in their attitude'. Chamberlain contended, however, that even if the admiralty felt it necessary to compete with the large American building programme, the United States could not equal Great Britain for many years, so that at least through 1921 a much greater proportion of the royal navy's capital ships could be safely kept in reserve.

Having denied the need for any immediate anxiety over the eventual possibility of an Anglo-American naval race, Chamberlain then considered Japan. He admitted that 'Japan may be suspected by some to have ambitious designs in the Pacific which in the long run will bring her into collision with this

[1] CAB 24/83, Admiralty Memo. to the War Cabinet, 'Navy Estimates 1919–1920', G.T. 7645, 5 July 1919, Secret.

country'. Yet he noted that since the admiralty's capital ship distribution put none nearer to Japan than the Mediterranean,

> A *coup de main* by Japan, if such were contemplated, could not be anticipated by any Fleet action even under the intended Admiralty disposition of the Fleet, and an interval would have to intervene during which we should collect our ships for an Eastern expedition.

The chancellor of the exchequer therefore concluded that Great Britain's strategic position with regard to Japan would not be seriously weakened by the immediate relegation of a larger proportion of capital ships to reserve.[1]

Austen Chamberlain's attack incensed the admiralty, and on 17 July the board discussed a proposed reply. To the chancellor's argument on far eastern defence the admiralty could only respond weakly that in the event of a Japanese *coup de main* the time factor would be all-important, since if Japan should succeed in taking Singapore 'the position would be so difficult to retrieve as to be impossible'. On policy with respect to the United States, however, the admiralty draft paper claimed that new and additional information on the American building programme now revealed that the kind of reductions Chamberlain proposed would put the royal navy 'in a *position of actual inferiority in respect of Dreadnoughts*' to the United States fleet.[2] To accept this, it was suggested, would be generally regarded 'as the handing over of sea-supremacy by the British Empire to the United States of America.' Agreeing that a war with the United States was improbable, the admiralty board nevertheless insisted that they 'would be failing in their duty if they did not recommend a policy of keeping the British Navy, upon which the Empire depends, at a strength at least equal to that of the United States Navy'. Since this was the first admiralty intimation that mere equality with the American fleet might be acceptable, it is perhaps significant that in the event this paper was not submitted to the cabinet.[3]

By the time he had seen the chancellor of the exchequer's memorandum the assistant secretary to the cabinet, Thomas

---

[1] CAB 24/83, Chancellor of the Exchequer to the War Cabinet, 'Navy Votes', G.T. 7646, 8 July 1919, Secret.

[2] Emphasis in the original.

[3] ADM 167/59, Memo. for the Board, 'Naval Policy', n.d.; discussed: ADM 167/76, Board Minute No. 814, 17 July 1919, Secret.

Jones, was concerned enough by the admiralty's proposals to write to his chief, Sir Maurice Hankey, on the subject of naval estimates. 'You will have seen', he wrote on 11 July,

> the two papers by the First Lord and the paper by Chamberlain on this most important question. I am deliberately delaying their consideration by the Cabinet until the P.M.'s return as they raise issues of the first importance. The crux of the matter—as it seems to me—is, having squashed Germany are we now going to start building against America? It is clearly in the minds of the Sea Lords. If they get their way we shall manufacture Bolsheviks faster than Hoover produced his pigs.

He suspected that even Hankey, with his love for the navy, would hesitate to endorse the new estimates. 'The world's capital is now practically controlled by the U.S.A.' he concluded, 'and it is sheer madness for us to try to compete with them or to do anything to provoke building by them.'[1]

It was at this point that Sir Maurice Hankey produced a memorandum for the prime minister which appears to have played a crucial role in the future direction of British defence policy, and especially with respect to the navy. On 16 July 1919 Hankey, as cabinet secretary, accompanied Lloyd George to Criccieth, in the prime minister's constituency in Wales, for a conference on economic policy, and more specifically on the coal industry. Apparently in the course of this meeting Hankey found time to draft a paper for the prime minister entitled 'Towards a National Policy. July 1919.' Noting the wartime practice, from 1916 through 1918, of periodically reviewing the entire national situation, to focus on the principal problems and the means of tackling them, Hankey suggested in his introduction that the same method would be useful in dealing with the 'problem of reconstruction'. In this wide-ranging introduction Hankey advanced the principle that

> Non-productive employment of manpower and expenditure, such as is involved by naval, military, and air effort, must be reduced within the narrowest limits consistent with national safety.

Since the application of this principle to the armed services depended upon British foreign policy, Hankey then turned to this subject in the second part of this paper, 'Foreign

[1] Thomas Jones, *Whitehall Diary*, (1969), i, 89. Hankey was then a lieutenant-colonel of the royal marines.

Policy, Overseas and Defence Policy'. After discussing the league of nations and the problems of relations with European countries, Hankey came to the question of Anglo-American relations. 'The United States of America', he stated flatly in opening this discussion, 'is the most powerful nation in the world'. It was, he wrote, almost completely self-contained and self-supporting, endowed with immense financial and economic strength, and the possessor not only of the world's second navy and mercantile marine, but also of one of the world's most powerful armies. 'It is quite out of the question', Hankey declared, 'that we could make successful war against her, and it is doubtful whether all Europe combined could do so'. He added that in any war with the United States Great Britain would not only lose Canada and the West Indies and jeopardize her South American trade, but she would also find her economic situation difficult without American resources.

'Fortunately,' Hankey continued, 'such a war is almost unthinkable.' Although finding the 'principal point of danger' for Anglo-American relations in the Irish question, Hankey considered that in the main 'American ideals are our ideals'. Furthermore he reminded the prime minister that before the war British military preparations, coast defence plans, and shipbuilding programmes, had all been made without reference to the United States; on this point Hankey spoke with special authority, since he had been in the secretariat of the committee of imperial defence since 1908, and secretary of that body since 1912. 'In view of these considerations,' he continued, 'there seems little ground for basing our naval and military establishments on the possibility of War with the United States.'

Having stated this rule, Hankey immediately declared one exception to it. It was his view that 'even though some other pretext for its maintenance is found, our fleet should not be allowed to sink below the level of the United States fleet'. He justified this position on defensive grounds. 'We must always', he wrote,

> be able to protect our home waters, the approaches to our shores, and our main trade routes, other than those contiguous to the United States, which are not defensible without immense forces. If we failed to maintain this standard we might be exposed to unbearable pressure, if a truculent overbearing and anti-British President should secure

election. If we cannot have local command of the North-Western Atlantic and North-Eastern Pacific, we must not abandon general command of the sea to the United States.

Thus, although Hankey began by sounding like Austen Chamberlain and Thomas Jones, he drew close to Walter Long's position in this passage. Significantly, Hankey added that 'At the same time no opportunity should be lost to induce the United States to abate their naval armaments in accord with us'. He considered the American decision not to extend the 1916 programme under construction with a new programme a good beginning in the direction of reduction.

Hankey concluded that while a war with the United States was the maximum danger, it was nevertheless an 'extremely remote contingency'. Although responsible statesmen should never entirely exclude the possibility of such a calamity from their minds, he insisted that it

> ... could never form the basis for our published policy. It could never be alluded to in public, and should only be spoken of in the most secret and intimate discussions.

To reconcile this reticence with his insistence on the maintenance of naval equality with the United States Hankey suggested that

> A possible basis for a public policy would be a two-power standard, excluding the United States of America, which would probably provide for the more remote contingency also. Moreover, it is simple and should not offend the mass of public opinion.

It is difficult to see how a two power standard nominally directed against the next two naval powers after the United States, Japan and France, would improve relations with those two countries—or with the United States, if it actually produced a British navy matching or exceeding the American navy.

Hankey recognized, however, that simply maintaining naval parity with the United States, under whatever pretext, would not necessarily reduce naval expenditure. For 'real saving in Navy Estimates' Hankey looked to naval disarmament, the first step in which he suggested should be

> to invite all the Naval Powers to concert a scheme, reducing to the absolute minimum the number of ships in commission and in immediate reserve, thereby reducing personnel to the lowest possible limit.

Hankey thus recommended to Lloyd George not only a renewed effort to reach agreement with the United States on naval reduction, but also British support for general international naval disarmament. An international disarmament conference, at Washington, was arranged only two years later, but within weeks of Hankey's paper the prime minister had organized a new diplomatic effort to negotiate a naval agreement with the United States alone.

In his discussion of naval policy Hankey had also insisted that a 'principle' should be established upon which the navy could base its estimates. In the conclusion of his paper he went further and recommended that the first step in coordinating defence and foreign policy should be for the committee of imperial defence, or a sub-committee of it, 'to draw up a basis of policy on which the Royal Navy, the Army, and the Royal Air Force should work out their estimates. . . .' He urged that this inquiry should begin at an early date, and that 'The Committee should be instructed as to the necessity of preparing a minimum basis in view of the need of economy or [sic] non-productive expenditure.' No committee was set up in the C.I.D., but in less than a month the newly-formed cabinet finance committee, in its second meeting, drew up the kind of principles for future defence policy and expenditure which Hankey had proposed, and which the cabinet then imposed on the three services at their 15 August 1919 meeting.[1]

In the meantime the admiralty had succeeded in getting war cabinet approval for their 1919–1920 estimates of £170 million, in spite of the opposition of the chancellor of the exchequer. When the first lord, Walter Long, presented these estimates to the house of commons on 24 July 1919 he cautiously avoided any reference to possible naval rivalry with the United States. Although it was clear enough that the sea lords in their own deliberations were determined not to let 'naval supremacy' slip into the hands of the Americans, the first lord chose in parliament to emphasize the rapid pace of the royal navy's demobilization.[2] He made no mention of the American construction programme, and he gave no indication of the strategic

[1] CAB 21/159, Hankey Memo. to Lloyd George, 'Towards a National Policy. July 1919', 17 July 1919, Secret.
[2] *H.C. deb.*, 118, c. 1598 (24 July 1919).

use or purpose the naval staff had in mind for the royal navy, other than to declare his own conviction that 'the advantages which follow from our flag being shown all over the world are enormous'.[1] In the debate which followed the opposition liberals were especially insistent in denouncing any possible movement towards naval rivalry with the United States.[2]

The pressure for the reduction of expenditure continued to mount, and on 26 July the chancellor of the exchequer, at the prime minister's direction, circulated a treasury memorandum on the 'Financial Position and Future Prospects of this Country'. In his cover note Chamberlain declared:

> The position grows daily more grave. No estimates hold good, and the Cabinet sanctions increase after increase with, as it seems to me, an insufficient appreciation of the aggregate result.
>
> Our capital commitments are already enormous. Borrowing is difficult and rates will be exorbitant. If we cannot balance revenue and expenditure next year, our credit—national and international—will be seriously shaken and the results may be disastrous. . . .[3]

The treasury memorandum pointed out that army and navy expenditure already contributed heavily to the expected further 1919–1920 deficit beyond the budgeted deficit of £200 million. The treasury demanded an immediate reduction in both personal and public expenditure, to make savings available for investment. It was suggested that the government should give a notable—indeed an exaggerated—example, since it was held that a substantial reduction of the estimates 'would produce effects reaching considerably beyond the actual money involved'. 'It is difficult to see', the treasury memorandum concluded, 'where such substantial reduction can be made except on the expenditure of the Army, Navy and Air Force.'[4]

---

[1] Ibid. 1606. Probably at about the time of this debate Admiral Lord Fisher wrote to Lloyd George that an 'immense economy' was possible in navy estimates: 'We are what the Silly Tories call "*Showing the Flag*" by a Multitude of Squadrons all over the face of the Earth?

'WHAT FOR?

'*Is the German Fleet at the bottom of the Sea or not?*

'It makes me weep!'

(Lloyd George Papers, F/16/6/4, n.d.)

[2] *H.C. deb.*, 118, c. 1610–1611 & 1694–1695.

[3] CAB 24/5, 'Note by the Chancellor of the Exchequer', 26 July 1919.

[4] CAB 24/5, Treasury Memo. to the War Cabinet, G-257, 18 July 1919, Secret.

By the end of July 1919 the British government had decided to seek special negotiations with the United States on several outstanding problems. Colonel House reported to President Wilson that he had dined in London on 27 July with Viscount Haldane of Cloan and the former foreign secretary, Viscount Grey of Fallodon, 'to discuss the Government's request to Grey to become Ambassador at Washington'. Lord Curzon, then acting foreign secretary, had asked Haldane, who had been a cabinet colleague of both Grey and Lloyd George in the prewar Asquith government, to use his good offices in persuading Grey to accept the offer. Haldane told Grey and House that the three matters the government wished to settle with the United States were the naval building programme, the Irish question, and the league of nations. Grey responded that while he would 'in no circumstances' become ambassador, he would consider undertaking a special mission to Washington to discuss these three matters, 'providing the Government agreed with him about these'. In this July conversation Grey saw no difficulty in dealing with the league or the naval question, and he was mainly concerned with the government's Irish policy. Grey promised Haldane a memorandum for the government outlining his position on the naval question, which, according to House's report, was

> That in no circumstances would Great Britain build against the United States no matter how many keels we laid. However, England would hold herself free to build against any European power in any quantity that seemed to her best. On the other hand, the United States could exercise her own judgment about building without regard to Great Britain as against Japan, and they would consider it a matter of no concern to them.

Grey's position was in fact, if not in intention, quite similar to the scheme Hankey had recently proposed. The problem with both was that while the United States and Great Britain could each piously pronounce that her naval standard did not include the other, the two fleets were bound to be compared and to appear as rivals. Grey's scheme required that each nation decide that it was a matter of no moment if the other possessed a larger navy. There was no reason to expect either nation to adopt this attitude. Indeed, in Hankey's similar scheme for excluding the American navy from the official

British standard of strength it was assumed that Great Britain would nevertheless actually maintain fleet equality with the United States by the subterfuge of using another two naval powers as the ostensible standard of comparison. There was, of course, nothing to prevent the same policy of tacit competition from prevailing in Grey's scheme.

Lord Grey was profoundly influenced in his position by the British government's policy, when he had been in office before the war, of disregarding the American naval programme. Grey admitted to House, however, that his was a Liberal view, and not that of the Conservatives or of those in naval circles. In his report to President Wilson House predicted that when the government received Grey's memorandum on naval policy 'they will soften their insistence that he go to Washington'.[1]

Colonel House was wrong. Grey's memorandum did not deflect Lloyd George from enlisting his help. 'The Prime Minister urged very strongly yesterday the good I might do by going to the United States', Grey wrote to Curzon on 5 August. He was willing to go, he explained, if he could be given written instructions which he could accept as clear statements of government policy 'likely to diminish friction and strengthen cordial feeling between the two countries'. Grey then outlined the kind of policy instructions he could accept. On the naval question he emphasized, as he had previously to House, that between 1905 and 1914 the cabinet had unanimously held that under no circumstances should the government increase navy estimates to build against the United States. They had then been convinced, and Grey considered it even more evident since the war, that England could gain nothing in a war with America, while the United States could not be prevented from building, if they chose, a bigger fleet than England's. Grey therefore declared that 'Competition in navies between us and the U.S.A. would be from every point of view, disastrous'. He continued:

> The only way (but I think almost a certain way) of avoiding it is to base our next navy estimates upon a European standard and to

[1] House to Wilson, 30 July 1919, House Papers, Yale University Library. This letter is also printed in Seymour, *The Intimate Papers of Colonel House*, iv, 494–8, and in *Foreign Relations of the United States. The Paris Peace Conference 1919* (Washington, 1943), ii, 621–2.

defend them in the House of Commons by saying frankly that what we want is security, that we do not aim at purely British supremacy on the other side of the Atlantic and in the Pacific and that we leave the United States programme out of account as a rival or enemy in framing our own.

Grey was convinced that such a statement of British policy would 'put an end to a big naval programme in the United States'. On the other hand, if this policy was not adopted, and the government produced a naval programme so large that it would have to be justified in Parliament by an admission that to some extent it was based on rivalry with the United States, he predicted that America would 'go one better', and that the friction from this naval issue would affect the discussion of all other subjects at Washington. Grey insisted that the government would have to be quite clear in their naval policy, since he anticipated 'an attempt in some quarters to put the U.S. navy in the place of the German navy as the rival against which we have to build or maintain a navy'.[1]

Grey told Curzon that he had substantially presented these same views in his paper of the preceding week (presumably the paper he had promised Haldane), which the prime minister had seen and approved.[2] For his part Grey entirely accepted Lloyd George's sole reservation, that 'if such a naval policy was adopted here, there must be a response and reciprocity in the U.S.A. naval policy'. Grey added, however, that he would have to know in advance, at least approximately, the government's naval construction plans, and the total amount of the next navy estimates, since he expected to be challenged in America on some of the enormous armaments estimates figures which had appeared in newspapers.[3]

Grey therefore demanded of the government, before he would undertake the mission to Washington, not only the promise of a public statement that the United States was excluded from British naval strength standards, but also assurances (and advance information to support them) that the navy estimates

[1] Lloyd George Papers, F/12/1/35, Grey Memo., enclosure to Grey letter to Curzon, 5 Aug. 1919.
[2] Ibid. I have been unable to find Grey's earlier memorandum on naval policy in the relevant files at the P.R.O. or in the Lloyd George Papers.
[3] Ibid.

would be reduced and that construction which could be considered inspired by American rivalry would be eliminated.[1]

Grey had made his conditions quite clear, and on 6 August Curzon sent Grey's memorandum on to Lloyd George with a note stating that there was 'no difficulty about [the] Navy. . . .'[2] A week later on 13 August Bonar Law, then lord privy seal and leader of the house of commons, announced in parliament that

> Pending the appointment of a permanent Ambassador, which will be made in the early part of next year, Lord Grey of Fallodon has consented to go on a mission to Washington to deal especially with questions arising out of the Peace. . . .[3]

On 5 August, the day after he had talked with Lord Grey about his proposed American mission, Lloyd George surveyed in cabinet the government's position on a whole range of problems, mostly domestic or Irish. The prime minister's review emphasized the nation's severe financial difficulties, and at its conclusion Walter Long complained that while the admiralty had often been accused of extravagance, it was impossible to reduce naval expenditure more than was being done. The admiralty's uncertainty about future naval policy was strikingly evident in Long's following remarks. First, he promised the cabinet a memorandum showing 'the duties upon which the Navy was at present engaged', and declared that after considering this 'it would then be for the Cabinet to decide our future Naval policy'. But when Lloyd George asked Long the size in numbers of men of the United States navy, the first lord left the present duties of the royal navy behind and launched into the question of American rivalry. Claiming that the United States intended to keep up to full strength for the first time three fleets, the Atlantic, Pacific and China fleets, he offered to produce complete figures on American naval numbers for the cabinet.

Lloyd George then suggested that the cabinet could either deal in detail with the question of future defence policy itself

[1] Ibid.

[2] Lloyd George Papers, F/12/1/35, Curzon to Lloyd George, 6 Aug. 1919, Confidential. Grey lunched with Lloyd George on 7 August and confirmed their understanding. (House Diary, 7 Aug. 1919, House Papers, Yale University Library.)   [3] *H.C. deb.*, 119, c. 1288 (13 Aug. 1919).

or set up the committee of imperial defence again, to consider and report to the war cabinet on the service departments' proposed policies. It was first necessary, the prime minister continued, to determine the length of time policy should cover; not 20 years, in his opinion, but perhaps ten or five years might be appropriate. He asked for war office and admiralty advice on this question and Winston Churchill suggested that the war office, admiralty and air ministry should each prepare memoranda showing 'the particular responsibilities which it was anticipated they might have to meet during the next five or ten years'. The cabinet decided that the war office, admiralty and India office should provide this information on defence responsibilities for the next five or ten years, and the admiralty was also asked to report on the present and future strength of the American navy.[1]

The admiralty's response to these requests was prompt. On 8 August Walter Long sent Lloyd George figures on the size of the American navy.[2] Four days later on 12 August the admiralty board produced a new memorandum on 'Post-War Naval Policy', which also included appendices detailing the strength of the United States and Japanese navies. This second paper was circulated to the cabinet on 13 August, the same day that the government announced Lord Grey's forthcoming mission to Washington.[3] It seems clear from the paper's contents, however, that the admiralty was quite ignorant of the commitments on future naval policy which Lloyd George had already made to Lord Grey. The admiralty's position was revealed in the four questions the paper posed to the cabinet for decision before a definite naval programme for 1920–1921 could be drawn up. These questions, the first lord wrote, involved the government's general policy, especially in regard to foreign relations, and in fact all four questions principally concerned Great Britain's attitude towards American naval policy.

[1] CAB 23/15, W.C. 606A, 5 Aug. 1919, Secret, ('A' Minutes).
[2] Lloyd George Papers, F/33/2/69, Long to Lloyd George, 8 Aug. 1919, enclosure: 'Note on strength & distribution of the U.S. Navy'.
[3] CAB 24/86, Admiralty Memo. to the War Cabinet, 'Post-War Naval Policy', G.T. 7975, 12 Aug. 1919, Secret. ADM 116/1774, Admiralty letter of transmittal of the above, to Hankey (enclosing 40 copies), 13 Aug. 1919.

The memorandum first asked:

> What is the policy of the Government as regards the supremacy of the seas—(a) over the United States of America? (b) over any probable combination?

The paper declared that hitherto in 300 years of British naval supremacy the question had been simply to decide how many and which powers were to be regarded as potential enemies, over whom Great Britain ought to have supremacy. There had never been any dispute, the first lord contended, '... that no one Power could be permitted to surpass us in Naval strength'. The discussion here of naval supremacy amply demonstrated that the admiralty considered this achieved so long as Great Britain maintained in home waters the world's most powerful capital ship fleet.

As for potential enemies, the first lord was evasive. He admitted that none of the European powers posed a naval threat, and that Japan too could be put aside for the present. The United States, Long stated, possessed 'the only Navy for which we need have regard, and in respect of which we desire a decision of the Government.' Having pointed to the magnitude of American postwar naval expansion Long then admitted that it seemed unlikely that the United States would so alter her traditional policy as to become an aggressive power. Yet although he refused to identify the United States explicitly as a potential naval enemy the first lord declared that if she continued to maintain such a large fleet even a moderate reduction in the admiralty's capital ship proposals would place England 'in a position of manifest inferiority'. Reminding the cabinet of the strength of feeling in Great Britain and the empire 'in favour of the maintenance of our sea supremacy', he concluded that the government would have to decide 'whether . . . to maintain the supremacy which we have held for so long'.

The admiralty's second question concerned Great Britain's attitude towards the league of nations and disarmament. Long suggested that to maintain the principle of mutual reduction Great Britain should invite the United States to join her in calling upon all the allied powers to reduce armaments under the provisions of the league covenant. In this way Long thought it would emerge

> . . . whether the object of the U.S.A. in projecting this big Fleet [is]

(as some people think) merely to have a powerful weapon with which to obtain a general reduction of Armaments, or whether it is really their intention to force us to the alternatives of either competing with or accepting numerical inferiority to them.

Long's assessment of the American motives does not seem in doubt. In any event, one can assume that it was neither his faith in the league nor his hope for early general disarmament which led him to suggest that Great Britain should avoid any reduction of her navy independent of the league.

The third question posed to the cabinet concerned the resumption of the prewar policy of 'showing the flag' in foreign waters, which the first lord contended had only been abandoned before the war because of the preoccupation with the danger of Germany across the North Sea. Reports to the admiralty convinced him that the white ensign should again be seen all over the world, and this required a considerable number of light cruisers. 'There is every indication', he concluded,

> that the U.S.A. and Japan are both well aware of the advantages which flow from the presence of their ships in foreign waters, and that they are doing all that they can to push their trade and their general interests, by sending their ships to stations where prior to 1904 we had the monopoly.

Finally, Long came to the admiralty's fourth question—'the time during which we may reckon on immunity from war with a great Power or combination of small powers . . . and therefore a reduction in our naval preponderance'. Weighing the arguments for and against a period of either five or ten years, Long noted that 'if we could fix upon the longer period, it would undoubtedly enable us to make more effective reductions at present'. He concluded, however, that since accurate information on the projected strength of the American and Japanese navies was available only for the shorter period of five years, the admiralty view was that the question of adopting the longer ten year period would depend upon whether the league of nations 'makes an auspicious beginning'.[1]

Although this admiralty memorandum clearly revealed the board's position on these pressing questions, it was not, as it has sometimes been supposed, this memorandum which moved Lloyd George towards a new formulation of naval policy. This

[1] Ibid.

new policy began to take shape two days before the admiralty submitted this memorandum to the cabinet office, when on 11 August Bonar Law, Austen Chamberlain, and Lord Milner met with Lloyd George in his room at the house of commons as the 'Cabinet Committee on Finance'. The secretary to the cabinet, Sir Maurice Hankey, and his assistant, Thomas Jones, were also present at this second meeting of the newly-formed finance committee. Taking up 'the method of tackling the cutting down of expenditure and particularly of naval, military and air expenditure', the committee agreed that neither treasury nor departmental financial experts could produce results unless the government first laid down policy. The committee then produced a wealth of proposals for defence policy decisions, most of which were adopted by the government at the meeting of the war cabinet later that week, on 15 August.

In the discussion of naval expenditure it was immediately suggested that 'the first steps in economy would be to stop all new construction and to cut down the number of ships in commission at least to the pre-war standard'. It was pointed out, however, that the effect on British public opinion might be serious if the United States kept a larger fleet in actual commission than the British empire, and the first lord's report that the United States intended to keep all the larger fleet units in commission was noted. This brought the suggestion that 'the U.S. Government might be approached with a view to an arrangement for a reduction of the number of ships maintained in commission'. All of these proposals seemed tailored to support the promises made to Lord Grey, but the projected mission to Washington is not mentioned in the minutes of this meeting. Of the four ministers present, however, Lloyd George naturally knew of it, and Bonar Law was to announce the mission just two days later in the house of commons. It seems likely that Chamberlain and Milner also knew of the mission, and it is almost impossible to believe that anything could have been kept secret from the ubiquitous Hankey.

The committee later examined the last prewar army and navy estimates to get '. . . a very rough calculation of the cost under present conditions of an army and navy of the same size as before the war'. After taking into account several new postwar factors, the committee agreed that 'it ought to be possible to frame satisfactory estimates for the forthcoming year at figures roundabout the following:

Army and Air	£75 millions	
Navy	£60 millions	
Total	£135 millions	

After reaching these figures the committee then produced what the minutes called 'Principles on which our naval, military and air estimates should be based'. Hankey, who was responsible for the minutes, had of course recommended that such principles be formulated, in his 17 July memorandum to Lloyd George. The fighting services were to be asked 'to draw up fresh estimates on some such bases as the following:

(1) They should proceed on the assumption that no great war is to be anticipated within the next ten years. . . .

(2) The Admiralty, War Office and Air Ministry should assume that their principal responsibility is the provision of sufficient forces to keep order in the United Kingdom, India, and all British (other than self-governing) territory.

The first of these principles is, of course, the original statement of the famous 'ten year rule'. The second principle apparently accepted Walter Long's endorsement of the royal navy as 'the cheapest and most efficient police force that the Empire can possess', but if it had been adopted by the cabinet (and it was not) it would have left Long with very little fleet except for his flag-showing light cruisers.[1]

The finance committee concluded its discussion of naval and military expenditure by agreeing that the prime minister should discuss the question in the first instance with the first lord of the admiralty and the secretary of state for war.[2]

If Lloyd George did in fact discuss with the first lord the proceedings of this finance committee meeting before the cabinet met on Friday morning 15 August, the conversation, like Long's 12 August memorandum, can have had little effect on the cabinet's adoption of the committee's proposals. When Lloyd George met the cabinet that morning at 10 Downing Street, Bonar Law and Austen Chamberlain who had been at the finance committee meeting were present, along with George

---

[1] See pages 196 and 209 above for Long's comments on 'showing the flag'.

[2] CAB 27/71, Finance Committee, 2nd Minutes, 11 Aug. 1919, Secret.

Barnes and Sir Eric Geddes. In addition to these members of
the war cabinet a large number of other ministers, including the
first lord and war secretary, and officials were also present.
Winston Churchill brought an entourage of four senior civilian
and military officials, including the chief of the imperial general
staff, Field Marshal Sir Henry Wilson. Walter Long attended
the meeting alone.

The only business taken up at this meeting was 'Naval,
Military and Air Estimates', and the discussion was initiated
by two memoranda on shipbuilding, from the minister of
shipping and the first lord, which were the only documents
before the cabinet. These papers were relevant to only one of
the decisions of this meeting, but the admiralty's very pertinent
12 August memorandum was not placed before the cabinet.[1]

Of the seven decisions announced at this notable cabinet
session as bases for new admiralty, war office and air ministry
estimates, four were of special concern to the admiralty. All
four had been agreed to, in substantially the same form, by the
finance committee at its meeting the beginning of the same week.
For the admiralty (and for British defence policy in general)
the most far-reaching decision was the so-called 'ten year rule',
which, in its final form, instructed the service departments to
assume

> for framing revised Estimates, that the British Empire will not be
> engaged in any great war during the next ten years, and that no
> Expeditionary Force is required for this purpose.

This decision was not unexpected, since the question had been
raised at the 5 August cabinet meeting. Furthermore, the
admiralty had gone on record as desiring to know how long the
navy could count on 'immunity from war', and had stated only
a qualified preference for a five rather than ten year period.[2]

For the admiralty the most controversial—and unwelcome—
conclusion to emerge from this cabinet meeting was the
admonition that

> No alteration should be made, without Cabinet authority, in the
> pre-war standard governing the size of the Navy.

[1] CAB 23/15, W.C. 616A, 15 Aug. 1919, Secret, ('A' Minutes). The two
documents before the cabinet were a note by the minister of shipping
(CAB 24/86, G.T. 7899, 5 Aug. 1919), and the admiralty's reply (CAB
24/86, G.T. 7959, 11 Aug. 1919).   [2] See above, page 209.

The admiralty was also directed to undertake no new naval construction, to make every effort to stop work on vessels of no mercantile value, and to aim, in framing new estimates, at a maximum figure of £60 million.[1]

The minutes of this cabinet meeting simply list the seven conclusions, without any account of the discussion which may have occurred at the meeting. Thus there is no record of any discussion at this meeting either of the general desirability of reaching a naval agreement with the United States, or specifically of the prospective mission of Lord Grey to Washington, with such an agreement as one of its objectives. It is evident, however, that all the cabinet's decisions affecting navy estimates —with the exception of the ten year rule—were necessary for Lloyd George to honour his commitments on future naval policy to Lord Grey. In any event, it seems clear that Lord Grey's special mission to the United States in the autumn of 1919 was not a result, as often assumed, but rather an important and immediate cause of the government's new naval policy adopted in mid-August 1919.

The following Monday, 18 August 1919, the first lord explained to the admiralty board the implications for the navy of the cabinet's momentous decisions the previous Friday. The ten year rule was apparently accepted with equanimity, since it provoked neither discussion nor dissent at this meeting. Nevertheless, this decision alone provided the logical justification for the other decisions. If a major war was to be excluded as a possibility for at least ten years then there could be no potential enemy, in any immediate sense, to support an admiralty case against the new budget limit, the stopping of new construction, and the reduced standard of naval strength. The only comment on the ten year rule at this meeting, however, was the observation that 'on the assumption of ten years' peace it was unlikely that any new programme [of construction] would be required for another six years'.

As for the cabinet's ambiguous limitation of the navy's size to the 'pre-war standard', the first lord explained that this 'was intended to prevent the inclusion of comparisons with the United States, the Prime Minister having stated that the United States had always been omitted in Pre-War Estimates'.

[1] CAB 23/15, W.C. 616A, 15 Aug. 1919, Secret, ('A' Minutes).

This interpretation of the cabinet's ruling conformed to Lord Grey's terms, but the actual exclusion of the United States from calculations of British naval strength proved not only unacceptable but inconceivable for the admiralty.

At this meeting the admiralty board agreed that a 'considered statement' should be prepared to show the cabinet not only the action the admiralty proposed to take to conform—'so far as possible'—to these new rulings, but also the consequences of the cabinet's decisions, for example, 'in the support which the Fleet will be able to give to diplomatic action.'[1]

In fact the cabinet's decisions to reduce the strength and standard of the navy served to support the diplomatic action Lord Grey was to undertake in his mission to Washington. On 20 August the war cabinet approved the terms of the formal letter of instruction to be sent to Lord Grey upon his appointment to the Washington embassy.[2] Lord Curzon, in transmitting the official letter of appointment and instruction to Grey on 9 September, noted in an accompanying personal letter that he had

> with the consent of the Admiralty, introduced a passage about Naval Estimates and construction which goes further than your original draft, and as far as we discussed at our last meeting.[3]

Under the heading 'Armaments' the government's letter of instruction first set out the substance of Grey's own interpretation of prewar British policy as excluding rivalry with the United States, and then declared that this was still the policy of his majesty's government. The letter further promised that 'The strength of the British Navy next year will be based upon a standard of security that does not take account of the United States Navy as a possible enemy'. While the exact figure for the 1920–1921 navy estimates could not yet be fixed,

> it is confidently hoped to reduce ... [them] ... to a figure which, having regard to the difference in value in money, is relatively less than that for 1914–1915. It is contemplated that the number of capital ships in full commission will be materially reduced below the pre-war figure. No new construction will be undertaken.

[1] ADM 167/56, Board Minute No. 924, 18 Aug. 1919, Secret.
[2] CAB 23/12, W.C. 619(4), 20 Aug. 1919, Secret.
[3] F.O. 800/158, (Curzon Papers), Curzon to Grey, 9 Sept. 1919; enclosure: formal instructions, Curzon to Grey, 9 Sept. 1919.

These were the assurances on the naval question which Grey had demanded, and the instructions continued to promise the publicity which Grey considered essential for his success. The new navy estimates, the letter declared, would be 'fully explained in the House of Commons early in the Autumn Session this year. . . .' Lloyd George's reservation, the necessity for 'response and reciprocity' in American naval policy, appeared in the letter's concluding statement on this subject:

> . . . if, as His Majesty's Government confidently expect, the policy they intend to adopt and explain meets with a similar response in the naval policy of the United States Government, this policy will, His Majesty's Government believe, continue from year to year to the mutual satisfaction of both countries and the advantage of the world.[1]

By the time Lord Grey set out for Washington in the latter part of September 1919 the naval staff had calculated the composition of the postwar fleet on the assumption 'that for the present the security of the country will be provided for if the number of Capital Ships in commission and reserve is equal to those of the United States Navy'. At their 22 September meeting, however, the admiralty board noted that

> . . . if the Fleet were reduced to this extent, it must be clearly understood that the British Empire had relinquished the supremacy of the sea. We should remain easily supreme in European Waters, but as regards the seas as a whole the supremacy would be shared with the United States.

Furthermore it was pointed out that Great Britain's naval equality with the United States would rapidly decline to a position of inferiority in the absence of new British construction while the American programme continued. Considerations of strategic security played virtually no role in the admiralty's reluctance to accept this kind of declining equality with the American navy, for it was candidly admitted that 'Our Naval strength would . . . be sufficient to secure us against *attack* by the United States or any other Power for some years to come.' In any event the discussion at this board meeting made it patently clear that the admiralty had in no way excluded the

[1] Ibid. (formal instructions) (Both Curzon's personal letter and the formal instructions are also in D.B.F.P., *1919–1939*, 1st ser. v, No. 360).

United States from its strength calculations; the arguments were rather directed at establishing the dangerous consequences of even naval equality with the United States on the 'Empire's prestige and its diplomatic and commercial interests'. The board decided that a memorandum should be prepared for the war cabinet 'setting forth clearly what is involved and urging that the position should be clearly explained to Parliament and to the Empire. . . .'[1]

Thus both Lord Grey and the admiralty urged the government to explain its new naval policy fully and frankly in parliament. Lord Grey hoped that a government pronouncement in parliament that the United States was now excluded from the royal navy's new postwar standard of strength would help persuade the American government to reduce its naval building programme. Grey genuinely wanted the government to speak out. For the admiralty, however, the demand that the government explain its new policy on naval strength and standards to parliament and empire was a challenge. The admiralty trusted that the government would shrink back from admitting that it had sanctioned the surrender of traditional British naval supremacy to the United States. As it turned out the admiralty was right, for Lloyd George's government never did fulfill the promise of a full explanation in parliament of the new naval policy, which it had given Grey in September.

It took the naval staff a month to produce the proposed cabinet memorandum, which was discussed and approved at the admiralty board's 23 October meeting. This memorandum incorporated, with only slight changes, the board minute of 22 September with its warning of the imminent passing of British sea supremacy if equality with the United States were accepted. Indeed this memorandum rehearsed almost the entire repertoire of admiralty arguments against the surrender of British naval supremacy which were used again and again from this time through the Washington Conference some two years later. It was, however, easier to advocate the retention of naval supremacy than to define what it meant in the world of 1919. In this October memorandum the naval staff characteristically assumed that supremacy was essentially a question

[1] ADM 167/56, Board Minute No. 939, 22 Sept. 1919, Secret.

of capital ship strength, or of main fleet pre-eminence, without reference to its possible use or purpose. While an enormous naval superiority would obviously be necessary to defeat the United States in a naval war in American waters, it was generally conceded, even in this paper, that for a defensive war against the United States in British home waters equality in main fleet strength would suffice.

Strategic requirements for British security against the United States continued, however, to be considered of less importance, or relevance, than other more subjective factors. 'Already the mere rumour of the passing of our sea-supremacy has called forth emphatic protests from other parts of the Empire,' the paper declared, 'and it will . . . have important effects on our prestige and our diplomatic and commercial interests.'

It should be noted that the admiralty did not accuse the United States of being unjustifiably threatening or belligerent in her naval aspirations. Indeed, the admiralty considered that in their determination to have a navy 'second to none' the Americans had grasped 'the truth that a Navy, to be an effective weapon, should be at least equal in strength to the possible antagonist. . . .'

This statement might logically seem to imply that an Anglo-American all-out naval building race could only be avoided if Great Britain were willing to allow the United States to achieve the naval equality which she sought, and which sound naval doctrine prescribed. The admiralty warned, however, that while American naval equality might have been acceptable in prewar conditions, it was not in the postwar world, in the light of the new American merchant marine competition for the world carrying trade. 'They propose to protect that trade with a strong Navy,' the admiralty explained, 'and the fact cannot be ignored that conflict of interests may arise with the United States in the same way as with other Powers in our history.'

In spite of these warnings the admiralty steadfastly refused to suggest that these conflicts would involve war between the United States and the British empire. 'Having acquired by peaceful means the supremacy of the sea', the memorandum declared,

their subsequent victories are probably destined to be commercial and diplomatic, but the effect of these upon our trade and Empire may be no less serious on this account.

The board stated their unquestionable conviction that Great Britain owed her leading position among nations to her long-maintained pre-eminence upon the sea, and added that 'this pre-eminence cannot be relinquished without her . . . position being profoundly affected, with all that that position involves in respect of prestige, authority, and commercial advantage.' The board of admiralty's particular responsibility for the empire's safety and welfare impelled them, the memorandum concluded,

> to urge that the sea supremacy, which is vital to us, should not be sacrificed, and that if the United States cannot be induced to abandon or modify their 1916 Programme . . . provision should be made to undertake the construction required to counterbalance it. . . .[1]

By the time of their 24 October memorandum the admiralty was well aware that Lord Grey had gone the previous month to Washington to seek, among other things, by diplomatic means to induce the United States to abandon or modify her naval building programme. Grey's diplomatic inducement for the United States, however, was supposed to be the government's announcement of its decision to exclude the United States from British naval strength calculations. The government had still made no pronouncement, while the admiralty had demonstrated their inability to conceive of any other standard for British naval strength than superiority over the United States, as the world's second naval power. Yet both government and admiralty apparently nourished hopes that Lord Grey might somehow be able to convince the United States that Great Britain should retain her world naval preponderance unchallenged by American expansion.

When Lord Grey got to Washington on 27 September 1919 he immediately found that the illness of President Wilson made negotiations on any question exceedingly unlikely. On 5 October he wrote to the prime minister that while the special reason for his coming to Washington had been Lloyd George's belief that he could help Anglo-American relations by dealing personally with President Wilson, it now seemed improbable that he would ever see the president or that the president would

[1] ADM 167/56, Board Minute No. 1004, Appendix I, 'Naval Policy and Expenditure', 23 Oct. 1919, Secret. This memo. was circulated, on 25 Oct., only to the cabinet finance committee. (ADM 116/1774.)

ever take up public business again during the remainder of his term. 'Within a week, therefore, of my arrival,' Grey wrote, 'the reason for my coming has disappeared. For some time, with no one to take the place of the President, there will be chaos in American policy.'[1]

Grey stayed on, but he never succeeded in seeing the president, and we have the unfriendly testimony of Josephus Daniels, Wilson's secretary of the navy, that Grey never sought to discuss the naval building programme.[2] Yet by the latter part of November 1919 reports reached England which indicated that the United States was reducing her postwar navy. On 24 November the finance committee noted reports that the American navy 'had been demobilised to a far greater extent than was generally supposed'. The finance committee agreed that while the United States fleet was not the standard by which the British fleet was to be reckoned, 'a big demobilisation of the United States Fleet would not be without influence on our own measures'. The committee therefore agreed to telegraph to Lord Grey for official information on American demobilization and fleet statistics. The first lord, Walter Long, was present at this meeting, and he approved the telegram which Lloyd George sent to Grey the next day, 25 November 1919.[3] It was perhaps the first lord's influence which widened the scope of the telegram's queries, and gave them a sharper, more suspicious character. In this telegram Lloyd George told Grey that the 'fullest possible information' on United States naval policy was urgently required for the cabinet's consideration of navy estimates. 'We have no desire to enter into naval competition with United States', he continued, 'but cannot afford to ignore what they are doing.' Unofficial reports of great reductions in United States naval personnel, rumours of pay increases to retain men and obtain recruits, and the apparent intention of the United States to proceed with the full 1916 building programme, all caused concern. Lloyd George therefore asked Grey to get 'authoritative official information' on the existing

[1] Lloyd George Papers, F/60/3/7, Grey to Lloyd George, 5 Oct. 1919, Private.

[2] Josephus Daniels, *The Wilson Era, 1917–1923*, 455.

[3] CAB 27/71, Finance Committee, 16th Minutes, 24 Nov. 1a19, Secret. This meeting was devoted solely to naval affairs.

numbers and proposed eventual establishments of the United States navy in personnel, and in ships in commission and in reserve.[1]

As the prime minister had requested, Lord Grey telegraphed the results of his inquiries on these matters immediately, on the next day, 26 November. His reply showed that the existing strength of 107,400 officers and men, compared with the proposed establishment of 150,000, left the American navy seriously undermanned. Having listed the ships in commission and reserve, Grey further noted that because of the shortage in personnel the majority of the American ships had only reduced crews on board at that time.

Grey then commented on the inherent difficulties in determining the lines of American naval policy:

> It is undesirable to make official enquiries of United States administration as to their . . . [prospective] naval expenditure for (1) They would probably decline further information. (2) Information if given would be (?unreliable) as friction between administration and Congress and illness of President prevent any (?settled) policy in any Government Department.[2]

Grey's assessment of the Washington situation was sound, and he concluded his telegram with his own recommendation on the direction British naval policy should take in the existing circumstances:

> I am convinced that best course for us is to produce moderate navy estimates as stated to me in London in September in expectation that example set by us will be followed here. Attempt to strike a bargain with Americans in advance about navy estimates will probably have contrary effect and stimulate agitation for biggest in the world navy.

In any event, he reassured the prime minister, Great Britain had the situation in hand for the moment, since the United States navy could not be raised from its existing condition to a really efficient state for at least a year.[3]

---

[1] F.O. 371/4249, telegram, (unnumbered), Curzon (for Lloyd George) to Grey, A501/501/45, 25 Nov. 1919. (Also in DBFP, *1919–1939*, 1st ser., v, No. 411.)

[2] F.O. 371/4249, telegram, (unnumbered), Grey to Curzon (for Lloyd George), A505/501/45, 26 Nov. 1919. (Also in DBFP, 1st. ser., v, No. 412.)

[3] Ibid.

Yet when Grey's telegram was received at the foreign office 27 November the foreign secretary, Lord Curzon, minuted on it:

> It was a part of Lord Grey's instructions that if we reduced, the Americans should be asked & should promise to do the same. He took out our pledge and now we are to forego theirs.[1]

In spite of Curzon's indignation Grey's advice was well-founded. He obviously could not negotiate an Anglo-American agreement while a leaderless Democratic administration quarrelled with a Republican congress—and elections were yet a year ahead. The failure of Grey's mission, however, left Lloyd George without the assurance of American naval reductions which would help make his own programme of retrenchment politically feasible. He was well aware that the government's secret decisions in August 1919 on naval policy could be attacked—and not only by the admiralty—as the surrender of England's traditional naval supremacy to the United States.

Lloyd George proved unwilling to take a clear position either for drastic naval economy, if it meant admitting that the United States navy would surpass the royal navy, or for British naval supremacy, if this meant undertaking an expensive naval building race with the United States. He therefore attempted, for almost two years, to support both these contradictory policies simultaneously, or alternatively. Thus the reassessment of British naval policy in the second half of 1919 produced not one new policy, but two competing and largely incompatible policies. The result was, on the one hand, a gradual and reluctant adoption—or admission—of a naval one power standard for capital ship equality with the United States; and, on the other hand, a general continuation of the restrictions on naval planning and expenditure—such as the ten year rule—imposed on the admiralty at the 15 August 1919 cabinet meeting. This ambidextrous policy continued, with increasingly apparent inconsistency, as the question of the future of the Anglo-Japanese alliance promoted Anglo-American suspicion and rivalry in the next two years. The problem of the Pacific and far east eventually provided the occasion for Great Britain to reconcile its two contradictory naval policies into one new

[1] Ibid. Curzon minute, 27 Nov. 1919.

policy. Although the first attempt for an Anglo-American naval agreement had failed in the autumn of 1919 the vastly more ambitious effort in the autumn and winter of 1921–1922 succeeded, not only in resolving far eastern differences, but in establishing on the basis of mutual reductions naval parity in capital ships between the United States and Great Britain.

The George Washington University,
Washington, D.C.

J. KENNETH McDONALD

VIII

LLOYD GEORGE'S STAGE ARMY: THE COALITION LIBERALS, 1918–22

KENNETH O. MORGAN

KENNETH O. MORGAN

Age 36

Oriel College, Oxford B.A., M.A., D.Phil.
Currently Fellow and Praelector in Modern
History and Politics, The Queen's College,
Oxford

LLOYD GEORGE'S STAGE ARMY:
THE COALITION LIBERALS,
1918–22

LLOYD GEORGE's Coalition Liberals are the most unloved of
political parties. Ever since the 'coupon' election of December
1918 they have been treated as universal whipping boys. Even
at the time they won little enough respect. They were the butt
of their Unionist allies. J. C. C. Davidson derided them as
Lloyd George's 'stage army—the same faces at every show—
a façade of gilded or gold bricks with no real fabric behind it'.[1]
The Asquithians and Labour, naturally enough, were vehement
in their abuse of 'the conscript ranks on the Coalition benches'.
Subsequently, the 'Coalie Libs' have suffered a consistently
dismal reputation. Trevor Wilson's otherwise admirable
volume is unbalanced by his antipathy towards them as 'a kept
party'.[2] They have failed even to inspire the affection reserved
for good losers. From the outset, they were ineradicably tainted
with the 'coupon'. Thereafter they were saddled with the
damned inheritance of the Lloyd George fund. Not once have
they been rehabilitated. Somehow it seems appropriate that,
with the sole exception of H. A. L. Fisher's slight volume, the
Coalition Liberal voice has been silent among the memoirs of
domestic politics in the post-war period. Here again, the
Asquithians hold the field triumphant.

The bad press to which the Coalition Liberals have been
subjected is not in any way surprising. They contributed to it
themselves. They complained that their principles were obscure
and their function ambiguous. If they stood anywhere in
politics, it was presumably in the middle ground, standing in
Lloyd George's own vague phrase 'between the reactionary and
the revolutionary'.[3] But the limits and the nature of that

---

[1] 'David' (J. C. C. Davidson) to Bonar Law, 13 Jan. 1922 (Bonar Law
Papers, 107/2/2a).

[2] Trevor Wilson, *Downfall of the Liberal Party, 1914–1935* (1966), 237.

[3] *Lloyd George Liberal Magazine* (October 1920), p. 12.

mysterious terrain and how it differed from that occupied by other political factions were never made clear. They pleaded with their leader to clarify their identity for them. The vice-president of the Manchester Reform Club, J. Walter Robson, complained in 1920 that 'Coalition Liberalism is a difficult thing to define . . . Without any definition of Coalition Liberal principles and policy the party is "in the air" '. He protested that they represented 'not a principle but merely a form of support for the government'.[1] But the appeal was in vain. When the government fell from power two years later, their quest for an identity remained unfulfilled.

Even so, the Coalition Liberals are worth closer and more dispassionate examination than they have hitherto received. After all, they included some impressive and creative personalities—Herbert Fisher, Edwin Montagu and Alfred Mond, Christopher Addison, Gordon Hewart and Hilton Young, and of course, Winston Churchill. These were hardly a negligible band of supporting players, and their influence on post-war policy was considerable. More crucial still was their role in the fluid party political scene. Without their support, Lloyd George could never have become premier at all, nor could he have made the transition to his peacetime premiership after 1918. His Liberal supporters were a vital element in a political revolution which was to shape the character of British politics for a generation to come. They left a permanent stamp on the Liberal Party in its final agonizing phase. Perhaps the time has come, therefore, to re-examine the Coalition Liberal idea. Perhaps 'Lloyd George's stage army' is after all too serious to be left to its generals.

The Coalition Liberals were conceived during the negotiations that led to the 1918 'coupon election'. Here were their origins and they never outgrew them. The party did not exist prior to the autumn of 1918. All Lloyd George had behind him on the Liberal side was an outgrowth of perhaps forty members from Sir Frederick Cawley's 'Liberal War Committee', together with other shifting groups of supporters. The government's Liberal whip, Freddie Guest, advised against forming a distinct Lloyd Georgeite Liberal Party at the end of 1917. Lloyd George's

---

[1] Annual Report of the Coalition Liberal Organization, 1920 (Lloyd George Papers, F/168/2/16), 24.

Liberal supporters in parliament and in the country still had hopes of reunion: their sympathies with the fallen Asquith were still very pronounced. In any event, the official Liberal machine under Gulland was too powerful to be challenged.[1] As a result, in a crisis like the Maurice debate on 9 May 1918 the exact strength of the Lloyd George Liberal element in parliament was uncertain and its constituency organization non-existent.

However, in July and August 1918 a new party came into being. As a result of secret negotiations between Guest and Bonar Law, 150 Liberals were guaranteed Coalition backing in the event of a post-war election.[2] Lloyd George was closely involved in these discussions: it was apparently he who insisted on the magic number of 150, a remarkably generous allocation which the Unionists accepted with great reluctance.[3] In the ensuing general election after the armistice, the terms of the agreement were carried out with an astonishing lack of friction. About 150 Liberal candidates, of varied background and mixed voting record, were given the 'coupon' of Coalition endorsement. According to Guest's own tally, 129 of them were returned, while other recruits after the election swelled their numbers to 136.[4] The electoral arrangements were steam-rollered through by Lloyd George and Bonar Law. Even a local Unionist potentate like Salvidge in Liverpool was coerced into accepting a Liberal candidate for the traditionally Unionist Fairfield division.[5] Only in very rare cases did local Unionists refuse to give way to Central Office pressure. The most striking was Swansea West where a local editor fought, and almost defeated, Sir Alfred Mond. Swansea Unionists could hardly claim that Mond was not a supporter of the government since he had been a member of it since December 1916. However, racial prejudice was overwhelming against a 'Teuton' with Jewish ancestry and

[1] F. Guest to Lloyd George, 3 Dec. 1917 (ibid., F/168/2/3).

[2] Guest to Lloyd George, 20 July 1918 (ibid., F/21/2/28).

[3] Sir George Younger to J. C. C. Davidson, 2 Dec. 1918 (Bonar Law Papers, 95/4).

[4] Guest to Lloyd George, 30 Dec. 1918 (Lloyd George Papers, F/21/2/56). Estimates of the number of Liberals receiving the Coalition whip after 1918 were given annually in the *Liberal Year Book*.

[5] Archibald Salvidge to Bonar Law, 22 November 1918 (Bonar Law Papers, 95/4).

with 'not one drop of British blood in his veins'.[1] But almost everywhere else the 'coupon' arrangements were put through with comparative ease.

However, the way in which the election had been conceived left a legacy of resentment between the two main Coalition groups. They had won the election in parallel rather than in alliance. They remained separate parties still, with only Lloyd George's personal leadership as a precarious bond of union. Unionists were bitter at the large Liberal representation which Lloyd George had exacted as his price for the bargain. The Coalition Liberals, for their part, were hardly less resentful. They felt that they had been absurdly generous in handing over 41 Liberal seats to the Unionists, especially in 'such typically Liberal centres as Manchester'.[2] Their grievances continued to rankle during the two years ahead. Against this background of mutual suspicion, the two main Coalition parties faced the unknown hazards of the post-war world.

One undeniable element, however, was the important role of the Coalition Liberals in the 'coupon election'. Their eventual tally of 136 seats was a formidable haul when set against the shattered remnant of 57 Labour members and barely 20 Independent Liberals. They had polled almost 1,400,000 votes. Further, the Coalition's election manifesto had carried clear Liberal overtones. It had been vital to Lloyd George's designs that he win over substantial Liberal backing before the general election. This was largely ensured at a meeting with his leading Liberal colleagues, Churchill, Fisher, Addison, Hewart, Munro, Guest and Montagu, on 6 November. These ministers had few illusions about the split that they were causing in their own party. Montagu wrote in a private memorandum: 'My own belief is that he (Ll.G.) has already made his agreement with the Conservatives. I wish he had said so, it would have been franker'.[3] But none of the Liberal ministers displayed any eagerness to obtain this information. After all, their govern-

[1] The Bonar Law Papers, contain a good deal of material on Mond's candidature in Swansea West. There is an admirable account of Mond's career in G. M. Bayliss, 'The Outsider: Aspects of the Political Career of Sir Alfred Mond, First Lord Melchett' (Ph.D. thesis, University of Wales, 1969). Cf. Frances Lloyd-George, *The Years That Are Past* (1967), 142–3.

[2] Guest to Lloyd George, 23 Dec. 1920 (Lloyd George Papers, F/22/2/24).

[3] S. D. Waley, *Edwin Montagu* (1964), 184–5.

ment's policy had now a clear Liberal emphasis in the three major areas on which the discussions between Lloyd George and Bonar Law had concentrated. In commercial policy, while there would be limited protection of key industries and the prevention of the unfair 'dumping' of foreign imports, the main outlines of free trade would be upheld. Ireland was promised home rule, although without the coercion of Ulster. And the Welsh Church would indeed be disestablished, with readjustment of the terms of disendowment. Elsewhere too, the Liberal ministers had received clear guarantees. Fisher was given a pledge about educational reform, Churchill promised that a peacetime cabinet would be restored, Montagu assured that Indian policy would proceed on Liberal lines. Fisher himself drafted the Coalition manifesto (later amended by J. C. C. Davidson). The winning over of the Liberal ministers was consolidated on 12 November when Lloyd George won the enthusiastic and unanimous endorsement of a large gathering of over a hundred Liberal backbenchers. During the subsequent election campaign, even in the occasional bouts of 'hang the Kaiser' hysteria to which all parties made some contribution, the old Liberal ideals were far from muted. On the contrary, the election returns seemed to confirm that, in the transition from war to peace, the historical continuity of the Liberal tradition would be fully sustained.

The character of the Coalition Liberals in the peace-time parliament was clear from the outset. To a unique extent, they were a ministerial party, rather than a parliamentary one. Still less were they based on the constituencies. While over 130 Coalition Liberals sat in the legislature, it was in the executive that their essential strength lay. For the Coalition Liberals at least, the war had never ended: politics were still being run from the front benches. In the post-war government, the Liberals had a remarkably strong representation. The reconstituted cabinet of October 1919 gave them seven members, quite apart from the Prime Minister who contrived to be a minister of all departments himself. They included Edward Shortt at the Home Office, Ronald Munro at the Scottish Office and Edwin Montagu at the India Office. Later they were to be joined by Hamar Greenwood (who succeeded Ian Macpherson) at the Irish Office, and by Dr. T. J. Macnamara

at the Ministry of Labour in 1920, and by Sir Alfred Mond at
the Ministry of Health and Gordon Hewart as Attorney-General
in 1921. These Liberal ministers were not, in general, men of
great executive experience—but, then, Lloyd George much
preferred to have 'good counsellors' rather than 'first class
statesmen' around him.[1] In addition, the Liberals were also a
target for anti-semitic abuse: with a Montagu and Mond, as
well as an Isaacs in Washington and a Samuel in Palestine
(the last admittedly an Asquithian), there was ready fuel for
die-hard 'patriots' still mindful of the irregularities of the
Marconi affair. Nevertheless, these Liberal ministers were more
than adequate in office. Only one could plausibly arouse criticism on grounds of incompetence—Christopher Addison, the
controversial Minister of Health and Housing until April 1921.
Addison's housing schemes soon showed signs of being disas-
trously inflationary in cost and Lloyd George eventually lost
patience with him. Addison, however, was valuable in other
ways. It was he who had estimated Lloyd George's parliamentary
following among the backbench Liberals in the critical months
of April-December 1916. He remained the only one of the lesser
Liberals at all close to his leader until the spring of 1920.
When he resigned in July 1921, protesting bitterly at the way in
which the government had betrayed its pledges on housing
policy (and, in the view of Thomas Jones, serving as a scapegoat
for the incompetence of his predecessor, Auckland Geddes)[2] it
notably weakened the strength of the Coalition Liberals in the
ministerial ranks wherein alone they had real status. The
departure the following March of Edwin Montagu was further
evidence of the undermining of what had always been in
essence a ministerial party.

Only two of the Coalition Liberal ministers were consistently
near to the centre of decision-making—H. A. L. Fisher and
Winston Churchill. Fisher's may seem a surprising name. He
had been plucked by Lloyd George from the vice-chancellorship
of Sheffield University in December 1916 and placed at the
Board of Education. A distinguished historian of nineteenth-

---

[1] Keith Middlemas (ed.), *Thomas Jones: Whitehall Diary. Volume I:
1916–25* (1969), 201.

[2] Addison to Lloyd George, 14 July 1921 (Lloyd George Papers, F/1/6/30);
Thomas Jones: Whitehall Diary, 229.

century France, he had had no previous political experience. But he proved to be a skilful and ambitious administrator with expansive ideas. His handling of the complex 1918 Education Act won widespread applause. To Lloyd George, Fisher was a figure of real stature in his post-war government, his sole link with the Liberal intelligentsia amidst the professional politicians who largely filled the ministerial ranks. By the end of 1919, the Prime Minister was singing Fisher's praises—'another Morley', 'most popular also and influential in the Cabinet and a thorough Liberal'. C. P. Scott felt that Fisher was 'evidently [Lloyd George's] chief support on the Liberal side'.[1] Fisher's cabinet responsibilities soon went far beyond educational matters. Most important, he chaired the vital Home Affairs committee where the main sifting of domestic legislation took place and which seemed to have largely supplanted the cabinet itself. Fisher was also much involved in policy towards Ireland until the summer of 1920, especially in drafting the Government of Ireland Act. Even more, Lloyd George frequently deferred to Fisher's reflections on foreign affairs. In preparing the Prinkipo summons for negotiations with the Russian Bolsheviks, on disarmament and the League of Nations, Fisher provided a Liberal intellectual's counter-blast to Curzon. At the same time, Fisher, for all his ambition, was very far from being a servile lieutenant. He sprayed his leader with uncompromisingly Liberal views on all issues, from the Anti-Dumping Bill to the Genoa conference. He was a living proof that an active Coalitionist could remain a committed Liberal. On Ireland, on the peace treaties and, above all, in fighting the Geddes economies, Fisher's was a constant voice of radical protest, whose resignation the Prime Minister would go far to avoid. Fisher may reasonably be regarded as one of the positive successes of the Coalition Liberals, not least in serving as Lloyd George's Liberal conscience. Partly due to him, Lloyd George, even as the head of an all-party 'national' government, remained in some sense an active and persevering Liberal.

The relationship of Lloyd George and Churchill was far more complex. 'Landing Winston' was a vital element in Lloyd George's designs in November 1918. Once caught,

[1] C. P. Scott's diary, 30 November–1 December 1919 (Add. MSS., 50905), f.211.

Churchill was often treated with indifference amounting to contempt. His leader variously accused him of personal ambition, of departmental irregularity and an 'obsession' with the menace of Bolshevism. But Churchill submitted to his master's verbal chastisement with surprising equanimity. Not until the spring of 1922, over the issue of the recognition of Soviet Russia, was he moved seriously to offer resignation. The extent to which Churchill could still be considered to be a Liberal was much debated in the press. Lloyd George confided to C. P. Scott in January 1922 that Churchill (whom he now called 'his second in command of the Coalition Liberal organization') was 'not a Liberal: his sympathies were all with the Imperialists'.[1] He later told Donald Maclean in 1924 that 'for three years he and Winston were at direct variance on many vital questions'.[2] Certainly the advent of Bolshevism in Russia unhinged Churchill's judgement and invested his pronouncements on foreign and colonial affairs with a new tone of chauvinism. In the labour unrest of 1919–1920, he was an ardent advocate of the use of force. Even so, Churchill's can also be held to be a Liberal voice on many public issues. In foreign policy, his could be a moderating influence, as when he urged a less aggressively pro-Greek policy in the Near East upon Lloyd George in 1920 and 1921. At home, he pressed for a more enlightened financial policy, urging Unionist chancellors (in vain) 'to budget for hope and not for despair'.[3] He also fought vigorously in the cabinet in resisting the Geddes 'axe'. Most important of all, Churchill's Liberalism remained active on the issue of free trade. This had been the cause of his original defection from the Unionists back in 1904. Even now, Churchill was 'almost fanatical' on free trade, as Lloyd George admitted.[4] He resisted the encroachment of protectionism in the post-war period with a passionate, unrelenting zeal. He fought hard against the abuse of the Safeguarding of Industries Act, especially in the extension of the provisions relating to 'key industries'.

---

[1] Ibid., 17–20 Jan. 1922 (ibid., 50906), f.133.

[2] Donald Maclean's interview with Lloyd George, 17 Jan. 1924, Viscount Gladstone Papers (Add. MSS., 46474), f.68.

[3] Churchill to Lloyd George, 12 April 1922 (Lloyd George Papers, F/10/2/63). By this, he meant cuts in direct and indirect taxation.

[4] C. P. Scott's diary, 17–20 Jan. 1922 (Add. MSS., 50906), f.133.

In 1923, his passion for free trade was to keep Churchill fiercely independent of the Conservatives, now led by the protectionist Baldwin; he fought the general election of December 1923 as a Liberal still. In the latter months of Lloyd George's administration, Churchill was to form, with Chamberlain and Birkenhead, one of the government's inner triumvirate. His presence helped to ensure that at the highest level the Coalition still kept faith with its Liberal origins.

Apart from the cabinet ministers, a key role was also played in the government by the two successive Liberal chief whips, Freddie Guest and Charles McCurdy, who succeeded him in April 1921. Guest was a genial playboy whose talents hardly lay in the realm of ideas: Montagu cruelly dismissed him as 'the half-wit'. Guest's lengthy analyses of the political scene were unimaginative, stereotyped and always mindlessly optimistic. Even so, his value as a personal adviser to the Prime Minister was immense. It was Guest who handled the delicate negotiations with the Unionist whips in July 1918, striking a remarkably favourable bargain. Later he handled some even more covert transactions, especially the traffic in peerages and baronetcies that led to the building up of the mighty Lloyd George fund. In handling the more orthodox side of a whip's work, however, Guest proved less effective. The central Coalition Liberal organization in Abingdon Street had an office, a small office staff and an effective publicity department, but not much else.[1] Not until after the decisive breach with the Asquithians after the Leamington conference of the National Liberal Federation in May 1920 did Guest face the facts of the coupon election and turn to building up a national party. His efforts made little impact on the constituency associations, most of which were now moribund. Finally in May 1921 he was removed to the Air Ministry, by now a virtual sinecure which left Guest ample scope for such activities as reorganizing the stock-holding of the *Daily Chronicle* and building up the Lloyd George fund still further, with his Lancastrian associate, Captain William Edge. When Lloyd George fell from office, Guest's assiduity had provided him with a working capital of over £3,000,000. At least Lloyd George had a party campaign fund, even if he had apparently no party and no campaign.

[1] Guest to Lloyd George, 29 Dec. 1919 (Lloyd George Papers, F/21/4/33).

Guest's successor, Charles McCurdy, was a more impressive figure who had already served as Food Controller. He was more at home in the realm of ideas and of policy-making. He threw himself also into the task of building up the Coalition Liberal party in the country, supplanting the existing constituency associations where necessary. Alfred Cope, a 'man of push and go', was put in charge of the central party machinery. By January 1922, McCurdy had become a figure of some influence and a major force in persuading Lloyd George to appeal to the country.[1] But this election plan was thwarted by the Unionist party chairman, Sir George Younger, who revealed the whole affair to the press, and something of McCurdy's influence evaporated as a result. He strove desperately to maintain the Prime Minister's interest in building up his party in the hope of uniting with the Unionists after the next election. But Lloyd George showed little interest: instead, as a reward, there was a suggestion that McCurdy be replaced as chief whip by Hamar Greenwood.[2] Yet it was largely due to McCurdy's persistent efforts in trying to galvanize local party workers into life that Lloyd George was left with any bargaining position with the Unionists at all.

A final important source of Coalition Liberal influence within the government was the Prime Minister's own secretariat or 'Garden Suburb'. Its most authoritative voice, until his departure early in 1921, was Philip Kerr, a powerful advocate of moderation in foreign policy, of appeasement towards Germany and of conciliation towards Russia. When he turned instead to managing the pro-Coalition *Daily Chronicle*, C. P. Scott noted that Kerr was 'a stronger Liberal than one had supposed and that George & his entourage are moving decidedly in the same direction'.[3] Kerr's successor, Edward Grigg, although a former Unionist, also helped to permeate Liberal principles throughout the government's foreign policies, especially at the time of the Genoa conference when he addressed a passionate appeal to Lloyd George. 'I write like a Liberal, you will say. I am one on this issue ... At present the Die Hards are watching you as the old reactionaries in Europe watched Napoleon in 1814'. The

---

[1] McCurdy to Lloyd George, 5 and 6 Jan. 1922 (ibid., F/35/1/3-5).
[2] Mond to Lloyd George n.d. (Aug. 1922), (ibid., F/37/2/15).
[3] C. P. Scott's diary, 17-20 Jan. 1922 (Add. MSS., 50906, f.139).

conflict lay now between 'peace, appeasement and reconstruction' and 'the old doctrines of intervention, ascendancy
and vengeance' which, Grigg alleged, were upheld by so many
of the Unionists.[1]

Yet another apostle of Liberalism in the 'Garden Suburb',
in his own eccentric way, was Sir William Sutherland, Lloyd
George's press secretary down to 1918 and now Liberal M.P.
for Argyllshire. Much of Sutherland's immense energy was
consumed (in Thomas Jones's words) by the 'hawking of
baronetcies in the clubs' to swell his master's coffers—a task
for which 'Bronco Bill's' Rabelaisian and convivial tastes were
ideally suited. In other ways, his activities were directed more
specifically towards Coalition Liberalism. He helped in building
up the party organization in Scotland, and also took charge of
the publicity programme. He even tried his hand at providing
a new Liberal philosophy for his leader. He urged that the
older Liberalism associated with the ageing Asquith was
moribund. 'The really vital thing is that we must break through
the "bourgeoisie" crust that the populace associate with
Coalition Liberalism and really get down to the masses'. He
went on in mellow, philosophic vein: 'the average voters are
grim realists today; in only too many cases unfortunately
casting about for life lines in their sea of troubles'.[2] In his own
way, Sutherland reinforced the appeal of Liberal principles in
ministerial and prime ministerial circles.

At the centre of decision-making, then, Coalition Liberalism
was a potent force. But the further away from Downing Street,
the more peripheral its influence. Certainly the Coalition
Liberals were never an effective parliamentary force, and their
function in the House was ambiguous. They met as a parliamentary group under the chairmanship of George Lambert
(South Molton), a man who had not received the 'coupon' in
1918 and was frequently to disobey the voting instructions of his
own whips. This curious selection was presumably intended as a
bridgehead to the Asquithians in the vain hope of reunion, but
it made the role of the Coalition Liberal party appear even
more obscure. It had its own whips, yet it never occupied a

---

[1] Edward Grigg to Lloyd George, 23 March 1922 (Lloyd George Papers,
F/86/1/35).
[2] Sir William Sutherland to Lloyd George, 2 Jan. 1922 (ibid., F/35/1/1).

distinct place in the House, separate from the Unionists. It never formally assumed the guise of an independent party. *The Times* commented quite fairly that 'the Coalition Unionists are a separate party, the Coalition Liberals are not'.[1] In addition, events soon showed that very few of the 130-odd members of the group were figures of any consequence. Only one of their number, Hilton Young, member for Norwich, rose from the ranks to major government office. Nearly sixty of the Liberal members were recruits from business or commerce: many of them had little experience of politics and little inclination to carve out their careers anew. It soon became apparent that only on free trade did 'Lloyd George's knights and baronets'[2] make any impact at Westminster. They were soon losing strength not only in by-elections but also by defections to the Asquithians. By February 1920, five had crossed the floor, among them General Seely who resigned from the government in protest at the virtual abandonment of the Air Ministry. Losing support from without, the Coalition Liberals were being undermined from within. By 1921 an active cabal of backbenchers, led by D. M. Cowan, Gerald France and John Hinds, was working hard for reunion with J. M. Hogge and the more radical 'Wee Frees'. Long before the government fell from office, the parliamentary feebleness of the Coalition Liberals was beyond dispute.

In the country they were weaker still. They had over a million votes behind them. They had a powerful organ in the *Daily Chronicle*: under Kerr's direction, it improved in quality even if its circulation now fell below the million mark. Yet as a national party they barely existed. Save only in Wales, most Liberal Associations remained solidly in Asquithian hands. Local party workers and activists rebelled against coalition with the Tories from the outset. Moreover, official Liberal agents were often reluctant to join Lloyd George for fear of loss of pension rights. In the South and West Midlands, it was reported that all but six agents were hostile to the Coalition.[3]

[1] *The Times*, 4 Dec. 1919.

[2] A. H. D. Acland to J. A. Spender, 31 Dec. 1918; Spender Papers (Add. MSS., 46392, F. 285).

[3] Annual report of the Coalition Liberal organization, 1920 (Lloyd George Papers, F/168/2/16), 32.

Some agents did indeed join the Lloyd George Liberals after
the Liberal fracas at the Leamington conference in May 1920,
but they had to be kept on the payroll of party headquarters at
considerable expense, since there was no local constituency
party to support them. After Leamington, a central party
organization did come into being, with Colonel Scovell as
general secretary. It issued its own *Lloyd George Liberal Magazine*
from October 1920, a monthly which printed over 30,000
copies.[1] Under McCurdy's guidance, regional councils were
formed in many parts of the country, most numerous in the
North of England, weakest in the Home Counties. Yet at the
constituency level, these remained largely paper organizations:
'apathy and nervousness have been the bugbear of our efforts'.[2]
Even in Wales, where twenty-five Coalition Liberals had been
returned in 1918 and where the Welsh National Liberal Council
under Lord St. Davids remained faithful to Lloyd George, there
was intense hostility to the Coalition and pressure for union
with the Asquithians or even with Labour. Local party
organization was decrepit, as by-election defeats in Gower and
Caerphilly showed in July 1922. In Cardiganshire in February
1921, the local Liberals adopted a fervent Asquithian, Llewelyn
Williams, when a by-election was due, and the Coalitionist,
Ernest Evans, had to construct his own *ad hoc* organization.
Even in the Prime Minister's native land, Coalition Liberalism
found little nourishment at the grass roots. It remained an
army of generals without much of a rank and file.[3]

This feebleness at the local level might seem surprising. After
all, Lloyd George's Liberals were no mere phantoms. Especially
in Wales, Scotland and the North of England they included
many stalwarts of local business—men like Max Muspratt of
Liverpool, Sir Charles Sykes of Huddersfield or Sir Beddoe Rees
of Cardiff, with occasional major tycoons like the Lords
Inchcape and Leverhulme. Again, especially in the Celtic
fringe, Coalition Liberalism contained some of the leading
patriarchs of nonconformity, men like J. H. Shakespeare and

[1] Ibid.   [2] Ibid.
[3] On this, see Kenneth O. Morgan, 'Twilight of Welsh Liberalism:
Lloyd George and the Wee Frees, 1918–35', *Bull. Bd. Celtic Studies* (May,
1968), 389ff.; and 'Cardiganshire Politics: the Liberal Ascendancy,
1885–1923', *Ceredigion* (1967), 332–7.

Towyn Jones who could enlarge on 'our moral debt to the Coalition'.[1] Lloyd George's Liberals seemed to have as much potential vitality as did Asquith's. Why then were they so ineffective? The answer lay in a basic fear of commitment, stemming from a rooted doubt as to whether the alliance of 1918 was merely transitional or a permanent arrangement. Every advance towards a closer liaison with the Unionists, every joint operation at a by-election or in supporting 'Ratepayer' candidates in local elections, every insidious approach towards 'fusion', aggravated this political schizophrenia. Macnamara was disowned by his own Liberal Association in Camberwell for speaking in support of Fairfax, the Coalition Liberal candidate, in the Spen Valley by-election. Even after Leamington, most of the Coalitionists still nourished the hope of reunion with the Independent Liberals. Since, however, Asquith viewed reunion with utter disdain and Lloyd George could never give the idea any encouragement without antagonizing his Tory partners, the result was a complete paralysis of will. Threatened in its industrial strongholds in South Wales, Scotland and the North by the rising power of Labour, Coalition Liberalism in the constituencies simply melted away.

The results of all this were very evident in by-elections. Between 1919 and 1922 the Coalition Liberals lost in ten of the nineteen seats they defended. Even in Wales, successive by-elections in Swansea East, Abertillery, Cardiganshire, Gower and Caerphilly showed a marked erosion of organization.[2] More serious, there was an erosion of morale. In Wales, as elsewhere, old objectives like disestablishment of the Church were either attained or else had become irrelevant. No new priorities had been formulated instead. Not until January 1922 did the Liberal ministers make a real effort to try to set up their party on a nation-wide basis. They held a great meeting at Westminster Central Hall on 19 and 20 January. Here the 'National Liberal Party' was launched, amid fervent orations by Lloyd George and Churchill. But the *Manchester Guardian*'s parliamentary correspondent, not an unfriendly critic, com-

[1] The Rev. W. Kingscote Greenland in *Lloyd George Liberal Magazine* (November 1920), 110–11.

[2] Sir Alfred Mond to Lloyd George, 10 Aug. 1922 (Lloyd George Papers, F/37/2/17), enclosing memorandum by W. C. Jenkins.

mented on the 'curious languour' of the proceedings and the
conspicuous absence of missionary zeal.[1] The impact of the
conference was non-existent. Lloyd George promptly retired to
Criccieth for three weeks: thereafter his energies were mainly
absorbed by foreign affairs, especially the Genoa conference.
Constituency parties continued to wither away and the
Coalition Liberals as a national party remained as dormant as
before.

Not surprisingly this caused much difficulty with the
Unionists, who found themselves forced to pour out money and
men for their Liberal partners in constituencies where they were
unable to fend for themselves. Younger wrote despairingly to
Bonar Law after the loss of the South Norfolk seat to Labour in
August 1920: 'This constant loss of C.L. seats becomes serious
and I see no chance of any improvement. With poor candidates
and no organization of their own, the attrition is bound to go
on and the inclusion of the Downing Street staff does no good.
They arrive, spend money lavishly, but cut little ice'.[2] Coalition
Liberal losses at Spen Valley, the Wrekin, Dartford and South
Norfolk during the year gave point to Younger's fears. In seats
held by Coalition Liberals, the local Association was likely to
nominate an Asquithian when the sitting member died or
retired, as happened at Spen Valley and South Norfolk. Since
the local Unionists had accepted a Liberal member here only
with sullen reluctance, the Coalition's local machinery remained
chaotic. In seats held by Coalition Unionists, the local Liberals
were usually 'Wee Frees' anyhow. More and more, Coalition
Liberalism in the constituencies needed the artificial stimulus
of ministers like Addison or Macnamara leaving their departments to try to breathe life into the inert bodies of local associations, or else the shock treatment of electoral organizers
imported from the Garden Suburb. In Wales, for example,
the main driving force for the Coalition Liberal machine
came from Evan R. Davies, a former town clerk who was
now Lloyd George's personal secretary, rather than from
the Welsh National Liberal Federation and its apprehensive
secretary, D. T. Salathiel. With the Prime Minister's own

[1] *Manchester Guardian*, 21 Jan. 1922. Among the speakers was Seely who
had rejoined the Coalition Liberals.

[2] Younger to Bonar Law, 12 Aug. 1920 (Bonar Law Papers, 99/4/16).

supra-party position now less of an electoral asset, after labour conflict at home, deadlock in peace conferences and 'always Ireland',[1] the Coalition Liberal Party, beyond the narrow hothouse world of Westminster politics, seemed to offer neither a present nor a future.

And yet, despite all this, the Coalition Liberals' influence on post-war events was far from negligible, both in relation to policy and to the evolution of the parties. As regards their policy, the Coalitionists like all Liberals faced the dilemma of a vanishing programme. The Welsh Church was duly disestablished amidst general apathy, licensing reform excited little interest save in Scotland and Wales, home rule all round was a dead issue even there, and few cared about the Lords' veto any more. Nevertheless, while the Asquithians tended to repeat the old shibboleths of pre-1914, in the new political world of post-war the Coalition Liberals had their own positive role to play.

First of all, it could reasonably be argued that the Coalition Liberals were largely responsible for the government's imaginative new departures in social reform. Whatever the enthusiasm of radical Tories like Steel-Maitland before 1914, none of the Unionist ministers now had any practical interest in social welfare, apart from spending less money on it. Lloyd George himself was largely absorbed in European affairs and 'felt we must go slow on domestic reform'.[2] Nevertheless, thanks mainly to its Liberal members, the government pursued a bold and courageous social policy. Admittedly, many of the Liberal ministers occupied posts where social reform was a natural departmental interest, but their personal commitment to it was the decisive factor. It was Addison who supplied most of the momentum behind the dramatic new housing programme which, however mismanaged in its financing, helped to make housing a social service for the first time. Macnamara played a somewhat similar role in relation to unemployment. After Spen Valley, he urged Lloyd George ungrammatically: 'Cost of Living! Housing! There it is.'—although there was probably something in Addison's charge that Macnamara tended to deal

---

[1] Lloyd George to Bonar Law, 7 June 1921, cited in Lord Beaverbrook, *Decline and Fall of Lloyd George* (1963), 264.

[2] H. A. L. Fisher's diary, 24 March 1921 (Bodleian, Fisher Papers).

only in generalities.[1] Mond also pressed the supreme importance of employment policies and their connection with such issues as transport and public works programmes. He used the Cabinet's Unemployment Committee as a platform for his schemes.[2] Fisher spearheaded the Coalition's educational policies. With his Welsh colleague, Herbert Lewis, he fought hard and long to save the day continuation schools and teachers' salary scales from the hands of Tory 'economists'.[3] When the Geddes recommendations threatened the entire social policy of the government, it was exclusively the Liberal ministers, especially Fisher, Mond, Montagu and Churchill, who led a spirited counterattack in the Cabinet.[4] Fisher almost resigned; Addison actually did so, when his housing programme was left in ruins by the cabinet Finance Committee. Mond, however, kept up Addison's fight against 'surrender to the reactionary, anti-waste crowd'.[5] Even Sutherland joined in the cry for the Prime Minister to attract younger voters by coming out as 'an 'enthusiastic progressive' on the social front.[6] All this was an unpopular line to follow in the post-war years. In the constituencies, Coalition Liberals were generally advocates of 'drastic economy' and an end to 'fruitless expenditure' on education and houses for the people. Lloyd George's 'knights and baronets' in Lancashire and Yorkshire called for the wielding of the axe of Geddes with the utmost vigour. Unionists were even more passionate on this theme and crusaded against the extravagant social policies of 'Addison, Fisher and company'.[7] In the end, of course, the 'economists' won all along the line: the Geddes reports left the government's social policies in tatters. Even so, they could not wholly undo the

[1] Macnamara to Lloyd George, 3 Jan. 1920 (Lloyd George Papers, F/36/1/13); Addison to Lloyd George, 22 Sept. 1919 (ibid., F/1/5/27).

[2] Mond's Cabinet memorandum, 6 Sept. 1921 (CAB. 24/127); Mond's memorandum, 7 Sept. 1922 (Lloyd George Papers, F/253).

[3] Herbert Lewis to Lloyd George, 'Nadolig' (Christmas Day), 1920 (ibid., F/32/1/24).

[4] H. A. L. Fisher's diary, 2 Aug. 1921.

[5] Mond to Lloyd George, 1 July 1921 (Lloyd George Papers, F/37/1/26). On the other hand, it should be noted that Mond completely reversed Addison's programmes by stopping the grants for new houses.

[6] Sutherland to Lloyd George, ? March 1920 (ibid., F/242).

[7] Joseph Nall to Younger, 3 Dec. 1920 (Bonar Law Papers, 99/8/4).

achievements already gained—Addison's houses, Fisher's schools, the important extension of national insurance in 1920. Not only was Labour pressure for direct action much blunted by this extension of social reform. The pattern of welfare policy in twentieth-century Britain was in some measure the achievement of the derided and despised Coalition Liberals.

Elsewhere, the impact of Coalition Liberal influence on policy varied considerably. Over Ireland, Liberal members of the government kept up a refrain of ineffective protest as the atrocities of the Black and Tans went on. Shortt, Addison and Fisher fought hard in 1919 for a less provocative policy towards Sinn Fein. But the arrival of Hamar Greenwood, a ferocious hard-liner, at the Irish Office in April 1920 weakened the impact of Liberal principles. Several backbench supporters of the government viewed with dismay the subsequent course of 'murders and irresponsible reprisals' in Ireland and the new bellicosity of Lloyd George's own utterances on the subject. Guest reported to Lloyd George on a protest meeting of Coalition Liberal M.P.'s in March 1921, chaired by the respected Lancashire member, Sir Ryland Adkins. Guest added: 'I am convinced from this meeting and from other sources that it is *only sheer loyalty* that restrains a large number of Coalition Liberals from openly opposing certain aspects of the Irish policy'.[1] From his own Caernarvon Boroughs constituency, Lloyd George was warned that '*Ireland* is being run for all it is worth against you'.[2] But these protests had no discernible effect, and the eventual reversal of policy that led to the Irish treaty in December 1921 owed nothing to them.

Coalition Liberal influence was more evident in policy towards India. This was due almost solely to the heroic stand taken by the Secretary of State, Edwin Montagu. He was never a popular figure in the House. A belated renegade from Asquith, he was detested by the 'Wee Frees' while his Old Testament radicalism and his Jewish blood excited Tory back-benchers to virulent protest. Sutherland reported casually how, in the Amritsar massacre debate, Montagu, 'more racial and more Yiddish in screaming tone and gesture', roused even 'normally placid

[1] Guest to Lloyd George, 9 March 1921 (Lloyd George Papers, F/22/3/6).
[2] Winifred Coombe Tennant to Lloyd George, 31 March 1921 (ibid., F/96/1/15), quoting the Liberal Woman Organizer for North Wales.

Tories'.[1] Despite all this, Montagu laboured with dignity and some success in implementing a moderate and rational policy for India after 1918. He firmly disciplined General Dyer after the tragedy at Amritsar; the governmental reforms worked out with Lord Chelmsford were carried through; the repression of Gandhi's passive resistance campaign through the Congress movement was greatly moderated. Further, Montagu strove, though with little result, to get Indian (more specifically Moslem) opinion brought to bear in the consideration of the peace treaties, especially in relation to Turkey. The result was to make Montagu an almost completely isolated figure in the Cabinet. He had no close allies among his fellow Liberals, while Unionists accused him of voting against the government in the South Norfolk by-election. Lloyd George, plagued by Montagu's penetrating criticisms of his Turkish policies, charged him with behaving more like 'a successor to the throne of Aurangzeb' than a member of the British government.[2] When Montagu finally rebelled against the government's Near Eastern policy in March 1922, he was ruthlessly cast aside. At the general election, he was heavily defeated and his career was at an end. For all that, the die-hards had been frustrated in India as (prior to Geddes) they had been at home. Montagu was in his way a martyr for the government's imperial policy as Addison, another Liberal, had been for its social policy.

In one supreme area, however, Coalition Liberals were intimately involved in the formulation of policy. This was the symbolic issue of free trade, the ultimate touchstone of their faith to Liberals of all factions. Soon it was being put to a crucial challenge. There was a suspicious delay in abandoning the wartime restrictions on imports first introduced through the Paris resolutions in 1916. When they were finally done away with in September 1919, Lloyd George then announced that, to protect British industry against the hazards of post-war conditions, some new measures would be adopted.[3] The dumping of foreign goods sold below the selling price in the country of origin would be prohibited. There would be protec-

---

[1] Sutherland's memorandum (ibid., F/22/2/5).
[2] Lloyd George to Montagu, 25 April 1920 (ibid., F/40/3/5); cf. also *Thomas Jones: Whitehall Diary*, i, 92–3, 112.
[3] *H.C. deb.*, 5th ser., vol. 119, 2010–12.

tion of some key industries such as the manufacture of scientific instruments. Finally, there would be measures to prevent British goods suffering from 'collapsed exchanges', that is unfavourable conditions arising through the rapid depreciation of foreign currencies like the German mark. These measures amounted to the most formidable challenge to free trade since the days of the Corn Laws. Lloyd George himself seemed casual to the point of irresponsibility about free trade principles. He ignored the vital difference between goods sold below British production cost (which might be cheaper simply because of greater efficiency in manufacture) and below production cost in the country of origin. Again, he seemed oblivious to the huge encroachment of protectionism that was possible under the 'collapsed exchanges' clause, which could theoretically eliminate trade with every country in the world save only for Japan, Holland, Portugal, Sweden and the United States. With an undisguised imperialist like Austen Chamberlain at the Treasury and Auckland Geddes at the Board of Trade, there seemed to be a vital challenge to the very fundamentals of Liberal economics.

The Coalition Liberals rose nobly to the defence of their Cobdenite traditions. When the government introduced its first anti-dumping measure, the Imports and Exports Regulation Bill, the Coalition Liberal members of parliament led by George Lambert were vehement in their objections. On 5 December 1919 they presented formal detailed objections to the bill, while Fisher led a free trade counter-attack in the cabinet. Lloyd George treated this 'little peccadillo' with some flippancy.[1] He used debating tactics to show that it was McKenna and Runciman, both Asquithians, who had first introduced identical policies during the war. But for once he had overreached himself. The Liberal backbenchers refused to yield and on 20 December the bill was quietly dropped. Throughout the 1920 session, the Liberal Coalitionists managed to block its re-appearance, although they suffered a major setback when a bill introduced in December 1920 to regulate the import of dye-stuffs made another dent in the fabric of free trade.

A far more serious threat came in the King's Speech for 1921

[1] C. P. Scott's diary, 30 November–1 December 1919 (Add. MSS., 50905), F.209; *Manchester Guardian*, 6 Dec. 1919.

which announced a Safeguarding of Industries Bill. This would impose a 33⅓ per cent duty on the import of certain key products, with an additional 33⅓ per cent duty on goods dumped below the cost of production or given a competitive advantage through depreciation of foreign currency. With the Coalition Unionists now in earnest, the Liberals could only hope for delay. They gained some minor victories, such as the power given to the Board of Trade to decide whether dumping had actually taken place; for the rest they were brushed aside. By 19 August the Safeguarding of Industries Act was on the statute book. Nevertheless, throughout its passage, the Liberal backbenchers had fought an unusually spirited rearguard action, led by France, Cowan and J. M. Wallace. Fifteen of them, including four of Lloyd George's Welsh contingent, voted against the second reading, while a further 56 abstained.[1] Mond, now a zealot for imperial development, was virtually the only Liberal minister to speak in support of the bill. Liberal attachment to the Coalition was undoubtedly weakened by this entire episode. The threat to free trade continued to overshadow the 1922 session. A motion by Wedgwood Benn in February to repeal the Safeguarding of Industries Act saw an astonishing protest—on a free vote, only eighteen Coalition Liberals, all ministers, voted with the government, while nineteen voted against and a further 87 were absent or abstained. These last included four ministers, Shortt, Munro, McCurdy and Churchill.[2] A new crisis loomed up in July when Baldwin, to the fury of Lancashire textile interests, announced that the Safeguarding of Industries Act would be extended to cover the import of fabric gloves. On this occasion, 76 out of 122 Coalition Liberal members either were absent or voted against the government, while Captain Edge, a junior minister, threatened to resign.[3] Certainly the result of all these measures was a sequence of inroads into free trade that gravely weakened Coalition Liberals' morale. On the other hand, their resistance had something to show also. Even after the Safeguarding of

[1] *Liberal Magazine*, July 1921, 348.

[2] *Manchester Guardian*, 15 Feb. 1922; cf. Churchill to Lloyd George, 15 June 1922 (Lloyd George Papers, F/10/3/5), in which he protests vehemently at the abuse of the 'key industries' clauses.

[3] William Edge to Lloyd George, 28 July 1922 (ibid., F/35/1/48).

Industries Act, Britain was still basically a free trade country. When in October 1923 Baldwin was openly to advocate protection of the home market, he was soundly defeated at the polls. Coalition Liberalism left few legacies but free trade could be numbered among them.

The influence of the Coalition Liberals on the development of party politics was even more profound. In 1919–1920 Lloyd George's supreme political objective was the creation of a 'fusion' party which would unite the Coalition Liberals and Unionists at all levels, and provide him with a permanent base from which to fight off the challenge of socialism. He broached this idea with Fisher and Addison as early as September 1919.[1] The main obstacle seemed to be the Unionists. Their attitude became critical in March 1920 when it appeared that the Coalition Liberal candidate might not receive the backing of Unionist votes in a forthcoming by-election at Stockport. But, after some persuading, Bonar Law and, less enthusiastically, Younger agreed to accept 'fusion' as the price to be paid for retaining the leadership of Lloyd George. His own party Lloyd George took for granted. The approach to fusion took place on two levels. In the first place, there was the New Members Coalition Group, consisting of over 150 backbenchers who sought a centre party; they were presided over by Oscar Guest (Loughborough), the brother of the chief whip, while another Liberal, Colin Coote (Isle of Ely) was co-secretary. Secondly, Lloyd George was applying severe pressure to his Liberal ministers. On 4 February, he urged them: 'Liberal labels lead nowhere: we must be prepared to burn them'.[2]

But these ministers were much less pliable than he assumed. Men like Fisher, Montagu and Hewart simply could not accept that Bonar Law and Chamberlain had suddenly embraced the central tenets of their faith. They (and their constituents) felt that on free trade, Ireland, disarmament and social reform, the differences between the parties were still very real. Only two Liberal ministers were enthusiastic for 'fusion', Churchill and Addison. But their motives were totally different. Churchill saw in a united 'constitutional' party the one sure means of rallying the forces of property and order against the

---

[1] Fisher's diary, 23 Sept. 1919.

[2] Ibid., 4 Feb. 1920; cf. Colin R. Coote, *Editorial* (1965), 103.

Red peril. Addison, by contrast, saw a Coalition as the only effective instrument for a national programme of radical reform. He wanted fusion at the constituency level first. 'At the first opportune moment, the Party fusion that we have often discussed should be pressed on with a proper declaration of policy. I think, however, it should be possible *even before this* to form a central Coalition Whips Organization'.[1] But his Liberal colleagues refused to be persuaded. At a crucial meeting with them on 16 March 1920, intended as a formal preliminary to a public union with Bonar Law, the Prime Minister found the Liberal ministers strangely adamant. They would not lose their identity; even more, they refused to shed their historic name. Why should they mortgage their future to Bonar Law and his increasingly 'die-hard' supporters? The fate of Joseph Chamberlain was a reminder of the perils of following that path. Even a Coalition Liberal had principles and pride. As a result, when Lloyd George met the Coalition Liberal backbench M.P.s two days later, instead of asking for fusion he only made a vague appeal for 'closer co-operation' in the constituencies with the Unionists.[2] Even this led to critical comment from such normally docile backbenchers as Tudor Rees (Barnstaple). The result was a complete anti-climax. Unable even to deliver his own party's support, Lloyd George could not approach the Unionists. The Coalition Liberals remained Liberals still, and, whether he liked it or not, so did he.

This was a historic turning-point in twentieth-century British politics. The one real opportunity that Lloyd George ever had permanently to transform the party system on his own terms had passed by for ever. His future was now uncertain as the older parties regained their pre-war position. Thereafter Lloyd George could pursue no consistent policy. He could veer towards an aggressive right-wing policy of anti-socialism and then back again to a radical programme of peace and social reform. Increasingly he was becoming a political anomaly. The Coalition Liberals, on the other hand, had served as their own grave-diggers. With fusion off and Liberal reunion out of the question, they had no discernible role. They found their

---

[1] Addison to Lloyd George, 3 March 1920 (Lloyd George Papers, F/1/6/4).
[2] Transcript of meeting in Lloyd George Papers (F/242). As usual, several notorious 'Wee Frees' were present at this meeting.

position harder and harder to bear. Their discontent reached a climax when the Unionists (backed up by Churchill) refused to endorse the recognition of Soviet Russia at the forthcoming Genoa conference in April 1922. Fisher and Hilton Young now urged that the Liberal ministers should resign as soon as the conference ended, but Lloyd George, backed up by McCurdy, turned down this suicidal appeal. The purpose of Coalition Liberalism was now wholly obscure. In March 1922 Hilton Young tried to definite it: 'to consolidate the party of the right under (Lloyd George's) leadership and, under the shadow of his wing, to do what we could to make that party a liberal and not a reactionary party ... I dream of a constitutional union of the liberal and conservative parties, within which those parties would work for a common policy, and with a common plan of campaign, as the British and French armies worked in the last year of the war, the P.M. our Foch'.[1] But since 16 March 1920 this had been nothing more than a pipe-dream. The so-called '1920 Club' at Whitehall Court was an empty memorial to it. There was no hope of a 'national' party now until after the next election, after which Coalition Liberalism might be hardly worth the Unionists' allying with at all. Its cause seemed finally lost. Its advocates had safeguarded their principles at the cost of destroying their future and probably that of their leader also.

In the latter months of 1922, Coalition Liberal discontent became more pronounced. Lloyd George himself treated his Liberal backbenchers with complete indifference and seldom met either them or their leaders. He took little interest in his party's organizational structure or in its by-election performance, apart from the fratricidal Welsh conflict in Cardiganshire in February 1921. His main associates within the government now, Churchill apart, were all Conservatives— Chamberlain, Birkenhead, Horne, Worthington-Evans. The departure of Montagu left his Liberal colleagues, Fisher, Mond and Shortt, the more exposed to Unionist sniper fire. Not until August 1922, when a general election again seemed imminent, did Lloyd George set up a committee to investigate the Coalition Liberal party machine—consisting, appropriately enough, entirely of ministers, Mond, Macnamara and Kella-

[1] Hilton Young to Edward Grigg, 23 March 1922 (ibid., F/86/1/35).

way.[1] Belatedly also, he sought the assistance of Mond, McCurdy, Neal and Sutherland about the main lines of a Liberal programme when the next election came.[2]

By this time, Lloyd George seemed to have little interest in Coalition Liberal politics or indeed in conventional politics at all. He saw himself as a kind of free-floating agent attracting particles of support from all over the political field. He would win working-class support from Labour by his well-tried appeal to 'the underdog'. He already had the Liberal vote in Scotland, Wales and the North. He would detach Chamberlain and the other Unionist ministers from their party by the same means through which the Liberals had won over the Peelite Conservatives back in the 1850's. Chamberlain, he maintained, was now 'a Liberal', Birkenhead 'a democrat', Balfour 'has become a Liberal in his old age—like Gladstone'. Horne was 'a Tory with a difference': he was 'the son of a Scottish Presbyterian minister—not much of Toryism in that'. As an added endorsement, Horne was 'a Gladstonian in finance'.[3] Lloyd George was far more involved with the fascinations of new party combinations than with shoring up his own sagging Liberal machine. The record of Joseph Chamberlain reminded him of the perils of a radical being simply swallowed up by the Tories. But any new combination would be achieved by the manipulation of leaders, not by the re-shaping of mass support. The Coalition would become not so much a party as a mood, a mystique that would appeal to 'the people' against 'the interests'. In this calculation, the Coalition Liberals often seemed to be numbered amongst the sectional 'interests' (on free trade, for instance) and their role therefore became expendable.

By September 1922 Coalition Liberal morale was desperately low. There had been recent by-election disasters in South Wales. Liberals had been rebuffed by Baldwin over the fabric gloves issue. Many of them were also intensely uneasy at Lloyd George's belligerence over the Turkish crisis. His stand at Chanak may have been partially intended to appeal to 'the Gladstonian tradition which regards the Turk as a curse'.[4] But most

[1] Mond to Lloyd George n.d. (August 1922), (ibid., F/37/2/15).
[2] Memoranda by Mond and others, Sept. 1922 (ibid., F/253).
[3] C. P. Scott's diary, 23 Oct. 1922 (Add. MSS., 50906), f.196.
[4] Ibid., 15 Sept. 1922.

Liberals were repelled by this crude jingoism, while all his close
allies in this final crisis, save for Churchill, were Unionists.
Only after Bonar Law's intervention in the Chanak controversy, with his famous letter to *The Times* on 7 October, was
Lloyd George forced back into the arms of his long-suffering
Liberal comrades. By now his government was manifestly
disintegrating. Baldwin and Griffith-Boscawen were near to
resignation; other Unionists might follow them, perhaps even
Curzon. Lloyd George's own response, at Manchester on
14 October, was a belligerently Liberal assault on traditional
lines. It was laced with rhetorical onslaughts on the unspeakable
Turk and the even more unspeakable Viscount Gladstone, 'the
finest living embodiment of the Liberal principle that talent is
not hereditary'. At the same time, he tried to persuade his
Liberal colleagues of the desirability of remaining in the Coalition as long as possible. Despairingly, they all agreed, save only
for Mond, who again faced Unionist opposition in his constituency. As a result, he 'saw little future in clinging to the
Tories'.[1] When the government finally fell on 19 October, after
the Unionist revolt at the Carlton Club, the Coalition Liberals
were left in a vacuum. They were coalitionists in a post-coalition
world. Despite protests from younger men like Samuel Hoare,[2]
Bonar Law agreed not to oppose the Coalition Liberals at the
polls. In spite of this, however, their representation fell by over
half, from 122 to 57. Had it not been for the absence of Tory
opposition in English and Scottish constituencies, this representation might have been cut by at least two-thirds. Only Bonar
Law's charitable impulses saved the 'Coalie Libs' from total
annihilation.

The fifty-seven members who emerged from their electoral
travails were not a negligible band. True, they had suffered
grievous losses—Churchill, Guest, Montagu, Greenwood and
Kellaway had all fallen. On the other hand, they had some
able new recruits in Archibald Sinclair, Edward Grigg and
Geoffrey Shakespeare (the last two from the Garden Suburb),
to be followed by Leslie Hore-Belisha in 1923. They had won
back five of the ten seats lost in by-elections and compared

[1] Fisher's diary, 16 Oct. 1922.
[2] Samuel Hoare to Bonar Law, 27 Oct. 1922 (Bonar Law Papers,
108/1/21).

favourably enough with the Asquithians whose representation (60) was almost identical.

Even so, the Coalition Liberals' disappearance from the scene was pre-ordained. The 1923 general election, with its deceptive signs of revival for a reunited Liberal Party, was basically a victory for the Asquithians. From now on, the ranks of the old Coalition Liberals were being inexorably diminished by a drift to the right. Churchill and Greenwood now enlisted in the Constitutional Party which ran twelve candidates, all of them former Coalition Liberals, in the 1924 general election; afterwards it merged with the Conservatives.[1] Men like Guest and Hilton Young (both recently chief whips) had electoral pacts with the Conservatives in their constituencies and threatened to cross the floor also. Guest's backbench rump of self-styled 'Coalition Liberals' at the time of the general strike in 1926 was simply an anti-socialist pressure-group.[2] By 1929 Guest had definitely moved over to the Conservatives, as also had Mond and Hilton Young, the last two finally alienated by the 'socialistic' land schemes contained in Lloyd George's 'green book'.[3] Other losses followed. McCurdy, after some harassing years as managing director of United Newspapers, became a Liberal publicist for Lord Beaverbrook's Empire free trade crusade, while Addison had been a rare defector to Labour. The one badge of identity for those Coalition Liberals who remained was one they would willingly have shed—the glittering millions of the Lloyd George fund, carefully hoarded by their leader as a weapon with which to coerce Maclean and Asquith. By the end of the twenties, the last remnants of the old Coalition Liberal party were fast fading away. Except for Macnamara, its former leaders were little involved in the

[1] Although four of the seven 'Constitutionalist' candidates actually returned in 1924 sat in the House as Liberals—J. Hugh Edwards (Accrington), Lt.-Col. A. England (Heywood and Radcliffe), Sir T. Robinson (Stretford) and Lt.-Col. J. Ward (Stoke-on-Trent).

[2] Guest to Lloyd George, 1 June 1926 (Lloyd George Papers, G/8/13/4). Guest listed here ten members of the 'Coalition Liberal' group together with another ten possible recruits. Some of the latter are very doubtful: for instance, Ellis Davies (Denbigh) who was later to join the Labour Party.

[3] Mond to Lloyd George, 25 Sept. 1924 (ibid., G/14/5/8); Hilton Young to Lloyd George, 26 Aug. 1925 (ibid., G/10/14/18). Young was to become Minister of Health in the National government, 1931–35.

formulation of Lloyd George's new quasi-Keynesian policies to grapple with unemployment. Many of them retired: Fisher found tranquil release as Warden of New College. Former Lloyd George men like Shakespeare and Hore-Belisha were prominent in the break-away group of right-wing 'National Liberals' under Simon's leadership in June 1931. The final demise of the Coalition Liberals came in the electoral débâcle of the following October. Thereafter, Lloyd George and his family entourage of three were left to face the future all alone.

In essence, Coalition Liberalism was an a-political concept. It was above all the union of opposites, the child of Lloyd George's own erratic dialectic. He wanted his party to be both ardently radical and staunchly coalitionist, wedded to the old Liberal faith and yet new-born in the novel conditions of post-war, distinct from the Tory Party and yet indistinguishable from it. This circle just could not be squared, even by Lloyd Georgian geometry. Walter Long very reasonably pointed out the contradictions. 'We have been patient, self-sacrificing, loyal and what do we find? Our Liberal colleagues go down to Leamington and ask the audience to believe that they are just as Liberal as they ever were. In other words, that there has been no Coalition, no mutual concessions, but that they have swallowed us'.[1] This was not the politics of party but of instinct, conceived by the erratic genius of Lloyd George himself. He rightly took pride in his government's liberal measures—'the greatest measure of Irish self-government ever proposed or thought of, a very great measure of franchise extension, a remarkable temperance measure, a not insignificant measure of land reform which accepted my land val[uatio]n survey as its basis, an important international agreemt. as to disarmament'.[2] (Addison's housing policies he chose to forget). But his policy of intermittent peace, occasional retrenchment and piecemeal reform lacked inner coherence. It bore no relation to the world of party which alone could lend it reality. This was an element which Lloyd George himself largely ignored. Never in his entire career, from his first steps in Caernarvonshire politics in the mid-1880's, had he been a machine politician. His political

[1] Walter Long to Bonar Law, 8 May 1920 (Bonar Law Papers, 102/5/16).
[2] C. P. Scott's diary, 16 Dec. 1922 (Add MSS., 50906, ff.207-8). The reference to disarmament relates to the Washington naval treaty.

style was a mixture of Wesley and Rousseau, of the nonconformist conscience and the general will. Certainly, he could whip
up an ephemeral campaign directed towards a specific objective, like the Cymru Fydd League of the 1890's or the land
crusade before 1914. But the stern labour of building up a
permanent party organization, of looking after agents and
registration and ward councils was a world of which he knew
little. Lloyd George operated essentially at the summit. This was
the initial strength of Coalition Liberalism and its ultimate
contradiction. As the world of the party regulars returned after
1918, Lloyd George's stage army simply disbanded.

If, however, Coalition Liberalism be considered not an
academic exercise in political theory but as a practical response
to particular challenges, its influence in the post-war political
scene is seen in a very different light. It clearly served to
liberalize the coalition government—at a time when its Prime
Minister strove to claim that Arthur Henderson and Lenin were
virtually indistinguishable. Whatever Lloyd George's government was, it was not a die-hard one, and for this its Liberal
members deserve much of the credit. They fought for social
reform against the critics of 'extravagance' and the apostles of
'de-control'. They fought for peace in Ireland, for conciliation in
India, for freedom of trade. Most important of all, they fought
for themselves. No episode in this post-war period is of greater
importance than the failure of 'fusion' in March 1920. The one
real attempt ever made to remodel the face of politics, to re-
mould the Conservatives and to rehabilitate the moderate left,
to break through the set dialectic of capital and labour, was
thwarted. Lloyd George's attempt to make himself a truly
'National' leader had collapsed. The immediate cause of this
failure lay primarily in the ethic of the Coalition Liberals.
They genuinely believed that they had maintained their
Liberal creed in full. They could put up with creeping protection, with the Black and Tans, with re-endowing the Welsh
Church or the abolition of the land taxes of 1909. But they
could never abolish themselves. They may not have been a party
in the orthodox sense. In many cases, they may not have been
Liberals at all. More important, they thought they were, and
Lloyd George neglected them at fatal cost. He crucially under-
estimated his own 'cabin boys', as Birkenhead underestimated

his own Youngers and Davidsons. The Coalition Liberal ministers reflected the proud spirit of independence still vigorous in their party up and down the land, in the chapels, in the Celtic fringe, in old Liberal citadels like Manchester and Bristol and Leeds. The Prime Minister, intent only on winning over Bonar Law and the Unionists, had simply lost touch with his own party and his own past. In the ultimate crisis, the principles of the forgotten and derided Monds, Montagus, Munros, Shortts, Fishers and Hewarts were still a part of the living political world as Lloyd George's chimerical pipe-dreams were not. The Coalition Liberals condemned their party to extinction but preserved their principles intact.

Perhaps they did Lloyd George himself an ultimate service. They materially contributed to his eventual downfall but at least, when he fell, he remained a Liberal. He avoided the fate of Joseph Chamberlain—still more that of Ramsay MacDonald. At the end, in the agonizing crises of Liberal humiliations in the thirties and forties, even when disguised as Earl Lloyd-George of Dwyfor, Lloyd George remained a man of the Left. Perhaps it was the Coalition Liberals who kept him one.

The Queen's College, Oxford   KENNETH O. MORGAN

I am grateful to Mr. Robert Blake, Provost of the Queen's College, and to Dr. Cameron Hazlehurst for some very helpful comments on this chapter.

IX

LLOYD GEORGE AND THE GREEK QUESTION, 1918–22

A. E. MONTGOMERY

DR A. E. MONTGOMERY

Age 32

Birkbeck College, London B.A., Ph.D.
Currently Lecturer to HM forces, Extramural
Studies, University of Birmingham

LLOYD GEORGE AND THE GREEK
QUESTION, 1918–22

I N November 1922 the former prime minister of Greece, M. Gounaris, together with his cabinet colleagues, was tried and condemned to death by a military tribunal upon the charge of leading his country to disaster in Asia Minor. In his defence Gounaris claimed that he had been urged on and encouraged by the British government. Shortly afterwards, the texts of letters exchanged between Gounaris and Lord Curzon, the British foreign secretary, appeared in the French and British press. Upon the evidence of these letters, Lord Birkenhead and Lloyd George, Curzon's former colleagues in the coalition government, accused him of having acted without proper consultation with the cabinet of the day. This charge the Foreign Office was able to refute, and Curzon himself wrote an indignant rebuttal from Lausanne where, as Britain's representative, he was attempting to restore peace in the Near East:

> I am amazed at the audacious attempt by some of my recent colleagues to throw upon me the blame for a policy which, as everyone knows, the late Prime Minister carried on, sometimes in cabinet, more frequently outside it and behind the back of the Foreign Office, in favour of Greece. . . . I am not willing that this gross and malicious travesty of my conduct, which is simply designed to cover up the deplorable policy of the late Prime Minister, should pass unchallenged.[1]

This view, that Lloyd George conducted, single-handed, a devious and machiavellian Greek policy, which Lord Curzon had tried manfully but vainly to prevent, has become the generally accepted interpretation of Britain's role in the Greco-Turkish war of 1919 to 1922, the more so because it ended in ignominious failure and precipitated Lloyd George's fall from power following the 'Chanak Crisis'. Moreover, the published texts of Venizelos's alleged reports to Athens during 1920 seemed to add substance to these charges.[2] The true story, however, now revealed in the archives of the Public Records

[1] FO. 839/8, Curzon to Foreign Office, 8 Dec. 1922.
[2] FO. 839/8, 293, Hardinge to Curzon, 1 Dec. 1922.

Office and the Lloyd George papers, is less clear-cut than Curzon would have had us think, or which he himself for that matter believed.

The story begins in 1918, when the Ottoman Empire, its armies defeated in the field, sought an armistice with the victorious *entente* powers. Few at that time doubted that this signified the final demise of the 'Sick Man of Europe' and the opportunity for the 'removal as far as possible from Turkish dominion of all non-Turkish peoples'.[1] For almost a century the Balkan states had been establishing their independence and extending their territory at the expense of the moribund multi-national Ottoman empire. Amongst these emergent nations, none had a more spectacular record than Greece. Since gaining her independence in 1832, she had greatly increased both her territory and her population by the absorption of Southern Epirus, Thessaly, Macedonia and Crete. Nevertheless, there remained in 1918 numerous territories which the Greeks regarded as their legitimate irridenta—territories in which Greek inhabitants, if not in a majority, constituted the largest significant element in the population. Of these, two, Cyprus and the Dodecanese, were in the possession of Greece's allies, Britain and Italy, respectively, and here Greece anticipated that the goodwill of these powers would result in their making the islands over to her in due course. But her other claims could be satisfied at the expense of the defeated enemy powers, Bulgaria and Turkey, and thus she had good reason to hope that she might prove successful in obtaining some at least of these. The most obvious areas for direct annexation were those contiguous with the existing Greek frontier, Northern Epirus (Southern Albania), and Western Thrace (part of Bulgaria), but she had a stronger ethnographical basis for her claims in the Turkish territories of Eastern Thrace; the area of Western Asia Minor adjoining the city of Smyrna; Pontus (the region of North Eastern Asia Minor); and finally Constantinople itself.

To achieve these claims, the astute Greek premier, Venizelos, had co-operated with the allies to bring Greece into the war in 1917. When, in the autumn of 1918, the end of the war was in sight, he commenced an assiduous campaign with the support

[1] *The Times*, 11 April 1918.

of the leading statesmen of the *entente* including the British prime minister, Lloyd George.[1] While refraining from making embarrassing demands for Cyprus or Constantinople,[2] he urged Lloyd George that in view of the fact that there had been two and a half million unredeemed Greeks under Turkish misrule before the war, the allies should consent to offset the postwar aggrandisement of Rumania and Serbia by a comparable accretion of territory to Greece.[3] In reply Lloyd George (according to Greek sources) gave this assurance:

> Great Britain will support Greece in all her legitimate aspirations in the hope that she will become a powerful, liberalizing factor in the Eastern Mediterranean.[4]

Thus, at the Paris Peace Conference in 1919, the British delegation accepted Venizelos's demand for the city of Smyrna with its hinterland, though they rejected his bolder claim to all Asia Minor, west of Castelorizzo.[5] When the Italians, who also aspired to play a role in Anatolia, landed troops at Adalia and began to advance towards Smyrna, Lloyd George immediately brought the matter before the supreme allied council.[6] Declaring that the Italians were encouraging Turkish persecution of the Greek population of the coastal region, he proposed that, to prevent further Italian encroachment, the allies should give to Greece a mandate to occupy Smyrna for the purpose of protecting the local Christians. The American President, Wilson, welcomed this idea,[7] and both he and Clemenceau, the French premier, expressed themselves willing for the Greeks to land at once. On 7 May, therefore, the three allies authorized Venizelos to land troops in Asia Minor.[8]

The Greeks landed at Smyrna on 15 May and lost no time

---

[1] Lloyd George Papers, F/55/1/10, Venizelos to Prime Minister, 15 Oct. 1918.

[2] Lloyd George Papers, F/205/2/1, Venizelos to Prime Minister, 15 Oct. 1918.

[3] Lloyd George Papers, F/55/1/11, Venizelos to Lloyd George, 2 Nov. 1918.

[4] D. Kitsikis, *Propaganda et Pressions* (1963), 372.

[5] FRUS, III, BC-21, 3 Feb. 1919; Lloyd George Papers, F/20/2/5.

[6] CAB 29/38, 171B, 2 May 1919. The Italians were not present at this meeting.

[7] CAB 29/37/181C, 6 May 1919.

[8] CAB 37/39, IC-181-F, 7 May 1919.

in expanding from the bridgehead they had established. At first
Venizelos had no difficulty in obtaining the allies' approval for
further advances, upon the pretext of ensuring the safety of his
troops,[1] but within a short time it became known that the
Greek forces had marred their arrival in Asia Minor by the
murder of Turkish prisoners and by atrocities against the local
Moslem population.[2] Thereupon the supreme council, though
it refrained from ordering the Greeks to withdraw, established
a commission of enquiry to investigate the allegations and
appointed a British general, Milne, to exercise overall command
in the area and to demarcate boundaries both between the
Greeks and the Italians and between the Greeks and the Turks.[3]

For the Greeks, by their very presence in Anatolia, had
provoked a spontaneous Turkish resistance, which, though
initially confined to guerilla operations around the zone of
occupation, soon developed into a national defence movement
directed against the allies as a whole. It operated from the
inaccessible heartland of central Anatolia and had found a
leader of genius in Mustapha Kemal Pasha, a general of the
Sultan's regular army. Kemal (the future Atatürk), brought to
the movement a singleness of purpose born out of national pride
and personal ambition. Without his ruthless dominance and
political acumen the movement would not have survived the
vicissitudes of the next three years. The rapid growth of
'Kemalism' impressed both British and French representatives
in Turkey, who became correspondingly dubious as to the value
of the Greek presence at Smyrna. When, in November, the
allied commission of enquiry, finding Greece guilty of precipi-
tating the disorders which had attended her landings, drew the
conclusion that she would prove unable to maintain her position
in Asia Minor,[4] it seemed possible that the allies would revoke
their mandate.

But Venizelos, meanwhile, had done much to strengthen the
Greek position. He had increased his troops to 75,000 men and
had established a perimeter against Italian and Turkish
encroachment. Moreover, he had persuaded Italy to drop her
opposition to his claims and even to promise to cede to Greece

[1] CAB 29/38, CF 19, 19 May 1919.
[2] F.O. 4218/79356, Granville to Curzon, 24 May 1919.
[3] DBFP, I, 14.   [4] DBFP, II, 17, 18.

the Dodecanese.[1] He therefore begged Lloyd George not to expel Greece from Smyrna adding that his personal position in Greece was at stake.[2] To this Lloyd George replied that the Greeks should certainly stay in Smyrna. Britain's policy was to support Greece, and especially Venizelos as a close and friendly ally.

In accordance with this assurance Lloyd George defended the Greek position at an Anglo-French meeting held in London in December 1919.[3] Clemenceau suggested that the allies should settle the Greco-Turkish question by offering to Greece the provinces of Thrace instead of Smyrna. But Lloyd George, suspecting that the desire of France to restore Turkish integrity in Anatolia cloaked her own ambitions in Asia Minor, objected to the proposal which he considered unfair to Venizelos.

Subsequently there was an exchange of views between the British and French Foreign Offices. Lord Curzon, desirous of enhancing Britain's imperial stature by a gesture worthy of her victory over the Ottoman Empire, was primarily concerned with obtaining the expulsion of the Turks from Europe, including Constantinople. He was therefore disposed to accept the French proposal to offer the Greeks Thrace in return for relinquishing their claim to Smyrna, a claim with which he had never sympathized. Nevertheless neither he nor Berthelot, the shrewd and realistic Director-General of the Quai-d'Orsay, believed that it would be possible to exclude Greece entirely from Smyrna. For the safety of the minorities, both agreed it was essential to establish some form of autonomy in the region.[4]

This enabled Lloyd George to secure a solution which ensured a dominant Greek influence in the Smyrna Zone. Convinced that Venizelos would fall from power if Greece relinquished Smyrna,[5] Lloyd George determined to save his friend from this humiliation, and, at a conference held in London from February to March, 1920 to settle the Turkish peace terms, he exploited his position as chairman to overcome all opposition. To the French premier, Millerand's, argument

[1] DBFP, IV, 95.

[2] Lloyd George Papers, F/92/12/5, Prime Minister/Venizelos conversation, 31 Oct. 1919.

[3] DBFP, II, 55. The United States had now relapsed into isolationism.

[4] DBFP, IV, 631, 665.   [5] DBFP, VII, 24.

that Greece must leave Asia Minor to secure a lasting peace, he retorted that Smyrna constituted the bridgehead of the *Entente*. He refused to betray the allied promises to Venizelos merely in order to placate the Turks, and on 16 February, 1920, ignoring Millerand's previous objections, he appointed a commission to hear the Greek claims. Its brief was to make recommendations concerning the geographical boundaries of the district of Smyrna upon the assumption that this district would be subject to Greek administration, though not necessarily Greek sovereignty. This commission, after due deliberation, unanimously recommended a Greek administration for a limited zone around Smyrna, in which (it was said) there was a substantial majority of Greeks.[1] This proposal offered to Greece a greater measure of control than either the British or the French Foreign Offices had envisaged. Nevertheless, Lloyd George succeeded in securing its acceptance.[2] Not only this, but he also won for Greece both Eastern and Western Thrace in full sovereignty. By astute bargaining, he persuaded the French to agree that the Chatalja lines should constitute the Greco-Turkish frontier in Europe in return for a token concession to the Turks—the retention of nominal suzerainty over the Smyrna zone.[3]

In the drafting of these terms Curzon had somewhat feebly acquiesced, unable, so he said, to resist the inexhaustible eloquence of Venizelos.[4] Nevertheless, he had grave misgivings, and in an attempt to secure some modification of the terms, wrote personally to Lloyd George expressing his concern:

> We must be on very sure and strong ground if we are to over-ride all this. I am the last man to wish to do a good turn to the Turks . . . but I do want to get something like peace in Asia Minor, and with the Greeks in Smyrna, and Greek divisions carrying out Venizelos's orders and marching about Asia Minor I know this to be impossible.[5]

Lloyd George was not prepared to change his views. He did not apparently reply to this letter, but in his papers are two

---

[1] The Committee based its findings on American figures: Moslems 325,000, Greeks, 375,000. Lloyd George Papers, F/206/3/18.

[2] DBFP, VII, 24.   [3] DBFP, VII, 14.

[4] F.O. 5043/1207, Minutes, 11 March 1920.

[5] Lloyd George Papers, F/12/3/24, Curzon to Prime Minister, 9 April 1920.

documents drawn up by his secretariat which strongly endorse
the Greek case. The first, of 7 April, by his private secretary,
Philip Kerr, set out the Greek case and argued that it would
be absurd to abandon the principles of self-determination
when the allies enjoyed all the advantages including 150,000
troops with more Greeks in reserve.[1] The second was forwarded to Montagu, the Secretary of State for India, who
was a strong advocate of the pro-Turkish case. It asserted
that after careful consideration of all the available figures
there was no doubt that the areas assigned to Greece had contained predominantly Greek populations before the war,[2] and
it continued:

> If Mr. Montagu's argument means that the peace terms should be
> determined not by considerations of justice, but by ease of enforce-
> ment, it is a plea that the Allies impose a peace which they think
> unjust to the Greeks, Armenians and other peoples, and biassed in
> favour of the Turks because they have not the resolution or the
> courage to insist on what they believe to be right . . . the truth would
> seem to be that it is difficult to realise that the war has shattered once
> and for all the ancient but tyrannical and oppressive Empire of the
> Turks over their neighbours.

These arguments Lloyd George employed at the Conference
of San Remo, where he resisted every attempt by the French
and the Italians to modify the London terms.[3] He stubbornly
defended the acquisitions of Greece, upon whom he placed his
hopes of enforcing the treaty, and he rejected the conclusion of
the military advisers that the allies would require twenty-seven
divisions to execute the peace terms. He had no doubt that the
Greeks, with six divisions in Smyrna and three in Macedonia,
could enforce the sections of the treaty relating to themselves.
Nor would he countenance the Italian premier, Nitti's, suggestion that Greece should not control Gallipoli and that her
presence in Asia Minor would lead to war. He steadfastly refused
to modify the frontiers of either Thrace or Smyrna, insisting that
the allies could not drive out Greece who was a civilized power.
The French, despite their misgivings, were anxious to avoid
alienating the British whose support they needed on the Rhine,

[1] Lloyd George Papers, F/90/1/44, Kerr to Prime Minister, Memorandum,
7 April 1920.
[2] Lloyd George Papers, F/40/3/5, Lloyd George to Montagu, 25 April 1920.
[3] DBFP, VIII, 11.

and they therefore refrained from endorsing the Italian arguments. Thus Lloyd George was able to maintain the London terms with only minor modifications.

Through Lloyd George's support, Venizelos had achieved the substance of his demands, and this he acknowledged in a letter of 26 April.[1] But he was under no illusions that he could rely upon the unequivocal co-operation of the British government. On March 19th at a meeting with the Secretary for war, Churchill, and the CIGS, Sir Henry Wilson, he had learnt that the Chief of Staff foresaw for Greece a long and exhausting struggle in Asia Minor.[2] Furthermore, Churchill explained that although Greece might obtain sympathy, and perhaps arms and ammunition, from Great Britain, she could expect neither financial aid nor troops. Nevertheless, Venizelos remained confident that he was undertaking nothing which was beyond the power of Greece.

At this point it may be opportune to consider what Lloyd George was attempting to achieve for Great Britain by his support of the Greeks. Perhaps the clearest definition of the aim is contained in a memorandum of 29 December, 1920 by Harold Nicolson, the British representative on the Greek committee of 1919, one of the strongest advocates of the Greek case:[3]

> The policy of HM Government ... is of necessity more nebulous [than that of her allies]. The idea which prompted our support of Greece was no emotional impulse, but the natural expression of our historical policy—the protection of India and the Suez Canal ... Geographically the position of Greece was unique for this purpose: politically she was strong enough to save us expense in peace, and weak enough to be completely subservient in war.

In June 1920, an opportunity arose for the Greeks to consolidate their position. The Turkish Nationalist movement, which had grown steadily since its inception in 1919, had now established firm control over the centre of Anatolia, with its capital at Angora. From here it was exerting military pressure against the foreign encroachments upon Turkish soil, notably the French who had forces in Cilicia, and the British troops

---

[1] Lloyd George Papers, F/55/1/8, Venizelos to Prime Minister, 26 April 1920.

[2] Lloyd George Papers, F/199/9/2, Meeting, 19 March 1920.

[3] DBFP, XII, 488.

who were garrisoning the Ismid peninsular which defended the
approaches to Constantinople.[1] This pressure the British military
felt unable to withstand. The cabinet, however, concluded

> ... that having regard to the very strong and even dramatic line of
> policy taken by the British plenipotentiaries in regard to the Treaty of
> Peace with Turkey, to retire from Constantinople before a bandit
> like Mustapha Kemal would deal a shattering blow to our prestige
> in the East.[2]

When it became apparent therefore that neither the French nor
the Italians were prepared to send out the reinforcements which
General Milne deemed necessary,[3] the British military, despite
their disdain for the Greeks, sought their help to relieve the
situation.[4]

On June 18th, Venizelos informed the British cabinet that he
was prepared to increase his forces at Smyrna and to conduct
a major operation against the Nationalists provided that it was
understood that he would advance no further into Anatolia.
Moreover, he offered to relieve the British position at Ismid at
once, by placing a Greek Division under General Milne's
command. This offer the Cabinet decided to accept, and they
resolved to consult their allies concerning Venizelos's proposal
for a Greek offensive against the Nationalists.

In accordance with this decision, Lloyd George met Millerand
at Hythe on June 20th.[5] There the French premier, anxious to
relieve the pressure on his forces in Cilicia, agreed not only to
the initiation of a Greek operation in Asia but also to the
immediate Greek occupation of Thrace, hitherto garrisoned on
behalf of the allies by a predominantly French force. For his
part, Lloyd George welcomed the opportunity to strengthen
the Greek position in Asia Minor and to make the Thracian
part of the Treaty a *fait accompli*. He took the view, as he
explained to Lord Riddell a few days later, that Britain must
decide whom she was going to back:

> The Turks nearly brought about our defeat in the war. It was a near
> thing. You cannot trust them and they are a decadent race. The

---

[1] DBFP, XIII, 90. (The Italians in Adalia had no perimeter against the
Turks whom they were actively assisting in their military reorganisation.
F.O. 5052/7721, War Office to Foreign Office, 3 July 1920.)
[2] CAB 23/21, 53(20), Appx. II, 17 June 1920.   [3] DBFP, XIII, 87.
[4] CAB 23/21, 38(20), 18 June 1920.   [5] DBFP, VIII, 26.

Greeks, on the other hand, are our friends, and are a rising people . . .
We must secure Constantinople and the Dardanelles. You cannot do
that effectively without crushing Turkish power.[1]

The Greeks acted rapidly and efficiently. With British naval
support, they occupied Thrace within five days, and proceeded
to drive the Nationalists from Brusa and Panderma, completing
their planned operation by the end of July.[2] Lloyd George,
confident that the Greek successes had vindicated his policy,
declaimed to the Commons, 'Turkey is no more'.[3] His confidence
in Venizelos was now unlimited and he suggested to the Italian
premier, Giolitti, that the allies should assign to Greece the task
of providing the garrison for Gallipoli thus giving her a
permanent role in the defence of the Straits.[4]

But although the Greek successes had revealed the comparative weakness of the Turkish forces, the limited character
of the Greek operations had enabled the Turks to withdraw
beyond the Greek zone and thus escape annihilation. Venizelos
realized that Kemal would constitute a standing menace to the
Greek provinces unless his forces were completely destroyed.
He therefore offered to launch a further operation to accomplish
this object, provided that the British government undertook
responsibility for initiating the offensive, participated in the
operations, and supplied Greece with the necessary financial
and military aid. For his services Venizelos demanded a
substantial political price: the creation of a Pontine Greek state;
the expulsion of the Turks from Constantinople; and the
formation of an independent state comprising Constantinople
and the Straits. On October 10th, the British Cabinet gave
these proposals serious consideration.[5] There was no longer
any doubt that the Greek army was a first-class weapon.
Indeed the CIGS, hitherto sceptical of the quality of the Greek
troops, now believed that they might be able to reach the
enemy capital. But the adoption of Venizelos's plan implied
the destruction of the peace treaty which the Sultan had signed
at Sèvres on August 10th. Moreover, the government, conscious

---

[1] Lord Riddell, *Intimate Diary of the Peace Conference and After* (1933), 208.
[2] DBFP, XIII, 102.
[3] *H.C. deb.*, 132, 21 July 1920.
[4] DBFP, VIII, Lucerne Conversations, 22 Aug. 1920.
[5] CAB 23/22, 55(22), 12 Oct. 1920.

of a growing domestic opposition to its eastern policy, had given an explicit assurance to the Commons that it was under no obligation to the Greek army.[1] For these reasons, and because it appeared improbable that either France or Italy would give their consent, the cabinet decided to shelve Venizelos's proposals.

Nevertheless the Greeks' position seemed secure. In Thrace their control was unchallenged, and although in Asia Minor they remained upon a war footing, they had received a mandate from the allies to occupy a much wider area than that laid down in the treaty and were the appointed guardians of the allied position at the Straits. Then, in November, the situation was unexpectedly transformed. The tragic death of the young Greek King, Alexander, resulting from a monkey's bite, altered the complexion of the impending Greek general elections, turning them into a test of confidence in the Venizelist regime. On 15 November Venizelos and his supporters were overwhelmingly defeated.[2] In their place was elected a government pledged to recall to the throne ex-King Constantine, whom the allies had expelled from Greece as a Germanophil in 1917. Lloyd George, in a letter commiserating with Venizelos, declared that the result made him 'despair of democracy'.[3]

This turn of fate seemed to the French a convenient pretext for the allies to reverse their policy and seek a reconciliation with the Turks.[4] But this Lloyd George was not prepared to do. Defending his policy in the Commons on 22 December[5] he declared that it was impossible to alter it merely because of a Greek election. Stressing the importance to Great Britain of Greek friendship in the Mediterranean, he refused to 'purchase a way out of our difficulties by betraying others'. Within the Cabinet he resisted the pressure of his colleagues to modify the treaty, and he secured their agreement to uphold the Sèvres policy until such time as a change of circumstances should warrant its revision.

In maintaining this course he had the support of Curzon,[6]

---

[1] *H.C. deb.*, 131, 20 June 1920.
[2] DBFP, XII, 420, 428.
[3] Lloyd George Papers, F/55/1/41, LG to Venizelos, 17 Nov. 1920.
[4] *Le Temps*, 23 Nov. 1920.
[5] *H.C. deb.*, 136, 22 Dec. 1920.
[6] CAB 23/23, 70(20), Appx III, 2 Dec. 1920.

who despite his former opposition to the Greek presence in Smyrna considered that Great Britain, having signed the Treaty of Sèvres, was bound by her promise to the Greeks, and that modification of the terms would constitute a humiliating concession to the Turks.[1] Thus when Cambon, the French ambassador, suggested that in the event of Constantine's recall the allies should make a joint declaration refusing to recognize him, Curzon emphasized that he regarded such action as impracticable and unwise. The allies' main duty was to save the treaty if they possibly could, for no-one could tell what might happen if they themselves proceeded to destroy it or allowed it to founder without making an effort to save it.

From 26 November to 4 December, 1920, the allies met in London to discuss the new situation.[2] Lloyd George had kept in touch with Venizelos who, though hopeful that a concerted allied threat might prevent Constantine's return, took the view that the essential task was to preserve the treaty and had advised the British government to recognize the ex-King if necessary in return for a firm promise to execute the peace terms.[3] In accordance with this advice Lloyd George, anxious to prevent a premature condemnation of Greece, proposed that the allies should invite the royalist regime to explain whether or not it was still prepared to excute the treaty. But the French opposed the proposal and refused to co-operate with the Constantinist politicians. They demanded drastic action—the allies should refuse to recognize Constantine, break off diplomatic relations with Greece, terminate financial aid, and give notification that they could not entrust important strategic positions to an unfriendly government. Against this proposal, Curzon reasoned that the allies should trust Greece until she should prove either unable or unwilling to co-operate. He denied that her presence at the Straits, could, as the French had suggested, constitute a threat to the allies, and he declared that it was a practical impossibility to expel the Greek forces from Smyrna. He proposed that if Constantine returned he should be asked to accept a set of stringent conditions which would give the allies effective control over Greek policy. But the French insisted upon immediate counter-measures against

[1] Lloyd George Papers, F/13/1/34, Curzon to Derby, 22 Nov. 1920.
[2] DBFP, VIII, 95–100.　　　　[3] DBFP, XII, 451, 453.

Greece. These Lloyd George rejected, saying that the allies had no power to modify the provisions of the treaty and he categorically refused to replace Smyrna under the 'Turkish heel'. Nevertheless, he expressed his personal hostility to Constantine and agreed that the allies should issue a formal warning to the Greek government that they held themselves free to take what action they thought fit if the ex-King were recalled.

On 3 December, the French again pressed for a revision of the Treaty, suggesting that the return of Smyrna might reconcile Kemal to a peaceful settlement. But Lloyd George refused to reconsider the terms until the policy of the royalists became clear. It was quite possible, he said, that the Greeks would reject Constantine, but if on the other hand the King returned, the allies had given fair warning that they would wash their hands of their responsibilities towards Greece. The following day, the allies determined to inform the Greek government that in the event of Constantine's return they would withdraw all financial aid from Greece.[1]

Thus, despite his desire to maintain the treaty, Lloyd George, partly because of his personal antipathy to Constantine, had allowed the French to manoeuvre him into an equivocal position. He had committed Great Britain to punishing Greece if Constantine returned, despite the fact that his policy depended upon Greek co-operation. When, on 6 December, Greece recalled the ex-King, the British government had no choice but to collaborate with the French in accordance with the declaration of 4 December.[2] They imposed a financial embargo upon Greece and suspended the dispatch of war material.[3] These drastic measures notwithstanding, Lloyd George still hoped that Constantine might yet complete the task assigned to Greece under the Treaty of Sèvres. Thus, when Venizelos sought British support for a coup at Smyrna similar to that which he had carried out at Salonica in 1917, Kerr replied that although Lloyd George was favourably disposed to the idea, nothing was to be attempted until Constantine had failed to maintain the Treaty of Sèvres.[4]

On 29 January the cabinet discussed the situation. There

---

[1] DBFP, VIII, 100.   [2] DBFP, XIII, 466.
[3] FO. 6077/137, Waterlow to Secretary of Admiralty, 5 Jan. 1921.
[4] Lloyd George Papers, F/20,90/1/34, Kerr to PM, 15 Jan. 1921.

was general agreement that Great Britain could no longer resist some revision of the peace terms,[1] and it was decided to approve Curzon's proposal that the allies should invite both the Turks and the Greeks to an international conference to discuss the problem. Lloyd George emphasized however, that if concessions were to be made, they must be at the expense of the allies as a whole, and not merely of Greece.

On 24 January, Lloyd George and Curzon visited Paris to discuss the position with the new French premier M. Briand.[2] They had no difficulty in securing his agreement to an international conference, but when Curzon suggested that the allies should recognize Constantine upon agreed conditions, Briand replied that the Greek forces (which had suffered a minor reverse at Inönü) were unreliable and that the allies should exploit Constantine's difficult position and put pressure on Greece. To this Lloyd George retorted that there could be no question of 'throwing over the Greeks', but he added that he would try to persuade them to accept a compromise in respect of Smyrna.

Meanwhile, Venizelos continued to furnish a constant stream of advice. He disliked the idea of an international conference and urged Great Britain to collaborate with Constantine rather than abandon the Greek cause.[3] Yet he still hoped that it might be possible to get rid of his enemy thus enabling the allies to return to their original policy. To this end, he suggested that Great Britain should offer the Greek government a financial inducement to persuade Constantine to abdicate.[4] But Lloyd George was by now convinced that the best course for the allies was to rely upon the Constantinist regime standing firm. He told Curzon that he doubted whether the allies could force Greece to leave Smyrna. If Constantine put up a good fight and if the allies offered some concessions on their part there was a good chance that the Kemalists could be bought off and persuaded to turn their ambitions eastwards.[5]

On 19 February, Lloyd George met the Greek premier, Kalogeropolous,[6] whom he questioned as to the ability of

---

[1] CAB 23/24/3 (21), 20 Jan. 1921.   [2] DBFP, XV, 12.
[3] Lloyd George Papers, F/90/1/36, Kerr to Venizelos, 26 Jan. 1921.
[4] Lloyd George Papers, F/90/1/37, Kerr to Prime Minister, 4 Feb. 1921.
[5] Lloyd George Papers, F/13/2/32, Lloyd George to Curzon, 16 Feb. 1921.
[6] DBFP, XV, 13.

Greece to defend her new frontiers. Kalogeropolous, assured of Great Britain's friendship, answered confidently that the Greek army was in a position to scatter the Kemalist forces if the allies gave the word. When Lloyd George explained that Curzon had proposed making Smyrna an autonomous province under Turkish sovereignty, Kalogeropolous stressed that Greece could never agree to return the province to the Turks. This answer delighted Lloyd George, who declared that he relied upon the spirit of the Greeks. Nevertheless, they should be prepared to compromise a little for it was important that if the conference broke down the onus of responsibility should fall upon the Turks.

Having assured himself of the Greeks' determination to maintain the Sèvres policy, Lloyd George set out to shelve Curzon's autonomy proposal.[1] He informed the French that the Greeks were determined to keep Smyrna and that they could not be driven out by force of arms. The allies were really being bluffed by Kemal, whose forces the Greeks could defeat with ease. He refused to listen to Briand's arguments that the Greek position in the Balkans was insecure and they were in need of financial aid. Kalogeropolous, meanwhile, had received instructions from his government in Athens to take an uncompromising stand, and on 21 February, he informed the conference that Greece would not abate her claims in either Thrace or Asia Minor.[2] Nor would he modify this position under pressure. In reply to the French argument that the Turkish opposition was formidable, he asserted that Greece was best fitted to judge the military situation, a contention which Lloyd George endorsed. Thereupon the French and the Italians proposed that since Greek intransigence had precluded the autonomy proposal, the allies should attempt to resolve the deadlock by appointing a commission of enquiry to investigate the ethnographic figures for both Smyrna and Thrace.[3] This proposal Lloyd George felt unable to reject, but he insisted that a corollary to the offer must be the Turks' unconditional acceptance of the remainder of the Peace Treaty. On 25 February Lloyd George sent Hankey (the British secretary to the conference) to advise the Greeks not to incur the odium of rejecting the allied proposal out of hand, but to consult the

[1] DBFP, XV, 14.   [2] DBFP, XV, 15.   [3] DBFP, XV, 22.

Greek National Assembly.[1] The Greeks, however, regarded the proposals as unjust; they feared that the enquiry would be virtually pre-determined by the biassed attitude of the French and the Italians; and they could not contemplate the possible loss of both territories.[2] On 4 March, Kalogeropolous informed Lloyd George that Greece rejected the allied proposals.[3] He offered Great Britain political guarantees in return for credits for her impending military operations, but this offer Lloyd George ignored. He warned the Greeks that the French were taking an increasingly pro-Turkish line, and that the Turks had agreed to accept an enquiry. In these circumstances Greece should reconsider the possibility of offering Kemal a fair compromise. She should be prepared to accept the administrative control of a reduced Smyrna zone, under Turkish sovereignty, and should make the Turks a financial offer (in the form of payment of tribute) to induce them to accept such an arrangement.

Although he had counselled the Greeks to compromise, Lloyd George was convinced that feeling was now so high on both sides that the issue would probably be settled by force of arms.[4] He therefore determined to ensure that in the event of the conference failing the Greeks should be at no disadvantage. On 4 March, when Briand and the Italian delegate, Count Sforza, proposed that the allies should throw upon Greece the onus for rejecting the enquiry, Lloyd George retorted that the Turks, who had refused to accept the rest of the treaty unconditionally, were equally intransigent.[5] The Greeks might yet respond to pressure on the Smyrna issue. In any event, if the conference broke down, the allies must observe strict neutrality. Moreover, if the Greeks found their positions threatened, they should be in no doubt as to their right to retaliate. The allies should therefore tell the Greeks that they were free to take any action they deemed necessary lest they should subsequently blame a disaster upon the allies. To this Briand agreed, and after this meeting, Lloyd George sent

[1] Lloyd George Papers, F/25/1/11, Hankey to Prime Minister, 26 Feb. 1921.
[2] F.O. 6467/3101, Granville to Curzon, 1 March 1921.
[3] DBFP, XV, 32.
[4] Lloyd George Papers, F/9/3, Lloyd George to Winston, 16 March 1921.
[5] DBFP, XV, 35, 50.

Hankey to inform Kalogeropolous, who thereupon notified Athens:

> ... [Lloyd George] had no objection to their undertaking operations against Kemal in the event that their advisers consider it necessary for the security of their army.[1]

Nevertheless, Lloyd George now took the lead in initiating a fresh attempt to reach a peaceful settlement. The allies should offer to Greece some modification of the original 'autonomy proposal', and to the Turks further revision of the main clauses of the treaty.[2] On 10 March, together with Curzon, he put the new proposal to Kalogeropolous and to Gounaris, his war minister (the 'strong man' of the Greek government).[3] There would be no question of Greece having to leave the whole of the Smyrna zone where she would retain full control wherever a Greek majority existed. Gounaris, however, insisted that Greece must complete her mission of implementing the Treaty of Sèvres by military force. Thereupon Curzon withdrew-Gounaris then asked Lloyd George to confirm Hankey's message. This he did, saying that if the Greeks considered an attack vital the conference could no longer take the responsibility for restraining them. Following this 'assurance' Gounaris and Kalogeropolous informed Athens: 'The beginning of these operations has been suitably intimated as being the essential argument in favour of our case', and they ordered the Greek offensive to proceed.[4]

Although both Lloyd George and Briand were convinced that the issue would now be settled by war[5] the allies nevertheless proceeded to draft a set of 'autonomy' proposals upon the lines suggested by Lloyd George. The Greeks, however, laid down impossible conditions for their acceptance. This perturbed the French and the Italians, who were anxious to issue further warnings to both belligerents of the consequences of their intractability, but Lloyd George vigorously defended the Greek position, which he argued was not unreasonable, and he refused to participate in any measure which might inhibit the Greeks' freedom of action. On 18 March, however, on learning from Gounaris that the Greek government proposed

[1] Frangulis, A. P., *La Grèce* ii, 207.   [2] DBFP, XV, 51. [3] DBFP, XV, 52.
[4] Frangulis ii, 210; F.O. 6467/3343, Minute, 16 March 1921.
[5] DBFP, XV, 53.

to resume hostilities without further delay,[1] he again emphasized the importance to Greece of ensuring that the onus for any resumption of hostilities should fall upon the Turks, and he gave an explicit warning that the consequences to Greece of a military failure might well prove irreparable. Gounaris, however, was clearly determined upon force and, thanking Lloyd George for obtaining for Greece her freedom of action, he requested British aid in the form of a loan or financial credit. But although Lloyd George authorized discussions with the British Treasury, Gounaris's subsequent negotiations for a loan came to nothing.[2]

The Greek dispatches recording Lloyd George's conversations with Kalogeropolous and Gounaris, which were intercepted by both the French and the British Foreign Offices, offer the principal evidence for Curzon's charges (made in December 1922) that Lloyd George 'directly encouraged the Greeks to go ahead in Asia Minor while the London Conference was sitting in March, 1921'.[3] At the time Curzon minuted:

> I think it a great pity that the fighting has been encouraged to begin for it can hardly help a settlement unless by a complete defeat of one or the other party who precipitates it.[4]

and the Foreign Office official D. G. Osborne, commented:

> HMG if they did not actually encourage the offensive at least did nothing to discourage it—which in the circumstances, amounts to much the same thing.

But Sir Eyre Crowe, the permanent under-secretary at the foreign office, was more sceptical, considering that the Greeks had chosen to read more into Lloyd George's words than he had intended.

The resumption of hostilities by Greece on 23 March, 1921 was widely attributed in both France and Italy to direct British encouragement. But the British government immediately took steps to establish its neutrality. It relinquished control over the Greek Division at Ismid and informed the Greek chargé that in agreement with the allies an attitude of strict neutrality would be adopted.[5] Furthermore, Curzon, on the

---

[1] DBFP, XV, 69.   [2] F.O. 6511/5142, Greek Chargé, 29 April 1921.
[3] Bonar Law Papers, 111/12/37, Curzon to Prime Minister, 2 Dec. 1922.
[4] F.O. 6467/3343, GHQ to War Office, 14 March 1921, Minutes.
[5] F.O. 6510/4746, Memorandum, 22 April 1921.

advice of his legal advisers, imposed an embargo upon arms exports including private sales. This, Lloyd George complained to Curzon, was contrary to the normal rules of neutrality and he argued that Greece should be entitled to normal belligerent rights to purchase in the open market,[1] but Curzon was adamant. He replied:

> I have always thought it very important not to take sides—we have on the whole successfully preserved neutrality. If we help Greece we will take their side and will lessen the chance of coming to terms with the Turks.

The Greeks' spring offensive[2] met with stiff Turkish opposition. The reorganized Turkish regular forces proved much superior to the irregular units of 1920, while the Greek army itself had deteriorated following a winter in Anatolia and political purges in the ranks of the officers after the royalist victory at the polls. The northern army failed to reach the strategic railway junction of Eskishehir and by 4 April Greek forces had withdrawn to their positions before 23 March. This was a severe setback for the Greek government, which immediately wrote to Lloyd George expressing the hope that this 'temporary and local reverse' would not shake his confidence or deprive Greece of his support.[3]

But Lloyd George's confidence was indeed shaken and when the British military told the cabinet on 31 May that the situation was serious, he was prepared to listen.[4] Harington, the British Commander-in-Chief at Constantinople, feared a Greek collapse with dire consequences to the allied cause, and the cabinet decided to appoint a special committee to consider the best course of action. This committee decided, in the light of advice tendered by Venizelos, to revive the London proposals with a view to imposing these impartially upon whichever belligerent refused to accept them. It was agreed that France should be asked to co-operate, and Curzon took pains to ensure that Lloyd George's draft proposals should make clear to the French that there was no intention of giving unilateral assistance

---

[1] Lloyd George Papers, F/13/2/15, Curzon to Lloyd George, 20 April 1921.
[2] CP. 46/4372, Rumbold (Sir Horace Rumbold, British High Commissioner at Constantinople) to Curzon, 5 April 1921.
[3] F.O. 511/5142, Granville to Curzon, 29 April 1921.
[4] CAB 23/25/45(21), 31 May 1921.

to Greece. She would receive aid only if she put herself in the hands of the powers while the Turks for their part rejected the allied peace proposals.[1] On 19 June Curzon put these proposals to Briand, who though willing enough to support a fresh peace initiative refused to contemplate any proposal to coerce the Turks.[2] Thus the scheme was emasculated from the start, and Gounaris, now prime minister, had no incentive to accept the allied terms which differed little from those offered to him in March.

On July 2nd Greece opened a fresh offensive. Her forces were now more efficient than ever before. Deficiencies had been made good and the changes of leadership had on the whole proved beneficial.[3] On 20 July the Greeks occupied Eskishehir and paused to regroup their forces. In Greece this success was acclaimed as a decisive victory and there was a burst of exaggerated exuberation. All Lloyd George's hopes in the Greeks revived and he complained bitterly to the War Office of its ignorance of the impending hostilities and its failure to assess the quality of the Greek army accurately.[4] In a speech to the Commons on August 16th, he defended the Greek presence in Smyrna, and made it clear that he considered 'fighting it out' to be the best solution. Though he spoke of the Greeks learning their limits, he castigated the arrogance of the Turks, and he hinted that a Greek victory would lead to a revision of the treaty of Sèvres in their favour.[5]

Anxious that nothing should impede the Greeks' chances of success, Lloyd George raised the question of the arms embargo at an allied conference on 10 August.[6] He complained that the restriction exceeded the legitimate rules of neutrality and discriminated unfairly against the Greeks since the Turks suffered from no such impediment in their acquisition of arms from the Bolsheviks. In the transformed situation the Greeks might well become the arbiters of the peace, and the allies should therefore do nothing to estrange them. To these argu-

[1] Lloyd George Papers, F/13/2/29, Curzon to Prime Minister, 11 June 1921.　　　　　　　　　　[2] DBFP, XV, 88.

[3] CAB 29/37, 289, Greco-Turkish operations, July-August, 1921.

[4] Lloyd George Papers, F/16/3/27, Lloyd George to Worthington-Evans, 21 July 1921.

[5] H.C. deb., 146, 16 August 1921.

[6] DBFP, XV, 94.

ments Briand retorted that the Greeks had had no difficulty in getting round the restrictions and obtaining supplies from France. Nevertheless, under pressure from Lloyd George, he agreed to a joint declaration which reaffirmed the principle of neutrality, but added a qualification that this would not prevent the purchase of arms through normal commercial transactions.

On 13 August the Greeks resumed the struggle in the hope of capturing Angora itself and permanently destroying the Kemalist threat. Since at this time Kemal's personal position was, due to internal rivalries, extremely precarious, this objective was not as unrealistic as has been sometimes supposed.[1] At first the Greeks made steady progress, but at the Sakharia river the Turks halted at prepared positions and checked the advance. A ten-day struggle ensued during which the Greeks took the first line of the Turkish defences and approached within thirty miles of Angora. But, despite high morale, they failed to turn the flank of the Turkish positions and in September, abandoning their campaign, they retraced their steps to Eskishehir. Their losses had been heavy and there was now every indication that the relative quality of the Nationalist army would improve.[2]

For the present, however, the position was a stalemate. The Turkish forces proved too exhausted to harass the Greek retreat, and Curzon was optimistic that the opportunity was ripe for the allies to make a fresh attempt to mediate between the two sides. Gounaris was anxious to come to London and discuss the situation and it seemed likely that he would accept some face-saving formula. Curzon therefore determined to press the Greeks to accept the June proposals and to abate their claims to Smyrna.[3] If he succeeded, he planned to summon an allied conference to reach agreement on the precise terms.

On 27 October he met Gounaris, whom he reminded that the British attitude towards Greece had been friendly and sympathetic throughout.[4] In his opinion the Turkish demand for Greece to withdraw from Smyrna was unreasonable, but in the circumstances he saw no choice for Greece but to agree.

[1] CP. 47/9560, Granville to Curzon, 10 August 1921.
[2] CP. 48/10272, Rumbold to Curzon, 7 Sept. 1921.
[3] CP. 11096, Curzon Memorandum, 7 Oct. 1921.
[4] CP. 11922, Gounaris/Curzon Conversation, 27 Oct. 1921.

Moreover, in view of the hostile attitude of France, she would probably have to accept also some modification of the frontier in Thrace. He advised her to place herself in the hands of the powers. There was no guarantee that either the French, the Italians or the Turks would accept the solutions he had outlined, but it would immensely strengthen the Greek position to accept mediation. In response to these urgings, the Greeks formally accepted Curzon's proposals on 2 November.

Curzon was now ready to launch his peace initiative when news arrived that the French had concluded a separate agreement with the Kemalists.[1] By this arrangement, signed at Angora on 20 October as the culmination of months of secret negotiation, the French undertook to withdraw their troops from Cilicia in return for an unmolested evacuation and vague promises of future concessions by the Turks. They also agreed, though the British did not secure confirmation of this until January 1922,[2] to leave behind large supplies of military equipment and arms, including aeroplanes, on their withdrawal from Cilicia. This agreement, which clearly aligned the French alongside the Turks, Curzon regarded as blatantly disloyal. Nevertheless, since neither Great Britain nor France desired an open breach, the *entente* survived.

Before serious negotiations on the eastern question could be resumed it was essential for Great Britain to restore a working relationship with France. In December Lloyd George attempted an all-round settlement of Anglo-French differences by offering the French a 'Pact' assuring them of British military aid in the event of German aggression against the soil of France.[3] In return he expected their co-operation upon a number of outstanding points, including a pacific settlement in the Near East. For a time it seemed that despite French dissatisfaction with the terms of the British offer, a deal would be possible, and at the Cannes conference in February 1922, Lloyd George told Gounaris that the guarantee Pact offered the chief hope of reaching a settlement.[4] Even so Greece must be prepared for substantial sacrifices—a complete withdrawal from Smyrna and the modification of her frontier in Thrace. The only course

[1] CP. 11937, Rumbold to Curzon, 25 Oct. 1921.
[2] CP. 1179, Memorandum, 27 Jan. 1922.
[3] DBFP, XV, 110.   [4] CAB 23/35/38, Conversation, 12 Feb. 1922.

for Greece was to place herself in Curzon's hands. This Gounaris agreed to do, saying that although Greece could no longer force an issue, she could maintain her existing position in Asia Minor. Almost immediately, however, French opposition to the terms of the Pact led Briand to resign. His successor, the right-wing former president, Poincaré, immediately laid down unacceptable conditions for the Pact and told Curzon that he was not prepared to attend a conference on the Near East until the British came closer to meeting the French view.[1]

For the Greeks this further postponement of allied intervention was serious. In November Gounaris had impressed upon both Lloyd George and Curzon the Greek government's desperate need of funds. On 21 December the British cabinet had decided that it was essential to keep the Greek army in being as a lever during negotiations and had therefore agreed to authorize the Treasury to approve a Greek attempt to raise a loan from the City.[2] On 23 December therefore, Lloyd George had raised the lien on Greek securities imposed in December, 1920.[3] But on 15 February, Gounaris, in a mood approaching desperation, asked Curzon for positive guidance.[4] He revealed that Greece, despite the consent of the British Treasury, had failed to raise a loan on the London market and had almost exhausted her resources. The Turks, on the other hand, were receiving arms not only from Russia but also from France and Italy. Greece could no longer undertake to hold a Turkish offensive unless she received arms, reinforcements and financial assistance. This letter Curzon circulated to the Cabinet, but he delayed an immediate reply pending reports from Britain's representatives at Athens and Constantinople. On 27 February, Gounaris wrote to Lloyd George in a sense similar to that of his letter to Curzon and requested an interview but this Lloyd George refused.[5] Meanwhile, Curzon had ascertained from his agents that the Greek condition appeared less serious than Gounaris had depicted. Lindley, the representative at Athens, was of the opinion that the Greek move was a

---

[1] F.O. 7853/692, Curzon/Poincaré Conversation, 16 Jan. 1922.
[2] CAB 23/27, 93(21), Appx III, 21 Dec. 1921.
[3] F.O. 6087/24060, Nicolson to Rangulis-Rabé, Conversation, 23 Dec. 1921.   [4] CP 49/1931, Gounaris to Curzon, 15 Feb. 1922.
[5] Premier, 1/18, Gounaris to Lloyd George, 27 Feb. 1922.

bluff intended to drive Great Britain into supplying aid. He believed that Greece had no intention of evacuating Asia Minor. Curzon therefore replied to Gounaris on 6 March in a carefully considered letter.[1] He declared that the wisest solution was to expedite a diplomatic settlement through Allied mediation adding:

> I can only express the hope that the military position is less immediately critical than your note would lead me to think and that the remarkable patriotism and discipline of the Hellenic army of which so many illustrations have been furnished in the campaigns of the last few years, will not fail them in any emergency which may conceivably arise.

At the end of March, the conference on the Near East finally met in Paris and devised fresh compromise proposals.[2] In these negotiations Lloyd George played no part. During the conference, Curzon found himself defending the Greek position against Poincaré whose aggressive hostility towards the Greeks complicated negotiations. Eventually, unable to match the obstinacy and sharp tactics of his opponent, Curzon was forced to go much further to meet the Turks than he had originally anticipated. The basis of the new allied proposals was the conclusion of an immediate armistice which would be followed by a conference at which the allies would ask the belligerents to accept a package settlement. This included the total withdrawal of Greek troops from Smyrna and a substantial modification of the frontier in Eastern Thrace.

This offer the Turks rejected, fearing that the armistice would enable the Greeks to recuperate.[3] They demanded an immediate Greek withdrawal from their front-line positions, or alternatively a preliminary conference at which the allies should discuss the general peace terms with the belligerents. Thereupon the Greeks accepted the armistice but reserved their reply to the other proposals since these went much further than Curzon had led Gounaris to expect.[4]

The situation had again reached deadlock. The French categorically refused to consider imposing the allied terms

[1] CP. 471, Curzon to Gounaris, 6 March 1922.
[2] CP. 3274, 3290, 3427, 3428, 3507–10. 22–27 March 1922.
[3] CP. 4028, Youssouf Kemal to French government, 5 April 1922.
[4] F.O. 7860/3493, Lindsay to Curzon, 31 March 1922.

upon the belligerents and wished to accept the Turkish proposal for a preliminary conference, but this the foreign office refused to consider, regarding it as a deliberate attempt to modify the March decisions in the Turks' favour. It continued to count upon the Greeks' ability to maintain their position in Asia Minor. So did Lloyd George. On 30 May he told Venizelos that he had no objections to a delay provided that the Greek army held.[1] To this Venizelos replied that though the troops could stand firm indefinitely, the cost to Greece was excessive and she was bleeding to death financially. The allies should coerce Kemal who would otherwise accept no terms of any kind. They should present him with an ultimatum which would force him to reveal his true character to the French. The allies might then be in a position to offer Greece support in return for the abdication of King Constantine, thus making possible the expulsion of the Turks from Constantinople. But Lloyd George pointed out that little hope could be placed upon a French *volte-face*, since their policy was too closely related to financial interests. The only course was for Greece to stick to her policy.

> He would never shake hands with a Greek again who went back on his country's aims in Smyrna. If he was out of office he would speak freely on this point. In office he could not do so but he felt strongly that this was the testing time of the Greek nation and that if they persevered now their future was assured. It would be a great mistake to press for a settlement now. A quick settlement would be a bad settlement for Greece. They must be patient and stick it out.

In June, however, Lindley, the British representative at Athens, informed the government that Greece could not hold out much longer.[2] Thereupon Lloyd George attempted to press the French to expedite a diplomatic solution but Poincaré refused to discuss the question until July.[3] The foreign office was convinced that the French policy was to delay negotiations, while supplying Kemal with the arms and ammunition to enable him to launch a final offensive.[4]

The Greek government became desperate. Although,

[1] Lloyd George Papers, F/86/2/3, Lloyd George/Venizelos Conversation, 30 May 1922.   [2] CP. 5887, Lindley to Balfour, 1 June 1922.
[3] F.O. 7866/6283, Meeting, 19 June 1922.
[4] F.O. 7866/6136, Hardinge to Balfour, Minute, 21 June 1922.

according to the British liaison officer, the army was still reliable,[1] the failure of the allied attempt to mediate had lowered morale. On 27 July the Greek government notified the powers that it was considering measures to end the conflict and on the 29th it requested allied authority to enter Constantinople.[2] To accomplish this end the Commander in Chief had transferred two divisions to Thrace from Asia Minor. But the allied governments took a firm stand against what they regarded as a threat and refused to countenance the Greek demand. In the face of this unanimity the Greek government thought better of the challenge and refrained from further action complaining bitterly that the allies had gravely complicated the issue.[3]

This situation exasperated Lloyd George who had followed the Constantinople affair closely (though it seems improbable that, as the Greek chargé alleged, he had directly encouraged the Greeks to occupy the city).[4] On 4 August he left no doubt as to his sympathies in a notorious speech.[5] He reminded the Commons that the Turks, Great Britain's wartime enemies, were untrustworthy and had rejected all the peace overtures of the allies. Their atrocities necessitated the provision of suitable guarantees for the minorities of Asia Minor. The Turks had enjoyed the inestimable advantage of having their capital defended for them against the Greeks by the allies and they had received supplies of arms from Europe. Greece, on the other hand, deprived of the right to blockade Asia Minor was unable to wage war with her full strength. This state of affairs could not be permitted to continue indefinitely.

This speech, Lloyd George's last effective intervention on behalf of the Greeks, was perhaps his most disastrous. Temporarily, it buoyed up the hopes of the Greek government, which, anticipating real aid from Great Britain, included extracts from the speech in its Military Orders of the Day and requested the British government to facilitate a loan.[6] But there

---

[1] CP. 88/90, Bentinck to Balfour, 29 July 1922.
[2] CP. 7351, Lindley to Balfour, 1 June 1922.
[3] CP. 122, Bentinck to Balfour, 3 Aug. 1922.
[4] Bonar Law Papers, 111/12/47, Curzon to Bonar Law, 17 Dec. 1922.
[5] *H.C. deb.*, 157, 4 Aug. 1922.
[6] CP. 8556, Bentinck to Balfour, 5 Aug. 1922.

seems little doubt that Lloyd George's words convinced Kemal that he must strike before the British could terminate their policy of neutrality and lend their aid to Greece. He delayed no more. On 26 August his forces (which had received substantial supplies of arms from the French) launched an offensive which split the Greek armies and drove them from Asia Minor. There followed the evacuation of most of the Greek population of Asia Minor, the burning of Smyrna and the advance of the Turkish troops to threaten the British positions at Chanak and Ismid.

During the crisis which followed, the Greeks played a small but significant role. Their defeat had deprived them of the power of independent action, but they remained a vital factor in British resistance to Kemal at Chanak, for despite their expulsion from Asia Minor they remained in occupation of Thrace which they held with several undefeated divisions (including the Northern Army group from Asia Minor which had been evacuated virtually without loss). Lloyd George and Churchill realized that an invasion of Europe by Turkish forces lacking naval and air support was improbable. They determined to stand firm in the knowledge that in the event of an outbreak of hostilities, British forces at Ismid and Chanak could rapidly be reinforced from Greece.[1] Nevertheless in view of the hostility of the British public to the government's policy and the resolute opposition of the French, who insisted upon conceding the full Turkish claims, the cabinet resolved to endorse Curzon's decision to purchase the safety of the British positions by returning Eastern Thrace to the Turks.

Of Lloyd George's policy as a whole it can be said that he never sought to hide his whole-hearted enthusiasm for the Greek cause. For the decision which embarked Greece upon her adventures in Asia Minor he shares responsibility with Clemenceau and President Wilson. Subsequently neither his colleagues nor his allies proved capable of standing up to his enthusiasms and he overrode their objections to the Greek policy without serious difficulty. For every major development in the Greek involvement in Asia Minor, he secured the consent of both his cabinet and the French and Italians.

[1] Lloyd George Papers, F/29/4/110, Lloyd George to the King, 18 Sept. 1922.

After Constantine's return his judgment was less sure, and he himself seems to have sensed this for he allowed the burden of the eastern policy to fall increasingly upon Curzon's shoulders. Henceforth his interventions upon the Greeks' behalf were almost invariably disastrous. In March 1921, the offensive which he had tacitly encouraged came to grief. In August, his successful raising of the arms embargo paved the way for the massive supply of European arms to the Turks. Finally, his speech of August 1922 precipitated the Turkish offensive. He was perhaps too sympathetic to Venizelos, for the Greeks' major difficulties arose from the allied financial blockade, a measure of which Lloyd George had himself approved in the hope that it would bring about the fall of Constantine.

A wiser course would have been Curzon's proposal to recognize the Greek King and assume control over his policy. Such a step might well have resulted in an early compromise agreement. But for the charge that Lloyd George conducted a secret policy behind the back of his ministers there is little evidence. He kept in close touch with Venizelos, whose advice was often at fault, but this was a very different matter from conducting secret negotiations with the actual government of Greece. Curzon claimed that while he had been attempting to get the Greeks out of Smyrna, Lloyd George had undermined his policy by secret machinations, yet as Lloyd George pointed out in a letter of 15 September, 1922, he had been careful to leave the conduct of affairs to Curzon.[1] Indeed there is every indication that Lloyd George, never quite certain that Constantine would not mishandle the situation, took pains to ensure that while there should be as few impediments as possible to a Greek victory, there should be no cause for anyone to blame him for a Greek defeat.

Birmingham University   A. E. MONTGOMERY

[1] Lloyd George Papers, F/13/3/33, Lloyd George to Foreign Secretary, 15 Sept. 1922.

X

A STRANGER DEATH OF
LIBERAL ENGLAND

CHRIS COOK

CHRIS COOK

Age 25

St Catharine's College, Cambridge B.A. 1967
Currently Senior Research Officer and Head
of the Political Archives Investigation at the
London School of Economics

A STRANGER DEATH OF
LIBERAL ENGLAND

THE downfall of the Liberal Party remains a theme which exercises a fascination over historians. Despite this attraction, much of the history of the Party after 1918 remains unwritten. There is no published work on the constituency Liberal Associations: the decline of the Party at municipal level remains uncharted.

A similar neglected period of Liberal history concerns the electoral revival of December 1923 and the débâcle of October 1924. Despite the value of Trevor Wilson's work on the downfall of the Liberal Party, his account of the events from November 1922 to October 1924 is open to serious criticism.[1] This essay gives a rather different interpretation of the election results of December 1923 and the subsequent Liberal decision to support a Labour Government without guarantees or conditions.

The essay is not an attempt to deny that, with the emergence of a firmly-based Labour Party, and with the combined effects of the war and of the party split, the former position of the Liberal Party had been eroded. It does, however, seek to question the *degree* of erosion: in particular, it will be argued that, although the party in industrial England was perhaps already in irreversible decline, in rural England the Liberal Party remained the major opposition party to the Conservatives, and could, with a reform of the voting system, as the party of rural radicalism, have remained a major party in a system of three-party politics.

The vital distinction drawn in this essay is between the *decline* of the Liberal Party and its *downfall*. In the last resort, the decline of the Party was transformed into its downfall between December 1923, when the party held 159 seats, and October 1924, when it retained only 40.

Prior to 1923, the Liberal Party, though facing all the obstacles of a third party, was still thought of as a party which might again form a government. By October 1924 this was no

---

[1] See Trevor Wilson: *The Downfall of the Liberal Party.*

longer true. The irony was that the success of the party in the 1923 election was the cause of its downfall: a slightly greater transfer of votes to the Liberals in December 1923 would have given them victory in a score of rural seats. The party would have been again the major opposition: a minority Liberal government would probably have followed. On a date and issue of their choice, the Liberals could have avoided the electoral débâcle of October 1924.

As it was, the party faced a difficult but not impossible position in December 1923. The position was made impossible by the divisions and mistakes of Asquith and Lloyd George. The final section of this essay concentrates on the role Lloyd George wished to pursue during these months.

To understand the events of 1923 it is necessary first to examine the state of the Liberal Party prior to that election. For this reason the structure of this essay falls into three parts: the position of the party in 1923; the campaign and results of December 1923 compared to November 1922; and finally, the debate over the course the Liberal Party should adopt, with the consequences of that decision.

The organization of the independent Liberal Party presented in mid-1923 a picture of almost unrelieved decay.

Herbert Gladstone, the Asquithian Liberal organizer, had no illusions. On the gravity of the position of the party at constituency level, Gladstone could only observe that

> Liberalism as an active missionary force is almost dead in numbers of constituencies and needs strengthening in almost all.[1]

These words were not exaggerated: the Secretary of the Midland Liberal Federation summarized the state of the party in his area in his report on the 1922 Election:

> The most dreadful feature of our work during the past four years has been the difficulty of arousing any interest whatsoever.[2]

The accuracy of these reports can be substantiated from an examination of two areas of Liberal organization in which

---

[1] Memorandum on Organisation: 7 April 1923; in the Herbert Gladstone Papers: Ad. MSS. 46480/52.

[2] Report of 1922 General Election: Midland Liberal Federation Executive Committee Minutes.

records are still extant: the numbers of party agents and the organization of the women's sections.

The steady decline in the numbers of party agents is recorded in the Annual Reports of the Society of Certificated and Associated Liberal Agents.[1] From 357 subscribing members in January 1920, total membership had fallen to 337 a year later, and to 289 by January 1922.

Although, by December 1922, there was no further fall in membership, the position of many Liberal agents was critical: a voluntary levy was held after the 1922 election, 'to assist out of work agents who were in distress', while the year concluded 'in a most depressing manner for agents generally'.

Despite reunion in November 1923, membership of the Society in December 1924 had increased by only three: since the 1924 figure included former National Liberal agents in such areas as Wales, the slight increase conceals a net decline: by December 1925, the figure had slumped to 258.

Even the above figures, however, exaggerate the number of Liberal agents in the constituencies. Of the total membership of 292 in 1924, a closer analysis reveals that 90 of these were employed at Federation or National headquarters, or had retired. A further 13 were unemployed, thus leaving only 189 full-time agents in the constituencies. The position was hardly encouraging.

Whilst any statistics of party membership need to be used with the greatest caution, they possess a value in indicating an overall trend towards decline or expansion. In this connection, the records of the Women's National Liberal Federation, even if suspect over details, present a trend of substantial decline.[2]

This was reflected in the 3rd Annual Report, for 1921–1922, which observed: 'some of our associations have still not regained the strength and membership of pre-war days'. This was a disastrous understatement: in mid-1920, the Women's National Liberal Federation claimed 732 branches with

[1] The following material has been compiled from the S.C.A.L.A. Annual Reports and Account Books, in the possession of Leeds Public Library.

[2] The following material has been compiled from the Annual Reports of the Women's National Liberal Federation, from 1918 to 1925. (In possession of the Librarian, National Liberal Club.)

95,217 members. Two years later, their numbers had fallen by 30% to 67,145. The report for 1921–1922 claimed that 'almost the whole country was covered with a network of Women's Liberal Associations:' in reality, there were scores of constituencies where branches and members had vanished like snow in spring. Once-flourishing branches had entirely disappeared by mid-1923: Grimsby and Kendal, each with 1,500 members in 1919, had vanished: it was a similar story in such seats as Bournemouth, Brighton, Wimbledon or Frome.

These were not isolated examples: the following table lists the extent of the decline in ten of the branches once among the most flourishing:

Branch	1919	1923
Darwen	1500	1051
Lincoln	1071	636
Colchester	750	263
Hartlepools	710	300
Rochdale	540	360
Exeter	1000	240
Hastings	730	180
Barnstaple	1000	120
Boston	550	210
Blackburn	2500	252
	10351	3612

Thus, whereas in 1919, these ten branches had a total membership of 10,351, this figure had slumped in 1923 to 3,612, a 65% fall.

To present a comprehensive picture of constituency Liberal organization is impossible within a short essay. The following case-study of East Anglia, however, gives a representative survey of the decay of constituency Liberal organization in a rural area in mid-1923. The main features can be paralleled in similar case-studies of Scotland, Yorkshire and the Midlands.

Following the Redistribution Act of 1918, the number of seats within the Eastern Counties Liberal Federation fell from 36 to 28. Prior to 1918, these 36 seats had returned the following members:

	Unionist	Liberal
1885	14	22
1886	31	5
1892	16	20
1895	26	10
1900	24	12
1906	5	31
1910	16	20
1910	15	21
Total	147	141
1892–1910	102	114

Thus, overall in the period 1892 to 1910, the Federation had sent 114 Liberals and 102 Conservatives to Westminster. Alongside this traditional Liberalism, the Federation contained many constituencies with a strong Nonconformist vote. Nine constituencies exceeded a proportion of 10% Nonconformist, while Horncastle, Gainsborough, Ipswich and Lincoln exceeded 12%. The average for the 28 constituencies was 8·4%.[1]

A third characteristic of these Eastern Counties was the high percentage of the working population engaged in agriculture. Of the twelve constituencies in Britain with an agricultural vote exceeding 50% of the working population, nine seats were concentrated in East Anglia. Of the 21 county divisions within the Federation, all except Lowestoft boasted an agricultural vote of over 20%.

This background of a Nonconformist rural area with a developed Liberal tradition might suggest an area in which active constituency Liberalism still persisted. The picture which emerges is very different.[2]

To the Liberal Federation Secretary, the single most alarming aspect of the position in 1923 was the decline in the numbers of full-time agents. Of 28 constituencies, only 15 now possessed agents: many of these were retained despite a precarious financial position. Thus, in Lincoln, the Liberal Association still existed,

[1] Statistics derived from M. Kinnear: *The British Voter* (1968), 125–9.

[2] The following account is based on the report of the Federation Secretary on constituency organisation, to be found in the Eastern Counties Liberal Federation Executive Committee minutes for October 5th 1923.

but was in debt: there was no money for an agent. In Huntingdonshire, financial necessity had caused the dismissal of a full-time agent, though the former agent was continuing in a voluntary capacity.

Of Gainsborough, the Federation Secretary observed 'Our prospects are hopeful if organisation can be maintained'. In fact, the Gainsborough division was also in financial difficulties, only retaining an agent with difficulty: the Federation was assisting with a £50 grant. Peterborough likewise lacked an agent.

Lack of agents was only one aspect of the problem facing the Federation Secretary: there was the major problem of constituencies with almost totally defunct organization, where activity was dormant to the point of prolonged hibernation.

Thus, the Federation Secretary could only list the two North Lincolnshire divisions of Brigg and Grimsby as 'dormant: no agent'. As one journal observed of the Brigg division, there had been a time when this old North Lindsey constituency used to be a stronghold of Liberalism: since 1918 however, old-fashioned Liberalism had died a lingering death.[1]

Suffolk provided an equally desolate Liberal scene: at Ipswich, a Liberal seat after 1895, the association was moribund and the agent had left. Perhaps the most derelict of all constituencies within the Federation was to be found in Bury St. Edmunds. Here the Federation Secretary possessed the name of one Liberal contact, a journalist on the Bury Free Press: otherwise there were no signs of Liberal life, however lowly.

The Rutland and Stamford division presented a similar sorry scene: in mid-1923 the Association was without an agent and badly in debt. A by-election occurred in the division in October 1923: no Liberal candidate appeared, despite the warning of the Federation Secretary that 'if we leave this seat to Labour our position for the future will be sadly prejudiced'.[2] No improvement in Liberal organization had occurred by the time of the General Election.

To add to the plight of Liberal organization was the damaging

[1] *Yorkshire Post:* 14 Nov. 1923.

[2] Minutes: Executive Committee: 1 Oct. 1923: Eastern Counties Liberal Federation.

effect of the party split. This was particularly noticeable in the case of Norfolk. Thus, in South-West Norfolk where the sitting member, Sir Richard Winfrey, was a National Liberal, the Federation Secretary reported that the old Liberal Association was practically non-existent: the agent had gone: no Liberal candidate appeared in either 1923 or 1924. In the North Norfolk division the Association had collapsed following the defection of Noel Buxton, the unsuccessful Liberal candidate in 1918, to the Labour ranks: by mid-1923, the association was defunct and the agent had left.

The split in the Liberal ranks had also played an important part in South Norfolk: two rival Liberal candidates in the by-election of July 1920 gave the Labour candidate victory. Since that by-election, Liberal organization had languished to the verge of non-existence.[1]

This account of derelict constituencies and indebted associations, widespread though it was, needs a qualification. There was nothing permanent or irreversible about this weakness of organization. After 1923, the tonic of that electoral revival resuscitated many associations. The malaise of constituency Liberalism in rural areas was one of organization rather than of voting strength. It was the temporary loss of organization rather than the permanent alienation of former supporters.

This account of constituency Liberalism has so far examined only the organization of the Asquithian Liberal Party. To complete the survey, a brief examination of the Lloyd George Liberal Party is necessary. Such an analysis provides a picture that mirrors the most decadent of the Independent Liberal associations. With inactive associations, expensive but ineffective organization, the National Liberals had become a parliamentary group without a constituency base; parliamentary heads without constituency bodies.

After the National Liberal Federation Annual Meeting at Leamington in May 1920, the Lloyd George Liberals had begun the creation of separate organizations at constituency level. The first such association appeared at Maldon. Money was generously provided, and in London new associations mushroomed.

Sir William Sutherland had warned Lloyd George in March

[1] *Norwich Mercury:* 17 Nov. 1923.

1922 that unless the Coalition Liberals were fully organized in every constituency they would never possess effective local influence.[1] His warning passed unheeded. Apart from London, only 21 local Lloyd George Associations were established outside those constituencies in which there were already Coalition Liberal candidates.

In all, only 224 constituencies possessed any form of Lloyd George Liberal organization.[2] Many of these existed in name only. Kinnear's analysis of the activity of these local associations for the period August 1922 to October 1923 reveals that no mention was ever made in the Lloyd George Liberal Magazine of 123 of them; a further 69 associations had met on only three occasions or less; only ten had met on more than six occasions.

Perhaps the most vivid example of the almost complete lack of coalition Liberal activity at constituency level can be seen in the area where Lloyd George Liberalism might have been expected to be most alive—in Wales itself.

With the exception of rural North Wales, an analysis reveals a Liberal Party disillusioned, disheartened and decaying. A useful insight into the extent of the decline can be found in a letter of Mond to Lloyd George, in which Mond conveyed the dismal scene presented to him by a Swansea Liberal, W. C. Jenkins.[3] Jenkins was forced to admit that the Liberals, in their Rip Van Winkle slumbers, had made only sporadic efforts to counter the march of Socialism. In several South Wales constituencies the party was without full-time agents or any form of political activity. The only hope for the Liberal Party was reorganization on new lines with an industrial policy.

Reorganization never came: the position in November 1923 was, if anything, worse than when Jenkins had observed the situation a year before.

Thus, the Cardiff Liberals had no agent, no executive and no offices in the city.[4] At Merthyr, Liberal organization had collapsed: the same was true of Newport.[5] In such mining

[1] Sutherland to Lloyd George: 18 March 1922: Lloyd George Papers F 35/1/39.
[2] Kinnear: *The British Voter*, 88–90.
[3] Mond to Lloyd George: 10 Aug. 1922: Lloyd George Papers F/37/2/17.
[4] *Manchester Guardian:* 14 Nov. 1923.   [5] *Western Mail:* 17 Nov. 1923.

divisions as Abertillery nothing had been heard of the Liberals.[1] The overall picture was one of almost unrelieved breakdown in organization and morale.[2]

The conclusion from the preceding analysis is clear: the Liberal Party in 1923 remained, in terms of organization and morale, in a state of chronic weakness. Few parties have been so ill-prepared for a General Election as the two wings of Liberalism were before Baldwin's conversion to Protection brought a new factor into the political scene.

To gauge accurately the nature and extent of the Liberal revival in December 1923, it is necessary to review also the electoral position of the party following November 1922. The results of 1922 were as follows:

Party	Votes	%	Seats
Official Conservatives	5,281,555	36·7	327
Other Conservatives	309,267	2·1	20
Lloyd George Liberals	1,320,935	9·2	47
Asquith Liberals	2,098,732	14·6	40
Prefixless Liberals	763,315	5·3	29
Labour	4,237,769	29·4	142
Others	382,059	2·7	10
	14,393,632	100·0	615 |[3]

In all, some 116 Liberals were returned to Westminster: if those Liberals elected without prefix are allocated according to their general sympathies, the Lloyd George Liberals number 60, the Asquithian wing 56.

These national figures, however, really exaggerate the strength of the Lloyd George group: except in Wales, no Coalition Liberal was elected in the face of Conservative opposition. As Wilson has written, the Coalition Liberals survived, where they survived at all, as a kept party.[4]

For those Lloyd George Liberals who faced Conservative opponents, the results of November 1922 were an unmitigated disaster. The National Liberal casualties included Churchill in

---

[1] *South Wales News:* 14 Nov. 1923.

[2] For a fuller discussion of the 1923 election in Wales, see C. P. Cook: Wales and the General Election of 1923, in *Welsh History Review*, December 1969.

[3] Kinnear: *The British Voter*, 40.

[4] Wilson: *The Downfall of the Liberal Party*, 237.

Dundee, Hamar Greenwood in Sunderland, Kellaway in Bedford and Guest in East Dorset.

Whereas 138 Coalition Liberals had been returned in 1918, only 60 were elected in 1922. Some 81 seats were lost; 21 of these were not even defended. While 57 seats were retained, only three were won: only one seat, Wellingborough, was taken from Labour. In Yorkshire, the rout of the National Liberals by Labour assumed the proportions of a massacre: in Sheffield, only the Park division survived as the lone outpost of Lloyd George Liberalism: Attercliffe was lost on a swing of 33·5%, Hillsborough fell to a 29·6% swing.

South Wales was the scene of similar disaster: Neath was lost on a 24·3% swing to Labour: Labour victories followed in Llanelly, Aberdare, East Swansea, Merthyr and Aberavon.[1]

Despite the continuation of the Conservative-National Liberal alliance, Scotland portrayed the same story of Liberal seats swamped on a Socialist tide: 8 of the 12 Coalition seats in industrial Scotland were lost. The following table indicates the extent and uniformity of the Labour avalanche in the eight comparable contests.

Constituency	% 1918	% 1922	NL % loss
Dumbarton	52·6	35·5	17·1
Edinburgh Central	48·7	42·1	6·6
Bridgeton[2]	55·2	36·3	18·9
Montrose	76·0	54·4	21·6
Stirling and Falkirk	64·3	46·7	17·6
Kilmarnock	67·1	54·7	12·4
Rutherglen	59·1	44·9	14·2
Renfrewshire West	61·8	46·0	15·8

Only in the stronghold of rural North Wales was Coalition Liberalism able to withstand Conservative and Labour attacks: seats such as Denbigh and Flint were won despite Conservative opponents.

For the Asquithian Liberals, fielding 325 candidates, the results were a profound and bitter disappointment. Admittedly, their members returned increased to 56, but this was a meagre advance. Even these gains could scarcely disguise many disheartening

[1] For a detailed analysis of Welsh politics during this period, see K. Morgan: The Twilight of Welsh Liberalism: Lloyd George and the Wee Frees; Bulletin of the Board of Celtic Studies, xxiv, May 1968.

[2] Excluding the votes of an independent in Bridgeton.

features. They had lost 14 of the seats won in 1918, nine of them to Labour; in such industrial strongholds as Durham, Consett, Seaham and Spennymoor were all lost. In Scotland, Donald Maclean's constituency of Midlothian and South Peebles was lost, as were such other mining divisions as North-East Derbyshire and Leigh.

To compensate for these losses, the Independent Liberals gained 43 seats. Only one seat, however, was taken from Labour, whereas 10 Coalition Liberal and 32 Conservative or Independent seats were won.

The best Asquithian performance was made in those traditional rural strongholds lost in the 1918 débâcle, such county constituencies as Tavistock and Mid-Bedfordshire, or in Scotland in Forfarshire, Dumfries and East Fife.

However, the most disturbing feature of this revival, outside the occasional area such as Devon and Cornwall, was the lack of any really secure geographical or regional base.

Indeed many of the Independent Liberal gains were in territory which had previously proved infertile soil for the Liberal cause. The victory of R. R. Fairbairn in Worcester was the first ever in the 1885–1918 period; in Oxford, Frank Gray was the first Liberal the city had elected since 1885.

A perfect illustration can be found in the series of victories in agricultural constituencies in 1922. Thus in Lincolnshire, where farming was as depressed as anywhere in the country, Grantham and Horncastle were gained: in the Yorkshire East Riding, the Holderness division, which had returned a Conservative at every election since 1885, similarly elected a Liberal.

At Taunton, the very heart of agricultural Somerset, the former Minister of Agriculture, Sir Arthur Griffith-Boscawen, lost the seat he had won in April 1921, providing the Liberals with their first success since 1885. The backlash against the Coalition's agricultural policy can be gauged by the fact that, in 1922, the Conservatives won only 48 of the 86 constituencies in which more than 30% of the working population were engaged in agriculture: their lowest figure for any inter-war election, except 1923.

It is vital to understand that the Liberal victories of 1922 came almost entirely in straight fights with Conservatives, with Labour absent.

Where their only opponents were Conservative, Asquithian Liberals achieved a distinct revival. In the 31 constituencies which saw only Conservative and Independent Asquithians in 1918 and 1922, the Conservative percentage share of the vote fell from 61·8 to 51·6, a Liberal swing of 10·2%. The problem was that these seats were highly unrepresentative: they were mainly rural or residential. Much more representative are the 54 constituencies which were contested by Independent Liberal, Conservative and Labour candidates in 1918 and 1922. Overall, the Liberal vote increased by 4·5%, from 22·7% to 27·2%. By contrast, in the ten constituencies in this group where those engaged in agriculture exceeded 20% of the working population, the figures were very different.

	%1918	%1922
Conservative	48·9	45·4
Liberal	22·5	31·1
Labour	28·6	23·5

Here, the Liberals had increased their percentage by 8·6%, while Labour had fallen by 5·1%.

Liberal victories in urban seats were conspicuous by their absence: the occasional exception, such as Walsall which was won for the Liberals by Pat Collins, only made the general pattern more obvious: these were isolated oases in an industrial Liberal desert.

In his report on 1922, the secretary of the Midland Liberal Federation stated: 'The most disappointing feature of the election . . . is the fact that the old electoral system has broken down with the arrival of a definite third party.'[1] Certainly, his remark could be understood from an analysis of votes within his Federation.

Whereas the Liberals had polled 33·5% of the votes cast in the 33 constituencies, they had received only 24·2% of the seats; the Conservatives, with 34·4% of the votes held 51·5% of the seats.

The extent to which the electoral system worked against the Liberal Party needs to be considered in assessing their performance in 1922: allowing for this, however, the results registered only a tentative revival.

[1] Report of the Federation Secretary: 1922 General Election, in Executive Committee Minutes: Midland Liberal Federation.

This essay is not the place to examine either the motives or the wisdom of Baldwin's decision to embark on a programme of Protection. It is necessary to stress, however, the chaos into which Baldwin plunged his party, the extent of which the recent biography of Baldwin very much avoids.[1] Similarly, Barnes and Middlemas reveal only the tip of the iceberg of criticism which poured in from Baldwin's colleagues over his policy.

The net result of Baldwin's action was that, in attempting to unite his own party, he effectively divided it, at the same time re-uniting the severed wings of Liberalism. Any doubts over Lloyd George's future course of action rapidly vanished when, landing at Southampton on his return from the United States, he declared himself unreservedly for Free Trade: the road to reunion was open. On the morning of 13 November, Lloyd George and Mond met Asquith and Vivian Phillipps to arrange the details of reunion and to plan the campaign.[2]

The details were soon settled: all candidates in the election were to fight as Liberals without suffix or prefix: to settle any rival candidatures, a committee was formed of Edge and Cope for the National Liberals and Phillipps and Howard for the Asquithians. A united Liberal Campaign Fund to finance the campaign was agreed upon; Mond and Maclean were delegated to attend to the details.

The most interesting discussion centred on the general campaign strategy that the Liberals would adopt. Free Trade presented no problems: Lloyd George confirmed his position as a Free Trader without any qualifications. In view of the lack of time to prepare for the election, it was agreed that nothing in the style of a 'Newcastle Programme' could or should be attempted. This was a vital decision: the whole of the subsequent Liberal campaign was noticeably lacking in constructive and detailed radical proposals.

Before examining in more detail the nature of the election campaign, mention needs to be made of the results of the

---

[1] Barnes and Middlemas: *Baldwin: A Biography*, 212–49. The authors' account of Autumn 1923 is very nearly as confused as Baldwin's own actions.

[2] The following account is based on the evidence in the Gladstone Papers: Add. MSS. 46475:F253/259.

nominations, and, with particular relevance for this argument, the relations of Liberal and Labour in the rural constituencies.

As Lyman notes, it is true that Labour intervened more often to force a three-cornered contest than they withdrew to leave the Free Trade Liberal a clear field.[1] However, Lyman significantly underestimates the lingering Liberal-Labour co-operation which survived in several constituencies. A formal rapprochement in the Eastbourne division left the Liberals a straight fight against the Conservative.[2] At Newark, it was widely reported that a Labour candidate would stand aside if a Liberal sympathetic towards Labour were adopted. There was a similar sentiment within the constituency Liberal Association: in the event, a joint committee was formed and a candidate acceptable to both sides adopted.[3] The Leek Liberals claimed in 1924 that Labour broke a pact by intervening in the neighbouring Stone division, and that in 1923 the understanding had been for the Liberals not to contest Leek, with its mining population, if Labour did not intervene in Stone. There was a similar understanding in Shropshire: Labour left the Liberals a clear field in the Shrewsbury division on the implied understanding that no Liberal intervened in the Wrekin.

More numerous were those constituencies where, once Labour found itself without sufficient funds or organization to contest, the local Association then gave active and public assistance to the Liberal candidate: thus, at Denbigh, the local Labour chairman publicly urged the 3,000 pledged party members to vote for Ellis Davies.[4] In Huntingdonshire, where lack of finance had prevented a Labour candidate, the Divisional Association issued a manifesto calling on all members to vote Liberal.[5] In such divisions as Finchley and Hemel Hempstead the successful Liberals subsequently thanked Labour for their platform assistance.[6]

Likewise, radical Liberals returned the compliment by urging pledged Liberals to cast their vote for Labour: the

---

[1] See R. Lyman: *The First Labour Government* (1957), 63.

[2] *Times:* 21 Nov. 1923.

[3] *Yorkshire Post:* 16 Nov. 1923.

[4] *Times:* 26 Nov. 1923.

[5] *Peterborough and Hunts. Standard:* 16 Nov. 1923; 14 Dec. 1923.

[6] *Finchley Press:* 14 Dec. 1923; *Bedfordshire and Hertfordshire Telegraph:* 24 Nov. 1923.

Liberal member for Louth addressed an open letter calling on Liberals to 'vote solid' for the Labour candidate in Holland with Boston: Nonconformist Liberal ministers took the chair at Labour meetings.[1] The Mitcham Liberal Association likewise issued a manifesto calling on all members to vote Labour: at Maldon, a constituency in which for the first time in its history there was no Liberal candidate, Labour received active Liberal platform support.[2] There was similar assistance in South Norfolk.[3]

These examples give an indication that relations between the Liberal and Labour Parties in the rural constituencies were not so absolutely hostile as the speeches of some Labour leaders might suppose.

To understand the nature of the 1923 Liberal revival, brief attention needs to be devoted to the campaign waged by the Party in opposition to Tariff Reform.

The decision of the Liberal leaders to attempt nothing in the way of a 'Newcastle Programme' resulted in the overriding emphasis of the Liberal campaign being centred on a negative defence of Free Trade.

Both Conservative and Labour opponents were able to attack the Liberals as a party bereft of constructive policy. In an editorial attacking the Liberals, the *Western Mail* could declare:

> Every speech delivered in the course of this electoral campaign lends emphasis to the fact that Liberalism is living in the dead past . . . and that only Conservatism gives useful thought to the affairs of the living present.[4]

In fact, when the Conservative candidate at Stockport accused the Liberals of 'repeating the old Shibboleths of years ago', the speeches of many Liberals came uncomfortably close to doing just that.[5] Henry Mond, fighting the Isle of Ely on the slogan 'Peace, Retrenchment and Reform' might have gladdened the heart of Gladstone.[6]

The essential paradox of the 1923 campaign is that Liberalism was fighting on a conservative policy: as one correspondent

[1] *Lincolnshire Free Press:* 27 Nov. 1923; 4 Dec. 1923.
[2] *Surrey County Herald:* 17 Nov. 1923; *Essex County Telegraph:* 11 Dec. 1923.
[3] *Norwich Mercury:* 15 Dec. 1923.   [4] *Western Mail:* 20 Nov. 1923.
[5] *Stockport County Borough Express:* 22 Nov. 1923.
[6] *Times:* 30 Nov. 1923.

observed of the contest in West Leicester, it was the Conservative candidate who desired change and the Liberal who feared it.[1]

Though the metaphors changed, the essence of the Liberal attack remained the same: the election was 'a vote in the dark': Baldwin was 'blindfolding the electors', or, as the imaginative Liberal candidate for Melton declared, it was 'a leap in the dark on the slippery slope of Protection'.[2]

The absence of constructive alternative proposals was especially noticeable in the case of Liberal agricultural policy. The party manifesto spoke in general terms of credit facilities, of co-operative marketing on a large scale and more generally still of raising the position of the agricultural labourer. Once again, the emphasis of the Liberal campaign was a negative attack on the hastily-improvised Conservative subsidy proposals. Impetus was given to this Liberal attack by the fact that, a year ago, Baldwin had himself declared at Worcester:

> Neither agriculture nor any other industry in this country can look to this or any other government for a direct or indirect subsidy of public money.[3]

More recently, Sir Robert Sanders in a speech in Lincolnshire had declared that, for reasons of expense:

> It is no use considering such heroic measures as subsidies or protective duties on foodstuffs.[4]

Apart from these opportunities of attacking Conservative policy, the Liberals in the rural constituencies were on the defensive: indeed, the *Yorkshire Post* taunted the Liberal leaders for 'having shown no enthusiasm for campaigning in agricultural districts'.[5] Occasional Liberal candidates either supported the Conservative subsidy, or suggested similar schemes of their own. The prospective Liberal candidate for the Cirencester division withdrew to support the Baldwin policy declaring in a letter to the Swindon Advertiser 'The Government's new policy respecting agriculture is one that all parties can and ought to support'.[6] In the Penrith Division, the Liberal approved

---

[1] Ibid.: 27 Nov. 1923.
[2] Quotations respectively from the Election Addresses of the Liberal candidates in Bodmin, Basingstoke and Melton.
[3] *Times:* 29 Oct. 1922.   [4] *Daily Chronicle:* 17 Feb. 1923.
[5] *Yorkshire Post:* 24 Nov. 1923.   [6] *Swindon Advertiser:* 21 Nov. 1923.

Baldwin's schemes,[1] while in the Eye division, the Liberal policy as stated in his election address advocated a subsidy of £2 per acre for 1924–1925, and a minimum wage for agricultural labourers of 32s. 6d.[2]

The negative nature of the Liberal campaign has a double significance: it enabled the party to secure many Free Trade Conservative voters: secondly, and more significantly, despite their lack of a radical constructive policy, the Liberals were still able in rural England, not merely to retain their traditional vote, but in several areas to win back votes which had gone to Labour in 1922 and 1918.

The extent to which the Liberal Party had both gained Conservative votes in the middle-class residential areas and retained its votes in the shires of England, becomes apparent from an analysis of the 1923 election result.

The results of 1923 confirmed the worst fears of the Conservative pessimists on the likely outcome of Baldwin's electoral gamble. The first results revealed a steady pattern of Liberal and Labour gains from the Conservatives.

The most immediate feature of the results was the series of Liberal gains in Lancashire: the party swept five Manchester seats, taking Blackley, Moss Side, Exchange, Rusholme and Withington from the Conservatives. In Liverpool they gained Wavertree and West Derby, both constituencies which had returned Conservatives at every election after 1885.

Outside Lancashire, it was Labour rather than the Liberals who were taking borough constituencies from the Conservatives. Except in the North-East, where the Liberals recaptured such seats as Gateshead and Cleveland, the 1923 results demonstrated the Liberal inability to recapture lost industrial territory from Labour, although they made a series of gains in middle-class Conservative urban seats.

Perhaps the greatest Conservative disappointment came with the rejection of Protection in those areas most likely to benefit from its introduction. Thus, an 11th-hour Liberal candidate, fighting solely on the Free Trade question, won the Nottingham East division, the centre of the depressed lace industry. The motor industry showed an equal lack of gratitude: Coventry was won by Labour.

[1] *Times:* 30 Nov. 1923.   [2] Eye Division: Liberal Election Address.

The Conservative Party might still have survived with a small overall majority had not their losses increased as the rural returns became known. Liberal gains in Free Trade Lancashire might have been expected: the Liberals, however, swept to victory in areas where correspondents had rated their chances as remote.

Thus, in the Hemel Hempstead division, the first Liberal candidate since 1910 uprooted J. C. C. Davidson by 17 votes, in a constituency with no Liberal organization and with an 11th-hour candidate. The Liberals won a variety of seats which seemed equally unlikely territory: Basingstoke, Blackpool, Chelmsford, Chichester, Lonsdale and Shrewsbury had all, prior to 1923, returned Conservatives at every election since 1885.

The nature and substance of this Liberal revival are crucial to any study of the decline of the party: although it is not possible, for reasons of space, to give a full statistical analysis, it is necessary to look closely at the results of December 1923.

Nationally, the voting figures for 1923 were as follows:

Party	Total votes	Seats	% vote
Conservative	5,538,824	258	38·1
Liberal	4,311,147	159	29·6
Labour	4,438,508	191	30·5
Others	260,042	7	1·8
	14,548,521	615	100·0[1]

Since 11 Liberals were returned unopposed, compared to only 3 Labour unopposed returns, the aggregate Liberal and Labour votes were almost identical. For the argument of this essay, it is useful to break down these overall figures into borough and county constituencies. Excluding Ulster and the University seats, these figures are set out in the following table:

(a)

Boroughs	Seats	Con.	Lib.	Lab.
Metropolitan	62	429,023	337,707	422,706
Provincial	193	2,028,783	1,504,791	1,794,339
Wales	11	69,126	94,148	141,803
Scotland	33	219,550	226,441	312,210
	299	2,746,482	2,163,087	2,671,058

[1] Source: Constitutional Year Book; 1925: 274.

(b)

Counties	Seats	Con.	Lib.	Lab.
English	230	2,297,966	1,723,647	1,331,571
Welsh	24	108,987	217,635	213,369
Scottish	38	248,976	196,554	220,240
	292	2,655,929	2,137,836	1,765,180[1]

From this table it can be seen that, in voting strength, the Liberals remained the second largest party in the English counties behind the Conservatives, the largest single party in the Welsh counties, and the second largest party in the borough seats in Wales and Scotland.

In terms of gains and losses, the Liberals gained 69 Conservative seats, losing 16 themselves, to emerge with a net gain of 53. In contrast to this, they gained 13 Labour seats, but lost 23, a net deficit of 10.

These statistics of gain and loss are deceiving. At first sight they suggest that the whole Liberal revival in 1923 was based on gains from the Conservatives: this is a cardinal error. The seats were won from Conservatism, but in rural and residential England votes were won from both Conservative and Labour.

To pursue a closer analysis of the votes cast, it is necessary to group those constituencies in which comparisons can be made between the Liberal performance in December 1923 and their record in 1922. On this basis, the following main groupings are useful:[2]

(1) the 63 seats contested by Conservative and Independent Liberal in both elections.
(2) the 94 seats contested by the three major parties.
(3) the 25 seats in which Liberals had straight fights against Labour on each occasion.
(4) the 18 constituencies which Labour contested in 1922, but withdrew to leave a straight-fight between Conservative and Liberal in 1923.

In all, this represents a sample of exactly 200 seats.

[1] The votes for independents etc. are excluded.
[2] I am indebted to Trevor Wilson and Richard Lyman for the preliminary analysis on these lines.

The 63 seats fought only by Conservatives and Liberals in 1922 and 1923 provide an important, if unrepresentative, sample. A closer analysis presents an interesting diversity of electoral movement: residential Stoke Newington swung 16·5 % to the Liberals: rural Leominster 5·1 % to the Conservatives.

Overall, for these 63 seats, the results are set out below:

Party	1922	1923	% 22	% 23
Conservative	784,374	726,242	55·1	49·3
Liberal	640,398	745,641	44·9	50·7
	1,424,772	1,471,883	100·0	100·0

Whereas, in 1922, the Conservatives had polled 55·1 % of the votes cast, in 1923 this had fallen to 49·3 %. Admittedly, much of this was due to the fall in turnout, most particularly in the commercial, residential and middle-class constituencies: very heavy swings from the Conservatives occurred in Southend (11·7 %), Thanet (11·1 %), Waterloo (15·7 %), Windsor (12·8 %) and Wallasey (12·1 %). There were similar heavy swings in such mixed residential and agricultural seats as Chislehurst, Hertford and Knutsford.

By contrast, the wholly or largely agricultural seats were more favourable to the Conservatives: of the 25 seats in which more than 27·5 % of the working population was engaged in agriculture, only eight swung Liberal by more than 2 %.

Ten constituencies actually swung Conservative: quite distinct Conservative movement occurred in Holderness (3·5 %), Taunton (3·9 %) and Leominster (5·1 %). The Conservative vote held in agricultural Scotland, with slight swings to them in Forfar, Dumfriesshire, East Fife and Central Aberdeenshire: for once the country north of the Tweed had failed the Liberals.

Perhaps the most important category of contests are those in which the three major parties fought in both elections. They provide a particularly representative cross-section of constituencies: of these 94 contests, 17 were in the Metropolitan boroughs, 41 in the provincial boroughs, 28 in the English counties, with 8 in Scotland.

The votes cast in December 1923 compared to November 1922 are set out in the following table:

Party	Votes: 1922	%	Votes: 1923	%	% +/−
Conservative	1,079,070	43·0	954,123	38·1	− 4·9
Liberal	676,494	27·0	779,695	31·1	+ 4·1
Labour	754,528	30·0	771,203	30·8	+ 0·8
	2,510,092	100·0	2,505,021	100·0	

A very different result is obtained when these 94 contests are divided into borough and county divisions.

(a) *English Boroughs*[1] (66 seats)

Party	Votes: 1922	%	Votes: 1923	%
Conservative	740,686	42·5	643,044	37·0
Liberal	440,969	25·3	492,264	28·4
Labour	559,708	32·2	600,672	34·6
	1,741,363	100·0	1,735,980	100·0

(b) *English Counties* (28 seats)

Party	Votes: 1922	%	Votes: 1923	%
Conservative	338,384	44·0	311,079	40·4
Liberal	235,525	30·6	287,431	37·4
Labour	194,820	25·4	170,531	22·2
	768,729	100·0	769,041	100·0

The differences which appear in these figures are considerable. Whereas in the boroughs, the Conservative share of the poll had declined by 5·5%, in the rural constituencies the fall was only 3·6%. It is the difference in the Liberal and Labour performance which is even more important: whereas in the boroughs, the Labour share of the poll increased by 2·5%, and the Liberal share by 3·1%; in the rural divisions, the Labour

[1] The three-cornered contests in Scotland, all in industrial seats, are included in the borough totals.

percentage decreased by 3·2, the Liberal rose by 6·8%. These figures quite clearly point to the fact that the Liberals were making inroads into the Labour as well as the Conservative vote in these rural seats.

Confirmation that, in urban England, the Liberals were still losing votes to Labour can be found in an analysis of the 25 contests in which Labour faced only a Liberal candidate on each occasion.

The following table sets out the position for this group:

Party	Votes: 1922	%	Votes: 1923	%
Liberal	292,060	48·1	277,184	45·4
Labour	314,543	51·9	333,073	54·6
	606,603	100·0	610,257	100·0

There had been a swing of 2·7% from Liberal to Labour, with particularly heavy movements away from the Liberals in mining areas. In the only two rural constituencies in this group, Merioneth and Caernarvonshire, there was a swing to the Liberals.

The final group of constituencies, the 18 seats in which Labour withdrew to leave a straight fight between Conservative and Liberal, provides a useful example of the willingness of Labour voters to transfer their allegiance to the Liberal.

Party	Votes: 1922	%	Votes: 1923	%
Conservative	220,738	47·9	208,065	45·7
Liberal	158,389	34·3	247,571	54·3
Labour	82,164	17·8	—	—
	461,291	100·0	455,636	100·0

These figures reveal that, while the Conservative share of the total vote had fallen by only 2·2%, an indication that some Labour votes had moved Conservative, the Liberals had nonetheless received much the greater part of the Labour vote. There is a peculiar irony in these rural returns: if Labour had possessed more money, their intervention would frequently have robbed the Liberals of victory, giving Conservatives these seats on minority votes. In this sense, the first Labour Government was a direct result of the lack of funds within the party.

This analysis of the results in 200 comparable constituencies gives an indication of the substantial nature of the Liberal revival despite their deplorable constituency organization. Whilst Trevor Wilson is correct to point out the narrow margin of many Liberal victories, it should also be emphasized that many Conservative seats were only retained in the face of the Liberal challenge by the narrowest of margins. Given a fractionally greater movement of votes to the Liberals, it is the Liberals who would consequently have been the second largest party again.

In view of the disaster which overtook the Liberal Party within a year of the electoral revival of 1923, it is essential to the argument of this essay to examine in greater depth the substance of the Liberal recovery. Was it merely the panic reaction of frightened voters over the issue of Protection? Or was it, perhaps, a sign that, despite the plight of the divided party after 1918, it still retained the allegiance of a substantial section of the electorate in rural England?

The evidence supports the latter view: if the rural returns for the 1929 election are examined, the party narrowly missed a major series of gains only through the unfairness of the electoral system. Such seats as Wells, Salisbury, Aylesbury, Chelmsford and Devizes, which Wilson lists as highly improbable victories in 1923, all polled well for the Liberals in 1929; in each case, the Conservatives won on a minority vote with Labour bottom of the poll. Under the single transferable vote, it is probable that the Liberal Party would have emerged with major gains in these areas in 1929.

In view of the persistent strength of Liberalism in rural England, how is the downfall of the Party from its revival in December 1923 to its collapse in October 1924 to be explained? Partly the answer is to be found in the electoral system: more than this, however, the decline of the party became its downfall through the mistakes, the miscalculations and the missed opportunities of the Liberal leaders after December 1923.

The result of the 1923 election left the Liberal Party holding the balance of power. Protection had been rejected with no uncertain voice: but what Government should take the place of Baldwin?

Wilson writes of Asquith's action in putting Labour in:

> His conduct at this juncture has been criticised. It has been said that
> he should have used his control of the situation to lay down clear
> conditions on which Labour might take office, including regular
> consultations with the Liberals. This misinterprets his position. He was
> not free to make and unmake governments on his own terms, and
> whatever he said in public he had some inkling of the fact.[1]

Wilson overstates the position here. It is true that, given the
nature of the campaign on Free Trade, for the Liberals to
maintain a Conservative Government would have been a gross
inconsistency. Any Coalition with Labour was likewise a
political non-starter. To this extent, the Liberal freedom of
action was limited.

It was clear that it would be the King's duty to send for
MacDonald, as leader of the second largest party, in the event of
Baldwin's defeat. One possibility is that, at this juncture,
Asquith could have proposed to MacDonald that the Liberals
would guarantee Labour a fixed term of office on an agreed
programme of reform, which excluded Socialism and included
a measure of electoral reform. Such a suggestion would give the
country its most needed requirement—the certainty of political
stability. If MacDonald refused such an offer, it would be
possible for the Liberals to portray Labour as men who refused
to put country before party, unwilling to abandon wild schemes
of Socialism to give the country much-needed tranquillity.
MacDonald could then have been unseated, and the Liberals
formed a 'Caretaker' government. Admittedly, such a scheme
was a very doubtful proposition, but it was a possible line of
action.

The result, in either event, might have given the Liberals a
reform of the electoral system. If they formed a minority
Government, at least the timing and issues of the next election
would be under some Liberal control.

Other possibilities were canvassed at the time: among the
schemes devised at the time to keep Labour from power, the
plans of Younger and Horne deserve mention.

Younger had his own clearly defined plan to solve the
political crisis. According to Younger, when Baldwin was
defeated, the King would send for MacDonald: MacDonald

---

[1] Wilson: *Downfall of the Liberal Party*, 264-5.

would be asked to give an assurance that he could govern for a reasonable time. This MacDonald, not having consulted the Liberals, would not be able to do. The King would reply that he must see if Asquith could give the necessary assurance: the Conservatives would then proffer support, and the Liberals would come in.[1]

Another scheme was devised by Horne, and communicated to Derby. Horne, like Younger, wanted 'to get an Asquith Government as quickly as possible'. Therefore, if Baldwin was defeated, and MacDonald formed a Government, he was to be immediately unseated: as he would not have had an appreciable term in office, the King would then be able to refuse a dissolution. Asquith would come in, and the Conservatives would give general support. The Liberals could pass legislation to create the alternative vote and then go to the country after a year of quietness. Such a development would start business again and cheer commerce.[2]

The major weakness of such schemes was that they would put public sympathy on Labour's side: the older parties would be appearing in open combination against the Labour Party. This would not be the case if the Liberals offered Labour a scheme of limited legislative cooperation to give the country a period of recovery. Although their success in 1923 put the Liberals in a delicate position, their freedom of manoeuvre was more than Wilson suggests.

Why then did the Liberal leaders not attempt more positive action in January 1924? There are two explanations. First, Asquith and Lloyd George were completely divided on policy: the crucial opportunity passed with the two leaders suspicious and fundamentally divided. Secondly, Lloyd George made the cardinal error of believing Labour would treat them in a co-operative way. When Lloyd George realized the error the Liberal Party had committed, it was too late.

When the Liberal leaders first met to discuss their future course of action, Asquith's own immediate idea, which received

[1] Related by Herbert Gladstone to Maclean: 12 Jan. 1924. Ad. MSS. 46474/64.
[2] Horne's letter to Derby is in the Derby correspondence. Horne communicated similar thoughts to Lloyd George: see Lloyd George Papers, G/10/6/1.

the support of Simon, was to turn the Conservatives out as soon
as possible, then to do the same with Labour through a combination with the Conservatives.[1] Lloyd George strongly opposed
this plan with the argument that any such minority Liberal
Government so dependent on Conservative votes would be
entirely without freedom of action.

However, the feeling of the meeting was against him: Lloyd
George then proposed an adjournment. Asquith, always ready
to adjourn anything, agreed.

When the leaders met again, Asquith had changed his views:
Asquith now wanted a policy of total independence. There was
to be 'no truck with the Tories', who were to be upset at the
first opportunity: there would then be a 'non-committal'
attitude towards Labour after it had formed a government.
Lloyd George accepted this as a first step in the right direction.

All the Scott evidence suggests that Lloyd George wanted a
policy of co-operation with Labour. Indeed, Lloyd George's
main fear was not that a Labour Government would go too far,
too fast, but that it would perish from lack of action. In
particular, Lloyd George realized that a Labour Government
would suffer from MacDonald's lack of experience in leadership
and from his vanity. According to Scott, Lloyd George would
have been willing to support nationalization of electricity and
railways, but not mines. Lloyd George envisaged Labour and
Liberal cooperation in a period of reform: it proved a sad
delusion.

Lloyd George later confided to Scott that the great mistake
of the Liberal Party was 'not the putting of Labour into office,
but doing so without any understanding or conditions'.[2]
Lloyd George continued:

> I confess it never occurred to me that we'd be treated as we were
> treated. I took for granted that the relations of the two parties would
> be analogous to those between the Irish and Liberal Parties in the
> Home Rule period.

This was the cardinal error: Lloyd George realized his mistake,

[1] The following material is based on C. P. Scott's diary, 5/6th January
1924. Ad. MSS. 50907. Scott obtained his information from Lloyd George.
[2] C. P. Scott's Diary: 27 Nov. 1924.

and in July 1924 he made an attempt to force a showdown. According to Scott, Lloyd George declared:

> ... in July I prepared to hold up the Labour Party on the unemployment question. MacDonald dare not then have dissolved: he was too keen about the London Conference and Foreign Affairs. But I was overruled and the party would not take the risk.[1]

Perhaps Lloyd George was right: perhaps as late as July 1924 the position of the Liberals could have been retrieved. It remains doubtful. The decisive moment was in January 1924. Asquith had sought to give the Party a policy of independence. This was a myth: either the Liberals supported MacDonald, or they forced an election in which they would be attacked from both sides.

When the election came in October 1924, the Liberal Party, for the first time in its history, was clearly not capable of offering an alternative government: it fielded only 346 candidates, 110 fewer than in December 1923.

The Liberal collapse was foreshadowed in the by-elections of the 1924 Parliament: by October 1924 the drift of votes had become a torrent. In the event, the Liberals won only 40 seats: their share of the total vote slumped to 17·6 %. The election had destroyed the party. Although Labour was reduced to 151 seats, the 1924 election was nonetheless a milestone in its advance. It had increased its vote by 1,050,000: its percentage of the total poll rose from 30·5 to 33·0. Above all, however, it had seen the elimination of the Liberal Party.

The Liberal revival of 1923 had become the disaster of 1924. The decline of the party had been transformed into its downfall, not by any 'inevitable' historical process, but, in the last resort, by a succession of accidents.

Nuffield College, Oxford   CHRIS COOK

[1] Ibid.

XI

IVAN MAISKY AND PARLIA-
MENTARY ANTI-APPEASE-
MENT, 1938–39

SIDNEY ASTER

SIDNEY ASTER

Age 28

McGill University B.A. 1963, M.A. 1965
London School of Economics 1969 Ph.D.
Currently Principal Research Assistant to
Martin Gilbert (official Churchill biographer)

IVAN MAISKY AND PARLIAMENTARY
ANTI-APPEASEMENT, 1938–39

THE nature of ambassadorial privilege has been defined as much by custom as by legislation. But the bounds of the diplomatically permissible have rarely been subject to as much strain as during the period from 1932 to 1943 when Ivan Maisky was Soviet ambassador to Great Britain. This manifested itself in his attempts to use the wide range of acquaintances and contacts he deliberately cultivated in order to influence the parliamentary process.

Maisky's acquaintance with Great Britain predates his appointment as ambassador. He had spent the years from 1912 to 1917 as a political exile in London. He took advantage of this unwelcome stay to master the English language, acquaint himself with British culture and make initial contacts with various left-wing personalities and movements.[1] He returned again to London to spent two years as a counsellor at the Soviet embassy until Anglo-Soviet relations were broken off in 1927. Hence, upon taking up his post as ambassador in October 1932, he could claim both a valuable familiarity with some aspects of British life and a modicum of established contacts.

Before leaving to take up his new post, Maisky had a long talk with Maxim Litvinov, Soviet commissar for foreign affairs. Litvinov, apparently foreseeing the rise to power of Hitler and assuming this would encourage Great Britain to search for allies against Germany, indicated that the ambassador's task would be to effect an Anglo-Soviet rapprochement. He was further to cultivate good relations with the Labour party and strengthen ties with the Liberals. But the onus of his mission, Litvinov instructed, was 'to break through the icy wall which separates our London Embassy from the Conservatives and establish the widest and most reliable contacts possible with them.'[2] The irony of Maisky's ambassadorship was that only war finally produced an Anglo-Soviet alliance. And as for the contacts he so ardently desired, these proved elusive.

[1] See Ivan Maisky, *Journey Into the Past* (1962).
[2] Ivan Maisky, *Who Helped Hitler?* (1964), 15–19.

317

When Neville Chamberlain became prime minister on 28 May 1937 the parliamentary opposition to appeasement, though perhaps numerically small, was led by various personalities who were eloquent, informed and articulate. While they all shared a critical attitude to Chamberlain's foreign policy, they differed on alternatives. But on one particular point they were most emphatic. It was believed that, despite any weakness resulting from Stalin's purges of the Soviet armed forces, the available strength of the USSR had to be added to a defensive bloc of the great powers willing to resist any future German coups. Only such a coalition, intended to deter or in the last result defeat Germany, could provide a viable alternative to appeasement. The other common thread shared by this group of anti-appeasers was their opinion that Maisky, while a loyal servant of Bolshevik Russia, was dedicated to the anti-Hitler struggle. He could therefore be a useful contact in bringing to bear informed criticism against the government. This could be managed principally through the acquisition of information normally available only to the foreign office. Also by imparting information and opinions useful to Soviet policy and thus sustaining the interest of that power in an anti-German orientation. Among this amorphous group, in contact in varying degrees with Maisky, were such disparate parliamentarians as Winston Churchill, Harold Nicolson, Robert Boothby, Archibald Sinclair, Hugh Dalton, Arthur Greenwood, and David Lloyd George. On the periphery stood the military strategist Basil Liddell Hart who was adviser on military affairs to Churchill and Lloyd George. The *News Chronicle* journalist Vernon Bartlett, along with several other diplomatic correspondents, was also in close touch with Maisky. Besides these, the Soviet ambassador was of course in communication with a multitude of left-wing groups, organizations and personalities. Beatrice Webb once noted in her diary that the 'Soviet Embassy is the only great house in London at which the left wing meet each other. . . .'[1]

The records kept by many of these individuals provide a unique source of historical information. Rarely has it been possible to document so accurately the statements and activities of a Soviet diplomatic representative abroad and relate these to

[1] Entry of 1 March 1935, *Beatrice Webb Diary*, Passfield Papers.

official narkomindel[1] utterances; rarely has it been possible to analyse the methods used by a Soviet diplomat to influence the foreign policy of his accredited country. In this respect, the papers of Lloyd George, by virtue of his continuous and close association with Maisky from 1937 onwards, are a unique source. The diaries and papers of Hugh Dalton are also invaluable.[2] Finally, Maisky's frequent visits to Sidney and Beatrice Webb, recorded at length in the latter's diary, provide intimate glimpses of a more relaxed and expansive ambassador, commenting on acquaintances and political events.

Maisky's 'acquaintance' with the former leader of the Liberal party was based, as he himself acknowledges,[3] on a distaste for Lloyd George's leadership of the coalition which sanctioned British intervention in the Russian civil war. But Lloyd George had also been responsible for concluding in March 1921 the first trade agreement between Great Britain and Soviet Russia. It was this which Maisky recalled in a letter of congratulation sent on 16 January 1943, on Lloyd George's eightieth birthday, and which took stock of the latter's career:

> ... in my estimation you are probably the most outstanding statesman Great Britain has produced throughout this period ... you were the first British statesman who understood the significance of the USSR and who, in the teeth of strong opposition from many quarters, established official relations with the Soviet Government. I remember also, with gratitude, that during the last twenty years or so you were one of the foremost to champion rapprochement and close collaboration between our two countries. ....[4]

Lloyd George returned the compliment by assuring the ambassador that from their first meeting—'I formed the highest opinion of your capabilities and insight.'[5]

It was Maisky's help in furnishing Soviet archival material for Lloyd George's *War Memoirs* which apparently began their

[1] Soviet Commissariat of Foreign Affairs.

[2] This collection is also in the British Library of Political and Economic Science.

[3] Ivan Maisky, *Vospominaniya Sovetskogo Posla*, II, *Mir ili Voina?* (Memoirs of a Soviet Ambassador, II, War or Peace? Moscow 1964), [hereinafter: Maisky, *Vospominaniya*, ii], 83.

[4] Letter from Maisky to Lloyd George, 16 Jan. 1943, Lloyd George Papers, G/14/1/27.

[5] Letter from Lloyd George to Maisky, 26 Jan. 1943, ibid., G/14/1/28.

friendship.[1] Their first extended discussion took place on 30 November, 1932 and covered a variety of topics. Among the many differences of opinion immediately evident was their estimate of the likelihood of war. Maisky argued that Japan was a potential source of danger. Lloyd George was not so pessimistic. When the conversation turned to Anglo-Soviet relations there followed an exchange typical of many the ambassador conducted. On the one hand, he offered full and frank details of current problems occupying London and Moscow. On the other, he carefully elicited both information and assessments of events and personalities of possible use to the narkomindel.[2]

In summing up their first meeting, Maisky's memoirs pay adequate compliments to Lloyd George's integrity, honesty and fearlessness. But he also criticizes certain 'defects' which lessened Lloyd George's reliability and reflected adversely on his judgment. One such example was of course the allied intervention in Russia. The other was Lloyd George's visit to Germany in September 1936. Maisky noted he found it 'difficult to believe' that Hitler favourably impressed Lloyd George and was much disturbed by the press reports Lloyd George made on his return. Soon afterwards the ambassador personally tried to persuade Lloyd George of Hitler's aggressive intentions. Maisky pointed out that the English translation of *Mein Kampf* possessed by Lloyd George did not contain the references to a future German campaign against the USSR.[3] In his memoirs Maisky omits mentioning that he had also tried unsuccessfully to dissuade Lloyd George from ever embarking on the visit.[4] Nevertheless, less than a year later and largely under the impact of the Spanish civil war, Lloyd George had also moved away from a position favouring revision of the Versailles treaty. By 25 July, 1937 Beatrice Webb, after a visit from Maisky, observed that he 'has become very intimate with Lloyd George'.[5] During 1938 and 1939 he became one of the most outspoken and articulate critics of Chamberlain's foreign policy and a

[1] See ibid., G/14/1/2; G/20/2/60, 90; G/213.
[2] Maisky, *Vospominaniya*, ii, 78–88.   [3] Ibid., 89–91.
[4] See Frank Owen, *Tempestuous Journey* (1954), 734; and Frances Lloyd George, *The Years that are Past* (1967), 256.
[5] Entry of 25 July 1937, *Beatrice Webb Diary*.

leading member of that group urging some form of Anglo-French-Soviet collaboration as an alternative to appeasement.

Maisky's first meeting with Chamberlain, after his appointment as prime minister in succession to Stanley Baldwin, took place on 29 July, 1937. During the course of their discussion, the prime minister outlined his plans for German appeasement. 'The general impression I have from the conversation with Chamberlain', Maisky reported afterwards to the narkomindel, 'can be reduced to the fact that he is now seriously concerned with the four power pact idea and the organization of western security, being ready for the achievement of this idea to go far to meet Germany and Italy.'[1]

As on so many subsequent occasions, the conclusion Maisky drew from his contacts with British officials faithfully echoed the content of his private conversations. He had in fact spoken to Lloyd George on 1 July. According to Maisky's record of the conversation, Lloyd George had stated:

> It is quite clear to me that Chamberlain's 'general plan' is leading to the following: during the next year to secure a settlement with Germany and Italy and conclude a four power pact. For Central and South-eastern Europe Chamberlain is ready to be satisfied by vague promises about non-aggression from the side of the dictators. Your country will be excluded from European security and left to itself.[2]

There was little in British foreign policy during the next fifteen months which could have disproved Lloyd George's assessment. British policy towards the Spanish civil war, Lord Halifax's visit to Germany in November 1937, changes in the foreign office in January and February 1938, the Anschluss, and the crisis over Czechoslovakia seemed to indicate, in Maisky's evaluation, the anti-Soviet nature of Chamberlain's foreign policy, the desire to conclude a four power pact without the USSR and, finally, to direct German expansion eastwards.

Halifax's conversations with Hitler in November 1937 appear in retrospect to have deeply troubled the Soviets. Maisky discussed this with Lloyd George on 21 November and asked for

[1] Foreign Policy Archives of the USSR, quoted in V. I. Popov, *Diplomaticheskie Otnosheniya Mezhdu SSSR i Angliei, 1929–1939gg.* (Diplomatic Relations between the USSR and Britain, 1929–1939, Moscow 1965), 328–9, 334–5. See also, Maisky, *Who Helped Hitler?* 68–9; and Entry of 27 Oct. 1937, *Beatrice Webb Diary*.

[2] Foreign Policy Archives of the USSR, quoted in Popov, op. cit., 333.

an assessment. Lloyd George replied that, while not completely abandoning the League of Nations, Chamberlain was pursuing a policy governed entirely by British interests. The prime minister therefore 'considers the most important task an agreement with Germany and Italy, for the sake of which he is ready to sacrifice Spain, Austria, Czechoslovakia and many others . . . Chamberlain will find support for his policy mainly from Halifax, Hoare, Simon and Hailsham.'[1] From other sources of information, Maisky formed the impression that the object of Halifax's visit was to search for an Anglo-German alliance and indicate British acquiescence in an eventual Anschluss.[2]

Important changes in the British foreign office appeared also to confirm the ambassador's information. Sir Robert Vansittart's promotion to chief diplomatic adviser on 1 January, 1938, and Anthony Eden's replacement by Halifax as foreign secretary in February were interpreted by Maisky as further evidence of Chamberlain's determination to press ahead with his programme. Both Eden and Vansittart, although not considered Russophil, were thought to understand the 'vital necessity for Britain to conclude an alliance with the USSR'.[3] After speaking to Maisky, Nicolson noted the ambassador 'minds very much the resignation of Eden who was working up to a London-Paris-Moscow triangle.'[4] What proved more important was that Vansittart's exclusion from the inner circle of policy formulation left Maisky without a sympathetic ear in the foreign office.

With Hitler intent on pushing for a solution of the Austrian problem, German policy in 1938 remained very much the topic of the day. This was the theme Maisky took up in a letter to Lloyd George on 10 February, 1938. In the ambassador's opinion the '"moderates"' in German policy 'are pushed back whilst the aggressive elements are brought to the fore'. It was this development which he suggested would find expression in future German policy.[5]

[1] Foreign Policy Archives of the USSR, quoted ibid., 339–40.
[2] Maisky, *Who Helped Hitler?* 73; and Popov, op. cit., 336–8.
[3] Ibid., 340. See also, Maisky, *Who Helped Hitler?* 70–1.
[4] Diary Entry of 7 March 1938, quoted in Nigel Nicolson, ed., *Harold Nicolson, Diaries and Letters*, i, *1930–1939* (1966), [hereinafter: Nicolson, I], 329.
[5] Letter from Maisky to Lloyd George, 10 Feb. 1938, Lloyd George Papers, G/14/1/3.

The Anschluss on 13 March, 1938 clearly designated Czechoslovakia as the next victim of Germany's attention. It is interesting that Lloyd George, unlike Chamberlain's other critics, at first viewed the Czech crisis with some indifference. He was dissatisfied with Prague's policy towards the incorporated Sudetenlands. Maurice Gerothwohl, a member of his secretariat, prepared for him a critical minute entitled 'Notes on Violations of Minority Treaties' [by Czechoslovakia and others].[1] As for the Czech president, Eduard Benes, Lloyd George had once described him as 'Poincaré's Jackal'.[2] It is thus not surprising that the Czech crisis saw Lloyd George rather reticent on this particular issue of foreign policy, though still very critical of appeasement.

Various attempts to solve the central European dispute continued throughout the spring and summer of 1938. Meanwhile, opponents of government policy proceeded with their own efforts to influence events. On 14 March, 1938 Churchill had crystallized a multitude of proposals with his 'grand alliance' speech in the Commons. In essence this suggested an offensive-defensive alliance between Great Britain, France and the USSR, backed by concerted staff arrangements and the moral authority of the League of Nations.[3] The scheme was decisively rejected both by the foreign office and the chiefs of staff.[4] Nonetheless, it served as a basis for discussion within anti-appeasement circles and, indeed, was propounded in various forms by the Soviet government during the months prior to the Munich conference.

When Maisky returned in May 1938 to Moscow, on leave, he kept Lloyd George informed of his departures and whereabouts.[5] It appears that Lloyd George also 'sent a warm message of admiration to Stalin, as the greatest living statesman alive'.[6]

[1] Minute by Gerothwohl, 8 June 1938, Lloyd George Papers, G/27/8/1.
[2] Memorandum of a Talk Between Lloyd George and Nicholas Titulescu, 11 June 1937, ibid., G/130.
[3] *H.C. deb.*, 333, 15 March 1938, cols. 99–100.
[4] Foreign Policy Committee of the Cabinet, Minutes, 18 March 1938, CAB 27/623; and Diary Entry of 20 March 1938, quoted in Keith Feiling, *The Life of Neville Chamberlain* (1946), 347.
[5] Lloyd George Papers, G/14/1/5–6.
[6] Entry of 16 May 1938, *Beatrice Webb Diary*.

This may not have been without ulterior motives. During this time, Lloyd George expressed his fears that Maisky might become a victim of the purges.[1] The London press carried the same stories which the ambassador felt compelled to deny through the columns of the *News Chronicle*.[2] In late July he was back at his post.

With Maisky's return, the Soviet government, after a period of fluctuating between bellicosity and passivity, began an intensive effort to consolidate an anti-Hitler front and stiffen the resistance of the western democracies. The ambassador played a key role in this diplomatic offensive. On 17 August he described to Halifax the disappointment in Moscow at what was considered the 'undue weakness' of Anglo-French policy, and urged that an 'absolutely firm front should be shown to Germany and Italy'. If Germany attacked Czechoslovakia, the USSR would ' "certainly do their bit" '.[3]

But from Lloyd George came words of caution. When asked by Maisky at the house of commons how Great Britain and France would react if the Czech crisis became serious, he replied: ' "Neither the British nor the French government will do anything really effective to defend Czechoslovakia against German attack." My intsinct', Maisky added, 'tells me the same.'[4] Nevertheless, he again reassured Nicolson on 22 August that if Great Britain and France went to war on behalf of Czechoslovakia the USSR would help. If Great Britain abandoned the Czechs, however, Moscow would become isolationist; confident in its own unlimited territory and resources.[5]

Plans for some form of great power cooperation to thwart Germany were generally current in late August and throughout September. As parliament was not sitting at the time, pressure was brought to bear through informal channels. Thus Nicolson repeated his conversation with the Soviet ambassador to Earl

---

[1] Louis Fischer, *Men and Politics* (1941), 504; and the same author's *Russia's Road from Peace to War, Soviet Foreign Relations 1917–1941* (1969), 289.

[2] George Bilainkin, *Maisky, Ten Years Ambassador* (1944), 204–5.

[3] Halifax to Chilston, 17 Aug. 1938, DBFP, 3rd Series, ii, no. 637.

[4] Diary Entry of 20 Aug. 1938, quoted in Ivan Maisky, 'The Munich Drama', *New Times*, no. 44, 1 Nov. 1966 [hereinafter: Maisky, 'Munich Drama'], 25–6.

[5] 22 Aug. 1938, quoted in Nicolson, i, 356.

De La Warr, lord privy seal. The latter considered the remarks
sufficiently important for a record to be made for transmission
to Vansittart.[1] 'The point being', Nicolson noted in his diary,
'that if Maisky can be induced to promise Russian support if
we take a strongline over Czechoslovakia, the weak will of the
Prime Minister may be strengthened.'[2] Indeed, Vansittart's
minute of his conversation several days later with Maisky was
calculated to play down Soviet isolationist tendencies and
encourage the foreign office to cultivate Soviet desires to
cooperate.[3] But the choice of Vansittart as an interpreter of a
message from Maisky was ill-considered and no doubt ensured
its unacceptability. In fact, De La Warr took more positive
steps. He wrote to Halifax on 2 September suggesting the
foreign office make a demonstration of consulting with the
Soviet and French ambassadors in London. Such a step
'would do good with the Russians whose help after all we may
need in the last resort. I gather from Harold Nicolson who saw
Maisky the other day that there is a certain amount of feeling
about being left out in the cold. . . .'[4]

Maisky also turned to Churchill. On 31 August Churchill
unfolded to the ambassador his now familiar solution to the
European crisis. Churchill suggested that, at the moment when
negotiations were finally deadlocked, Great Britain, France and
the USSR should send Hitler a collective note warning against
any possible attack on Czechoslovakia. 'This move . . . would
frighten Hitler and inaugurate the London-Paris-Moscow
"Axis" which could alone save the world from another
shambles.' Churchill asked what Soviet reaction would be to
such a plan. Maisky thought it had merit, but was unrealizable.
He commented with considerable justification: 'I could not see
Chamberlain agreeing to joint action with the U.S.S.R. against
Germany.'[5] Nevertheless, that same day Churchill wrote

[1] For Nicolson's Letter to Vansittart, see F.O. 371/22289, N4317/97/
38.

[2] Diary Entry of 26 Aug. 1938, quoted in Nicolson, i, 357–8.

[3] Minute by Vansittart, 29 Aug. 1938, F.O. 371/22289.

[4] Letter from De La Warr to Halifax, 2 Sept. 1938, F.O. 800/314. On
10 September, in another letter to the foreign secretary, De La Warr
repeated his suggestion. Ibid.

[5] Diary Entry of 1 Sept. 1938, quoted in Maisky, 'Munich Drama',
26.

Halifax a letter along the lines sketched to Maisky.[1] Further discussions on this theme took place in early September between Churchill, Nicolson and Boothby;[2] and it was also mentioned in a letter Boothby sent to eight cabinet ministers on 9 September.[3]

All of these suggestions had been anticipated by the cabinet and discussed on 30 August. At that time Neville Henderson, British ambassador in Berlin, had personally advised a conference of ministers 'that Herr Hitler attached little importance to Russia except as regards aeroplanes and that he would go forward against a combination of France, Russia and this country.' The ministers agreed that no such three power threat should be made[4] and resisted all subsequent suggestions to this effect.

Although September 1938 was a period of intense diplomatic activity in the international sphere, Anglo-Soviet relations bear only a peripheral relevance to events. On the official governmental level information as to Soviet intentions continued to derive mainly from the French government and was then passed to London. Thus official contact between the foreign office and the narkomindel was severely restricted. The importance of this arrangement was that one of the most crucial statements of Soviet intentions was so distorted when forwarded to London as to render it useless. On 2 September, in order to reply to an enquiry on Soviet intentions, Litvinov had received Jean Payart, the French chargé d'affaires in Moscow. Various records exist of what transpired. The French version claims Litvinov had merely indicated his intention to raise the whole Czech-Sudeten dispute at the League of Nations.[5] The Soviet record suggests the foreign commissar proposed that a conference of Great Britain, France and the USSR should issue a declaration, and that military consultations between the general staffs of France,

[1] F.O. 800/314; also published in Winston S. Churchill, *The Second World War*, vol. i, *The Gathering Storm* (London 1949), [hereinafter: Churchill, vol. i], 262–3.

[2] Entries of 3, 4 Sept. 1938, *Harold Nicolson Diary*, Balliol College, Oxford.

[3] Letter from Boothby to Lloyd George, 30 May 1939, Enclosure, Lloyd George Papers, G/3/13/9.

[4] Conclusions of a Conference of Ministers, 30 Aug. 1938, CAB 23/94.

[5] Georges Bonnet, *Défence de la Paix*, i, *De Washington au Quai d'Orsay* (1946), 197–9.

Czechoslovakia and the USSR should begin at once. Besides this Litvinov also advised an appeal to the League.[1]

It was this version which Maisky took upon himself to circulate in London. He had received no official instructions on the matter. On 3 September he journeyed to Chartwell to brief Churchill. The ambassador's approach in this context may not have been altogether propitious. The similarity in Churchill's and the Soviets' remedies for the crisis made him an obvious, but not a suitable, choice. He doubted whether Great Britain would as yet consider any of the suggestions. But inasmuch as this information fully coincided with his own ideas Churchill immediately informed Halifax. The foreign secretary replied that putting the Czech question before the League would not be helpful, although he would keep it in mind. The other points concerning a declaration and a conference seem to have passed without comment. Halifax did indicate that Great Britain must wait on continuing developments in Czechoslovakia.[2]

At the same time Maisky also informed Lloyd George and Arthur Greenwood, the deputy Labour leader, of the Litvinov-Payart conversation. The ambassador's motive in these lobbying activities, which increased during the coming months, was to give the Soviet proposals the maximum publicity in order to counter a 'whispering campaign' by the 'Cliveden set', which pointed to Soviet reticence as proof of a desire to avoid its obligations. Thereby political circles in London would know Russia's attitude. Furthermore, Maisky pointed out, if there were 'slanderous talks in Parliament about the "passivity" of the U.S.S.R. on the Czechoslovak question there could be a reply from the Opposition restoring the true facts.'[3]

Halifax finally invited Maisky for an interview on 8 September, mainly to express his inability to join the ambassador at the League meetings in Geneva. Only at the end of their talk did he broach the subject of Litvinov's latest proposals. Maisky was

---

[1] Litvinov to Alexandrovsky, 2 Sept. 1938, V. F. Klochko, et. al., *New Documents on the History of Munich* (Prague 1958), 62–3.

[2] Letter from Churchill to Halifax, 3 Sept. 1938, quoted in Churchill, i, 263–6. Churchill's explanation of why the Soviet ambassador chose him—to avoid a possible foreign office rebuff—differs from the reasons advanced by Maisky.

[3] Maisky, *Who Helped Hitler?* 79–80.

then thanked for information already familiar to the British government.[1] Maisky exaggerated when he wrote later: 'Apparently Churchill's letter had made some impression and he [i.e., Halifax] wanted to verify the information with me.'[2] But the curtness of the foreign secretary's reply confirmed that London was quite unwilling to consider such overt action in association with the USSR.

Maisky left London the following day, after having informed Lloyd George of his impending departure and indicating he would return at the end of the month. In his reply Lloyd George grimly forecast: 'I fear that the Czechs are being betrayed by Neville and Daladier.'[3] On 9 September, A. J. Sylvester, Lloyd George's principal private secretary, was received by S. B. Kagan, the counsellor of the Soviet embassy. Kagan denied press reports that Moscow had threatened to abandon Czechoslovakia if Benes made further concessions. On the contrary, the USSR had never interfered in Czech internal affairs. The Soviet position was

> that while Hitler had not gone too far in engaging himself there was still time to prevent him from committing an act of aggression and plunging Europe into a war. For this purpose the essential thing was to make it clear to Hitler that any act of aggression on his part would be met with the strongest resistance .... The British Government ought to say that the Czechs had made their last sacrifice, and that any attempt to impose force to terrorise the Czechs would result in the British siding with France and other countries to resist aggression. If Mr. Lloyd George would say something on these lines it would have a very important bearing on the situation.

Kagan could offer no information as to the number of troops his government had on its western frontier. But 'he assumed they were alive to the situation and that whatever measures their military people had taken were adequate.' The Soviet Union 'would not be found napping.'[4]

Efforts to ensure some form of three power co-operation continued. On 11 September Lloyd George took up Kagan's suggestion. In an article in *The Sunday Express* he urged that

[1] Halifax to Chilston, 8 Sept. 1938, *D.B.F.P.*, II, no. 808.

[2] Maisky, 'Munich Drama', 27.

[3] Letter from Maisky to Lloyd George, 6 Sept. 1938; Letter from Lloyd George to Maisky, 14 Sept. 1938, Lloyd George Papers, G/14/1/7–8.

[4] Minute by Sylvester, 9 Sept. 1938, ibid., G/27/3/42.

Hitler should be warned 'in time that if he attacks Czecho-Slovakia he will have the armies of France and Russia battering at his gates . . .' Both these countries have clarified their willingness to defend Czechoslovakia in case of attack. 'The attitude of Britain alone is in doubt.' Boothby referred favourably to this article in a letter he sent the same day to Oliver Stanley, president of the board of trade, and Walter Elliot, minister of health.[1] Three days later Churchill telephoned to Halifax and once again urged the scheme of an Anglo-French-Soviet joint note to Berlin. The record of their conversation was circulated to the cabinet.[2]

On 17 September Dalton had a meeting with Vansittart in order to be apprised of the latest developments. Vansittart wanted to keep Russia involved, but clearly feared the British government would act otherwise. Before parting, he cautioned Dalton against revealing the extent of his knowledge of foreign office telegrams. Vansittart later added that his position in the government was becoming more difficult and that they should no longer meet at the foreign office.[3] As Dalton frequently saw Maisky and was *persona grata* at the Soviet embassy, Vansittart's caution was understandable.

Following this meeting on the 17th, Dalton went on, in the company of Walter Citrine and Herbert Morrison, to a conference with Chamberlain, Halifax and Sir Horace Wilson. When the conversation turned to Soviet affairs, Dalton confronted the prime minister with having omitted Maisky's version of the Litvinov-Payart discussion; rather contrary to Chamberlain's statement that the Soviet government merely intended to raise the whole Czech question at the League. The prime minister was apparently unperturbed and suggested that the British general staff 'did not think the Red army could do much. In the air, of course, the Russians could do a great deal, but what *would* they do?'[4] In actual fact, the Chamberlain government believed the Russians were politically

---

[1] Letter from Boothby to Lloyd George, 30 May 1939, Enclosure, ibid., G/13/9.   [2] Cabinet Paper 200, CAB 24/278.

[3] Entries of Sept. 17, 19, 1938, *Dalton Diary*.

[4] Entry of 17 Sept. 1938, ibid.; and Hugh Dalton, *Memoirs*, ii, *The Fateful Years, 1931–1945* (1954), [hereinafter: Dalton, ii], 176–183. Cf. Lord Citrine, *Men and Work, An Autobiography* (1964), 361–6.

unreliable and could do little to aid Czechoslovakia. A report from the chiefs of staff sub-committee on 14 September had advised along these lines.[1]

With the Soviet foreign commissar at the League, the venue for a discussion of the alternatives to appeasement shifted to Geneva. On 21 September Litvinov publicly, but selectively, described the content of recent Soviet diplomatic moves. Two days later the British government made its first direct approach to the Soviet Union. The British delegation at Geneva, headed by De La Warr and parliamentary under-secretary of state, R. A. Butler, was directed to ascertain what action the USSR would take if Czechoslovakia was involved in war with Germany and at what point they were prepared to take it.[2]

There were several reasons which precipitated this action. The second round of Chamberlain-Hitler talks at Godesberg was running into difficulties. British public opinion was hardening against further concessions to Hitler. Alternatives had to be explored. Furthermore, the move appears to indicate some distrust of prior French information on Soviet policy. Finally, the usual advocates of Anglo-Soviet cooperation had been active. On 21 September Dalton arranged an appointment at the Soviet embassy to meet Kagan. Dalton was told of the lack of consultations between the foreign office and the embassy. He was given full details both of what Litvinov had conveyed to the French government in early September and of the content of talks between Litvinov and Georges Bonnet, the French foreign minister, in Geneva on 11 September. Then, along with other Labour leaders, Dalton had a meeting with Halifax at the foreign office. Dalton particularly criticized the government for having accepted Bonnet's version of French consultations with the Soviets and for not having initiated talks between Moscow and London.[3] He later suggested that this meeting prompted the British inquiry in Geneva.[4] Boothby also appears to have been partly responsible. On 22 September he saw Litvinov at Geneva. The latter 'burst into bitter complaint

[1] Cabinet Paper 199, CAB 24/278.

[2] Halifax to U.K. Delegation (Geneva), 23 Sept. 1938, D.B.F.P., II, no. 1043.

[3] Entry of 21 Sept. 1938, Dalton Diary. Cf. Dalton, II, 183.

[4] Hugh Dalton, Hitler's War, Before and After (1940), 77.

against the British Government' at the lack of consultation. He mentioned Russia had 1,500 first line airplanes to place at the disposal of Czechoslovakia. Boothby immediately saw De La Warr who wired for instructions to consult Litvinov. Returning to London the following day, Boothby gave an account of his meeting to Halifax.[1]

> I was not, by that time 'persona grata' in official circles; although . . . Halifax listened with great attention and courtesy, and apparent interest. I left the F.O. with the definite impression that it was his intention to make contact with Litvinov by one means or another, and I have good reason to believe that he did. This was my objective.[2]

Thus Litvinov was finally asked to develop his views directly to a representative of the British government. He replied that Russia 'would take action' if France assisted the Czechs. His government might raise the matter at the League. But the essence of his statement was a proposal for a meeting away from Geneva of Great Britain, France, the USSR and any reliable small power, when military discussions could also take place. The conversation concluded with hopes being expressed for continued consultations.[3]

For the foreign office in London there appeared little in Litvinov's remarks which differed from his previous declarations.[4] This approach nonetheless stands as an indication that certain elements in the British government, under the continuous pressure from the critics of appeasement, were anxious to explore the possibilities of a Soviet role. But these tentative beginnings were not followed up and no further discussions ensued.

The only other success achieved was a statement issued from 10 Downing Street on 26 September and published in the press the following day. It stated that if, in spite of Anglo-French

---

[1] Robert Boothby, *I Fight to Live* (1947), 160–2; and Memorandum from Boothby to Churchill, 1 Oct. 1938, Lloyd George Papers, G/3/13/9. See also, Diary Entry of 23 Sept. 1938, Nicolson, i, 365–6.

[2] Letter from Lord Boothby to the author, 8 June 1968. I am grateful to Lord Boothby for permission to quote from this letter.

[3] U.K. Delegation (Geneva) to Halifax, 24 Sept. 1938, *D.B.F.P.*, II, no. 1071. Maisky gives his version of this meeting with additional details, in Diary Entry of 23 Sept. 1938, quoted in Maisky, 'Munich Drama', 28.

[4] See the Minutes on the telegram from the Geneva Delegation in F.O. 371/21777, C.10585/5302/18.

efforts at conciliation, Germany attacked Czechoslovakia, the 'immediate result must be that France will be bound to come to her assistance, and Great Britain and Russia will certainly stand by France.'[1] The precise origins of this statement, after all the subsequent controversy it aroused, is now clear. Halifax met with Churchill and Chamberlain in the cabinet room where they 'spoke together and agreed together in the sense of the Communiqué'. In the evening Reginald Leeper, head of the foreign office news department, issued the communiqué with Halifax's authorization. To the foreign secretary's surprise Chamberlain, annoyed and upset, reproved him for its publication. The communiqué, Halifax noted, 'said publicly what we had all been saying privately.'[2]

The significant inclusion was of course the Soviet Union. This was the first time it had been publicly mentioned in a government statement. Presumably the basis for this action was Litvinov's Geneva speeches and his interview with De La Warr. Maisky's consistent lobbying activities had achieved some result. The advantage thereby gained was the impression created abroad of a united front. The communiqué precisely reflected the policy so long advocated as an alternative to appeasement. Eden later claimed in the Commons that it had helped to avert war.[3] But should the statement have had to be implemented the weak foundations upon which it rested would have been exposed. And, indeed, it was never brought to the test. The meeting of Chamberlain, Daladier, Hitler and Mussolini at Munich on 29 September decisively symbolized the rejection of the Soviet alternative to appeasement.

Excluded from the four power deliberations at Munich, the Soviet government immediately began to disassociate itself from recent events. The Moscow press repeatedly declared that the USSR had nothing whatever to do either with the Munich conference or its decisions. Maisky vigorously set to work in London to buttress this contention. Having previously met Lloyd George and discussed Anglo-Soviet relations, Maisky then sent him copies of two of Litvinov's most important policy declara-

[1] Halifax to Henderson, 26 Sept. 1938, *D.B.F.P.*, II, no. 1111, fn. 1.
[2] Letter from Halifax to Churchill, 24 July 1947, Hicklewood [Lord Halifax] Papers, A4/410/19/3.
[3] *H.C. deb.*, 339, 3 Oct. 1938, cc. 79–80.

tions: the 17 March, 1938 proposal for a conference and the 21 September speech before the League assembly. This material, Maisky wrote expectantly, 'will be of interest to you in the present circumstances.'[1]

Anglo-Soviet relations came up many times during the four day parliamentary debate on the Munich settlement. Chamberlain himself did not refer to Russia in any of his three contributions to the debate. But Attlee, Sinclair, Eden, Dalton and Churchill, among others, criticized the government for cold-shouldering the USSR and failing to explore adequately the possibilities of resisting Germany with Soviet help. It was alleged that only a united front of peaceful powers could have restrained Hitler. They also warned of a possible Soviet retreat into isolation as a consequence of Chamberlain's pursuit of a four power pact. Some predicted a Nazi-Soviet rapprochement.[2] Dalton supplemented his criticism with very explicit evidence, derived from the Soviet embassy, on the course of Anglo-Soviet discussions during September.[3]

Replying to these charges, Sir Samuel Hoare, the home secretary, suggested that France had been primarily responsible for consulting with the USSR. To talk of the 'cold-shoulder' was a 'complete exaggeration of the position.' He then confirmed Dalton's descriptions of Maisky's contacts with the government and added that at Geneva the British delegation maintained that contact.[4] Nonetheless, the Labour member, A. V. Alexander, returned to the subject. He claimed the government had received on 8 September a report on Litvinov's proposal to Payart for staff talks. But Sir Thomas Inskip, minister for the co-ordination of defence, denied the validity of the information, and repeated the official explanation as to why there had been no Soviet representative at Munich. He also condemned the solution based on a triple alliance. It would have offered 'no remedy for the disease', he declared, and would have been a return to 'power politics'.[5]

To counter what he considered the misleading impression

[1] Letter from Maisky to Lloyd George, 1 Oct. 1938, Lloyd George Papers, G/14/1/10.

[2] *H.C. deb.*, 339, 3, 5 Oct. 1938, cc. 57–8, 63–5, 74, 86–7, 141–4, 363–4.

[3] Ibid., 3 Oct. 1938, c. 141.   [4] Ibid., cc. 152–3.

[5] *H.C. deb.*, 339, 4 Oct. 1938, cc. 286–7, 297–8, 304.

given by Hoare, Maisky circulated a long memorandum
outlining the course of Anglo-Soviet relations during September.
In his covering letter to Lloyd George, the ambassador confidently wrote that the information was a 'statement of facts'.
The memorandum—interesting both for the explicit details
furnished to members of parliament for use in a foreign affairs
debate, and for the picture it presents of the Soviet view of
relations with Great Britain prior to the Munich conference—
stated:

> The Soviet Ambassador, during the crisis, visited the Foreign Office
> three times; on the 8th and the 29th September—on both occasions
> to see Lord Halifax—and on the 30th to see Sir Alexander Cadogan.
> Between the 9th and 28th September, the Soviet Ambassador was at
> Geneva and consequently there was no contact in London between the
> Foreign Office and the Soviet Charge d'Affaires.

Maisky then gave details of these three consultations. On 8 September 'simply an exchange of views on the situation' took
place. On 29 September Halifax explained the reasons for Soviet
exclusion from the Munich conference. The next day Sir
Alexander Cadogan, permanent under-secretary of state, described the results of the conference which were then discussed.
The memorandum continued:

> During the same period of crisis the British Ambassador in Moscow
> had not a single conversation with the Soviet Foreign Office on
> Czechoslovakia.
>
>   In Geneva, Mr. Litvinov and the Soviet Ambassador were meeting
> practically daily in the meetings of the Commissions or at lunches
> and dinners, Mr. Butler, the British Under Secretary for Foreign
> Affairs, and on several occasions (in the course of his comings and
> goings between London and Geneva) Earl de la Warr. But these
> meetings consisted in the exchange of the latest bits of news which
> either side had of the developments in Czechoslovakia and in the
> various capitals of Europe.
>
>   The only one occasion which approached something like consul-
> tation between the Soviet and the British Governments on the crisis
> occurred in the afternoon of the 23rd September—the day when
> Herr Hitler produced his ultimatum in Godesberg—when Earl de la
> Warr and Mr. Butler on instructions from London, invited Mr.
> Litvinov and the Soviet Ambassador to join them in a conversation
> of a quite 'informal' character. (The word 'informal' was particularly
> stressed.) . . .
>
>   All through this crisis the 'contacts' which the British Government

had with the Soviet Government were: (a) rare; (b) in the nature of an exchange of views on the situation or information given to the Soviet Government on the already accomplished facts; (c) except the meeting of the 23rd September at Geneva, which had no direct results, there was not a single case of consultation with the Soviet Government on the steps or measures contemplated by the British or by the British and French Governments in connection with the crisis. Therefore, all attempts which are being made at the present time to create an impression that the Soviet Government had something to do with the Anglo-French Plan of the 19th September or with the Munich 'settlement' are absolutely false.[1]

Lloyd George himself did not speak in the debate on the Munich settlement, but inevitably Maisky's information was brought up in parliament. Greenwood quoted almost verbatim from it when criticizing the government's handling of its relations with Moscow.[2] However, Sir John Simon, chancellor of the exchequer, closed the government's case by assuring members that there had been no intention of excluding Russia from any European settlement. Nor had Great Britain succumbed to four power diplomacy. Chamberlain's only oblique response was to dismiss excessive armaments and military alliances as a 'policy of utter despair'.[3]

Having succeeded in permitting informed parliamentary criticism to be made of government policy, though having failed to change that policy, Maisky continued to plead Moscow's case and influence opinion. He attempted to convince Nicolson 'that Chamberlain tried to trick the country into his four-power pact.'[4] On 11 October Dalton visited the Soviet embassy where he heard from the ambassador yet more particulars of Anglo-Soviet diplomacy during the previous month. This information, Dalton wrote in his diary, 'fills out a little a familiar story.'[5] Liddell Hart likewise was briefed on 1 November. Maisky also took the opportunity to accuse Chamberlain of having consistently sought any arrangement with the fascist powers, even to the point of surrender, rather

[1] Letter from Maisky to Lloyd George, 4 Oct. 1938, Enclosure, Lloyd George Papers, G/13/1/9.
[2] *H.C. deb.*, 339, 5 Oct. 1938, c. 356.
[3] *H.C. deb.*, 339, 6 Oct. 1938, cc. 549–50.
[4] Entry of 4 Oct. 1938, *Nicolson Diary*.
[5] Entry of 11 Oct. 1938, *Dalton Diary*.

than co-operate with the USSR. Liddell Hart tactfully suggested that while there might be some anti-Soviet prejudice there was no definite policy. But genuine doubt did exist in London as to Soviet ability and desire to co-operate.[1]

Soviet pronouncements on foreign policy, as typified by Maisky's private conversations during the next five months, alternated between sombre threats of isolation and assurances to the contrary. Immediately after the Munich conference he confided to Dalton that the Soviet government would not 'for the present do anything dramatic. They would wait for a month or so and watch developments.'[2] Speaking to Boothby at a later date, Maisky described his government as having decided after Munich 'to have done with Geneva and retire into a well-protected isolation.'[3] He told Liddell Hart the same, but added: '. . . whatever the immediate advantages of this policy the Government of the U.S.S.R. recognised its possible long-term dangers, and were thus inclined to defer any definite decision to cut loose from the West.'[4] On 3 February, during an extensive discussion with Maisky at the foreign office, Butler gained the impression that the USSR would pursue an isolationist policy.[5] Several days later Maisky told a group of English guests at the Soviet embassy that Russia was 'obviously much wounded by Munich', and Great Britain could 'expect no advances from her side.' But an approach from London might be reciprocated.[6] At about the same time, while entertaining the Anglo-Russian parliamentary committee at the Soviet embassy, Maisky warned that 'there might be a change of policy'.[7] On 9 March he stated the Soviets were 'hesitating before deciding on a policy of complete isolation.'

[1] B. H. Liddell Hart, The Memoirs of Captain Liddell Hart, II (1965), [hereinafter: Liddell Hart, II], 195.

[2] Entry of 11 Oct. 1938, Dalton Diary. See also Entry of 31 Oct. 1938, Beatrice Webb Diary.

[3] Letter from Boothby to Lloyd George, 18 Sept. 1939, Enclosure, Lloyd George Papers, G/3/13/12; and Boothby, op. cit., 189.

[4] Liddell Hart, II, 222.

[5] Halifax to Seeds, 14 Feb. 1939, D.B.F.P., IV (1951), no. 103.

[6] Diary Entry of 9 Feb. 1939, quoted in Nicolson, I, 391. The other guests included Boothby, Richard Law, M.P., Vernon Bartlett and J. B. Priestley.

[7] Memorandum on a Conversation Between Lord Strabolgi and Maisky, 20 Sept. 1939, Dalton Papers.

They had therefore agreed 'to wait and see how things developed.'[1] Soviet foreign policy from October 1938 to March 1939 seems to have been particularly unsettled.

Maisky's bewildering fluctuations were partly due to the changes in British policy towards the Soviet Union during this same period. From October to December 1938 the attitude of the foreign office was one of reserve but not hostility. However, in the opening weeks of 1939 the situation changed abruptly. Reports that Germany planned a military move westwards multiplied ominously. Germany and the USSR began to renew their economic contacts. Curiously, in a *News Chronicle* article on 28 January, 1939, strongly suggestive of Soviet embassy inspiration, Vernon Bartlett warned that the USSR might be driven into the arms of Germany.[2] Finally, the general tenor of information coming into the foreign office seemed to indicate a Soviet retreat into isolation, or even worse. On 1 February, 1939 Cadogan minuted: 'It seems that we shall have to watch very carefully the development of any tendency towards a rapprochement between Germany and the Soviet.'[3]

For the first time since the Soviets began to utter threats of isolation, these were being taken seriously in London. And as usual the unofficial advocates of closer Anglo-Soviet relations continued a campaign which seemed at last to bear fruit. Lloyd George particularly began more and more to turn his full attention to publicizing the need of an Anglo-Soviet understanding. He tried to counter the prevalent criticism of the military weakness of the USSR.[4] In the *Sunday Express* on 1 January, 1939, he criticized politicians of the right in both Great Britain and France 'for fostering this delusion' of the demoralization of the Red army. He returned to the attack in a speech at Llandudno on 19 January. Chamberlain, he declared, had refused to mobilize the powerful aid available from the Soviet Union, despite the Red army being 'three if

---

[1] Minute by Butler, 9 March 1939, *D.B.F.P.*, IV, no. 194.
[2] Cf. Vernon Bartlett, *And Now, Tomorrow* (1960), 36–7.
[3] Minute by Cadogan, 1 Feb. 1939, *D.B.F.P.*, IV, no. 76.
[4] His secretariat fully briefed him on this aspect. See Memorandum by Malcolm Thomson, [c. Nov. 1938], Lloyd George Papers, G/22/4/21; and Memorandum by T. F. Tweed, 4 Nov. 1938, ibid., G/130.

not four times as numerous in officers and men, as the German Army' and possessing vast armaments and immense industrial resources. Yet Russia was never approached. Surely this was not because of any aversion to authoritarian states, Lloyd George continued. The prime minister 'has been cringing and crawling before Dictators for months. . . . The supreme diplomatic imbecility of snubbing Russia ought to be repaired without loss of time. The peril is great—and it is imminent.'[1]

Such criticisms, although noticed by Chamberlain, left him personally quite unmoved. In a letter to his sister he wrote that he had been advised to 'make a grand alliance against Germany. In other words better abandon my policy & adopt Winston's! Fortunately my nature is as Ll[oyd] G[eorge] says extremely "obstinate", & I refuse to change. . . .'[2] But government thinking on the perennial question of Soviet military strength, as exemplified at least by Halifax, appeared to undergo a very slight shift. On 23 February Sylvester forwarded to Lloyd George a summary of a statement made by Halifax to the foreign affairs committee of the Conservative party. This was obtained from a 'very reliable source'. Halifax reportedly stated: 'Best way to describe Russia now is something between the 1914 attitude of "the unconquerable steam roller" and looking on her as entirely useless militarily. We cannot ignore a population of 180,000,000 people.'[3] Indeed, Halifax's was the only voice raised at this time in the cabinet against doing anything further to alienate Russia.[4] However, suggestions in parliament to institute some form of Anglo-Soviet military collaboration were turned down by the government.[5]

Nonetheless, it was quite true that in February and early March 1939 the British government attempted in various ways to improve relations with the kremlin. No concrete proposals were put forward; rather expressions of good-will and sugges-

[1] Lloyd George Papers, G/130.
[2] Copy of Letter from Chamberlain to Hilda Chamberlain, 8 Jan. 1939, Viscount Templewood Papers, XIX: (C)11, University Library, Cambridge.
[3] Summary of a Statement by Halifax, 23 Feb. 1939, Lloyd George papers, G/23/1/8. Maisky also heard a report of this address. Bilainkin, op. cit., 299.
[4] Cabinet Conclusions, 8 Feb. 1939, CAB 23/97.
[5] H.C. deb., 343, 8 Feb. 1939, cc. 929–30; vol. 344, 22 Feb., 8 March 1939, cc. 354–5, 2251–2.

tions for friendly contacts. The intention was one of insurance and not obligation. Russian aid was to be available if and when needed. Not unnaturally, the Soviet Union responded to these overtures with suspicion. In London Maisky's criticisms of Chamberlain's appeasement policies continued unabated. Moscow, he declared to a government official, 'would judge the seriousness of [British] intentions by the degree Anglo-Soviet relations were improved not by words but by deeds.'[1] He openly expressed his suspicions of Chamberlain's motives when talking to Butler. The latter concluded his report of their conversation by observing, with some justification, that Maisky 'thought that the reason why we were approaching them was that ... the Government were anticipating trouble and were therefore seeking the help of Russia.'[2]

Maisky also sought out independent opinion on developments. This time Liddell Hart was invited to the Soviet embassy and was asked how far recent British approaches to Moscow were genuine or not. Maisky suggested that the Soviet position was 'one of "wait and see".' His government considered 'that our apparent change of attitude might merely be a tactical move—to make the Germans more inclined to compromise. and that if it succeeded in this purpose we might again throw Russia overboard....'[3] Events were very shortly to ensure against any such possibility. But the attempts during the winter of 1939 to improve Anglo-Soviet relations proved a useful background to the tripartite political and military negotiations which shortly followed.

Unlike the previous year when the Anschluss was immediately followed by Litvinov's proposals for consultations, the German occupation of Czechoslovakia and the rumoured threat to Rumania's independence in mid-March 1939 witnessed Great Britain taking the initiative. Halifax instructed Vansittart to brief Maisky on the crisis. British thinking, it was emphasized, was taking a firmer attitude to Germany.[4] More important was the approach made to the USSR on 17 March. The Soviet

---

[1] Foreign Policy Archives of the USSR, quoted in Popov, op. cit., 384.

[2] Minute by Butler, 9 March 1939, *D.B.F.P.*, IV, no. 194.

[3] Liddell Hart, II, 222.

[4] Ian Colvin, *Vansittart in Office* (1965), 295. See also, Entry of 24 March, 1939, *Dalton Diary*.

Union was asked to help Rumania, if requested, to resist German aggression. The Soviet reply once again suggested convening a conference to discuss possibilities of common action. This was politely and, perhaps, impatiently declined. Instead, the narkomindel agreed on 21 March to a declaration proposal. Great Britain, France, Russia and Poland were to agree to consult together on possible steps to resist future acts of aggression. This declaration of intent would be followed by detailed consultations on specific situations. Polish distaste for collaboration with the USSR effectively stifled this approach. This four power plan was then allowed to lapse in favour of direct Anglo-Polish negotiations.

By the end of March the Soviet press was once again accusing the British government of returning to appeasement. Maisky explained to Dalton that his government interpreted recent British policy as follows: 'Chamberlain wanted (1) to frighten Germany by some evidence of a rapprochement with the S[oviet] U[nion], though he did not seriously intend the latter, and (2) to meet the electoral argument that he was cold-shouldering Russia.'[1]

The lack of further developments in Anglo-Soviet relations was producing the inevitable feelings of mistrust in Moscow and deepening suspicions of western plots to divert Germany eastwards. Maisky complained to all his political contacts and vented his irritation at not being kept in touch. His isolation, no doubt, reflected badly on his own position *vis-à-vis* his government. He was finally called to the foreign office on March 29 and for the first time officially informed that the four power declaration was being dropped. Cadogan explained that Great Britain and France were contemplating giving assurances, involving direct military assistance, to both Poland and Rumania. Such a course, Maisky noted, would be a 'revolutionary change in British policy'. The role envisaged for the USSR, according to Cadogan, was for 'sympathy and . . . active assistance . . . in whatever way might seem suitable and effective.'[2]

Maisky was thus briefed generally on developments prior to

[1] Entry of 28 March 1939, *Dalton Diary*.
[2] Halifax to Seeds, 29 March 1939, *D.B.F.P.*, IV, no. 565. Halifax to Seeds, 4 April 1939, *D.B.F.P.*, V, (1952), no. 4.

the Polish guarantee. But he certainly exaggerated when he let it be understood he had seen Cadogan 'merely on routine matters. We then exchanged little bits of information, but there was no sort of consultation at all.'[1] However, confronted by Sinclair who had the details of the conversation, the ambassador confessed having made the remarks about a revolution in British policy. Sinclair's information was derived from Vansittart and O. S. Cleverly, the prime minister's principal private secretary. When forwarding the details to Lloyd George, Sinclair noted that cabinet ministers 'have not yet managed to dispel the cold atmosphere which has enveloped the relations between the Foreign Office and the Soviet Embassy since Eden's resignation, and it is quite likely that Halifax himself does not appreciate the difference in the atmosphere which Maisky feels.'[2]

The various records of the ambassador's unofficial conversations at this point indicate a certain distortion of facts designed to put the Soviet issue directly before the government. To this end he succeeded in convincing his political acquaintances that Russia was again being cold-shouldered. In response to this, continuous pressure on the government was informally applied with the aim of getting Chamberlain to clarify his policy towards the USSR. The point was well taken by the prime minister. He stated in the foreign policy committee on 27 March that 'failure to associate with Soviet Russia would give rise to suspicion and difficulty with the left wing. . . .'[3] On 28 March, he managed to convince Greenwood of the problems involved in trying to bring in the Russians. But as he informed the cabinet a day later, 'Certain other members of the Opposition were . . . less amenable'.[4] On the morning of 30 March, Chamberlain briefly saw Greenwood and Sinclair. They were told of secret reports indicating an immediate German attack on Poland. The government was therefore considering a statement. To Sinclair's question—' "What about Russia?"', Chamberlain referred to Maisky's conversation with

[1] Minute by Sylvester of a Conversation with Maisky (I), 31 March, 1939, Lloyd George Papers, G/130.
[2] Sinclair to Lloyd George, 1 April, 1939, ibid., G/18/4/9.
[3] Foreign Policy Committee, Minutes, 27 March 1939, CAB 27/624.
[4] Cabinet Conclusions, 29 March 1939, CAB 23/98.

Cadogan the previous day.[1] (At that time, however, a unilateral guarantee had not yet been mentioned.)

Following this conversation, a special cabinet discussed a guarantee of Polish independence. Its terms were settled at a foreign policy committee meeting that afternoon, without the USSR having been consulted or officially notified. A visit by Maisky to Halifax scheduled for four o'clock was cancelled due to pressure of work at the foreign office. The ambassador's irritation at not having seen Halifax since 19 March was vented during a meeting two hours later with Dalton and Greenwood.

As a result of a Labour party executive meeting at nine o'clock, it was agreed to press Chamberlain 'to get something put in about Russia'. The dilemma facing the party was whether to support the guarantee as an 'instalment of collective security' and insist on a Soviet role, or else reject it altogether until Moscow was included. The first alternative prevailed. Consequently, that same evening (the 30th) Greenwood, Alexander and Dalton saw the prime minister in the cabinet room at No. 10.

> We told him that he would never get away with it to-morrow unless he brought in the Russians. We dwelt not only on the state of opinion in our own Party and elsewhere, but on the crude importance of having the Russians on our side if trouble should come. . . . The P.M. said the Government were anxious to consult the Russians and were keeping in touch with them, but he himself had been surprised at the strength of the objections taken by many States to having anything to do with Russia.

It was agreed, however, at Dalton's suggestion, that the parliamentary statement scheduled for eleven a.m. the following day should be postponed for several hours. This would enable Chamberlain to take into account the results of Halifax's early morning conversation with Maisky.[2]

This meeting having yet once again been delayed, Maisky instead saw Sylvester at the request of Lloyd George. The latter was seeking information both on the government's proposed statement and the Soviet position. Maisky proclaimed his ignorance as to precisely what the government intended; merely noting that he had '"heard in round about ways"' that an

---

[1] Entry of 30 March 1939, *Dalton Diary;* and Dalton, ii, 237.

[2] Entry of 30 March 1939, *Dalton Diary;* and Dalton, ii, 237–8.

Anglo-French pledge was to be given to Poland and Rumania. The Soviet government '"were not consulted about it and have not been informed . . . officially.'" Therefore, he could not say whether he was satisfied or not. Maisky then accused the foreign office of 'discourtesy' for not consulting him and for never having officially sent him a copy of the four power declaration.[1]

The meeting with Halifax finally took place at one o'clock and opened with apologies to Maisky for the repeated delays. The foreign secretary then read out the proposed statement. After dealing with criticism, he asked whether Chamberlain might say the Soviet government approved of the statement. According to Halifax's report of the conversation, this was to avoid 'any unnecessary appearance of divisions' between Great Britain and Russia. Maisky claimed the reason advanced was 'to prevent any quarrelling on the part of the Opposition.' He refused his approval, but consented to Chamberlain making some reference that British action accorded with the principles of Soviet policy. At the same time Halifax was twice warned that the Soviet government 'had no wish to force themselves on anybody, and would therefore take no initiative.'[2]

The desire to present as united a front as possible when announcing the guarantee in parliament led also to the first private discussion between Lloyd George and Chamberlain. Having heard from his chief whip, David Margesson, that Lloyd George was in a very critical mood, Chamberlain passed a note to him in the Commons on 31 March. This was an invitation to meet in the prime minister's room in order to impart 'the latest information.'[3] The two had a fifteen minute discussion without apparent disagreement, but with little

[1] Minute by Sylvester of a Conversation with Maisky (I), 31 March, 1939, Lloyd George Papers, G/130. The atmosphere of gloom in the Soviet embassy on this day is vividly described by Beatrice Webb who was there when Sylvester was speaking to the ambassador. Entry of 31 March, 1939, *Beatrice Webb Diary.*

[2] Minute by Sylvester of a Conversation with Maisky (II), 31 March, 1938, Lloyd George Papers, G/130; and Halifax to Seeds, 31 March, 1939, *D.B.F.P.*, IV, no. 589. For Maisky's description, in which he erroneously claims the talk was with Chamberlain, see his *Who Helped Hitler?* 107-8.

[3] Letter from Chamberlain to Lloyd George, 31 March, 1939, Lloyd George Papers, G/4/2/1.

rapport.[1] The acrimonious parliamentary exchanges between these two men in the coming months were doubtless the product of more than just political differences.[2]

On the evening of 31 March, Maisky gave Sylvester, for Lloyd George's information, the details of his conversation with the foreign secretary. Maisky complained of the liberty taken in the Commons of associating the USSR with the guarantee. He did not mention he had agreed to permit some vague reference. The Soviet Union, he explained again, was 'not prepared to be put into the position of *unwanted saviours.*' Therefore, they would 'not move unless or until they were asked to move'. Sylvester then informed the ambassador of Lloyd George's conversation with Chamberlain. '"I think Mr. Lloyd George is right in saying of Poland", Maisky observed, "that this is a reckless gamble on the part of the Prime Minister to believe that he can really stop Hitler by combining Britain, France and Poland."'[3]

The only full record of Lloyd George's conversation with Chamberlain comes in a telegram from Maisky to the narkomindel. According to this, Lloyd George had asked about Soviet participation in a guarantee and had been told that the objections of Poland and Rumania made this impossible.

> Then Lloyd George asked why, under such circumstances, Chamberlain had risked making his statement threatening to involve Britain in a war with Germany. The Prime Minister replied, that, according to information at his disposal, neither the German General Staff nor Hitler would ever risk war if they knew that they would have to fight at the same time on two fronts—the West and the East. Lloyd George then asked just where this 'second front' was. The Prime Minister answered: 'Poland'. Lloyd George burst into laughter and began to gibe Chamberlain, explaining that Poland had no air force to speak of, an inadequately mechanised army, worse than mediocre armaments, and that Poland was weak internally—economically and politically. Without active help from the U.S.S.R., therefore, no 'Eastern front' is possible.

In conclusion Lloyd George had warned that without the USSR the guarantee to Poland was an '" irresponsible game of

[1] See copy of letter from Chamberlain to Hilda Chamberlain, 3 April, 1939, Templewood Papers, XIX: (C) 11.

[2] On this point see A. J. Sylvester, *The Real Lloyd George* (1947), 238–9.

[3] Minute by Sylvester of a Conversation with Maisky (II), 31 March 1939, Lloyd George Papers, G/130.

chance which can end up very badly"'.[1] Maisky also briefed
Dalton on his talk with Halifax and repeated the substance of
the Chamberlain-Lloyd George interview. The ambassador's
knowledgeability provoked from Dalton the teasing remark:
'"I suppose the P.M. told you of this conversation."'[2]

Thus after several days of intensive lobbying Maisky had
again succeeded in bringing the Soviet issue to the attention of
the British government. As far as involving the USSR, if that
was his aim, then his efforts must be considered a failure. The
only acknowledgment he gained was this statement from the
prime minister, after announcing the Polish guarantee: 'I have
no doubt that the principles upon which we are acting are fully
understood and appreciated by that Government.'[3]

The records of Soviet comments on the guarantee indicate,
on the contrary, that it was neither understood nor appreciated
in Moscow. In London, this major British commitment in
eastern Europe unleashed one of the most sustained and
effective parliamentary campaigns ever conducted. Over a
period of four months the leading protagonists of Anglo-Soviet
cooperation succeeded in moving the government from a
position seeking only Soviet aid to Poland and Rumania, in
case of need, to acceptance of an Anglo-French-Soviet mutual
assistance pact. The lobbying activities of Maisky and the
effective parliamentary speeches of Lloyd George, Churchill,
Dalton and others were crucial in achieving this result.
Chamberlain frankly admitted to Admiral Drax, later to head
the British military mission to Moscow, that the Commons
'had pushed him further than he had wished to go.'[4] Moreover,
cabinet discussions from April to early August indicate that it
was fear of the parliamentary opposition which literally forced
the Chamberlain cabinet to continue the talks, when it would
have sometimes preferred a breakdown.

This parliamentary campaign began as soon as the guarantee
was announced. Greenwood, Sinclair, Churchill, Lloyd George

[1] Foreign Policy Archives of the USSR, quoted in 'Soviet-British-French
Talks in Moscow, 1939, A Documentary Survey', International Affairs
(Moscow), no. 7, July 1969, 80.

[2] Entry of 2 April 1939, Dalton Diary.

[3] H.C. deb., 345, 31 March 1939, c. 2416.

[4] R. P. Ernle-Erle-Drax, 'Mission to Moscow, August, 1939', Naval
Review, XL, no. 3, Aug. 1952, 252.

and Eden all emphasized the need to include the USSR. Both Churchill and Lloyd George, the latter having been previously briefed by Liddell Hart on the military implications of a guarantee and the need for Soviet support to make it effective, viewed the new British commitment as the first instalment of the 'grand alliance', the major component of which, a Soviet commitment, was missing. Lloyd George warned that the government was 'walking into a trap'. Russia was the only country strategically situated and with sufficient military strength to aid Poland.[1] Afterwards Nicolson, Churchill and Lloyd George discussed the situation with Maisky. Churchill stressed Polish and Rumanian fears of allowing Soviet troops into their country. Maisky merely expanded on his now favourite theme of Poland's weakness.[2]

Chamberlain's reaction to the debate was to complain privately of the 'almost hysterical passion of the Opposition egged on by Ll[oyd] G[eorge] who have a pathetic belief that in Russia is the key to our salvation.'[3] For his own part, the prime minister bluntly told the cabinet on 5 April 'that he had very considerable distrust of Russia, and had no confidence that we should obtain active and constant support from that country.'[4] The sentiment seemed reciprocated by Maisky who intimated to Beatrice Webb that 'Moscow did *not* trust him and it was doubtful whether they would join a pact if he remained Premier.'[5]

Discussion on how best to approach the USSR languished in the two weeks following the guarantee to Poland. Meetings between Maisky and Halifax on 6 and 11 April failed to produce anything more concrete than expressions of interest in continued consultations. Halifax admitted to Joseph Kennedy, the U.S. ambassador, that he hesitated to tell Maisky too much, because this was 'given over to the enemies.'[6] This accusation was not

---

[1] *H.C. deb.*, 345, 3 April 1939, cc. 2480, 2493, 2501–2, 2506–10, 2513–14; and Liddell Hart, II, 218–19.

[2] Diary Entry of 3 April 1939, quoted in Nicolson, ii, 394.

[3] Copy of Letter from Chamberlain to Hilda Chamberlain, 9 April 1939, Templewood Papers, XIX: (C) 11.

[4] Cabinet Conclusions, 5 April 1939, CAB 23/98.

[5] Entry of 8 April, 1939, *Beatrice Webb Diary*.

[6] Kennedy to Hull, 11 April 1939, *Foreign Relations of the United States* [hereinafter: *F.R.U.S.*], 1939, I, (1956), 125.

without considerable foundation. Indeed, almost every conversation between the Soviet ambassador and the foreign secretary was followed by a briefing to some member of the parliamentary opposition. Dalton appears to have been almost continuously in touch with Maisky. From the announcement of the guarantee until the ambassador's departure to Moscow for consultations on 18 April, three meetings were held. The fullest details of foreign office thinking and policy were given to Dalton. The tenor of this information as emphasized by Maisky was the doubt whether the British government '"really means business."'[1]

Although Dalton had managed to extract from Simon a parliamentary statement that the British government was not opposed in principle to an Anglo-Soviet military alliance,[2] the exact opposite was true. Moscow turned down yet another proposal for a declaration of Soviet intention to help its neighbours. Instead Litvinov offered on 17 April a counter-proposal for a comprehensive Anglo-French-Soviet mutual assistance pact; the simultaneous conclusion of a military convention; and a guarantee of all the states bordering on the USSR from the Baltic to the Black Sea.[3] This the foreign office found embarrassing, undesirable and bristling with objections. The chiefs of staff agreed.[4] But such a triple alliance, details of which Maisky circulated privately, was precisely the scheme most of Chamberlain's parliamentary opponents advocated. Lloyd George had termed this one of the 'two or three supreme and infallible tests as to whether he [i.e., Chamberlain] means business or not.'[5] On Maisky's return from Moscow, he twice saw the foreign secretary who gave him some indication of Britain's likely response to the 17 April proposals. When the ambassador received Dalton on 7 May he described Halifax's observations; this time adding that Great Britain's projected reply was likely to be rejected.

[1] See e.g., Entries of 2, 12, 17 April 1939, *Dalton Diary*.

[2] *H.C. deb.*, 346, 13 April 1939, c. 138.

[3] Seeds to Halifax, 18 April, 1939, *D.B.F.P.*, V, no. 201.

[4] Foreign Policy Committee, Minutes, and Appendix II, 19 April 1939, CAB 27/624; and Report of the Chiefs of Staff Sub-Committee, Cabinet Paper 95, CAB 24/285.

[5] Speech by Lloyd George at Pwllheli, 12 April 1939, Lloyd George Papers, G/189. See also, Sylvester, op. cit., 244, 248.

Interestingly, Maisky's unofficial briefings were beginning to have their complications. He warned Dalton that various Labour members of parliament were indiscreetly making use of information intended only for himself, Attlee and Greenwood. W. P. Coates, secretary of the Anglo-Russian parliamentary committee and a familiar figure in the parliamentary lobby, had already been cautioned. Maisky then added that '"at No. 10 Downing Street they think that I am an arch plotter. I do not mind that, but I hope you will ask your friends to be careful."'[1]

The 8 May British reply, essentially a restatement of earlier declaration suggestions, received the equally expected Soviet rejection on 14 May. Once more the British government was faced with the unwelcome demand for a mutual assistance treaty. But by the middle of May British policy was reluctantly moving towards acceptance of the Soviet position. One of the most important factors in this shift was the overwhelming support a triple alliance was receiving from the press and from parliament.

In a seemingly penultimate attempt to exert informal influence on the Soviets and arrest this current of opinion, Vansittart was authorized by the foreign policy committee of the cabinet to renew his contacts with Maisky and engage in some unofficial bargaining. Vansittart suggested to the ambassador that staff talks could be initiated if Russia agreed simply to unilaterally guarantee Poland and Rumania. But a commitment to a triple alliance was still withheld.[2] It is not surprising, therefore, that when discussing developments with Lloyd George's son, Gwilym, Maisky observed 'that Halifax did not give him the impression of being terribly keen on an out and out alliance with Russia.' Rather enigmatically he added: '. . . the need for some arrangement to be come to before a month was out was vital.'[3] The following day Maisky again saw Gwilym Lloyd George. This time the conversations with Vansittart were described. In conclusion the ambassador noted that Great Britain 'ultimately . . . would be compelled to accept the prin-

[1] Entry of 7 May 1939, *Dalton Diary.*

[2] Details in Foreign Policy Committee, Minutes, 16, 17 May 1939, CAB 27/625; and Minute by Vansittart, 16 May 1939, F.O. 371/23066 C7268/3356/18.

[3] Minute by Gwilym Lloyd George, 17 May 1939, Lloyd George Papers, G/130.

ciple of the Alliance, as it was the only possible foundation for peace in Europe.'[1] On 18 May Maisky also had a telephone conversation with Churchill. The latter bluntly asked for details of current Soviet proposals which were duly given.[2]

Having thus fully briefed two of the main protagonists of a triple alliance, Maisky no doubt witnessed with some satisfaction the 19 May foreign affairs debate in the Commons. Churchill, Lloyd George and Eden, among others, spoke forcefully and knowledgeably about the overriding necessity of constructing a strategically viable eastern front, and urged the immediate conclusion of a military alliance with the USSR. Chamberlain in his comments during this debate was unmoved, as indeed he was during cabinet sessions at this time. The fact that he was 'boggling' at an alliance was intimated to Nicolson by De La Warr.[3] However, the prime minister was gradually being overruled. On 16 May the chiefs of staff had advised that British policy would benefit from an Anglo-Soviet mutual assistance treaty.[4] Virtually the whole foreign policy committee of the cabinet had also by 19 May accepted this advice.

The results of conversations Halifax had with the French in Paris on 20 May, and with Maisky on 22 May, while in Geneva for the League Council sessions, suggested that the British government was faced with the choice between a breakdown in the negotiations or a triple alliance. Describing this meeting later to Gwilym Lloyd George, Maisky stated that at Geneva he had found Halifax 'much "freer" than at the F.O.', and a useful exchange of views took place.

> Maisky made it plain to H[alifax] that the acceptance without qualification of the Triple Alliance was fundamental for if . . . Russia was to abandon her position of isolation and thus her freedom of action she must be certain that what took its place did not endanger her position. He felt that H[alifax] appreciated this and he thinks made a favourable report to the Cabinet. . . .[5]

On his return to London Halifax did manage to secure cabinet support for a triple alliance. Chamberlain resigned

[1] Minute by Gwilym Lloyd George, 18 May 1939, ibid.
[2] Maisky, *Who Helped Hitler?* 125–6.
[3] Entries of 16, 24 May 1939, *Nicolson Diary.*
[4] Foreign Policy Committee, Appendix II, 16 May 1939, CAB 27/625.
[5] Letter from Gwilym Lloyd George to Lloyd George, 1 June 1939, Lloyd George Papers, G/130.

himself to the idea. But as Cadogan wrote to Halifax, the prime
minister 'has come to this point very reluctantly and is very
disturbed at all that it implies.'[1] Chamberlain was well aware
that a further 'refusal would create immense difficulties in the
House' even if he could persuade the cabinet.[2]

The Anglo-French draft treaty, communicated to Moscow
on 27 May, envisaged tripartite mutual assistance in case of
direct aggression against any of the three contracting powers.
But it still hedged round this commitment by reserving the
rights of other powers to accept assistance and by vague references to projected staff talks. Finally, the whole treaty was tied
to article XVI of the League covenant. It was precisely these
various reservations which, contrary to British expectation,
elicited Moscow's disapproval. Maisky complained to Gwilym
Lloyd George of the 'ambiguities' of the British draft. 'Bearing
in mind the fact that in our F.O. we had some of the most
experienced men in the world in writing notes', Maisky
continued, 'this ambiguity gave the impression that we wanted
to leave plenty of loopholes for ourselves.'[3] Judging by Chamberlain's attitude and his personal role in drafting this treaty, the
suspicion was well founded.[4]

At this point in the negotiations the Soviet ambassador
exuded confidence that an agreement would shortly be reached.
In his view the British 'Government has now come 75 % of the
way and are bound to come the whole 100 %.'[5] The prediction
was never fulfilled. From this stage onwards the venue of the
negotiations switched to the Russian capital. As a result of this
change Maisky's personal role diminished considerably. He
seems to have been kept ill-informed on the subsequent

[1] Letter from Cadogan to Halifax, 23 May 1939, F.O. 371/23066,
C7469/3356/18.

[2] Copy of Letter from Chamberlain to Hilda Chamberlain, 28 May 1939,
Templewood Papers, XIX: (C) 11.

[3] Letter from Gwilym Lloyd George to Lloyd George, 1 June 1939,
Lloyd George Papers, G/130.

[4] See Copy of Letter from Chamberlain to Hilda Chamberlain, 28 May,
1939, Templewood Papers, XIX: (C) 11; and Letter from Cadogan to
Halifax, 23 May 1939, F.O. 371/23066.

[5] Letter from Gwilym Lloyd George to Lloyd George, 1 June, 1939,
Lloyd George Papers, G/130. See also, Entries of 12, 18 June; 7 Aug., 1939.
Beatrice Webb Diary.

negotiations; having sometimes to ask Halifax for details of current draft treaties. His main usefulness for the narkomindel remained as a disseminator of available information behind the scenes; a role he busily filled.

The task for all concerned in these tripartite negotiations increased considerably in the following weeks, as their whole character altered. Mutual Anglo-Soviet mistrust strengthened as various proposals and counter-proposals were exchanged. These encompassed such questions as whether or not to publicize the list of states which were to be guaranteed; the definition of 'indirect aggression'; and the timing of military talks. The continued delay resulting from the ensuing exchange of views was reflected in the impatient volley of questions faced by the government in the Commons. But little concrete information was forthcoming. And with this circulated the inevitable flood of rumour and report, fuelled by private briefings. Sylvester informed Lloyd George that in 'Government quarters' there was dissatisfaction with Chamberlain's conduct of the negotiations. It was suspected he did not want an agreement with the Soviets.[1] Gerothwohl reported the frank disclosures made to him by a German embassy official on Berlin's attempts to secure Moscow's neutrality.[2] Dalton, dissatisfied with the optimistic forecasts privately given him by such foreign office officials as Ivone Kirkpatrick, Gladwyn Jebb and Vansittart on the one hand, and W. P. Coates on the other, visited Maisky on 25 June. He confessed to be searching for concrete information to criticize the government. His last such parliamentary performance, he told Maisky, had brought him a 'large mail, chiefly favourable'. The ambassador thereupon outlined the latest diplomatic correspondence. The two agreed that one point raised in the Moscow talks—Molotov's suggestion that perhaps a simple triple pact of mutual assistance would solve all difficulties—could appropriately be the subject of a question in the Commons.[3] This same tactic of concerting a parliamentary inquiry, but with an appropriate leak arranged beforehand by Maisky in the *News Chronicle*, was used on 5 July.[4]

[1] Minute by Sylvester, 8 June 1939, Lloyd George Papers, G/23/1/29.
[2] Minute by Gerothwohl, 26 June 1939, ibid., G/28/1/3.
[3] Entries of June 14, 21, 25, 1939, *Dalton Diary*.
[4] Entries of 4, 5 July 1939, ibid. See *H.C. deb.*, 349, 5 July 1939, c. 1265.

The seemingly endless talks were inevitably taxing the patience of all concerned. Chamberlain felt his suspicions of the Soviets better placed than ever. As for himself the prime minister noted: '. . . I am so sceptical of the value of Russian help that I should not feel that our position was greatly worsened if we had to do without them.'[1] Moreover, he informed the foreign policy committee that he 'now doubted whether the Soviet Government really desired an agreement with us.'[2] In private meetings of Labour party leaders, expressions of doubt as to the good faith of the Russians were at last beginning to be heard.[3]

Lloyd George seemed to sense the drift of events. In a conversation with Maisky on 14 July, he stated that the Chamberlain cabinet 'cannot to this day reconcile itself to the idea of a pact with the USSR against Germany. . . .' Accordingly, the prime minister was pursuing the following policy: pressure on Poland for a compromise over Danzig was being combined with a firm line towards Germany. If this succeeded in intimidating Germany or channelling her aggression elsewhere, then a pact with the USSR would lose its urgency. Chamberlain would then 'have another opportunity of trying to come to terms with the aggressor or, at least, delay signing a treaty with the Soviet government for a long time.'[4]

Events in London seemed to accurately fulfil Lloyd George's prognostication. The talks held between R. S. Hudson, parliamentary secretary of the overseas trade department, Horace Wilson and Helmut Wohltat, commissioner of the German four year plan, centred on plans for a far-reaching Anglo-German settlement. It is of interest that on 20 July, the day Hudson and Wohltat held their first talk, Maisky intimated to Nicolson (with distinct echoes of Lloyd George's analysis) that the prime minister hoped for a settlement of the Danzig question. Should this occur, the Russian negotiations would

---

[1] Copy of Letter from Chamberlain to Hilda Chamberlain, 2 July 1939, Templewood Papers, XIX: (C)11.

[2] Foreign Policy Committee, Minutes, 19 July 1939, CAB 27/625.

[3] See Entries of 5, 10, 11 July 1939, *Dalton Diary*.

[4] Foreign Policy Archives of the USSR, quoted in B. N. Ponomaryov, A. A. Gromyko and V. M. Khvostov, eds., *Istoriya Vneshnei Politiki SSSR 1917–1966gg.*, I, *1917–1945gg.* (The History of the Foreign Policy of the USSR 1917–1966, i, 1917–1945, Moscow 1966), 337.

lapse. Maisky had the 'definite impression that the Government do not really want the negotiations to go through.'[1] Given Maisky's particular network of private information, it is not inconceivable he had immediate knowledge of the Wohltat talks, which had in fact begun on 18 July.

From this point until the signature of the German-Soviet non-aggression pact of 23 August, Maisky steps into the background. He had his last talk with Halifax on 25 July at the foreign office. With parliament about to recess, with the political negotiations deadlocked on a definition of 'indirect aggression', and with the outcome awaited of the military conversations in Moscow, non-official political activity ground to a halt. The only recorded intervention is Maisky's attempt, on the instructions of his government, to influence the composition of the British military mission. He asked Greenwood to advise Chamberlain that Moscow expected Lord Gort, chief of the imperial general staff, to head the British military mission. The suggestion was turned down by the prime minister.[2]

To all those who had worked for an Anglo-Soviet agreement the decision of the Soviet government to sign a pact with Germany was an unpleasant event. The possibility of a Soviet retreat into isolation was entertained by all concerned on the British side. It was a subject continuously raised during cabinet meetings since April. But the actual pact must have caused considerable uneasiness. It appears that events may even have caught up with Maisky.[3] Having visited the Soviet embassy on 22 August, the day Ribbentrop's forthcoming visit to Moscow was announced, Dalton thought that Maisky knew nothing of what was going on and was 'as much surprised as the rest of us by the latest turn.'[4]

On 24 August the Soviet ambassador was a conspicuous absentee from his usual place in the diplomats' gallery in the Commons. But in the following days, despite the obvious embarrassment occasioned by the change of policy in Moscow, he continued to expound the principles of Soviet foreign policy

[1] Diary Entry of 20 July, 1939, quoted in Nicolson, I, 406.
[2] Maisky, *Who Helped Hitler?* 164–5.
[3] See Kirk to Hull, 22 Aug. 1939, *F.R.U.S., 1939*, I, 338.
[4] Entry of 22 Aug. 1939, *Dalton Diary*; and Dalton, II, 256.

to those British contacts who would still listen. At about this time he circulated a long memorandum outlining the course of the Anglo-Soviet negotiations.[1] This purported to show that the British government was responsible for continuously raising new points, causing endless delays and generally mishandling the negotiations.

During September 1939 Maisky did his best to repair his bridges so shattered by Stalin's pact with Hitler. Dalton told the ambassador on 3 September that the USSR '"has greatly disconcerted us, but I hope that some of us will still keep in touch with you from time to time."' Maisky replied: '" Do not believe everything you read about our Pact with Germany. . . . We are neutral now."'[2] Boothby was privately treated to a long justification of the Soviet-German pact. To his accusation that '"Nothing can get away from the fact that you double-crossed us"', Maisky replied that 'we were all now playing a cold game of power politics'. He disingenuously added, '" it was merely a question of technique'." Having been asked whether Churchill was angry with the Russians, Boothby recalled that Churchill had stated that '" it was the way he would expect that particular crocodile to behave."' Maisky seemed amused.[3]

Of all Maisky's contacts the source from which least criticism came was Lloyd George and his secretariat. For reasons entirely connected with the famous Lloyd George peace offensive of the autumn of 1939, a continuous flow of information passed between the Soviet embassy and Lloyd George's offices. W. P. Coates, described by Sylvester as a 'contact of mine . . . whom I have known for many years', forwarded to Lloyd George a detailed description of the Anglo-Soviet negotiations with the by now familiar criticism of Chamberlain's mishandling of them.[4] A copy of the 26 August, 1939 issue of *Izvestia* in which Marshal Voroshilov, Soviet defence commissar, explained the failure of the tripartite military talks, was also

[1] Copies are available in the Dalton Papers, and the Lloyd George Papers, G/130. The copy in the latter collection contains additional and fuller information dictated by the ambassador on 22 August 1939.

[2] Notes by Dalton, 3 Sept. 1939, Dalton Papers.

[3] Letter from Boothby to Lloyd George, 18 Sept. 1939, Enclosure, Lloyd George Papers, G/3/13/12; and Boothby, op. cit., 188–192.

[4] Minute by Sylvester, 6 Sept. 1939, Lloyd George Papers, G/23/1/30.

submitted to Lloyd George.[1] On September 18 Maisky received
Sylvester and put forward various justifications of the Soviet
invasion of Poland, but was vague as to its ultimate intention.
He was worried lest Great Britain declare war on the USSR. He
then added: ' "Things may not turn out so bad as they might
now appear." '[2] Indeed, in a subsequent conversation with Sylvester on 3 October, Maisky urged Lloyd George 'in advance
of today's discussion in Parliament' not to assume the existence
of a military alliance between Germany and the USSR.[3] But
these remarks already belonged to a new phase of Anglo-Soviet
relations.

Throughout the 1930's Maisky no doubt succeeded brilliantly,
from the point of view of the USSR, in giving the maximum
publicity to the foreign policy of his government. He also
managed to convince many of the suitability of that policy as an
alternative to appeasement. However, if an ambassador's duty
is also to interpret for his government the nature of inner
government thinking, as opposed to the whim of public opinion,
then Maisky's achievement must be questioned. For it is clear
that at many crucial points he based his analysis on what, for
example, his parliamentary contacts interpreted foreign office
thinking to be, rather than what it really was.

This discrepancy stemmed from the very nature of the sources
Maisky managed to tap. His acquaintances among the British
left wing were numerous. He also made himself indispensable to
various politicians, civil servants and members of parliament.
'What an ambassador has to aim at', Maisky once observed, 'is
intimate relations with all the live-wires in the country to which
he is accredited—among all parties or circles of influential
opinion. . . .'[4] But these peripheral contacts he cultivated with
such care were not responsible for policy and at least until 1939
had little influence on its formulation. What they could do was
to focus on the government informed parliamentary criticism.
During 1938 this deeply annoyed the Chamberlain government,
but had no real effect on policy. In his memoirs Hoare summed

[1] Letter from Flora McMillan to Sylvester, 14 Sept. 1939, ibid., G/130.
[2] Minute by Sylvester, 18 Sept. 1939, ibid.
[3] Notes by Sylvester of a Conversation with Maisky, 3 Oct. 1939,
ibid.
[4] Entry of 12 June 1939, *Beatrice Webb Diary.*

up the anti-Maisky case by accusing him of having been throughout the Czech crisis

> very active behind the scenes, stimulating criticism against the Government, and implying that it was only our hesitations and the cold-shouldering of Russia that were endangering peace. The critics of the Government were quick in rising to Maisky's fly. His story that the Soviet was only waiting for our invitation to help, was no more than the stock Communist propaganda for making mischief . . . The troubled waters were giving the Ambassador the best possible fishing conditions.[1]

Likewise during the negotiations of 1939, Maisky's continuous and close contact with the advocates of an Anglo-Soviet alliance aroused the most intense displeasure within the government. The information he imparted to members of parliament and the press corps, and the publicity which he so readily gave to supposedly secret diplomatic exchanges, severely handicapped Chamberlain's ability to negotiate on equal terms with Moscow. This problem was several times brought up at cabinet level. For the fullest details of the ambassador's private briefings were almost immediately known. In a letter on 14 May, 1939 Chamberlain bitterly complained that the Russians 'have no understanding of other countries' mentality or conditions and no manners, and they are working hand in hand with our Opposition.'[2] There is also ample evidence that it was uncertainty as to the effect on the pro-alliance faction in the Commons which never allowed the government to break off the negotiations even when this was entertained by the cabinet.

If Maisky, with the help of parliamentary critics of appeasement, managed to force Chamberlain into negotiating with the USSR in 1939, it is equally important that, by this same time, he had quite lost the good-will and confidence of the British government. For Maisky often overstepped the border between legitimate publicity for the policies of his government and the delicate, and questionable, use of public and parliamentary opinion against his accredited government. Where the ambassador unquestionably succeeded was that he kept the Soviet alternative to appeasement indelibly before the British govern-

---

[1] Viscount Templewood, *Nine Troubled Years* (1954), 302.

[2] Copy of Letter from Chamberlain to Hilda Chamberlain, 14 May 1939, Templewood Papers, XIX: (C)11.

ment and public, at a time when many would have preferred it to be dismissed and forgotten. A less energetic Soviet ambassador need not have produced closer ties between London and Moscow. But it was political circumstances and events, quite independent of Maisky's lobbying, which ultimately determined the course of Anglo-Soviet relations.

SIDNEY ASTER

XII

LLOYD GEORGE AND COM-
PROMISE PEACE IN THE
SECOND WORLD WAR

PAUL ADDISON

PAUL ADDISON

Age 27

Pembroke College, Oxford 1961–64
Nuffield College, Oxford 1965–67
Lecturer at Pembroke College 1966–67
Research Assistant to
Randolph S. Churchill 1967–68
Currently Lecturer in Modern History at
Edinburgh

LLOYD GEORGE AND COMPROMISE PEACE IN THE SECOND WORLD WAR

BIOGRAPHERS of Lloyd George have been embarrassed by the last chapter of the story. However many flaws could be seen in his career, it had been overall a record of constructive and liberal endeavour. But then Lloyd George faltered. From 1939 he put himself on the wrong side of historians by arguing that the second World war could scarcely be won and that a compromise could be achieved even with Hitler. World War one might be opposed or condemned on liberal grounds as a struggle among ruling cliques for territorial gain. But World War two was plainly a progressive cause in itself, a 'peoples' war against fascism' and a struggle with the Devil. In Britain, anyone suspected of half-heartedness in 1939–1945 has been vulnerable to the accusation of sympathy with fascism. In the case of Lloyd George, the recollection of his eagerly following the broadcasts of Lord Haw-Haw[1] must give rise to the same suspicion.

There have been many aspersions against Lloyd George's 'defeatism'. One of the first was a famous rebuke by Churchill. During a debate in the House on 7 May 1941 Lloyd George drew a grim picture of the state of the war and argued that any idea of eventually invading Europe was 'fatuous'. Churchill in winding up the debate referred to this as 'the sort of speech with which, I imagine, the illustrious and venerable Marshal Pétain might well have enlivened the closing days of M. Reynaud's Cabinet.'[2] Lloyd George's biographers have generally conceded that he was brooding over the possibility of returning to power as a peacemaker after the Churchill government had failed to win the war, and one or two sharper allegations have been made. Mr. Donald McCormick suggests that in 1940 a channel existed between Lloyd George and Nazi agents, via some Welsh nationalists. Elsewhere he is said to have

[1] Frank Owen: *Tempestuous Journey*, 1954, 752.
[2] *H.C. deb.*, 371, cc. 867–81, 929, 7 May 1941.

been in touch with the Nazis via neutrals, to discuss the terms of an armistice.[1] Was Lloyd George's career running parallel with that of Pétain or Quisling?

The simplest reply might be that by 1939 Lloyd George was an old man and a spent force, his actions part of geriatrics rather than politics. At least until 1943 this could not be maintained. Roosevelt's special emissary to Europe, Sumner Welles, reported home in March 1940 that he had found Lloyd George 'alert, mentally very keen, and minutely familiar with every detail of both British domestic affairs and British Foreign Relations'.[2] Unless Lloyd George had been capable of a rôle, there would have been no extensive lobby to make him a member of the War Cabinet in the summer of 1940, when it was supposed that he would act both as a counsellor to Churchill, and as a brake on him. He had even been suggested for the premiership. At the beginning of the war, Lloyd George was a little younger than Churchill when he began his second premiership in 1951, and in roughly comparable health.

What was Lloyd George's true position? During the first seven months of 'twilight war' he urged that since there was an unbreakable military deadlock in the West, more would be won from Hitler by a peace conference than by a long and ruinous war. Between 9 April and 19 June, Scandinavia, the Low Countries and France were conquered. Lloyd George still favoured a bargain with Hitler, but he sharply distinguished his rôle from Pétain's. Pétain had asked for terms when his homeland had fallen to the enemy; Lloyd George ruled out negotiations unless invasion were beaten off. Britain would then become an impregnable fortress, and the 'opportune' moment arrive[3]. As late as the autumn of 1942, Lloyd George talked of compromise peace. But when victory was assured, he made a *volte-face*. Attending a foreign office lunch in honour of the new Soviet ambassador early in 1944, he attacked his own government for defeatism in delaying the second front.[4]

[1] Donald McCormick, *The Mask of Merlin*, 1963, 288–95; Tom Driberg, *Guy Burgess*, 1956, 57.   [2] F.R.U.S., 1940: 185–6.

[3] Lloyd George gave a lucid review of his line over the first twelve months in one of his letters: Lloyd George to the Duke of Bedford, 14 September 1940 (Lloyd George Papers, G/3/4).

[4] Vincent Massey, *What's Past is Prologue* (1963), 379; *see also* Cecil Edwards, *Bruce of Melbourne* (1965), 389.

Why did Lloyd George brood for so long on peace with Hitler? In part because Britain's resources, until Pearl Harbor, were indeed only adequate for her defence, and not for the successful invasion of Europe—no justification, in itself, for Lloyd George's attitude. For at least the first twelve months of war, a similar vein of 'realism' was evident within some circles of the government.[1] Lloyd George's pragmatism was the more extreme as the result of his special *rapport* with Hitler. After meeting him in 1936, Lloyd George was enthralled. He thought he had found the German Lloyd George, and even in war felt that a bond of like genius was drawing them together. He was also deeply influenced by Soviet policy. If, as he argued, Great Britain must act in step with Russia, a policy of war with Germany made little sense after the Non-Aggression Pact of August 1939. Above all, this was Lloyd George's final plot. He calculated that Chamberlain would bungle the war through incompetence, Churchill through Chauvinism. Turning from the illusory policy of victory, the British would summon Lloyd George.

Lloyd George's perspective on the second World war was unique. With Clemenceau and Wilson he had fashioned the Versailles settlement which the dictators were destroying and had dissented from some of its provisions, pointing especially to the Polish frontier as unjust and provocative from the German viewpoint. But he must be absolutely distinguished from the group in Britain which carried a crown of thorns in repentance for the guilt of a dictated treaty. On the whole Lloyd George stood by the Versailles settlement and the League. 'I do not want to reverse the decisions of Versailles', he wrote to Kingsley Martin in 1936, 'I want them carried out honestly'. There should be minor revisions 'but these are mostly oddments'.[2] In *The Truth About The Peace Treaties*, completed by Lloyd George in the month of Munich, the settlement was strongly defended, and the blame laid on allied statesmen who had subsequently failed to implement it in Germany's favour; not

---

[1] For the limited and ambiguous aims of the Chamberlain government see D. C. Watt: *Les Alliés et la Résistance Allemande* in *Revue d'Histoire de la Deuxième Guerre Mondiale*, October 1959, 65.

[2] Lloyd George to Kingsley Martin, 28 March 1936, Lloyd George Papers, G/14/2.

the Führer, but Poincaré was 'the true creator of modern Germany with its great and growing armaments' and should there be another catastrophe it would be his fault.[1]

Lloyd George's response to the rise of Hitler is confusing. There were many in the democracies who praised the dictators, and of these two sublime flatterers stood out. There was Deputy Esmonde, who in 1935 described Mussolini, in the Dáil, as the 'Abraham Lincoln of Africa'; and Lloyd George, who declared in the *Daily Express* that Hitler was the George Washington of Germany.[2] On the other hand, Lloyd George had more than a foot in the anti-appeasement camp, as the opponent of Mussolini and Franco, Chamberlain's critic after Munich, an advocate of the League of Nations, and the collaborator of Ivan Maisky, the Soviet ambassador in Britain. As ever, Lloyd George stood for a balance or even a contradiction of forces. He stood, not for *entente* with Germany or the Soviet Union, so much as for the right relationship of those two powers from the British point of view. At least until 1937 he played the anti-Bolshevik card as an argument for conciliating Germany. From 1938 he argued more strongly for cooperation with the Soviet Union. But even then one feature was conspicuously lacking from the Popular Front politician's credentials. Broadly speaking, he was thoroughly hostile to Mussolini but admiring and conciliatory towards Hitler.

In September 1936 Lloyd George made his celebrated visit to Hitler. To Lloyd George, Hitler was one of the great architects of social reconstruction after 1931, together with Roosevelt and (though frustrated) himself. These men, he considered, stood high above the immobilized caucus politicians who dominated Great Britain and France.[3] The verdicts with which Lloyd George returned are well known—that Hitler was a man of peace, a genius bent on social reform and determined to avoid war.[4] An essential point is easy to miss. Lloyd George

---

[1] David Lloyd George: *The Truth About The Peace Treaties*, 252. See also the preface and introductory chapter.

[2] Conor Cruise O'Brien: *Ireland in International Affairs*, in Owen Dudley Edwards (edited): *Conor Cruise O'Brien Introduces Ireland* (1969), 114–15; *Daily Express*, 17 Sept. 1936.

[3] Thomas Jones: *Lloyd George*, 1951, 238.

[4] *Daily Express*, 17 Sept. 1936; *News Chronicle*, 21 Sept. 1936. There is a fine account in A. J. Sylvester: *The Real Lloyd George*, 192–227.

cared very little indeed for the Nazi system and admired only one man in Germany. The British ambassador wrote home privately to report that Lloyd George had simply refused to see Goering or Goebbels. Never before had anyone flouted their invitations in this way. 'Lloyd George', he wrote, 'must have been a sore trial to his hosts. Except at the interviews with the Führer he rode the high horse, and flatly refused to keep to the programme or play up to the local bigwigs'.[1] The visitor was especially bored and provoked to rudeness by tours of factories and educational institutes.

With Hitler all was different, and there is every reason to believe that Hitler for his part admired Lloyd George. Phipps reported that Hitler was impressed by his dynamism and energy, and relieved that the Jewish question had not been raised. In his wartime table-talk Hitler spoke admiringly of Lloyd George and harked back to their meeting.[2] Lloyd George for his part saw Hitler as one of the select club of great world leaders to which he himself belonged, a company that excluded the Goerings and the Goebbels as surely as the Baldwins and the Chamberlains. There was a flattery they alone could offer each other, as the man who imposed Versailles and the man who was overturning it, and this for both was the food of the gods. From that time onwards these two dynamic upstarts, risen from the petty bourgeoisie to the mastery of venerable ruling classes, were potential collaborators.

For Mussolini and for Italy Lloyd George reserved a stern contempt. 'Mussolini', he wrote to Professor Conwell-Evans at the close of 1937, 'is temperamentally an aggressor. I never thought that Hitler was'.[3] The following year the Cabinet Office, in the person of Hankey, requested excisions from passages dealing with Italy in Lloyd George's second volume on the Peace Treaties, and Hankey deplored the probable repercussions in Italy when it was published: he hoped that the *Daily Telegraph* would serialize only tactful extracts.[4]

The Spanish Civil War was far more an Italian than a German operation and Lloyd George was strongly for the Republic, as

[1] Sir Eric Phipps to Anthony Eden, 21 Oct. 1936, Simon Papers.
[2] Hugh Trevor-Roper (Ed.): *Hitler's Table Talk* (1953), 259–60, 579–80, 657, 677.   [3] Owen: *Tempestuous Journey*, 733.
[4] Hankey to Lloyd George, 11 July 1938, Lloyd George Papers, G/8/18.

he had been for Abyssinia. But on Czechoslovakia his line was not all it seemed. He called for an agreement with Russia to stop Hitler, and after a pause of three weeks condemned the Munich Agreement (which he had voted against in the House) as a surrender. Yet it was clear that Lloyd George was also inclined to be anti-Czech, and his attack on Munich was far more anti-Chamberlain than anti-Hitler.[1]

Lloyd George called insistently in the first eight months of 1939 for cooperation with the Soviet Union and condemned Chamberlain's guarantee to Poland as no better than a trap in the absence of agreement with Stalin. His convictions were thoroughly reinforced by the Russo-German Non-Aggression Pact in August, but when the outbreak of war was announced by Chamberlain Lloyd George was swept along by the powerful currents in the House: 'The Government could do no other than what they have done. I am one out of tens of millions in this country who will back any Government that is in power in fighting this struggle through, in however humble a capacity he may be called upon to render service to our country'.[2] A similar stand was taken in France, once the war had started, by Bonnet and Laval. Meanwhile the recurrence of war with Germany stirred popular memories of leadership in World War one, and re-established Lloyd George as a figure of at least symbolic importance, as was the case with Pétain in France.

In his temporary mood of truculence, Lloyd George hoped that the allies would strike a quick blow in the west to relieve the pressure on Poland, and praised 'the undoubted superiority of the French Army to any other Army in the field'. He also struck out with some rude remarks about Italy, which remained neutral. The Cabinet, walking on tiptoe to avoid fluttering Mussolini, was angry, and Churchill—now First Lord of the Admiralty—was deputed to rebuke him. '. . . I was asked to point out to you the very bad effect on our interests at the present moment which would be produced by sneers at Caporetto, about which the Italian Army is naturally so sensitive. The army is believed to be very much opposed to

---

[1] See for example his letter in the *Daily Telegraph* of 25 July 1938.
[2] *H.C. deb.*, 351, cc. 299–300, 3 Sept. 1939.

going to war with England and France, and the King's influence with them is great'.[1]

Then Lloyd George changed. The swift collapse of Poland underlined for him the mediocrity, not only of the Polish ruling class, but of the British and French. His attacks on Poland brought him into a quarrel with the Polish ambassador in London, Count Raczynski, and Lloyd George circulated a counterblast in the form of an open letter on 27 September: 'I am sure that the people of Britain are not prepared to make colossal sacrifices to restore to power a Polish régime represented by the present Government . . . we are fighting not to force back under Polish rule people of another race who objected to the imposition and were subjugated by the force of Polish arms, nor for the restoration of a particular régime which has failed in the hour of its country's distress.'[2] This opened the door for a peace based on the establishment of an 'ethnic' Poland, stripped of territory by Germany and by Russia whose claims to parts of it Lloyd George endorsed.

The fact that these two powers had partitioned Poland was disquieting for many: would all the king's horses and all the king's men ever recreate Poland? On 29 September a joint message from Hitler and Stalin called upon Great Britain and France to accept the *fait accompli* and end the war.

By the third week of the war Lloyd George, along with many who loathed Germany and wanted to see Hitler smashed, was becoming convinced of allied inability to win. On 27th he spoke to the All-Party Group of M.P.s and asked why the R.A.F. had not bombed German arms factories within twelve hours of the declaration of war. This must indicate weakness and if so we should never have begun to fight. There should be a secret session at which the Government would disclose the facts, and unless the chances were 50-50 peace should be made.[3] In private he was soon less tentative. To Lord Mottistone he wrote: 'If they reject the chance of making peace it will not be long

---

[1] *Sunday Express*, 10 Sept. 1939; Churchill to Lloyd George, 12 Sept. 1939, Lloyd George Papers G/4/4.

[2] I am most grateful to Lord Sorensen for letting me see his copy of this document, which was also partly reported in the Press.

[3] Harold Nicolson: *Diaries and Letters 1939–45*, edited by Nigel Nicolson, 1967, 35–6; Robert Boothby: *I Fight to Live*, 1947, 195.

before Britain will realise that they have committed the most calamitous mistake perpetrated by British statesmanship since the days of Lord North. Although many people will hardly believe it, I am only thinking of this grand old country of ours. I belong to a race which has lived in it and fought for it against every enemy, including the Italians and the Germans centuries ago'.[1]

His pessimism seeped into the minds of others. Boothby, a long-standing admirer of the social thought of Lloyd George, wrote that he felt strongly against rejecting a peace conference out of hand; he was worried that Chamberlain's personal anger against Hitler, and his hatred of Russia, would lead him into a long, bloody and indecisive war.[2]

In response to the Russo-German initiative, Lloyd George broached the idea of negotiating a settlement in two speeches of 3 and 21 October, the first in the House of Commons, the second in his constituency of Caernarvon Boroughs.[3] Before setting out from Euston for the second speech he was joined for a brief conference by Maisky, and when he came to address the crowd of 6,000 in North Wales he called for 'a man of real standing and influence' to be sent to Moscow. Defending the very idea of negotiating with Hitler, he had argued to the House of Commons that a tolerable settlement could be achieved if the three neutrals, Italy, Russia, and the United States, took part. Their pressure would oblige Hitler to be moderate, their strength would guarantee that he kept his promises. To this he added the humanitarian case against a second butchery, and ended his Welsh speech: 'Flood waters are stated to be holding up military activity on the Siegfried Line. It may be that, as in the time of the deluge, the dove of peace will appear with an olive branch in its beak ...'

There was a faint ripple of assent among Conservative backbenchers, but it was Duff Cooper, angrily denouncing Lloyd George, who best represented the mood of the house. All in all, Lloyd George found scarcely anyone of significance in public life to support him. However he began to receive a huge postbag of letters from private citizens, writing over-

[1] Lloyd George to Mottistone, 9 Oct. 1939, Lloyd George Papers, G/15/4.
[2] Boothby to Lloyd George, 29 Sept. 1939, Lloyd George Papers, G/3/13/13.
[3] *H.C. deb.*, 351, cc. 1870–4, 1874–80, 3 Oct. 1939; *Manchester Guardian*, *The Times*, 23 Oct. 1939.

whelmingly in support of him. These are stored in the papers in a dozen boxes, roughly sorted, and labelled 'Compromise Peace 1939'.[1] It is significant that the Prime Minister, Neville Chamberlain, was receiving a similar mail at the time.[2] Leaving aside the usual sprinkling of cranks, Lloyd George's correspondence was a testament of widespread and deeply felt longing for escape from another four years of trench warfare. This gave Lloyd George confidence that when the moment came he would be able to cut through the ruling class pretence of war spirit to the reality beyond.

Instead he was to find himself the false hope of minority groups and political eccentrics, some of whom hastened to get in touch with him. The Arabian explorer and ex-candidate of the pro-fascist British People's Party, St. John Philby, offered his services, was turned down, and went back to Riyadh, where in return for his illuminating defeatism, Ibn Sa'ud gave him a house on the outskirts of town.[3] Victor Gollancz, whose Left Book Club was locked in conflict over the war, thought that Lloyd George's speech in the house might prove to be 'the one sane utterance in an insane world'. This is a reminder that the Comintern Line still acted as a magnet for the Left, one of whose youthful representatives at Oxford, John Biggs-Davison, was another enthusiast for Lloyd George.[4] For good measure there was also a telegram from Lord Rothermere: 'You are a grand old warhorse to go ahead with your present policy and you will win hands down'.[5]

To edify his old friend, Churchill enclosed a copy of a telegram from Smuts, to the effect that a peace offer from Hitler would only be designed to weaken Great Britain, but Lloyd George obdurately replied that Great Britain should reply with a peace offensive to baffle *Hitler*.[6]

---

[1] Lloyd George Papers, G/50–60.

[2] Keith Feiling: *The Life of Neville Chamberlain*, 1946, 424.

[3] H. St. John Philby to David Lloyd George, 9 Oct. 1939, Lloyd George Papers G/60; H. St. J. Philby: *Arabian Days*, 1948, 311/16.

[4] Gollancz to Lloyd George, 4 Oct. 1939, Lloyd George Papers G/57; Biggs-Davison to Lloyd George, 17 Oct. 1939, Lloyd George Papers G/60.

[5] Rothermere to Lloyd George, 9 October 1939, Lloyd George Papers G/17/1/38.

[6] Churchill to Lloyd George, 6 Oct. 1939; Lloyd George to Churchill, 9 Oct. 1939, Lloyd George Papers G/4/4.

After 21 October 1939 Lloyd George kept quiet about his opinions in public, rehearsing them in private. In the New Year he was telling the editor of the *Sunday Pictorial* that neither side would win. The peoples would become bored and a demand would arise for peace. To Roosevelt's special emissary, Sumner Welles, he argued in March 1940 that the 'territorial and political questions should present no real obstacles; the economic postulates for a sane world commercial and financial relationship could be established with the aid of the United States; the problem of security could then be determined through disarmament and international control of armament'. The mass of the British people would support peace on these terms 'and he himself would publicly support it up and down the length and breadth of the land'.[1] It was of course known to British ruling circles that Lloyd George was 'defeatist'.

He had now attracted a strange assortment of politicians to his side, all of whom wished to curtail the war. It was natural that Lord Noel-Buxton and Charles Roden Buxton, lifelong liberal pacifists, should look to him. They busied themselves drawing up terms, circulating memoranda, and placing their last hopes, sagaciously, in Lord Halifax. They became associated with a nucleus of pacifist and neo-pacifist M.P.s in the Labour Party, who took the name Peace Aims Group, and included the rump of the I.L.P. In November 1939 20 M.P.s of this Group called for an armistice; the following signed the appeal: Rev. James Barr; George Buchanan; William Cove; T. E. Groves; Agnes Hardie; David Kirkwood; George Lansbury; William Leonard; Neil Maclean; Malcolm Macmillan; George Mathers; Henry McGhee; Rhys Davies; Alfred Salter; Sydney Silverman; Alex Sloan; Reginald Sorensen; Richard Stokes; Cecil Wilson.[2] These names recalled an ailing and remote political tradition. However, there was one odd man out, the remarkable Richard Stokes, Labour M.P. for Ipswich. He was chairman of the group, a Catholic, an arms manufacturer, land taxer, and a future minister in the 1945–1951 Labour government. Stokes, who was something of an amateur diplomat,

[1] Hugh Cudlipp: *At Your Peril* (1962), 62–70; *Foreign Relations of the United States 1940*, I, 85–6.　　[2] *New Leader*, 17 Nov. 1939.

[3] (Copy letter) Stokes to Halifax, 17 Feb. 1940, Lloyd George Papers G/19/3.

came forward as Lloyd George's lieutenant, forming a peace group which looked to him. At the beginning of 1940 Stokes was in Istanbul and managed to see von Papen, then German ambassador to Turkey. They talked generally about the outlines of peace, and notes of their talk reached Halifax and Lloyd George.[3] Stokes, who also had an audience with the Pope during his winter excursion, was a candid man: 'Are we really content', he wrote, 'to bring our own civilization to ruin in order that the Hammer and Sickle shall fly from the North Sea to the Pacific?'[1] It was probably Stokes who brought purported German peace terms to Lloyd George, and it was noticeable how much credence the latter gave them. Take, for instance, the terms which the Marquis of Tavistock claimed he had discovered from the German embassy in Dublin, in January 1940. Tavistock was Chairman of the British Council for Christian Settlement in Europe, to which Stokes, and an uneasy alliance of pacifists and neo-fascists, belonged. Tavistock produced the very moderate 'Nazi terms' with a flourish of publicity. The Germans denied them at the time, and the published records show that they were never authorized. Lloyd George, relying on Stokes, believed in them: moreover, he had had them confirmed 'from another source'.[2] It need hardly be added that there was a continuous buzz of rumour about peace terms from the beginning of the war until at least August 1940, some of which undoubtedly reflected the subtle means by which each side tested the determination of the other.

After the failure of the Norwegian expedition had become apparent the Chamberlain government began to lose ground rapidly to its critics. Chamberlain and Lloyd George were irreconcilable enemies from World War one, and no feelers had been put out for the return of the old war hero to office. There were now many attempts to propel Lloyd George forward. On 26 April Beaverbrook rang up Esmond Harmsworth (of the *Daily Mail*), to inquire what should be done if Norway turned out badly. Harmsworth replied that Lloyd George should become Prime Minister of a National Government, and Beaverbrook agreed. 'When the moment comes', Harmsworth wrote to Lloyd George, 'I intend to campaign for your recall as

[1] Memo 4 Oct. 1939, Lloyd George Papers G/19/3.
[2] Liddell Hart Papers, Notes for History, 6/7/8, March 1940.

P.M.'[1] The promise was almost redeemed. Lloyd George, Cripps and Harmsworth together arranged a trial balloon: a letter from Cripps signed 'A British Politician' calling for a new war cabinet under Halifax and including Lloyd George.[2] Churchill, too, took a hand. In theory he was a loyal member of the Chamberlain cabinet and had to defend it. But we have already been informed that before the crucial debate on Norway, of 7–8 May 1940, Churchill had asked Lloyd George whether he would serve in a Churchill cabinet, to which Lloyd George replied that he would.[3] The Astors made encouraging noises and had him to lunch on 6 May. This was the occasion when J. L. Garvin reported back to Tom Jones that Lloyd George 'was still good for six hours a day and it would be six hours of radium'.[4] It was said to be the opinion of Lord Salisbury's Watching Committee—a combine of Tory elder statesmen in the Lords with members of the Eden group in the Commons—that Chamberlain would fall and a Lloyd George government replace him.[5]

Lloyd George intervened devastatingly in the Norway debate. The fact that his speech was directed against Chamberlain has tended to mask its pessimism about the war, the old tunes played again. When Churchill intervened on an Admiralty point to take his full share of responsibility for the campaign, Lloyd George said: 'The right hon. Gentleman must not allow himself to be converted into an air-raid shelter to keep the splinters from hitting his colleagues.'[6] Two days later, Churchill emerged as prime minister.

The first idea for Lloyd George was that he should become chairman of a Food Production Council, that is 'prime minister' of three departments concerned with food supply. This would have been a valuable role in the war effort, have redeemed him from pessimism and associated him with Churchill. All of these things he did not want. Talk of who should be his civil servants

---

[1] Harmsworth to Lloyd George, 26 April 1940, Lloyd George Papers, G/17/1.

[2] Cripps to Lloyd George, 5 May 1940, Lloyd George Papers G/5/6; Laurence Thompson, *1940* (1966), 73–4.

[3] Sylvester: *The Real Lloyd George*, 263.

[4] Jones: *Lloyd George*, 154.

[5] Nicolson, *Diaries and Letters, 1939–45*, 74.

[6] *H.C. deb.*, 360, cc. 1277–83, 8 May 1940.

faded away, and when Churchill made a definite offer during the retreat from Dunkirk, Lloyd George declined on the ground that he could not work with Chamberlain. He did indeed hate Chamberlain, as the first angry drafts of the reply to Churchill confirm. One must sympathize with Churchill. Of his two old colleagues, Lloyd George and Beaverbrook, one was always about to come in, the other always about to go out.[1]

So anxious was Churchill for Lloyd George's support that he wrote to Chamberlain on 6 June asking him to withdraw his objections to Lloyd George's entry into the war cabinet. Chamberlain gave way and a second offer was made and rebuffed.[2] Not shyness, but a deeper motivation, was prompting Lloyd George to withhold his badly-needed moral support from his oldest political colleague. In the first World war he had established the unique Lloyd George War Cabinet, the ghost of which now haunted political discussion. The myth was that the Lloyd George cabinet had been an unfettered committee of wise men, chosen irrespective of party, and constantly evolving together policy decisions: men without departments, whose minds ranged freely and exclusively over the war. This model was constantly quoted against Churchill's own government. He had proceeded cautiously in reconstruction; the Chamberlain government, far from being overthrown, had been swallowed almost whole into the belly of its successor. Lloyd George commented: 'He will not smash the Tory Party to save the country, as I smashed the Liberal Party.'[3] This was true. Lloyd George had destroyed himself in this way, and Churchill had no thought of following suit.

A number of politicians cherished with Lloyd George the hope of a complete break with the 'old gang', notably Chamberlain and Halifax, who continued in the war cabinet. Notable in this group were Robert Boothby, L. S. Amery and Harold Macmillan (all of whom Churchill had brought into his government); Clement Davies, Arthur Salter, and T. L. Horabin (who remained backbenchers). Lloyd George spurred

[1] On the projected job in Agriculture see Lloyd George Papers G/8/17; for Lloyd George's draft replies, Lloyd George to Churchill, 29 May, 1940, Lloyd George Papers G/4/5.
[2] Feiling, *Neville Chamberlain*, 447; Sylvester: *The Real Lloyd George*, 269.
[3] Jones: *A Diary With Letters, 1931–1950*, 465.

them on. In the third week of June, as France was collapsing,
Churchill received letters from Clement Davies and Robert
Boothby, telling him in effect how to run the war. There was
also a visit by L. S. Amery to Churchill on 18 June, to represent
the views of the group. The key demand was for a Lloyd George
style war cabinet or 'Committee of Public Safety' composed of
non-departmental ministers irrespective of party position, which
implied the termination of Attlee and Greenwood besides
Chamberlain and Halifax. These ministers were to have the
whip hand over all civil servants in the departments which they
supervised. Churchill told Amery that he thought it was all a
plot to bring back Lloyd George. 'Winston flattened out Amery
completely by telling him that if he and his friends were not
satisfied the whole lot of them could resign, and he made it
perfectly clear.'[1]

There was an interesting sequel. Churchill's nerves, sorely
tried by the French armistice, were again upset. On 19 June,
the day after Amery's visit, Frances Stevenson was aroused from
sleep by a telephone call from Brendan Bracken, who said that
Churchill wished to offer Lloyd George a Cabinet place 'and
I gathered that L.G. could have anything he liked to ask for,
provided he would lend his name to Churchill's team, and his
policies.'[2] Possibly a critical leading article in *The Times*
contributed to Churchill's anxieties.[3]

Lloyd George would not lend his name to Churchill's policies
no matter whether Chamberlain were in or out of the cabinet.
For he very much doubted whether Churchill would succeed,
and if the lion exhausted himself, the day of the fox would
surely follow. Six months later the Prime Minister made his
last offer, so far as we know, and invited Lloyd George to
become Ambassador in Washington in succession to the late
Lord Lothian. 'I had a long talk with him in the Cabinet
Room, and also at luncheon on a second day. He showed

---

[1] For all of this see copy letters Davies to Churchill, 16 June 1940, Lloyd
George Papers G/5/14 and Boothby to Churchill, 19 June 1940, Lloyd
George Papers G/3/13; Minute, Sylvester to Lloyd George, 19 June 1940,
Lloyd George Papers G/24; and Robert Boothby: *My Yesterday Your
Tomorrow* (1962) 74.

[2] Frances Lloyd George: *The Years That Are Past*, 264.

[3] The editions of *The Times* for 19 June 1940 which I have consulted do
not contain the article referred to by Lady Lloyd-George.

genuine pleasure at having been invited.' But he declined saying that at 77 he was too old.[1] Though Lloyd George remained outside, he still saw Churchill from time to time and the Prime Minister sought his advice—on intervention in Greece, for example. Thus he took a hand in the Baltic States question in 1942. The war cabinet favoured recognizing the Soviet claim to the Baltic States, except for Churchill and Attlee, who opposed. Lloyd George—despite his close relationship with Maisky—advised Churchill that there was no need to grant recognition; it would be time enough for that if the Russians reconquered them and produced a *fait accompli*. So recognition was avoided.[2]

During the summer, Lloyd George had been very closely connected with the peace movement, as Churchill (who was a broadminded and subtle man, not a mere John Bull psychologically) must have known. On 20 June, after encouraging the Amery group and refusing an offer from Churchill, Lloyd George received a deputation from a group of M.P.s whose nucleus was the Peace Aims Group. At one of their meetings on 25 June Richard Stokes was instructed to take a message to Lloyd George, namely: 'That this meeting decided to urge on Mr. Lloyd George the critical situation which may arise from Herr Hitler's speech next Friday, as there is a possibility—however remote—that some utterances may be made which could be the start of negotiations. It would be disastrous in the opinion of this meeting if such an opportunity were destroyed as it undoubtedly would be by a rhetorically scornful speech by the Prime Minister or the ill-advised remarks which the Minister of Information[3] is inclined to make. This meeting therefore urges that every possible step be taken to prevent any utterances over the wireless or in the press by senior or junior Ministers following Herr Hitler's speech (if made) until both Houses have had an opportunity of discussing it, and all those assembled urge that Mr. Lloyd George be asked to present this opinion to the Prime Minister on their behalf in such a way as he may think fit.' According to Stokes, this was the voice of 'some 30 M.P.s'.[4] We know that at some point Lloyd George

[1] Winston S. Churchill: *Their Finest Hour*, 503–4.
[2] Liddell Hart Papers: Notes for History, 14 June 1942.
[3] Duff Cooper.
[4] Stokes to Lloyd George, 25 June 1940, Lloyd George Papers G/19/3.

did in fact urge upon Churchill the virtues of negotiation. The Prime Minister responded passionately, shouting, 'never, never, never', but he fell quiet when Clementine, looking up from her sewing, said: 'We all have the right to change our minds.'[1]

By 17 July Stokes was writing on behalf of 30 M.P.s and 10 peers, who had generally approved a memorandum to this effect: 'If he [Hitler] does offer a European conference or any other means of coming to an agreement without admission of defeat by either side, we ought to accept the offer without hesitation. . . . It is futile to talk as if all that mattered were the winning of the war. The war will not be won if it ends in a collapse of Europe. What does matter to everybody, except perhaps to the Third International, is that it shall end before Europe, including Britain, suffers economic collapse.' The argument that there could be no negotiation with Hitler was brushed aside, since the peace would restore prosperity and 'dictatorship cannot survive prosperity.'[2]

Who attended this kind of meeting? The Peace Aims Group, certainly. And possibly a handful of disaffected M.P.s in search of an opposition. In March 1941 Horabin, McGovern and Stokes decided to hold a meeting of those who were 'not bitter-enders'. The list of those invited and those attending is in the papers. 64 were invited, 23 attended. Of the 23 there were 11 from the Peace Aims Group and I.L.P., and the 12 others were William Gallacher, D. N. Pritt, Bevan, Jennings, Bennett, Culverwell, Sanderson and Arthur Evans from the House of Commons, and Buxton, Ponsonby, Darnley and Holden from the lords. The presence of any particular name may mean nothing, but the whole list of 64 is a fine general guide to the grumblers in both houses, some of whom were critical because they wanted the war won, others because they thought it was leading nowhere.[3]

Throughout his period of pessimism Lloyd George was confirmed in his beliefs by information from varied and

[1] Kingsley Martin: *Editor* (1968), 289–90.
[2] Stokes to Lloyd George, 17 July 1940, Lloyd George Papers G/19/3.
[3] Stokes to Lloyd George, 3 April 1941, with accompanying list dated for a meeting on 2 April, Lloyd George Papers G/19/3.

curious contacts. His Private Secretary Sylvester wrote racy minutes almost daily for his chief, designed to whet the old man's appetite for politics. According to Sylvester the Churchill government was constantly on the run from the firebrand Clement Davies. Also this, of 1 November 1940:

> KINDLY DESTROY THIS WHEN READ
> I am told on very high authority that the 'Beaver' is in touch with Hitler. I cannot tell you whether this is true or not but I can tell you that the authority for the belief is very high indeed.[1]

Among those who saw something of Lloyd George, and sent him appreciations of the war situation, were Basil Liddell Hart and Thomas Balogh. Liddell Hart was both a constant advocate of economy of effort in strategy, and convinced that every attempt should be made, in the interests of civilization, to work towards a negotiated and moderate settlement. Balogh, then a member of the gadfly '1941 Committee', urged the necessity for a siege economy and argued that civilian consumption was running at a dangerously high level. This reinforced Lloyd George's preoccupation with the war in the Atlantic and the slender lifeline of Britain's supplies. To Beaverbrook he wrote early in 1941: 'The time is coming when I think it will be urgent that I should have another talk with you. It is right that we should keep up a cheerful front, but amongst ourselves it is even more vital that we should understand the real and imminent peril of which you gave a hint in your broadcast to forewarn the public.'[2] The conviction that Churchill was a rash man ran through a speech drafted for delivery by Lloyd George by a member of the Government: Edward Grigg, a long-standing colleague and Surrey neighbour, who was also Under-Secretary at the war office. The speech recited Churchillian errors of judgment. In the reshuffle of February 1942 Grigg lost his job and was accompanied out of office by Maurice Hankey. Hankey was disgruntled after his long career in public life and sent Lloyd George waspish notes on the Churchillian record, claiming that it was a surprise that the government survived at

[1] Minute by Sylvester, 1 November 1940, Lloyd George Papers G/24.
[2] Lloyd George to Beaverbrook, 24 February 1941, Lloyd George Paper G/3/6.

all.[1] Of all the titbits sent to Lloyd George the most interesting
historically was the first intimation of the circumstances
surrounding the dismissal of Admiral North from his command
at Gibraltar at the end of 1940. His own personal account,
written shortly afterwards, made it clear that the first lord and
first sea lord, Alexander and Pound, had relieved him of his
command in order to cover up the guilt of the admiralty in
Whitehall over the Dakar affair.[2]

It is noticeable that Lloyd George balanced between two
rather anti-Churchillian groups, the critics who contended that
the Prime Minister was losing the war, and those who were
upset because he was fighting it so hard. This suited Lloyd
George well. He wanted the war fought toughly in the short
term, and wound up in the long term. He set down a lengthy
appraisal of the war, and definition of his own position, a few
days after the start of the blitz, and it marks him out very
distinctly from, say, Lord Brocket, who believed that a purely
Russo-German war would have been much preferable to the
second World war.[3]

Lloyd George started with fears where others hoped, for
he believed that the United States would not voluntarily enter
the war on the side of Great Britain, unless too late. His vision
was warped by continuing deference to Hitler, who possessed
'genius of an order which ranks him among the greatest leaders
of men in history.' It was unlikely that he would be foolish
enough to attack Russia and it would be 'the depth of folly' to
gamble on the possibility of a breach between Hitler and Stalin.
Meanwhile Great Britain would suffer defeats if she went on:
North Africa, Egypt, Palestine, even Kenya, might fall (did he
really believe the Italians would take Kenya?). What was the
possible solution? 'A Pétain peace is of course unthinkable', he
reflected. 'For instance no reputable British statesman or
General would consent to an Armistice which would permit
British soil to be occupied by German troops or place the

[1] Grigg, Lloyd George Papers G/8/11; Hankey, Lloyd George Papers
G/8/18, notably Hankey to Lloyd George 23 Oct. 1942 and accompanying
memorandum.

[2] 'The Circumstances Attending My Removal from my command at
Gibraltar by Their Lordships,' Lloyd George Papers G/15/12. In his *History
of the Second World War* Churchill passed over North's dismissal in silence.

[3] Brocket to Lloyd George, 7 July 1941, Lloyd George Papers G/68.

British Navy at the disposal of the Germans'. No doubt he was entirely sincere in arguing that 'it is better to be free men in rags rather than be slaves in fine linen.' However, his interpretation of Hitler led him to believe that the Führer would offer a generous and genuine peace, for once baffled in the Battle of Britain he would face only a long and dreary war of attrition. 'There is no glory in that. It only wears off and tarnishes the shine on the stars and epaulettes of a great conqueror. And he will gradually disappoint his people. . . . And all through he will have an uneasy feeling that there is a potent and potential enemy at his back. He may be a marauder but he is no fool.

'His repeated overtures to us are I am sure prompted by considerations of this kind. He has already won more than he can handle. . . . He is a shrewd man and he would therefore prefer a peace which will enable him to go on with his programme of building up a greater Germany into one of the most prosperous and well organised communities in the world.'

The conclusion was that Great Britain must continue the war for the time being in order to stir up trouble in the conquered territories, and, by announcing moderate war aims, within Germany. In this context it was vital to restore Anglo-Soviet relations, since Hitler would respect pressure from Stalin. In short, a limited British war would bring the best possible peace settlement in the military circumstances, and the alternative was a socially destructive five or ten year conflict ending in stalemate. That Lloyd George really did want a toughly-fought war in the immediate future is attested by his remarkable conversations with Sir Roger Keyes, the Director of Combined Operations, to whom he criticized Pound as 'too much of an old woman'; Lloyd George favoured coastal raids around Europe and was angry when Churchill postponed Keyes's plan for the capture of Pantellaria. So, Lloyd George declared, 'We shall emulate the immortal victories won by the Greeks when they threw back the hordes of the all-conquering Persian Empire. That is the time to make peace.'[1]

The arrival of Russia and later the United States in the war gave Lloyd George temporary encouragement in his gloom. But he harped on the desperate condition of Russia. Early in

[1] Memorandum by the Rt. Hon. D. Lloyd George, Lloyd George Papers G/81; On Keyes, MacCormick, *The Mask of Merlin*, 293.

1942 Maisky told him that Russia might consider a separate peace unless Great Britain and the United States accepted her claims in the Baltic.[1] And he continued to play his game with the Peace Aims Group. In the middle of 1942 they sent him another delegation to inquire about the appropriate time to call for an armistice, and he told them 'that Stalingrad would fall by the end of September and that, with the Volga route closed, the war would take on a new phase, especially if the Japanese attacked Russia. He advised that we should put down a motion with regard to an armistice, urging that it should appear before November, by which time he anticipated that Russia would be negotiating or that, at any rate, informal negotiations would be commenced.'[2]

From the beginning of the war in Great Britain, there were divergent feelings within the Cabinet, which occasionally made themselves known, about the purpose of the war. Chamberlain and Halifax during the phoney war would have been content with a relatively marginal change in Germany's internal affairs and frontiers, though they were not optimistic about achieving even this. It might be supposed that with the German occupation of the Low Countries and the capitulation of France the question of peace ceased to be relevant. On the contrary, it was relevant to any long-term consideration of strategy. Churchill's aim, from the day he joined the Chamberlain government, was to develop a strategy of total victory. If anything, the events of May and June 1940, though strengthening British anger and determination, weakened Churchill's position. The cabinet, and the political establishment, were none of them potential Pétains, for there was no parallel with the French situation. The two striking differences were these: (1) the strong possibility that Great Britain could fight a successful defensive war that would keep its soil and forces intact, and (2) the fact that Hitler would in all probability have considered much more favourable arrangements for Great Britain than he had done for France. In the first year of the Churchill government, the government was united in determining to fight on for British independence. No one would have agreed to a peace of German occupation, not even Mosley. But this left one key issue unresolved. If Great

---

[1] Liddell Hart Papers: Notes for History 22–3 March 1942.
[2] Fenner Brockway: *Bermondsey Story* (1949), 233–4.

Britain fought a successful campaign for its national independence, was this later to be converted, *supposing that neither Russia nor the United States entered the war*, into a long crusade to conquer Europe by force of arms? There is every indication that at this point was the dividing line which would have separated the Churchillians from the rest. It is important to understand that although Lloyd George was outside the Government he had not, as is generally supposed, lost his acumen altogether. His mind ran parallel with those of certain leading British politicians during the great crisis of the war effort. He represented, outside the government, the same kind of policy as Halifax and Butler represented inside. We may also take it that Churchill was aware of the potential division. In 1940 he was truly leading a coalition, of war aims as well as of parties. His power rested on the superb gamble that the war would run in the direction of his hopes and expand across the world. But he understood that this might not happen, and that if it did not, the Lloyd Georges would have their role to play.

The evidence can be considered only very briefly here. In the phoney war Butler had already contended that Churchill was a law unto himself. Speaking to the Italian ambassador Bastianini in November 1939 he referred to a recent speech by Churchill as in conflict with the Government's views: 'As a matter of fact he always spoke only as Mr. Churchill.'[1] Despite the intervening revolution in the military situation, Butler's conversation on 17 June 1940 with the Swedish ambassador Prytz reflected the same divergence in the new context. Butler assured Prytz that no reasonable terms of peace would be turned down, and that there were other views in the government apart from Churchill's.[2] These had emerged fitfully during the retreat from Dunkirk, on 26–27 May 1940, when there was a possibility that Mussolini might come forward as a mediator. The official historian of the foreign office indicates that Halifax considered that Hitler might be rendered more reasonable by Mussolini, and the next day (27 May), Halifax noted in his diary: 'At the 4.30 Cabinet we had a long and rather confused discussion about, nominally, the approach to Italy, but also largely about the general policy in the event of things going badly in France.

[1] *Documents on German Foreign Policy, Series D*, viii, No. 375.
[2] *The Times*, 9 Sept. 1965.

I thought Winston talked the most frightful rot, also Greenwood, and after bearing it for some time I said exactly what I thought of them, adding that if that was really their view, and it came to the point, our ways must part.' Indeed in seeking to defend the Foreign Secretary, Birkenhead reveals very distinctly the limited war which Halifax envisaged: 'The more I ponder it, the more convinced I feel that the Germans have got to be more knocked about before they will be in any mood to learn any lesson. If we can persuade them to get rid of Hitler, all the better, but at least we want them to learn that war does not pay them.'[1]

A similar argument exists in a letter from Viscount Simon to Noel-Buxton, of 1 August 1940. Simon argued (perhaps for the comfort of his correspondent) that while Hitler was at present unreasonable, he might conceivably become more reasonable when the war began to turn against him.[2] In brief the idea was precisely as sketched by Lloyd George, that a limited war, a punch rather than a fifteen-round contest, would either get rid of Hitler or make him more malleable. All this rested on the simple and true assumption that Great Britain alone, no matter what the false prophets of bombing and blockade might say, could not restore Europe by force.

What of Churchill? He appears to have said during the Dunkirk crisis that Hitler could not at present offer us acceptable terms, and that Great Britain might get better terms later on.[3] His attitude towards compromise peace seems to have been that while *he* would never agree to it, he recognized that others might negotiate an untreasonable peace. When he came to test out Lloyd George in June 1940, to see whether he was fit for office, he used a most telling choice of words. 'Winston told me' (Halifax wrote) 'that he meant to put him through an inquisition first as to whether he had the root of the matter in him. By this he means, so he explained to me, adopting a formula I suggested to him, that any Peace terms now or hereafter offered *must not be destructive of our independence.*' (My italics).[4] This indicates that Churchill accepted the existence of a minimum war commitment, which might in the end result in a compromise peace,

[1] E. L. Woodward: *British Foreign Policy in the Second World War*, 51–3; Earl of Birkenhead: *Halifax* (1965), 457.

[2] Viscount Simon to Noel-Buxton, 1 Aug. 1940, Simon papers.

[3] Woodward, op. cit., 51–3.   [4] Birkenhead: *Halifax*, 459.

alongside his own maximum aims of total victory over Germany. So while he wrote to Roosevelt of the possibility of a Quisling government in Britain, what was really on his mind was the possibility of a government under Halifax or Lloyd George securing 'reasonable' terms. He could allege afterwards that the issue had never been discussed. While this was true up to a point, the division was there. Churchill freely admitted that very generous terms might have been offered to Great Britain, as he explained to Stalin in 1944: 'We never thought of making a separate peace even in the year when we were all alone and could easily have made one without serious loss to the British Empire and largely at your expense.'[1] The situation of Great Britain and France was, then, different in that Great Britain retained the option of moving into isolation. Writing of Hitler, Churchill says that students of the Führer realized the possibility 'that he would consent to leave Britain and her Empire and Fleet intact and make a peace which would have secured him that free hand in the East of which Ribbentrop had talked to me in 1937.'[2] Churchill won his great war and thus his great victory, but some alternative line would have to have been devised in the absence of the Russian and American alliances, or in the event of the rapid defeat of Russia in 1941 and continued benevolent neutrality of the United States. Churchill appreciated Lloyd George's position and did not regard it as dishonourable, hence his offer to make Lloyd George ambassador to the United States. As a matter of fact the previous ambassador, also respected by Churchill, had briefly taken a Lloyd George line: 'Philip Lothian telephones wildly from Washington in the evening begging Halifax not to say anything in his broadcast tonight which might close the door to peace. Lothian claims that he knows the German peace terms and that they are most satisfactory.'[3] It was a mark of Churchill's brilliance that he could foresee a role for others should he fail. It is to be expected that as the thirty-year rule marches forward in its revelations, the Churchillians will be less understanding of those who differed from Churchill than he was himself.

[1] *Stalin's Correspondence with Churchill, Attlee, Roosevelt and Truman 1941–45* (1958); Churchill to Stalin 24 Jan. 1944, 189.
[2] Winston S. Churchill: *Their Finest Hour*, 199.
[3] Nicolson: *Diaries and Letters 1939–45*, 104.

Lloyd George survived to congratulate Churchill in the house of commons on the D-Day landings. The last fingerprints of his style were still distinctive: his vote cast against the government and for the Beveridge Report, and his criticism of the policy of 'unconditional surrender'.[1] Despite his great age, he remained an impressive figure, pottering about his farm, his face weatherbeaten beneath a shock of white hair. It was perhaps through reluctance to leave parliamentary life that he accepted from Churchill an earldom in the New Year's honours list of 1945; this would have enabled him to speak on the question of peace terms.

He died on 26 March 1945, and two days later Churchill reviewed his career in the house of commons, translating that most dialectical and complex career into his own bold, vivid and straightforward terms.[2] In his final years, Lloyd George was active enough in mind and body to have caused Churchill considerable anxiety had he seized the moment, as in May 1940, to attack the Government. But Lloyd George would have been too old. In this Churchill was fortunate. For as Hitler remarked: 'Churchill's predestined opponent was Lloyd George. Unfortunately he's twenty years too old.'[3]

Edinburgh University   PAUL ADDISON

[1] Malcolm Thomson: *Lloyd George*, 456.
[2] Winston S. Churchill: *Victory*, 87–90.
[3] Hugh Trevor-Roper: *Hitler's Table Talk*, 184.

Index